# Information Revolutions in the History of the West

# Information Revolutions in the History of the West

Leonard Dudley

*Professor of Economics, Université de Montréal, Canada*

**Edward Elgar**

Cheltenham, UK • Northampton, MA, USA

Published by
Edward Elgar Publishing Limited
Glensanda House
Montpellier Parade
Cheltenham
Glos GL50 1UA
UK

Edward Elgar Publishing, Inc.
William Pratt House
9 Dewey Court
Northampton
Massachusetts 01060
USA

A catalogue record for this book
is available from the British Library

Library of Congress Control Number: 2008927706

ISBN 978 1 84720 790 6

Printed and bound in Great Britain by MPG Books Ltd, Bodmin, Cornwall

# Contents

# Preface

The boundary was marked by a black, red and gold wooden post bearing a metal plaque with the country's seal. Running along the far side of a double barbed-wire fence beyond the post was a sand track checked daily for footprints. For 500 meters behind the track, all trees and shrubs had been cleared. In the distance stood a concrete control tower manned by guards with automatic weapons. On that side of the fence, non-residents were not allowed within a five-kilometer *Sperrzone* (prohibited area). It was November 1988, and I was visiting the University of Bamberg in northern Bavaria. My host, Ulrich Blum, had taken me to inspect the border of the German Federal Republic with the German Democratic Republic, on the boundary between Bavaria and Thuringia.

That evening, at 7:30 p.m., we tuned in to the East German television news, broadcast in black and white from East Berlin. An announcer with jacket, tie and horn-rimmed glasses sat at a desk in a bare studio reading from sheets of paper with few visual embellishments. We heard about the travels of party secretary Erich Honecker and the latest government projects. Heavily filtered news of events in the West completed the broadcast. Finally, when we could bear to watch no longer, we turned to ARD, one of the West German channels. There, in brilliant color, were commercials for cars, clothing and prepared foods that were unavailable in the East. Then at 8:00 p.m. came the West German news broadcast, *Die Tagesschau*, from Hamburg. A smartly-dressed young woman presented a report of discussions between the government and the opposition parties on the latest labor legislation followed by color film clips of events from around the world.

It was obvious to any viewer – whether in West Germany or in East Germany, where most residents had access to these same channels – that the discrepancies between the two systems of social organization were becoming too great to be blocked by barbed wire alone. Indeed, barely a year later, on 9 November 1989, the Berlin Wall was opened. Soon after, the fences disappeared, and the metal border plaques became collectors' items. The East German economy was about to be exposed to the winds of competition from the outside world. The question then arose in my mind: were the momentous political and economic developments of 9 November, somehow related to the changes in communications media? If so, what was the nature of the relationship?

The idea of a chain of causality linking communication technologies and human behavior dates back at least to Francis Bacon. In *Novum Organum* (1620), he observed that printing, gunpowder and the magnet had 'changed the whole face and state of things throughout the world'.[1] However, Bacon did not have at his disposal the data or statistical tools that would have allowed him to test this hypothesis. More recently, the Canadian economic historian Harold A. Innis delivered a set of lectures at Oxford University that was published in 1950 under the title, *Empire and Communications*.[2] In these talks, he sought to explain the extension of the world's great empires over space and time by the characteristics of the communications technologies they used. In particular, Innis emphasized the importance of the Caroline Minuscule script for the circulation of knowledge across state borders in the Middle Ages. Even as popularized by Marshall McLuhan, however, Innis's research lacked the theoretical and statistical underpinnings to convince many of his academic colleagues.[3]

Yet another source of inspiration for this book is Elizabeth Eisenstein's seminal study on the impact of the printing press and its influence on the spread of literacy in the vernacular.[4] Chapters 3 and 4 below, pick up her story a bit earlier than the invention of movable type with the career of Cardinal Nicholas of Cusa. In addition, the tale is carried beyond the Reformation to the English Civil War and the Glorious Revolution of 1688. The surrounding chapters show that Ms Eisenstein's analysis may be generalized to other media in other periods. Her approach complements Jack Goldstone's hypothesis that revolution is a reaction to a fall in real incomes. The economic crises he describes may trigger the release of tectonic stress that has been building up because of technical change.[5]

Since its publication in 1990, Joel Mokyr's *The Lever of Riches* has generated a burst of theoretical and empirical research on the economic impact of new technologies. To separate those innovations with important spillovers from more run-of-the-mill fare, Timothy Besnahan, Elhanan Helpman and Richard Lipsey and their collaborators have popularized the concept of General Purpose Technologies.[6] Although I do not disagree with their analysis, I nevertheless believe that communications media are somehow more basic than the steam engine and electricity.

As I suggest in the conclusion, changes in the relative importance of two key dimensions in information technologies have led to the restructuring of social networks. Indeed, this book may be viewed as a set of variations on a theme proposed recently by Mokyr in *The Gifts of Athena*: 'The inventions of writing, paper, and printing not only reduced access costs but also materially affected human cognition, including the way that people thought about their envirnoment'.[7] In particular, I suggest that we need to examine the impact of information technologies on our propensity to cooperate with one another.[8]

This volume is not intended as a text book. Rather it offers a set of case studies designed to provide the reader with detailed information on some of the crucial moments in the history of the West over the past millennium. The text brings together the results of a number of academic papers in what I hope is a more accessible form.[9] I am grateful to my co-authors on several of these papers – Ulrich Blum, Johannes Moenius and Ulrich Witt – for their cooperation and for their permission to use jointly developed material.

A word of explanation is perhaps in order. The introduction and the first nine chapters are essentially descriptive, concentrating on the origin and diffusion of a series of new information technologies. Each of the five key innovations to be studied will be shown to have been the unforeseen consequence of an attempt to solve a relatively minor social, political or management problem. The concluding chapter combines the results of experimental psychology, network theory and economic history to suggest *why* the information revolutions of the past millennium have triggered very different types of ruptures in social structure – and are continuing to do so.

Leonard Dudley, Montreal

## NOTES

1. Novum Organum, Aphorism 129.
2. Innis (1950).
3. McLuhan (1962).
4. Eisenstein (1979).
5. Goldstone (1991).
6. Bresnahan and Trajtenberg (1995), Helpman (1998), Lipsey, Carlaw and Bekar (2006).
7. Mokyr (2002, p. 8).
8. Mokyr (2002).
9. See the Epilogue for the studies in question.

# Acknowledgements

In the fall of 1994, Pierre Fortin kindly invited me to present the annual lecture named in honor of Harold A. Innis at the 1995 Canadian Economic Association annual meeting. The University of Toronto economic historian was well known a half-century ago for his contributions to the staple theory, an approach to a region's development that emphasized the impact of a dominant commodity. In the intervening years, however, Innis had been all but forgotten. Rather than talk about subjects I had been working on over the previous few years, as was the custom in these lectures, I decided to talk about Harold Innis himself. During the last phase of his career, Innis devoted his energies to exploring the impact of communications technology on the geographical limits and internal structures of the world's great empires. Little did I realize that this choice of topic would reshape my life over the following decade and beyond.

I would like to express my appreciation to William H. McNeill for encouraging me to work on a subject that he himself would have chosen 'had [he] been thirty years younger'. My co-authors Ulrich Blum, Ulrich Witt and Johannes Moenius have been continual sources of fresh ideas and tough criticism during the preparation of the journal articles and conference papers listed in the Epilogue. I particularly thank Ulrich Blum and Ulrich Witt for their invitations to visit the Technical University of Dresden and the Max Planck Institute of Economics in Jena respectively for extended periods. Jean-Michel Josselin and Alain Marciano have been generous in their invitations to participate in the Corsica Conferences on Law and Economics. Lieutenant Colonel (ret.) Pascal Daniel was good enough to invite me to present my ideas for several years to the cadets of the École Spéciale Militaire St-Cyr. Stan Winer and Michael Huberman have provided an invaluable sounding board for my interpretations of economic theory and historical facts. And I must express my profound debt to the numerous journal editors, anonymous referees and seminar participants who have struggled to correct my inchoate ideas as the papers and the book have evolved.

My daughter, Sonia Wheaton-Dudley, patiently read and vetted the final versions of the manuscript. Felicity Plester, Nep Elverd, Karen McCarthy and the rest of the team at Edward Elgar have been superbly efficient in the transformation of the manuscript into book form. Finally, I am most grateful to Brigitte and Étienne for their constant support.

# Introduction

Bands of young Muslims and other foreigners roamed the suburbs, occasionally penetrating into the central cities to loot and burn. Slow to respond, society's institutions for preserving law and order proved incapable of dealing with this new threat. With increasing frequency, property owners fell victim to thieves and kidnappers. The inner cores of many cities became neglected and run down, while taxpayers revolted against the confiscation of their wealth by public officials. As streets, highways and bridges fell into disrepair, the educational system was unable to maintain the standards of earlier years. Traditional religious institutions were no longer able to impose centralized discipline on their followers, who flocked to newer movements. In the political sphere, citizens looked in vain for leaders willing to put aside their personal interests and those of their inner circle in order to govern for the common good.

No, this is not a sequence from a recent newscast or from a science-fiction film portraying our society in the very near future. Rather, it describes Western Europe after the break-up of the Carolingian Empire, during the last half of the ninth century and the first half of the tenth. Yet the parallels between the creative destruction seen at that time and present-day events are quite striking. The similarities suggest that the West has come full circle since the final collapse of the institutions of the Late Roman Empire some 1200 years ago. If we are interested in what lies ahead for us, we might do well to attempt to explain a remarkable series of social, political and economic transformations that have brought us from the Carolingians to the present time.

This book looks at how new communications technologies affect political, social and economic institutions. In an attempt to identify patterns in the process of social change, it focuses on short periods of rapid transformation in the West over the past 1200 years. Yet the situations we will be discussing are so basic to human behavior that you will undoubtedly have experienced them yourself.

## WAVES OF DISCONTINUITY

Historians have often divided the history of the West since the fall of Rome into four distinct periods – the Middle Ages, the Early Modern period, the century from 1815 to 1914 and the twentieth century. For many, the late twentieth century marks the beginning of yet a fifth era, sometimes called postmodern.[1] A feature that distinguishes each of these periods is the relationship between the West and the rest of the world. From one era to the next, it was the West that changed the most dramatically, with the other major areas of civilization suffering the consequences or, after 1500, trying desperately to catch up. Let us consider each of these social revolutions in the West to see what they have in common and how they differ.

In January 1989, East German Party Secretary Erich Honecker predicted that the Berlin Wall would stand for another 50 or 100 years.[2] However, only ten months later, on the evening of 9 November 1989, the gates in the Berlin Wall were suddenly thrown open to allow free travel across the Iron Curtain for the first time in almost three decades. The event was spontaneous – the result of a minister's momentary confusion in answering journalists' questions on live television. Admittedly, pressure for reform had been growing in East Germany. In September, 1989, the *Neues Forum* was founded by a group of peace activists who called for the rule of law in place of the invasive one-party state.[3] In October and the first week in November, there had been demonstrations in Leipzig and other East German cities. Nevertheless, the outpouring of thousands of East Berliners who spilled through Checkpoint Charlie on to the streets of West Berlin on the night of 9–10 November took the East German regime by surprise.

What finally brought down the German Democratic Republic (GDR) was the exodus that followed over the next few weeks and months. It was very much a minority decision, as thousands of skilled East German workers realized that they could do better in the West than in their own country. The socialist country's leaders quickly realized that to avoid economic chaos, they had no choice but to proceed as quickly as possible with hitherto unthinkable German reunification. Indeed, less than a year after the fall of the Berlin wall, on 3 October 1990, the GDR formally disappeared, and the institutions of the Federal Republic were extended into the eastern part of Germany.

The momentous events of 1989 were not the first occasion on which small groups of citizens acted together to transform Western societies. There had been equally profound upheavals during the first decades of the twentieth century. However, the discontinuity that occurred then was far from spontaneous. During the First World War, there was an unprecedented increase in the power of the state to tax and to determine how resources were allocated in all of the combatant countries. Small groups of officials made decisions previously left to individuals or groups in the private sector. After the war's end, some of these powers were relinquished, but the degree of taxation never returned to its prewar levels. The extra resources were now channeled into social welfare programs. In country after country, the state began to provide unemployment insurance, old-age pensions and medical coverage to be paid for by progressive taxation. Prior to the First World War, government expenditures had averaged a modest ten per cent of GNP, a proportion that had been approximately constant in periods of peace for at least a century. The public share of total income then doubled before 1939 and doubled again after the Second World War.[4] The establishment of the welfare state and its extension in some countries to become totalitarianism involved unprecedented control by the state over individuals.

If we look at the three previous centuries (from 1600 to 1900), there had also been two waves of discontinuities in the West. However, the characteristics of these earlier sets of mutations were quite different from those of the twentieth century. It was accepted that the state would play a moderate role in each country's economic and social affairs. The government's principal activity during this period was the defense of its territory against invasion by foreign powers and the protection of property rights through the legal system. At issue, rather, was the degree of cultural homogeneity to be allowed within each society.

Was it acceptable to have multiple allegiances within a single society? At the end of the Middle Ages, the answer to this question was certainly yes. The societies of Europe were marked by strong class divisions. Also, many of the civil institutions of these societies were controlled by a powerful transnational organization distinct from the secular state, namely, the Catholic Church. In addition, there were strong regional loyalties reinforced by linguistic differences. Finally, people considered themselves subjects of the hereditary ruler who happened to govern their state.

During the seventeenth and eighteenth centuries, this structure of multiple identities was to a great extent destroyed. As wealthy commoners purchased titles or used their wealth to obtain power and influence, the distinctions between the social classes became blurred. As for religion, either the Catholic Church was brought under firm state control or it was replaced by weaker institutions subservient to the state. Common national vernaculars overrode regional dialects. Finally, in a series of great political upheavals, the citizens of three nations – England, the United States and France – each established their collective sovereignty.

Although these momentous events were spread out over a century and a half, there was a common theme. Absolutism was swept away in each case, to be replaced by constitutional regimes under a set of rules that in principle all accepted. Britain and France were now governed by hereditary monarchs who ruled with the consent of elected assemblies. It was generally accepted that the right to vote be restricted to white men of above-average income and wealth. Even in the United States, there were property-holding or tax-paying requirements for voting in many states until the 1820s.[5]

This broad consensus in support of national policies set by representative institutions broke apart in a second set of social upheavals in the second and third quarters of the nineteenth century. The United States was one of the first to abolish restrictions on the right to vote for white men. Nevertheless, the nation became increasingly divided over the question of slavery. In Europe, the nineteenth century saw the formation of new social classes and political movements that reflected their interests. Great Britain underwent a similar although more peaceful transition to broader democracy in three steps, in 1832, 1867 and 1884.

On the continent, in 1830 and again in 1848, political unrest spread from France to other countries. In the latter year, there was rebellion across much of central Europe, as people took to the streets in Germany, Austria and northern Italy. Just as the 'Second Empire' architectural style of the Paris boulevards was imitated with a delay in other major European capitals, so also were the institutions of the liberal state. To prevent social upheaval, those who controlled the political systems of Western states proposed constitutional reforms that diluted their own power and privileges.

The High Middle Ages are almost a millennium away from us in the distant past. However, those who have traveled in Western Europe will be familiar with the Tower of London, Notre Dame in Paris and the great Romanesque cathedrals along the Rhine in central Germany. These structures are reminders of yet another wave of social upheaval that marked the transition from the centralized successor states of the Roman Empire to the decentralized feudal societies of medieval Europe. As we will see in the next chapter, this period has much in common with the one which we are now experiencing.

We see that over the past thousand years, there have been several quite different types of transformation in the West. During the Middle Ages, the turn of the millennium saw a break-up of the centralized kingdoms that had formed as Roman civilization declined. There was no organized movement. Rather, a series of ad hoc contractual arrangements, at first oral and then written, gave rise to a social structure known as feudalism. Only a small faction of the population, namely the most capable warriors, was directly concerned. Accordingly, this mutation, supported by a minority and spontaneous, might be called contractual.

The transition from the medieval to the modern period was also marked by a series of spontaneous upheavals. However, these revolts against a hereditary monarchy to establish more representative governments quickly gained the support of the great majority of citizens. Examples are the English, American and French (1789) Revolutions. This second type of transformation, majoritarian and spontaneous, could be termed consensual.

In the second and third quarters of the nineteenth century, the previous consensus broke down, as important groups within Western societies threatened to take power into their own hands. To avoid anarchy, the previously dominant groups conceded written constitutions which guaranteed that all – or at least all men – would be represented. These planned but majoritarian mutations, carefully structured by groups that already held power but submitted to the approval of a majority of citizens, deserve the description pre-emptive.

Finally, during the years from 1914 to 1938, troubled citizens ceded to powerful leaders and government bureaucracies unprecedented powers to tax and redistribute income. These planned but minoritarian transformations might be termed a prescriptive mutation.

Where does the recent transition in Eastern Europe fit within this typology? The most recent mutation was characterized by spontaneous upheaval and ended when a minority drafted new codes of conduct that limited state power. In many ways, then, this latest transformation resembles the changes that marked the introduction of feudalism a thousand years earlier and might also be termed a contractual mutation.

In short, each of the five major periods of Western history over the past millennium began with a restructuring of society. The next section will discuss possible explanations for these discontinuous changes.

## THEORIES OF REVOLUTION

Can we be more precise about the nature of the transformations in the West over the past millennium? Ekkart Zimmermann has offered a definition of revolution that would probably be accepted by many social historians: 'A revolution is the successful overthrow of the prevailing elite by a new elite who after having taken over power fundamentally change the social structure and therewith also the structure of authority'.[6] It may be seen that there are three elements to this definition, namely, a rapid, contested transfer of power between elites, a transformation of relations between individuals within the society and a restructuring of political institutions. By this criterion, the rise of feudalism, the formation of nation states, the granting of democratic constitutions, the state takeover of responsibility for social welfare and the sudden collapse of socialism in Eastern Europe all qualify as revolutionary. But what caused these social mutations?

In a recent survey, Jack Goldstone (2001) suggested that over the past half-century there have been three successive generations of theories of revolution, namely, those focusing on institutions, those emphasizing social classes and, more recently, those suggesting factors that alter the probability of state breakdown. With each successive generation of theories, the set of phenomena to be explained has been enlarged.

The first generation of postwar revolutionary theorists emphasized the breakdown of political institutions during periods of technological and economic change. Proponents of this approach focused on the failure of the state to adapt to the demands of important groups within the society during a period of modernization. More generally, Samuel Huntington argued that there were two preconditions for revolution: first, institutions that are too rigid to cope with demands for change, and second, new political groups that aspire to participate in political decisions.[7]

This approach would seem well-tailored to fit the great revolutions such as the English rebellion of 1642, the French Revolution of 1789 and the Russian October Revolution of 1917. Indeed, the institutional hypothesis perhaps fits too well. It is virtually a tautology to state that regimes have been overthrown when a state's institutions have proved too inflexible to meet the demands of powerful aspiring groups. The question is whether such a theory can help predict which states will suffer institutional failure, when the break will occur and how the society will change.

A second generation of studies focused on conflict between social classes. In her studies of the French, Russian and Chinese Revolutions, Theda Skocpol (1979, 1986) attributed revolution to structural weaknesses of the state that allowed unfavorable external military or economic shocks to destabilize the social system. Marginal elites such as students, teachers or journalists could then seize power. In Russia, military defeat in the First World War destroyed the tsarist bureaucracy, leaving the poorly-organized peasantry open to exploitation by whoever could seize power in the cities. In China, war also weakened the central regime, but because the urban sector was underdeveloped, revolutionary success came from alliances in the countryside between peasants and the challenging elite.[8]

For Charles Tilly (1986, 1990) the increased frequency of conflict between social classes after 1500 was the result of changes in the structure of the state that raised the stake in such struggles. The modern period of history, he noted, has been marked by the concentration of power in the nation state and by a general rise in the level of organized violence due to inter-state wars. As a result, the principal ingredients of revolutions have been taxation to wage war, defeat in war, and the complicity of military leaders in attempts to overthrow existing regimes.

Jack Goldstone (1991) examined the interplay between demographic and environmental forces in generating class conflict. He observed that revolution repeatedly occurred when the majority of a society's members experienced sharp falls in their real income. Such shocks were likely to occur when population growth strained an economy's productive capacity, leaving its distribution system vulnerable to climatic disturbances or war. He pointed out that crop failures and high grain prices preceded the revolutions of 1640 in England, and 1789, 1830 and 1848 in France.[9]

Beginning in the 1970s, as Goldstone (2001, p. 141) noted more recently, there began a series of revolutions that did not fit easily into the frameworks proposed by either the institutional or the social class approaches. The overthrow of the Shah of Iran in 1979, the fall of the Philippines dictatorship in 1986 and the collapse of Communism in Eastern Europe in 1989 all occurred in states that were experiencing favorable external economic and military conditions. Moreover, the political changes were backed by broad alliances that crossed class boundaries.

The most recent generation of studies suggests there can be no general theory of revolution. At the very least, it would appear to be necessary to separate pre-1950 revolutions from the more recent upheavals in the Third World and Eastern Europe. Goodwin's (2001) inventory of revolutionary movements in the postwar period, Kurzman's (2004) detailed study of the Iranian revolution and Foran's (2005) comparison of 36 revolutions in developing countries imply that each instance of social breakdown and the transfer of power between elites is a special case that has its own unique causes and consequences. One can speak only of factors that increase or decrease the probability that a given social and political regime will be able to reproduce itself from one moment to the next. In addition to war and public finance, factors such as religion, ideology, leadership and the expectations of individuals can all play a role in destabilizing regimes.

A common failing of all three generations of revolutionary theory is their inability to explain the differences between the four types of revolution described earlier. Why were some spontaneous and others carefully planned? Why were some the result of actions by a small minority in a society while others received strong majority support? To help answer these questions, the next section points out a remarkable fact that most studies of revolution have overlooked. Each of the major turning points in the history of the West since the fall of Rome has coincided with the introduction of a radically new information technology.

## AN ALTERNATIVE APPROACH

A half-century ago, several observers noticed that the waves of social revolution described at the outset of this chapter coincided with the diffusion of new information technologies. But what exactly constitutes a major change in such techniques? In the 1950s, Harold Innis suggested that media may be biased towards either 'time' or 'space'.[10] A decade later, Marshall McLuhan spoke of the creation of the 'global village' in which 'Big Brother goes inside' the mind of each individual.[11] Unfortunately, neither author defined these terms precisely enough to allow his hypotheses to be tested. However, recent developments in the theory of information networks allow the possible links between media and social institutions to be expressed with greater precision. The key concepts are scale economies and network effects.

### Scale Economies

In the mid-1960s, graduate students in the social sciences began writing theses that required many numerical calculations. On some days, when there were just a few long divisions to do – for example, for a summary table – one could use an electronic calculator that cost a couple of hundred dollars. However, for more complex statistical estimates involving thousands of calculations, one had to go to the university's computer center to use an IBM 360 mainframe that cost many hundreds of thousands of dollars. On this machine, one first had to write a program in FORTRAN or some other friendly 'high-level' language. Once this program had been debugged, each operation required only a tiny fraction of the time and effort that it took by hand on the calculator.

The contrast between doing a small number of calculations on an electronic calculator and a large number on a computer is an example of the presence of scale economies – the extent to which unit costs fall when the volume of production increases. As the quantity of information to be treated rose, the cost of each additional transformation fell. First, however, there was a high initial cost – the financing of a university computer center and the preparation of a computer program for one's specific needs – that had to be met. It was efficient to use the computer only if one had a large number of computations to do.

In 1981, consumers were introduced to the IBM personal computer, a scaled-down version of the old IBM 360, with 64 kilobytes of random-access memory. After adding a bit of extra computing power, one could easily do statistical tasks that had previously required a mainframe. The difference was that instead of costing several hundred thousand dollars, the microcomputer sold for $4000. Because of the dramatic fall in the initial investment, it was now possible for an individual to afford doing calculations that only a large organization could have financed a decade earlier. After a decade and a half of innovation, unit costs no longer fell very much as volume rose; that is, there had been a sharp decrease in the scale economies of information processing.

**Network Effects**

The first home computers such as the Apple II and the IBM PC were stand-alone devices, useful for word processing or computation, but unable to communicate electronically with one another. Network effects – the gain to other users when an additional person bought a similar machine – were very low. However, a useful accessory soon available for home computers was the modem. Thanks to this marvelous device, one could subscribe to an electronic data service and buy the most recent economic statistics to be delivered electronically over the telephone line to one's computer. Electronic data transfer, formerly limited to large organizations with mainframe computers, was now open to individuals in their own homes. Nevertheless, as there were still relatively few individuals and firms linked to the internet, the connections to the existing subscriber base were still of low value to each subscriber. In other words, network effects were positive but modest.

Then in the 1980s, commercial internet providers such as Compuserve and Quantum (later America Online) began offering electronic mail, chat groups and on-line games to their customers in the United States. Many, many people began buying modems. By the late 1980s Western European universities, firms and government agencies were linked to their North-American counterparts through the internet.[12] In the early 1990s, individual households in Western Europe began to get internet access. Over the decade, as the number of internet users grew and the software to link them improved, there occurred a great increase in the importance of network effects – the rise in the value of a network to existing members when a new participant joins.

We see, then, that the revolutionary changes in Eastern Europe that began in 1989 were preceded by a remarkable fall in the importance of scale economies in information processing and a simultaneous rise in network effects. Using these concepts, we may perhaps better understand the terms used by an earlier generation of media analysts. Innis's 'bias' toward time and space may be expressed in terms of the relative importance of scale economies. When they were considerable, as with the Roman alphabet and centrally-manufactured papyrus, regimes tried to dominate an extended territory. However, when scale economies were low, as with locally-produced parchment during the Middle Ages, there were many political units concerned with transmitting knowledge and wealth across generations.[13] Similarly, McLuhan's distinction between the individualism of eighteenth-century 'typographic man' and the 'electronic interdependence' of the mid-twentieth-century 'global village' may be expressed as the effect of a decrease in network effects. The introduction of the telegraph, radio and television transformed a society of freely interacting individuals into a mass audience throbbing unconsciously to a common rhythm.[14]

Our task in the following chapters will be to see whether at the beginning of each period in the West over the past millennium a new technology altered the importance of informational scale economies relative to network effects and if so, whether the revolutionary social changes that defined the new era were related to the diffusion of this innovation. Unfortunately, there will not be enough space to do more than hint about how spillovers from these diffusion processes have affected social structures in the Third World.

## OUTLINE OF THE BOOK

One of the limitations of earlier studies of media – such as those of Innis and McLuhan – is their focus on causality in a single direction – from information technology to social structure. However, new media themselves are not created spontaneously: they are generated at specific times by individuals living in particular societies trying to solve certain problems. To be complete, our analysis must pay as much attention to the effects of social institutions on the innovation process as to the impact of innovations themselves on social behavior. Our proposed study should therefore have two components. First, we should explore the origin of innovations in information technology. Second, we should study the diffusion of the resulting techniques and their social effects. Analytically, then, it is convenient to divide each of the major periods in the history of the West into two phases, one explaining how a new information technology came to be developed and a second describing the impact of its diffusion.

In his study, *Capitalism Socialism and Democracy*, first published in 1942, the Austrian economist Joseph Schumpeter warned that the introduction of a major new technology would be followed by an initial phase of 'creative destruction'. Firms using earlier techniques would see their markets eroded and many would consequently perish in the 'perennial gale'. For example, the introduction of the railroad destroyed the jobs of many workers whose livelihoods depended on intercity transport by horse-drawn carriage. However, as the diffusion of the new technology progressed, there would be a second phase in which new relationships were formed. Invariably, in the longer term, the value of total output would rise and the society as a whole would benefit.[15] Let us call this second phase in the revolutionary cycle 'wrenching rebirth'.

The structure of the present book, with alternating chapters of creative destruction and wrenching rebirth, fits this Schumpeterian pattern. In the period from 800 to 1950, there were four sets of profound change in information technology in the West. Each altered the existing balance between scale economies and network effects. For each set of media breakthroughs, the book offers an initial chapter devoted to the innovation and the creative destruction it caused. The following chapter then describes how a new social structure formed. The ninth chapter in the book presents the latest innovation and the perturbations that its diffusion is presently causing.

The most convenient way to organize the material is by means of a series of questions, two for each of the four types of revolution and a final question for the reccurrence of one of these types. Here, then, is a preview of the following nine chapters, each a case study of a revolutionary new information technology's development or diffusion.

### The Contractual Revolution

#### 1. Why did the Carolingian Empire collapse?

Under Charlemagne, the Franks controlled an empire that covered a large part of Western Europe – Belgium, the Netherlands, Luxembourg, France, Germany and most of Italy, the original six members of the European Union. Yet within a century of his death in 814, this enormous state had broken up into dozens of autonomous petty kingdoms, duchies and counties. The usual explanation has been the invasion of Western Europe by Muslims, Vikings and Magyars.[16] Yet the brunt of these attacks came after 841, when the Empire had already broken up.

We will explore another approach. During the last two decades of Charlemagne's reign, there occurred a standardization of the Latin language used at the royal court and in the monasteries. This standardization made possible a considerable increase in literacy, thereby reducing the fixed cost of a scriptorium and raising network externalities. Might there be a link between the emergence of Medieval Latin and the break-up of the Carolingian Empire?

#### 2. Why were the Normans able to conquer and hold on to the Kingdom of England?

Beginning in the eleventh century, William the Conqueror and his descendants, unlike the Romans and the Danes before them, successfully invaded and maintained their conquest of England. Indeed, the present queen, Elizabeth II, is a direct descendant of Duke William. How could Normandy, with only 400 000 inhabitants, succeed in a sea-borne invasion of an island kingdom with four times its population? The usual explanation is that William's success was an accident. Barely two weeks before Hastings, the Anglo-Saxon army had fought and won a battle against another invader and his English allies.[17] However, it is difficult to believe that the fate of a country for a millennium depended upon the outcome of a single battle.

We shall see that the conquest took place shortly after the appearance on the continent of a convention that governed relations between a military leader and the mounted knights who followed him. Under what became known as feudalism, the followers and their heirs received permanent title to landed property. In exchange, they and their dependents were expected to provide the leader with annual military service. These changes in turn occurred during a period of a steady increase in the number of clergy and laymen able to read and write in a recently standardized form of the Latin language. Could the defeat of the Anglo-Saxon shield wall at Hastings in 1066 be connected with the diffusion of literacy in Medieval Latin across the English Channel and the accompanying spread of feudalism?

### The Consensual Revolution

**3. Why did Luther's movement to reform the practice of Christianity succeed where the earlier attempts of John Wycliffe and Jan Hus had failed?**

In 1415 the Church succeeded in stamping out heresy by setting fire to John Wycliffe's books and by burning Jan Hus himself at the stake. However, in 1450, Pope Nicholas V authorized the sale of letters of indulgence in Germany to finance the defense of Cyprus against the Turks. The production of these letters marked the first recorded use of Gutenberg's printing press. In 1517, this same invention was used to diffuse Luther's 95 theses attacking the sale of the letters of indulgence. Although Luther was undermining both the spiritual and the financial foundations of the Catholic Church, his ideas survived all attempts of the Church and its allies to suppress them.

The most frequent explanation for the success of the Protestant Reformation has been the popular rejection of growing secularization of the Church during the fifteenth century, indulgences being one example.[18] Yet as Diarmaid MacCulloch has recently observed, Luther himself considered the indulgences to be a minor issue.[19] Not only did Luther use the printing press but he also translated the Bible into German and insisted that all boys and girls be taught to read the scriptures. Might the Reformation's success be linked rather to the spread of literacy in the vernacular?

**4. Why did Charles I of England lose his kingdom – and his head?**

In 1611, King James I authorized the publication of a standardized English Bible, the result of seven years of labor by a royal commission. His heir, Charles I, followed his father's example by ruling over England for a long period without summoning parliament to approve his decisions. However, this time Parliament rebelled. In the 1640s, the king lost two civil wars against parliamentary armies and was subsequently executed. The usual explanation for the defeat of the Stuart monarchy refers to the character of the king. By his intransigence, his duplicity and his belief in the use of force to settle disputes, he incurred the wrath of his subjects.[20] However, neither the parliamentary leader, Oliver Cromwell, nor his eventual Stuart successor, James II, was able to impose personal rule on the English.

In 1688, William III, the Dutch stadtholder, was invited to take the throne provided that he accept the sovereignty of an elected legislature. When he and his wife Mary II signed the Bill of Rights, the elected Parliament was finally supreme. This remarkable expansion of the number of people participating in political decisions came at the end of a process of linguistic transformation. Over the course of the seventeenth century, the percentage of adult men able to read and write almost doubled, approaching the 50 per cent level. At the same time, written English became standardized, with present-day English emerging by the end of the seventeenth century. Was the diffusion of literacy in this standardized language somehow related to these tumultuous political events?

## The Pre-emptive Revolution

**5. Why did the British Parliament pass the Great Reform Bill of 1832?**

By the early nineteenth century, although Parliament was sovereign, it was far from representative of Great Britain's male population. At the beginning of 1832, only one adult male in eight was eligible to vote. However, in that year, the relatively small number of people who controlled political decisions suddenly agreed to dilute their power by eliminating 'rotten boroughs' and increasing the electorate by 50 per cent. Most historians would probably agree with Simon Schama that the reform was designed to pre-empt the type of revolution that France had experienced in 1830.[21] But why extend the right to vote in 1832 and not a quarter-century earlier or later?

Was it a coincidence that the preceding three decades had seen the first important improvements in the printing press since the days of Gutenberg?

First had come the all-metal Stanhope press and then the steam-powered Koenig press. Between 1780 and 1835, total stamped newspaper circulation more than doubled, rising from 14 million to 31 million despite crippling taxes that the Tory government placed on newspapers. In addition, by the early 1830s, there were numerous unstamped popular periodicals, some of them selling from 10 000 to 30 000 copies a week.[22]

### 6. Why did the Northern states not let the Deep South secede in April 1861?

By the beginning of April 1861, seven states in the Deep South had seceded. However, North Carolina and the Border States were still in the Union. Newly inaugurated president Abraham Lincoln then made a fateful decision. He sent ships without munitions to supply Fort Sumter, the federal stronghold that controlled access to the harbor of Charleston, South Carolina. This step led South Carolina to open fire on the fort – the opening shot in the Civil War. When Lincoln called for volunteers to maintain the Union, four other states seceded. But why did Lincoln refuse to abandon Fort Sumter? Why not simply let the defenders of the Union fort surrender peacefully and then try to make some accommodation with the rebelling states? Twice before, in 1820 and in 1850, compromise had preserved the Union. Why was the North so intransigent this time? The textbook answer is that Lincoln sent provisions to Fort Sumter because he felt it his duty as president to uphold the law of his country.[23] But were the lives of the soldiers who would die in the conflict that his decision provoked less valuable than the title to federal property?

Could the answer somehow be related to the tremendous expansion in newspaper readership and the great acceleration in the flow of information that had occurred over the preceding two decades?

## The Prescriptive Revolution

### 7. Why did the United States declare war on Spain in 1898?

In 1896, William McKinley became the first American political leader to master the art of campaigning through the mass media. At the beginning of his second year in office, on 27 March 1898, McKinley sent Spain an ultimatum that he hoped would end three years of fighting between Cuban rebels and the Spanish army. Spain over the following two weeks agreed to comply with the essential terms of McKinley's note, declaring an immediate armistice, abandoning its concentration camps and accepting autonomy for the Cuban legislature. Nevertheless, the president on 11 April sent a war message to Congress. The House and Senate then passed a resolution demanding Spain's immediate withdrawal from Cuba, in effect declaring war.

Was the American decision made simply because Spain's concessions were too little too late, as some have argued?[24] In the ensuing war, the United States inflicted a severe defeat on Spain. Although it then allowed Cuba to become an independent republic, it retained rights to the Guantánamo Bay Naval Base. In addition the US insisted on maintaining control of Puerto Rico, Guam and the Philippine Islands. Indeed, the American army subsequently fought a two-year war against a Philippine insurrection in order to establish its hold on the islands. These two wars marked the beginning of American military intervention beyond the North American continent and the founding of an American empire. Might the sudden belligerence of a nation that had previously opposed colonialism since its inception somehow be related to a circulation war that was raging between two American newspaper magnates?

### 8. Why did the United Kingdom enter the First World War?

In 1908, British Liberal ministers Winston Churchill and David Lloyd George both visited Germany, scoffing at the possibility of war between the two countries. In that same year Alfred Harmsworth, Lord Northcliffe, purchased *The Times*, thereby obtaining control of 40 per cent of the London daily press. Northcliffe had been predicting war with Germany since the turn of the century. Six years after these events, on Saturday 1 August 1914, Germany and Austria declared war on Russia. The following Tuesday, German armies invaded Belgium and Luxembourg, which lay on their route into northern France.

Britain was not directly threatened and need not have intervened. Indeed, a majority of the ruling Liberal Party's MPs were against war. However, Churchill and Lloyd George convinced their cabinet colleagues not only to declare war on the central powers but also to send an expeditionary force to northern France. The two ministers were not alone in their enthusiasm for war. Almost three million British men volunteered for military service. One in five would be killed in battle. Niall Ferguson has argued that Britain's intervention to aid France was the result of decade-long planning by 'a minority of generals, diplomats and politicians'.[25] However, on the eve of the war, Britain's foreign secretary, Sir Edward Grey, in a critical conversation with the German ambassador, referred to the pressure of public opinion.[26] Might the channeling of information through a few mass-circulation newspapers help explain this extraordinary willingness to sacrifice?

## Another Contractual Revolution

### 9. Was there a connection between 11/9 and 9/11?

On the night of 9 November 1989, East German authorities opened the border crossings between East and West Berlin for the first time in over

28 years. Within a few weeks, the Berlin Wall had been broken into pieces for souvenir sellers and the German Democratic Republic's one-party regime had ceased to exist. Then on 7 August of the following year, the first contingents of American troops arrived in Saudi Arabia to defend that nation from a threatened invasion by Iraq, which had just seized Kuwait. At that time, Osama bin Laden, a wealthy Saudi who had participated in the Afghan victory over the Soviet Union in the 1980s, resolved to do all he could to rid Islamic lands of the hated infidels. Twelve years later came the 11 September 2001 attacks on the World Trade Center and the Pentagon.

Most people would fail to see any link between the two key events that marked the transition to the new millennium. However, as Thomas Friedman has pointed out, in recruiting for, planning and financing the 9/11 attacks, the al-Qaeda movement made use of the latest electronic technologies.[27] Moreover, in losing its monopoly over the public distribution of information, the East German government on 9 November 1989 was also a victim of this wave of innovation. Might there be a technological link between 9/11 and 11/9?

In the concluding chapter, we will discuss *why* information revolutions have been followed by, to quote Zimmerman[28] once again, 'the successful overthrow of the prevailing elite by a new elite who after having taken over power fundamentally change the social structure'. We will see that on a much smaller scale, similar mutations in group behavior were the surprising outcomes of two controlled experiments in psychology. Indeed, careful examination of these experiments will perhaps enable us to understand the relationship between major changes in information technology and the revolutions that have featured so prominently in what William McNeill called the *Rise of the West*.[29] First, however, there are nine stories to be told.

## NOTES

1. Geoffrey Barraclough (1984b) used the first four periods in editing *The Times Atlas of World History*, as did Dudley Dillard (1967) in *Economic Development of the North Atlantic Community*. J.M. Roberts (1983) employed all five periods in *The Pelican History of the World.*
2. Ash (1994, p. 356).
3. Fulbrook (1991, p. 325).
4. Dudley and Witt (2004).
5. Nash *et al.* (1986, p. 330).
6. Zimmermann (1983, p. 298).
7. Huntington (1986, p. 45).
8. Skocpol (1986, pp. 68–88).
9. Goldstone (1991, pp. 290–294).
10. Innis (1950, 1951).
11. McLuhan (1962).

12. Dodge (2004).
13. Innis (1950).
14. McLuhan (1962, pp. 1, 166).
15. Schumpeter (1950, pp. 89–90).
16. Hollister (1968, p. 96).
17. Bates (2004, pp. 104–105).
18. Holborn (1982, pp. 123–125).
19. MacCulloch (2003, pp. 120–121).
20. Schama (2001, p. 121).
21. Schama (2002, p. 138).
22. Asquith (1978, p. 100).
23. Nash *et al.* (1986, p. 495).
24. Musicant (1998, pp. 182–183).
25. Ferguson (1999, p. 443).
26. Massie (1991, p. 886).
27. Friedman (2005, pp. 442–446).
28. Zimmerman (1983).
29. McNeill (1963).

# PART I

# The contractual revolution

# 1. Words and the man

In the mid-eighth century, the medium of communication that had once been used by millions across Western Europe was dying. It was not just the replacement of light, cheap papyrus by heavy, expensive parchment that marked the transition. After a thousand cuts from mutations, each region of the former Roman Empire now had its own version of spoken Latin. Increasingly, travelers from one region had difficulty making themselves understood in other areas. Meanwhile, with the disappearance of lay schools north of the Alps, knowledge of the Romans' phonetic writing system there was limited to a few thousand priests and monks. The written vocabulary and grammar were also beginning to diverge from classical Latin, although in different ways in each region. Since many monastic houses had their own scripts, even the learned had trouble understanding documents that were exchanged for copying.

There were nevertheless some grounds for optimism with regard to the survival of literacy. By the year 780, thanks to the efforts of a gifted tutor, the sounds of the oral Latin of northern Italy had replicated themselves in the brain of the powerful Germanic-speaking king of the Franks. Although Charles himself could not decode the mysterious scratchings of his scribes, he was troubled by the high cost of storing accurately the information required to administer his kingdom. Perhaps the royal power of selection could somehow be used to promote a reform that would make it easier for him and his advisers to recall what had occurred in the mists of the past.

## THE BIRTH OF EUROPE

Was it all because of a woman? In the late summer of 773, Charles son of Pippin surveyed the Frankish army assembled before him on the Field of Mars, the *Campus Martis*, near Geneva.[1] He had summoned the select levy, made up of all those warriors who held at least a *mansus* – an estate of from 25 to 45 acres (10 to 18 hectares). In total, there were some 3000 cavalry and 7000 infantry from across northern Europe.[2] The king, aged 41, was a blond giant over six feet three (190 cm) in height who towered above his subjects.[3] To later generations, he would be known as Charles the Great or Charlemagne.

Addressing the assembly, Charles announced that although it was late in the season, they were to set out on a campaign that promised glory and riches for all. They would cross the Alps into the fertile valleys of northern Italy in order to attack enemies of the holy church – the perfidious Lombard king Desiderius and his followers. Charles announced that he was dividing the Frankish host into two fighting units. He himself would lead one army by a southerly route across the Mont Cenis pass. Meanwhile his uncle Bernard would bring a second army across the Great Saint Bernard pass to the north.[4] The Frankish king was impatient to get under way for he knew that the mountain passes would soon be blocked with snow.

## The Conquest of Northern Italy

A few months earlier, Charles had been installed at his winter quarters in Thionville on the Moselle in present-day Lorraine, when he received an urgent message from the newly elected Pope, Adrian I.[5] The spiritual leader of Latin Christendom, son of a Roman nobleman, requested the aid of his Frankish allies to defend the church lands in central Italy. For several months, Desiderius, ruler of the Lombard kingdom in northern Italy, had been waging a merciless war, attempting to expand his territory at the expense of the church. The former Duke of Tuscany, who had been king of the Lombards for almost two decades, had seized the papal towns of Senigallia, Montefeltro, Urbino and Gubbio. At Blera, a town to the northwest of Rome, he and his Germanic followers had put the entire population to the sword.

The founding of Europe may in fact be due to a dispute over a woman. Charles was not surprised to learn that Desiderius had broken the peace. Officially, the Lombard ruler was still his father-in-law, but the Frankish king no longer considered himself wedded to the young Lombard princess he had married only three years before. When for reasons we can only imagine, she had proved unsatisfactory, Charles had sent her back to her father and quickly taken another bride. Charles was nevertheless furious to learn that Desiderius no longer recognized him to be the legitimate ruler of all the Franks. The Lombard king called for restoration of the eastern part of the Frankish kingdom to its supposedly rightful rulers, the two young sons of Charles's deceased brother Carloman.[6] Charles responded by sending to Rome a delegation that included the Anglo-Saxon scholar Alcuin.[7] When they confirmed the charges in the Pope's message, Charles offered a generous payment to Desiderius – provided that he end his invasion of papal lands. However, the Lombard ruler could not be persuaded. To Charles, it was obvious that compromise was no longer possible: Desiderius must be removed and his kingdom destroyed.

The wily Desiderius had anticipated Charles's reaction to the Pope's call for help. The Lombard king stationed the bulk of his troops so as to block the route down from the Mont Cenis pass, the traditional path for the invasion of Italy from the west. The stone defensive walls built by his men along the valley leading down to the town of Susa may still be seen today.[8] As Charles's troops descended into Italy, they met stiff Lombard resistance. The Frankish king was even contemplating retreat, when his troops one morning discovered that the enemy defenders had disappeared during the night. The Lombards had apparently learned of the approach of Bernard's troops from the north. The second Frankish army had succeeded in crossing by the undefended northern route and now threatened the Lombard flank. Desiderius withdrew his army behind the thick walls of his capital city of Pavia on the upper Po River. As the Franks lacked machinery to break down the city's ramparts, Charles had little choice but to settle down for a long siege.[9]

It was not until June of the following year, 774, that Pavia, its population facing disease and famine, finally surrendered. Charles spared the garrison and the civilian population but consigned the treacherous Desiderius to the monastery of Corbie north of Paris, where, surprisingly, he developed a reputation for piety.[10] On learning of Charles's clemency, the Lombard cities that had not already fallen surrendered to the Franks, one after the other.

## A Man with a Problem

Having successfully eliminated his most important rival, Charles was confronted with a dilemma. As a result of the final submission of Aquitaine in 768 and now Lombardy, the population over which he ruled had virtually doubled in six years, reaching some 12 million.[11] However, the subjects of these new territories spoke dialects of Latin rather than the Germanic tongue of the Franks. Regrettably, the Franks had few officials able to read and write Latin. Indeed, the Frankish language itself had as yet no written form and Charles himself was illiterate. Although he had united the three kingdoms under his personal rule, he was forced to leave northern Italy under the control of Lombard nobles.[12]

The disadvantages of this administrative structure were exposed in 776, two years after the capture of Pavia, when Charles was compelled to interrupt a campaign against the Saxons in northern Germany in order to put down a rebellion in Italy.[13] Although he left the Lombard dukes in place, he clipped their wings by naming a Frankish count to represent him in every city.[14] Yet this could be no more than a stopgap solution. With the increasing cultural diversity of the empire, some unifying factor was needed to hold the various regions together. One possible integrating element was the Christian religion. However, to spread the faith, he would need educated priests.

The conquest of northern Italy also had fiscal implications. With the integration of this wealthy region into the Empire, there were few possibilities for further expansion. Consequently, the king could no longer count on pillage and tribute to finance his household and numerous retainers. His attempt to conquer the infidels of Spain in 778 would prove a costly failure, although he would succeed in adding a strip of land south of the Pyrenees to his empire. The very structure of the Frankish state would therefore have to be reformed.[15] Instead of relying on pillage and tribute from their neighbors, the Franks would henceforth be required to live on the fiscal resources of their own subjects. Here again, educated officials would be necessary.

The Frankish conquest of northern Italy has been considered by many historians to mark the beginning of Europe. Indeed, this was the position of the Carolingians themselves when they revived the classical term of 'Europe' (from 'the land of the sunset', the territory to the west of Asia).[16] Of course such a focus on Latin Christendom neglects the vibrant development of the cultures of Eastern Europe. Nevertheless, for the first time since the fourth century, much of the territory of present-day Europe was now under the command of a single ruler. The response of Charles and his successors to the administrative and fiscal challenges that arose from governing a territory that lay on both sides of the Alps would play a major role in shaping Europe's future.

## The Emperor and the Deacon

In 781, five years after the rebellion of his Lombard vassals, Charles was back south of the Alps, but no closer to a solution to his administrative problem. Having spent the winter in northern Italy with his wife and children and the members of his household, he had stopped briefly in Parma on his way south to Rome. The Frankish ruler wished to assure a smooth succession at the end of his own reign. Accordingly, his two young sons, Pippin and Louis, were to be baptized by the Pope at an Easter mass and crowned kings of Italy and Aquitaine respectively. While staying temporarily in Parma, Charles learned that a former acquaintance, Alcuin of York, was also in town. Recalling the breadth of the Anglo-Saxon cleric's knowledge and his ability to communicate his ideas clearly and simply, Charles invited him to a private audience.[17]

Alcuin had been born into a noble Northumbrian family near York in northern England in about 732 – the same year that Charlemagne's grandfather defeated a Muslim army near Poitiers in one of the great battles of history. Alcuin was related to Saint Willibrord, the Anglo-Saxon missionary who had baptized Charles's father, Pippin III (the Short). While Alcuin was still a boy, he was left under the charge of the school that Archbishop Egbert had developed at the cathedral of York. There, among the sons of other noble families from the surrounding region, Alcuin stood out as a rapid and eager learner.[18] Already, by the age of 11, he had begun to show great interest in both the Holy Scriptures and the writings of secular Roman poets such as Virgil.[19]

York, a town of about 10 000 people, had been fortified in the first century AD by the Roman army as its headquarters in northern England. The site had access to the North Sea by the Ouse and Humber Rivers; yet it was set deep among the villages and the forests of central Northumbria. Under Egbert, the traditional religious program of the town's cathedral had been expanded to include secular literature and science. Here a difficulty had arisen. Virtually all of the manuscripts available to Anglo-Saxon scholars in the early eighth century were in Latin. But Egbert, like his colleagues and their students, spoke the local Northumbrian dialect, which was closely related to the language spoken by the Frisians and North Germans and very different from the vulgar Latin spoken in western Francia and Italy. As a result, Latin had to be taught as a foreign language.

Egbert's teacher, Bede the Venerable, had been the first to find a way to overcome this difficulty. It was Bede who wrote the first grammar intended to teach Latin as a foreign language. In England, Latin was generally learned by reading aloud or reciting by memory. But how was the language to be pronounced? It was discovered that the passage from the written text to the spoken word was easiest for non-native speakers if every letter was pronounced and always in the same way. The result was an oral Latin very different from that spoken in any of the Romance areas on the continent.[20]

As Alcuin was growing up, Archbishop Egbert gradually transferred more and more of the teaching responsibilities in the palace to one of his kinsmen, a young priest named Aelbert. Although religious studies were not neglected, the new head of the school gave considerable emphasis to Latin language and grammar as well as to mathematics and natural science. Aelbert traveled to Rome and Francia, using these occasions to gather new manuscripts for the cathedral library, often taking the young Alcuin with him.[21] During the 750s, as Alcuin came to manhood, he too was given teaching responsibilities. In 768, after Egbert's death, Aelbert succeeded him as Archbishop of York. At this time, Alcuin at the age of 36 was ordained deacon and eventually took over the direction of the cathedral school. However, he was never ordained as a priest; nor did he ever take monastic vows.[22]

Since Latin was a second language for Alcuin and his fellow scholars at York, it was particularly important that every character be clear. In their texts, the Romans had used large capital letters with no spaces between words. Not only was such writing hard to read, but also it consumed great quantities of precious parchment. The Irish missionaries who had converted Northumbria to Christianity had brought with them two more efficient scripts descended from sets of characters that had been developed in the late Roman Empire for use in place of capitals. One, a cursive, made up of attached lower-case letters, was used for day-to day writing. The other, called half uncials, consisted of detached lower-case letters and was preferred for books. Alcuin was well trained in both.

As mentioned, Alcuin's mentor Aelbert traveled on several occasions to Rome and to Francia. Accompanying him on these voyages, Alcuin made many contacts among scholars of Carolingian Europe.[23] As a teacher, Alcuin established a reputation for excellence across Western Europe. Students came to study under him from other kingdoms in England as well as from Ireland and the continent. In 778, when Aelbert retired from the post of Archbishop, Alcuin was placed in charge of the cathedral school and library.[24] Three years later, when one of his former classmates was appointed as Aelbert's successor, Alcuin was the logical choice to lead a delegation to Rome to make a formal request for the Archbishop's pallium.

In 781, approaching the age of 50, Alcuin had accomplished almost all that a scholar of his day could expect. He had a secure and respected position as head of the most important educational institution in Western Europe. He had traveled widely and had many friends scattered across England and the continent. For his two mentors, Egbert and Aelbert, such a career had been sufficient. Having attained these goals they had gone on to become church administrators as archbishops. However, Alcuin realized that from the basic elements of the communications technology developed in Northumbria – clear, simple scripts, and uniform grammar and phonetic pronunciation – something further could be attained.

## THE KINGDOM OF THE FRANKS, 780

Let us step back a moment to examine the place of Latin Christendom among the civilizations of the Eurasian landmass. In the year 780, the largest city in the Christian West was Rome, with a population of some 50 000. The other major cities in the Frankish realm were considerably smaller. The largest were Regensburg, Metz and Paris with 25 000 inhabitants each. The remaining large urban centers, Trier, Cologne, Reims, Speyer and Mainz, all had populations in the range of 15 000 to 20 000.[25]

If the degree of urbanization may be used to measure the capacity of a region to generate a surplus above the subsistence level, it is obvious that Western Europe fell far behind the other centers of civilization. At that time, the largest city in the world was Changan (Xian), the capital of the Tang Empire, situated on a tributary of the Huang Ho or Yellow River in north-central China. With a population of one million, this city was the administrative center of a vast empire of 60 million people that stretched from Indo-China into central Asia.[26] In comparison, Charles's kingdom with its population of about 12 million, was limited to present-day France, western Germany, Austria, northern Italy and the Low Countries.

Elsewhere, another rapidly growing city that would soon challenge its Chinese rival in size and importance was Baghdad, the capital of the Abbasid Caliphate, on the Tigris. Founded in 762, it was already spreading beyond the 1.6 mile (2.6 km) rampart built to protect it. By the time of Charles's death, it would have over a million inhabitants.[27] Its influence was felt throughout the Caliphate, from the Indus River to the Atlantic Ocean: in the Islamic world, only Spain under the Umayyad dynasty refused to accept Baghdad's authority. Most of the Abbasids' territory had been acquired at the expense of the Byzantine Empire, now reduced to Asia Minor, the Balkans and southern Italy. Yet even now, the latter empire's capital, Constantinople, with its quarter of a million inhabitants, outshone in brilliance any Christian city in Western Europe.[28]

By the late eighth century, there were considerable differences in both spoken and written Latin across the different regions of Western Christendom. Concerning the spoken language, linguistic historians believe that the non-Germanic territories of the former Roman Empire continued to form a single language zone. Nevertheless, the pronunciation of Latin in Gaul, influenced by the Germanic sounds, was distinct from that of Italy.[29] For example, the Anglo-Saxon Alcuin could converse in Rome but was unable to make himself understood in northern France.[30] There were also numerous differences in the written Latin that was used. There were at least a dozen regional varieties of pre-Carolingian scripts.[31] As mentioned, scriptoria in the British Isles used a half uncial as a book hand. Those in southern Italy used the rounded Beneventan form, while in northern Italy and France different lower-case forms derived from the late Roman cursive came to be used for documents and books.[32] Generally, the non-cursive scripts could not be written easily and compactly on parchment, the preferred writing medium. Although the cursives with their attached letters were easier to write, they were often difficult to read.[33]

Punctuation and spelling posed further problems in written texts. On the continent, before the late eighth century, there was no space left to indicate when a new word began.[34] Ends of sentences were frequently not marked, nor were the ends of paragraphs.[35] Further difficulties in exchanging written documents in the mid-eighth century arose from the growing frequency of irregularities in spelling. As the spoken vernacular in the Romance areas gradually diverged from classical Latin, writers were tempted to modify their spelling to reflect pronunciation changes. Instead of the correct *pago*, *robustus* and *persona*, one might find *bago* or *paco*, *ropustus* or *persuna*.[36] Moreover because western Romance speakers began to drop word endings from nouns, declensions began to disappear from colloquial speech.[37] It would take a further two centuries before the Romance languages began to be clearly distinguished from Latin.

By the middle decades of the eighth century, in the non-Germanic territories controlled by the Franks, the use of writing had declined dramatically compared to Roman and even Merovingian times. The number of new charters and diplomas issued had sunk to 'an alarming level'.[38] Data from the *Codices Latini Antiquiores* show that some 1750 Latin manuscripts have survived from the first seven centuries of the Christian era in continental Europe, an average of 25 per decade. However, only five exist for the half-century between 700 and 750, an average of one per decade. Lay education had become increasingly rare. Indeed, in northern Europe, urban schools had completely disappeared.[39] Outside of the clergy, even those at the summit of the political pyramid were illiterate. Despite the presence of scholars at his court, Charles was unable to read or write. Indeed one of his hopes in attracting Alcuin to his court may have been that the Anglo-Saxon scholar could grant him access to the mysterious symbols he saw on parchment. There is evidence that by the end of the eighth century, many Franks were beginning to be assimilated into the surrounding Latin culture.[40] Charles learned to speak Latin, probably initially with the soft north-Italian pronunciation of Peter of Pisa, his teacher after 776.[41]

Under the existing technology of oral communication supplemented by multiple writing systems, there were high fixed costs to storing information accurately over time. Essential information had to be kept in the memories of decision makers. Although use was made of written documents, these were usually not full texts, but simply notes or lists to aid in the recall of oral commands.[42] In effect they served to transfer information from long-term to short-term memory. Whenever the ruler or even his key advisers changed, much of the information necessary to interpret these notes would be lost. Once stored in the ruler's memory and complementary notes, any given set of information could be transmitted cheaply orally to an assembly of illiterate listeners. In other words, there were considerable scale economies in information processing. Unable to read or write, the listeners would be incapable of sharing complex information among themselves;

that is, network effects were low. With high scale economies and low network effects, one would predict that the Franks would maintain a highly centralized information network.[43]

Decision making in the Frankish kingdom was indeed highly centralized. Apart from several clerics attached to Charlemagne's household, there was nothing resembling an administrative bureaucracy in the empire of the Franks.[44] All important decisions were made by the king himself. Aachen (Aix-la-Chapelle), a town south-west of Cologne known since Roman times for its warm mineral springs, was Charlemagne's favorite place of residence. In the late eighth century it had a population of two to three thousand.[45] But during the first decade of Alcuin's stay in the kingdom of the Franks, Aachen was simply one of several royal residences among which the king circulated when he was not on campaign.[46] Over the fourteen years from 782 to 795, Charles would spend Christmas in ten different cities and only four times in Aachen.[47] Thus the central node in the Carolingian network was itself itinerant. For general policy, Charlemagne convened his some 250 counts annually. For more urgent administrative matters, he used a system of *missi dominici* (royal messengers).[48]

The danger of such an information structure is its vulnerability to seizure of the central node. By capturing this key point, a small group can monopolize the resources of the entire system for its own benefit, taxing income producers heavily at the level which maximizes short-run revenues. In effect, the Franks themselves were such a group. Clovis and his descendants had seized the rich lands between the Seine and the Rhine and gradually extended their territory from this base. Under the Carolingians, both tribute and plunder, the latter often in the form of slaves, continued to form an important part of public revenues.[49]

In an oral society, new ideas are quickly erased from short-term memory before they can replace existing ways of doing things. The odds against Alcuin in his mission to teach the Franks to read and write were therefore overwhelming. Let us now see how he fared under these challenging conditions.

## THE INVENTION OF A SYNTHETIC LANGUAGE

Alcuin's assignment on joining Charlemagne was to establish a program of secular education for the Frankish king's court. Previously, the training of the young members of the royal household had been limited to manners and court procedure.[50] Now the king intended to use the court school to provide formal instruction both for future priests who would go on to fill the top ranks in the clergy and also for lay officials. Several of Alcuin's students came from the royal family. Charles himself studied when he was not on campaign.[51] Alcuin also taught the three royal princes, Charles, Pippin and Louis, who all succeeded in learning to read and write. The king was sufficiently liberal to allow his successive wives, his sister and his daughters to receive instruction.[52] Numerous young men not from the royal family were also educated for the priesthood at the king's expense under Alcuin's guidance.

It is difficult to imagine a greater contrast than that between Charlemagne, the burly warrior, and Alcuin, the ascetic scholar. At the end of a day of hunting, Charles loved nothing more than a feast of roast venison, accompanied by his friends and mistresses. Alcuin, however, was content with porridge and cheese; he clearly frowned upon his patron's promiscuity.[53] In his personal correspondence with other men, Alcuin showed signs of intense emotion that may indicate homosexuality.[54] Yet the relationship between king and scholar was warm. Charles, to whom Alcuin gave the name 'David', called the teacher master, while Alcuin as 'Flaccus' (the family name of the Roman lyric poet Horace) called the king his disciple.[55] On one occasion, while Charles was giving a swimming-pool party in the warm springs of Aachen, he stopped amid the splashing to discuss a theological question with Alcuin.[56]

In the court school, acquiring literacy took the form of reading aloud. To aid the students, Alcuin prepared lists of words along with directions concerning their pronunciation. These notes were later assembled in manuscript form, under the title *De Orthographia*, probably between 796 and 800.[57] In this way there came to be two ways of reading a text aloud – one in the vernacular manner and one in a roughly phonetic, 'correct' fashion. The former, Roger Wright has argued, eventually evolved into the Romance languages, while the latter became the vehicular language used for scholarship well into the modern period – Medieval Latin.[58]

Alcuin was not the only learned person in residence: three north-Italian scholars were already present when he arrived at the Frankish court.[59] However, the Italians may have had difficulty teaching Latin to the Germanic Franks: the English cleric seems to have played the main role in organizing the school's curriculum. Alcuin divided the seven arts of classical education into two groups, which would later become the arts and science faculties of western universities. Grammar, rhetoric and dialectic were taught as the *trivium*, providing the fundamental elements of an education. The sciences of arithmetic, geometry, astronomy and music were grouped together as the more advanced subjects of the *quadrivium*.[60]

Instruction under Alcuin took the form of oral questions and answers. Indeed, for each of the subjects of the trivium, Alcuin prepared a textbook with both questions and answers in the form of dialogues between himself and his students. In *De Grammatica*, for example, he set forth a discussion between himself and two adolescent boys. 'Saxon', aged 15, does much of the explanation of grammatical rules, with the help of Alcuin, in answer to the questions of 'Frank'.[61] Further dialogues covered the subjects of rhetoric and dialectic.

There was not much point in setting up such a system if its effects were limited to a few dozen students at the Carolingian court. Alcuin therefore attempted to assure that his methods were extended to every town and village across the Frankish kingdom. In 789, he participated in the preparation of an edict issued by Charles, the *Admonitio Generalis* (General Admonition) that requested his bishops to make certain that every priest be able to read and understand the prayers he recites. In addition, there should be 'schools to teach boys to read' in each monastery and diocese.[62] In effect Alcuin, through Charles, was proposing a hierarchy of teaching centers, with the court school at the top, cathedral schools for training priests in every diocese, and parish schools at the elementary level in every village.[63]

By the early 790s, Alcuin had accomplished what he had been hired to do. With his patience, wit and great learning, he had brought continuous stimulation and knowledge to the Frankish king. Adapting Anglo-Saxon methods for teaching Latin as a second language, he had ensured that Charlemagne's children and others of the royal household were able to read and write. And under his direction, the king took steps to assure that in theory literacy would spread into every village in the vast kingdom.

Yet there was a fatal flaw in Alcuin's plans that must gradually have become evident to him. As described above, at the time of Alcuin's meeting with Charlemagne in 781, very little writing at all was being done in the government of the kingdom of the Franks.[64] Communication between the rulers and the nobility took place orally, either at an annual assembly or, when matters were more urgent, by messengers. Nevertheless, the Franks had available to them a language – Latin – that was spoken in one form or another by the majority of their subjects. In addition, like the Byzantines, they had access to a fully phonetic 24-character alphabet. Although the principal writing material, parchment, was expensive, it was ideal for storing written material over long periods in codex (book) format. Moreover, it could be produced locally in all corners of their realm. If necessary, parchment could even be recycled. Many medieval manuscripts were 'palimpsests' – texts written on top of an earlier text that had been scraped away.[65]

What the West lacked was a set of uniform writing standards. For three centuries, it had been ruled by illiterate warriors whose priority had been to use any surplus they could extract from their subjects in order to finance raids on their neighbors. Taking fierce pride in the oral bonds that linked a leader and his followers, they had failed to comprehend that by not maintaining uniform writing standards they were slowly strangling their source of rents. As a result, practices of written communication had gradually decayed to the point where, beyond the walls of a few monasteries, recording information for long-term storage had virtually disappeared. Under these circumstances, it is not surprising that the diffusion of technology had slowed to a bare trickle.

At about the time that Alcuin arrived at the royal court, Charles issued a request for books from all corners of his realm.[66] The result was the accumulation of what must have been the largest library in Latin Christendom. It comprised books written over a period of five centuries, although it is not clear where these books were kept prior to the construction of the palace at Aachen.[67] The most important volumes may have traveled with the king's household. Others may have been left at one or more of his favorite residences. Yet the results of this exercise presented a challenge to Alcuin and the other scholars at the Frankish court.

Today when one enters a library in Western Europe, North or South America or sub-Saharan Africa, one is confident that whatever the language, the vast majority of books will be printed in a uniform script composed mainly of lower-case Roman letters. Each word will be separated from the preceding and following words by spaces the width of an individual letter. Sentences will begin with upper-case letters and end with periods. Minor divisions in the text will be indicated by indented paragraphs, major ones by chapter headings. Such was not the case in the royal library to which Alcuin and his pupils had access. Some books were written with Roman capitals, others in uncials or half uncials, still others in semicursives or cursive script. In virtually all of these texts, there was no spacing between words. With experience, a Latin speaker could develop the ability to recognize the most important scripts and to break the stream of letters into individual words. For the Germanic speakers who formed most of Alcuin's pupils, however, the task would have been formidable.

After ten years of constant work, Alcuin began to realize the severity of the problem. He could not remedy the backwardness of the Kingdom of the Franks simply by teaching young nobles to read and to write under existing conventions. As long as script, vocabulary, and spelling varied from one scribe to another, and as long as individual letters could not be grouped easily by the reader into words, phrases, sentences and paragraphs, the probability that information recorded by one could be retrieved successfully by another was low. For those whose mother tongue was Germanic, there was an understandable problem. Yet as the regional pronunciations of Romance diverged further from the classical Latin of written texts, even native Romance speakers had difficulty learning to read and write. As a result, the accurate transmission of knowledge over time that was essential for the functioning of a complex society was unfeasible.

Consider Alcuin's most distinguished pupil. A native Germanic speaker, Charles had already learned to speak Latin and was strongly motivated to learn to read and write. His biographer, the German monk Einhard, noted that the king kept writing tablets and notebooks under his pillow in order to study if he should have trouble sleeping.[68] With today's materials for teaching reading to adults, Charles could probably have learned to read and write easily. As it was, there is no evidence that he was ever able to read, although like many others of his age, the king took great delight in listening to others read aloud.[69] On official documents, he signed by making a cross in the center of a symbol prepared by a scribe.[70] The greatest patron of the arts in the Middle Ages, taught by the most gifted medieval teacher, remained functionally illiterate.

Apart from the lack of standardization in writing, there was another problem that Alcuin and his pupils faced. The perpetual circuit of travel from one royal residence to another prevented the ready access to documentation. If the books were all left at one residence, they would be available for only part of the year. If they were scattered among the principal royal properties, each would be accessible only when the king's entourage happened to be there. As a result, for most of the year, Alcuin and his students would be cut off from the greater part of the stock of accumulated past knowledge. Furthermore, any contributions to written knowledge that they might make were likely to be discarded or lost while traveling or between visits.

It might seem that all of these problems could have been surmounted if only the court could have settled in one place. Between 791 and 796, Charles managed to crush the kingdom of the Avars, an Asiatic people who had settled in the central Danube valley. The Franks managed to seize the treasure hoard that the Avars had accumulated during their raids of Christendom over the previous century. Charles decided to use these windfall gains to help finance the construction of a permanent capital at Aachen. Accordingly, in 794, construction of a royal palace began, to be followed by a magnificent chapel, built in Byzantine style.[71] The opportunity to stay on within the new building complex, continuing his work through his patron by royal decree, must have tempted Alcuin.

One can only surmise that the realization must gradually have come to Alcuin that even from a permanent office in a royal palace, he could not achieve his ultimate goal. The highly centralized decision-making structure of the Carolingian state was ultimately inimical to the reforms he saw as necessary. After all, how could a decree imposing uniform standards of writing be credible when the king himself was unable to read or write? And how could a band of illiterate warriors ever enforce such a decree? Instead, Alcuin realized, writers of documents had to be persuaded individually that it was in their interest to harmonize their practices with those adopted by a group whose leadership they recognized. As teacher to a generation of Europe's scholars, Alcuin was in a unique position to accomplish this task. First, however, he must escape from Charles's entourage while still maintaining the prestige that came with royal patronage.

In 795, pleading fatigue after more than a decade of itinerant court life, Alcuin asked Charles to be transferred to a quieter, more sedentary position in the abbey of Tours. This request might have posed problems for a more conventional ruler than Charles. Although Alcuin had spent most of his life in institutions of the church, as mentioned, he had never been ordained as a priest. Charles clearly valued the Anglo-Saxon scholar's company but he could not refuse this request. Alcuin was appointed abbot of the monastery of St Martin at Tours.

**Alcuin at Tours**

Situated in the lower Loire valley, St Martin's was the richest abbey in the Frankish kingdom. Thousands of peasants worked its numerous estates, providing a flow of income that was the envy of many a secular noble. Upon his arrival in Tours in 796, Alcuin was about 64, an advanced age for his day. He could have left the administration of the abbey to younger men and retired to a life of study and contemplation. Instead, he decided to use his remaining years to convert the abbey into what may be described as the first node of a new communications network.

From his long experience as pupil, teacher and headmaster of the cathedral school in York and as head of the 'palace school' of the Franks, Alcuin knew how an institute of learning should be organized. His first priority was to assure the strict enforcement of Benedictine monastic discipline. He then set up a program of instruction at the abbey similar to that which he had developed at the royal court. Clerical and lay candidates would be given rigorous training in both religious and secular knowledge. Finally, he could set about the preparation of a scriptorium where scribes could be trained to produce books according to uniform standards.[72]

During his years at court, Alcuin had had the opportunity to read documents prepared at many different sites from all over Latin Christendom. He thus knew where to find the benchmark practices in every area of manuscript preparation. The ideal form of document for information that had to be preserved for frequent access over a long period was the parchment codex or book. But how would that text be written? What scripts would be used? How would the text be punctuated? And how would the page be laid out?

The script for the body of the text must be easy to read for non-Latin speakers. Yet it must be compact enough for many characters to fit easily on to a page of parchment. It must be as easy to write as the cursives used in France and Italy, yet as clear as the larger detached Anglo-Saxon half-uncials. Alcuin chose a semi-cursive that seems to have originated at the monastery of Corbie in north-eastern France around 770. Made up of lower-case, detached letters it could be written quickly, yet was easy to read. It was a judicious compromise between the large detached half uncials with which he was familiar from Anglo-Saxon manuscripts and the attached cursives found in France and Italy. Although variants of it had already become popular as a book hand in northern France, there was much work to be done. In individual manuscripts from this early period, multiple forms of some letters could be found.[73] Because of the official sanction the new script received from the court of Charlemagne, it has become known as the Caroline Minuscule.

To help the reader understand the structure of a text, Alcuin and his associates adopted a standardized punctuation. Sentences began with a capital letter and ended with a period. Words were separated by a space. In addition, a hierarchy of scripts was established. Chapter headings were in Roman capitals. The first line of a new chapter was written in half uncials. The beginning of a new paragraph was indicated by an enlarged capital that projected into the margin (indentation of paragraph beginnings was introduced only in the seventeenth century). To indicate the rising tone at the end of a question, a curving symbol was borrowed from musical notation.[74] The body of the text was in Caroline Minuscule.[75]

Not only was the new script easier to read and to write, but also it could be copied more cheaply than previous scripts. A lector or reader could read the text aloud using the revised Latin pronunciation that Alcuin had introduced to the continent. By translating the sounds back into phonetic characters, several scribes could make accurate copies of the original at the same time.[76] To assure that the religious texts which future priests would read aloud were pronounced correctly, it was essential that the spelling of written Latin be standardized. Alcuin therefore prepared the manuscript on spelling, *De Orthographia*, based on his teachings at the Palace school.

The scriptorium as an institution had emerged in earlier centuries, each monastic house tending to develop its own style. But the setting of rigorous standards for copying seems to have originated at Tours under Alcuin.[77] As one who himself had copied manuscripts, Alcuin knew well that long hours of careful training were necessary before a scribe could be assigned a manuscript to copy. As many as 30 scribes might collaborate on a single manuscript.[78] Unless their efforts were coordinated, the reader would have great difficulty in understanding the text. Alcuin was the first scholar to address scribes as a group. In his *titulus*, he instructed his scribes:

> May those who copy the pronouncements of the holy law and the hallowed sayings of the saintly fathers sit here. Here let them take care not to insert their vain words, lest their hands make mistakes through such foolishness. Let them resolutely strive to produce emended texts and may their pens fly along the correct path. May they punctuate the proper meaning by cola and commata and put each point at its proper hierarchy so that the lector reads nothing false nor suddenly falls silent when reading before the pious brothers in church.[79]

An opportunity to present the perfected medium to the world came at the beginning of the new century. In the fall of the year 800, Charles crossed the Alps to Rome to deal with charges of misconduct that had been made against Leo III, a man of humble origin who had been elected pope five years earlier. There, on 23 December, a great assembly of archbishops, popes and abbots cleared the pope of any wrongdoing. Then two days later at Christmas mass, in what was surely a prearranged gesture, as Charles was rising from prayer, the pope suddenly placed a golden crown on his head. Charles was proclaimed Emperor of the West. In a stroke, the church, by pretending that it alone had the right to bestow the imperial crown, had made a claim for precedence over the secular power.

Alcuin had been too infirm to make the trip to Italy with Charles; however, he made up for his absence by presenting his patron with a gift in honor of his coronation. The most important of all medieval texts was the Bible. Alcuin had prepared a new translation from the Greek, and in 801, he sent a magnificent copy of the corrected Latin text to his patron.[80] This work was to remain the standard version of the Bible in Western Europe over the following centuries. Although the original has been lost, for a half-century between 800 and 850, the scriptorium at Tours produced two such Bibles a year for export throughout Carolingian territory; 13 of which have survived. The typical Tours bible in codex (book) form contained about 435 folded sheets (folios) of parchment, each holding four pages of text divided into two columns.[81] In this work, the Tours scribes used standardized punctuation along with a 'hierarchy of scripts': capitals for the main headings, half uncials for the first line of a chapter, and a clear minuscule with detached letters.

The German paleographer Bernhard Bischoff suggested that these Bibles from Tours set the standards for ninth-century medieval manuscript writing.[82] From about 810 to 820, there occurred a great harmonization of Carolingian writing, as most other monasteries in the Frankish empire adopted the regularized script used at Tours.[83] By the middle of the ninth century, even the Roman curia had adopted the minuscule.[84] This standardization process was accompanied by a burst of production of manuscripts in Western Europe. At no other period during the Middle Ages were so many manuscript copies of the Bible made. In addition, the Carolingian scholars made copies of secular texts. Works of the major Roman authors such as Virgil had been transcribed on to parchment during the later Roman Empire. However, the works of secondary authors such as Caesar, Tacitus and Lucretius have survived to the present only through copies made by Carolingian scribes.[85] Some 7000 Latin documents have survived from the ninth century – roughly four times as many as survived from all eight preceding centuries together.[86]

Once the new medium had been developed, Alcuin quickly demonstrated another possible use for it. A full 300 of his letters have survived, some 250 of them written during the eight years of his residence at Tours, between 796 and 804.[87] Thanks to this correspondence and other texts he wrote, we know more about Alcuin than about virtually anyone else who lived before him in history.

For two decades, there had been no question of who was principal and who was agent in the relation between Charles and Alcuin. Then in 802, Alcuin granted refuge to a cleric from nearby Orléans who had sought pardon for a crime he had committed. When Bishop Theodulf of that city, one of Alcuin's longtime friends, sent his men to the abbey to bring back the accused, Alcuin refused to grant them admission. The bishop's men were beaten back when they tried to force their way into the monastery. Alcuin and Theodulf each wrote to the king to intercede. When Charles replied, it was to severely chastise Alcuin, who as a stranger and a foreigner had blackened the name of St Martin's.[88]

Such an incident could not, however, shake the friendship between the emperor and the scholar. His life's work accomplished, Alcuin wrote to Charles in 803 to bid him farewell.[89] The following year on the eve of Ascension, he suffered a stroke that left him paralyzed for over a week. Finally, on the morning of 19 May 804, the day of the Feast of Pentecost, Alcuin died, just after the singing of Matins. His innovation – a standardized vehicular language and a simply structured medium that made it accessible for non-native speakers – was a snowball that would gather mass and momentum with each year that passed.

## VERDUN, 843

Charlemagne experienced the sorrow of having his two eldest sons die before him – Pippin in 810 and Charles in 811. Finally, in 814, the old emperor himself died of pleurisy at the age of 72, after catching a chill while taking a bath.[90] He left his empire to his surviving son, Louis, who lived for another quarter-century. But during the last decade of Louis's life, the empire was shattered by a series of revolts on the part of his own sons. Full-scale civil war broke out among the sons when Louis died in 840. In 841, the two younger sons, Charles the Bald and Louis the German, defeated their elder brother Lothar at Fontenoy in Burgundy.[91] The following year, at Strasbourg, Charles and Louis swore to defend each other against Lothar. Charles addressed the troops of Louis in their Germanic tongue, while Louis spoke in Romance to the French soldiers of Charles. The bilingual text of their oaths constitutes the oldest surviving version of what would become the French and German languages.

Verdun lies on the Meuse River to the east of Paris, on the linguistic border between the Romance- and Germanic-speaking regions of Europe. There, in 843, Charles, Louis and Lothar agreed to split the empire into three kingdoms: the future France, Germany and Italy, with the ruler of the latter temporarily holding the key middle territories. Yet the fighting between the brothers and their descendants continued. By the end of the ninth century, effective central rule ceased to exist even in the component states.

The sudden collapse of the empire of the Franks after the death of Charlemagne has been something of a mystery to historians. Timothy Reuter has described how the Carolingians suddenly went from the offensive to the defensive at about this time.[92] The most frequent explanation is that their accumulated wealth made their territory a tempting target. Poorer groups of warriors such as the Vikings, Magyars and Muslims who lived on their borders were drawn by the possibilities of adventure and sudden wealth.[93] Yet this hypothesis fails to explain the civil wars that tore apart the empire from 830 to the end of the ninth century. It also offers no explanation of why the decline of central power should have been so complete in the Latin zone of the west and northern Italy, whereas the eastern Germanic lands were quickly re-consolidated. By the second half of the tenth century, this German Empire had become the dominant political force in Western Europe. The collapse of central authority in the Germanic territories would not occur for another two centuries. It almost appears as though the Carolingian Empire was attacked by a virus that infected the Latin territories first and then slowly spread eastward.

## Post-Imperial Decay

Consider the host institution, Carolingian society, at the time of Charlemagne's death. By the early ninth century, the post-imperial system of government that Western Europe had known since the fall of Rome was in an advanced state of decay. As we have seen, the semi-barbarian warrior kings who had seized the rich territories of the Western Empire had not understood that continued upkeep was essential to maintain the flow of income on which their prosperity depended. As a result, there had been a decline of literacy and of the infrastructure of the late Roman Empire. Roads, ports, courts and fortifications had been allowed to run down. Gradually, long-distance trade had fallen off, and production for market had declined. Tax revenue from these two sources had been reduced to a trickle.

By 719, when Charlemagne's grandfather, Charles Martel, as Mayor of the Palace, reunited the two halves of the Frankish kingdom, tax receipts were no longer sufficient to finance the state's defenses. In order to allow his followers to maintain the horses and equipment required for the new exigencies of cavalry warfare, Charles Martel gave them large grants of church lands. In return, he expected them to be at his call for military service. These concessions of land were not intended to be permanent, however. At the death of the vassal, the land could be granted to another warrior.[94] In effect, as Ganshof has pointed out, the Carolingians drew their enormous power from the combination of two existing institutions. One was the act of *commendatio*, by which a free man voluntarily placed himself in a state of dependence upon another man.[95] The other was the *beneficium* or benefice, according to which a landholder granted land to another person for a limited period under favorable conditions.[96]

Despite these grants of territory, Carolingian society had remained highly centralized. In the first century AD, the Roman writer Tacitus had mentioned the *comitatus*, a voluntary relationship of dependency of Germanic warriors upon their leader.[97] By the time of Charlemagne, this pattern had been reinforced by the asymmetric availability of reading and writing skills. Owing to his enormous landed wealth, the Frankish ruler could hire the best-qualified holders of a rare skill. The resulting zone of literacy around the Frankish court reinforced the traditional position of precedence of the warlord over his followers, the illiterate warriors whom the Carolingians appointed to positions of secular power across their territory. In effect, all recognized that in a predominantly oral society, information storage must be centralized to be managed efficiently. By assigning residual power to a single individual with access to some means of recording written information, the Franks could minimize conflicts over resource allocation while successfully defending the territory they had acquired.

With the decline of the exchange economy, urban centers had shrunk and the countryside had become increasingly self-sufficient. By the time of Charlemagne, as noted above, the agricultural surplus was no longer sufficient to support a large group of urban tradesmen and artisans. Now limited to serving as seat of the bishop and the local nobility, the town's role with respect to the surrounding countryside was largely non-economic.[98] Beyond the town's limits were to be found either great estates worked by servile labor or smaller plots belonging to free landholders. With few markets for their products, these property owners had little incentive to raise their productivity. Consequently, new technologies were rare and their diffusion was glacially slow. For example, the watermill had been known in Roman times, but in Charlemagne's day it was seldom seen.[99]

## THE PERIOD OF DARKNESS

Traditionally, the ninth and tenth centuries have been seen as a 'period of darkness' in the development of literacy, particularly among lay people.[100] By destroying the institutions of the Frankish state, the waves of invaders are thought to have severely interrupted the renaissance that had begun under Charlemagne. Yet if this position is correct, how can one explain the profound social transformations that began in the late tenth century, initially in the upper levels of the lay aristocracy? Between the death of Charlemagne in 814 and the beginning of the following century, not only did the entire decaying structure of post-imperial society collapse, but also the basic elements of a new type of society began to form. Western society was being restructured, from the most basic unit, the family, to the highest level, the state.

The key to understanding this transformation is to follow developments in the monasteries after the death of Alcuin in 804. Bischoff has described how between 810 and 850, most of the monasteries in Carolingian Europe adopted the simplified Carolingian script. As mentioned above, the Tours Bibles, distributed widely throughout Latin Christendom, were probably an important standardizing agent.[101] Although scriptoria at Corbie, Reims, Lyons, St Denis, St Germain des Prés and Fleury added some ornamentation in the last half of the ninth century, their house styles remained very similar.[102] The mutation in communications media introduced by Alcuin had begun to take firm root in its West Francian heartland.

Then, early in the tenth century an event occurred that would allow standardized Latin script to be diffused across Western Europe. In 909, William the Pious, Duke of Aquitaine, founded a new monastery at Cluny in the vicinity of Mâcon, Burgundy, just inside the eastern borders of the French kingdom. One of the conditions of the charter, unusual for its time, was the protection of the monastery from any secular interference: it was placed directly under the Holy See. In 927, the monastery came under the charge of Odo, a monk known for his asceticism, who remained abbot until his death in 942. Odo insisted upon the strict observance of the code of

Benedict of Aniane, which prohibited the eating of meat; he also extended the choir office and the rules of silence. As his own reputation for sanctity spread, Odo was requested to aid in reforming other monasteries, both in France and in Italy.[103]

Odo was a member of an Aquitanian noble family with close ties to Alcuin's former abbey at Tours.[104] He himself had been taught by Remigium of Auxerre, who had been at the monastery in Reims mentioned above. Once adopted by Cluny, the standards for writing set at Tours were diffused across Western Europe.[105] From 17 monasteries in 937, the reform movement led by Cluny climbed to about 60 by 1049. By the early twelfth century, there were some 2000 affiliated monasteries scattered across France, Italy, Spain, Germany and England.[106] Like Cluny itself, most of these monasteries were new foundations that had not existed at the time of Charlemagne.

As the number of men trained to read and write multiplied in the ninth century, it became conceivable to replicate the institutions of government developed by Charlemagne within smaller political units. As a result, the monopoly of the imperial court became increasingly contestable. Since Charlemagne's two elder sons had died relatively young, the succession by his third son, Louis I, in 814 went unchallenged. However, in 830, Louis's three oldest sons challenged their father's decision to bestow a part of his empire on his youngest son. And when Louis in turn died in 840, his three surviving sons fought among themselves and concluded by dividing the kingdom. Yet their authority was in turn challenged by their most important vassals. As Georges Duby has observed, the economic role that Charlemagne's court had formerly fulfilled, coordinating defense and dispensing justice, could now be played by the courts of these lesser lords.[107]

F.L. Ganshof documented the changes in contract underlying this breakdown of authority. By the early ninth century, the great royal vassals were granting benefices to their own vassals.[108] Naturally, the holdings most coveted were those in the hands of cathedrals or monasteries. By the middle of the ninth century, Charlemagne's grandsons were distributing church lands to their vassals or commanding the church to accept their own followers as vassals.[109] Gradually, in West Francia, it became accepted that the benefice was hereditary.[110] In addition, the lines of obligation became crossed, as the vassal of one lord received a second benefice from another noble.[111]

The use of written documents for administration requires a permanent capital where records can be stored. By the third quarter of the ninth century, Charles the Bald had established his court at Laon, north of Paris, while his half-brother Louis the German had chosen Regensburg, on the upper Danube.[112] Meanwhile, their nephew Louis II of Italy ruled from the former Lombard stronghold of Pavia. These cities thus experienced a brief period of rapid growth in the ninth century before the further disintegration of political power passed them by. Then, at the turn of the millennium, from the wreckage of the Carolingian Empire, a new structure began to emerge.

## NOTES

1. Collins (1998, p. 60).
2. Butt (2002, p. 40).
3. Chamberlin (1986, p. 30).
4. Chamberlin (1986, pp. 73–74).
5. Chamberlin (1986, p. 72).
6. Gobry (1999, p. 56).
7. Gobry (1999, p. 59).
8. Chamberlin (1986, p. 74).
9. Gobry (1999, p. 62).
10. Chamberlin (1986, p. 86).
11. Maddison (2001, p. 241).
12. Depreux (2002, p. 40).
13. Gobry (1999, p. 65).
14. Chamberlin (1986, p. 128).
15. Reuter (1990, p. 404) suggests that after their campaign against the Avars in 794, the Franks ran out of conquerable and profitable victims.
16. Davies (1996, pp. xvii, 302).
17. Duckett (1951, p. 33).
18. Duckett (1951, pp. 14–16).
19. Duckett (1951, p. 17).
20. Wright (1982, pp. 98–99).
21. Godman (1982, p. xxxvi).
22. Duckett (1951, p. 26).
23. Godman (1982, p. xxxvi).
24. Duckett (1951, p. 32).
25. The urban population data are for the year 800 and come from Bairoch *et al.* (1988).
26. Barraclough (1984a, p. 127).
27. Ibid.
28. Ibid.
29. Wright (1997, p. 267) expresses the consensus among linguistic historians over the essential unity of the Romance regions in the early Middle Ages. Keller (1978, p. 151) notes the impact of the Germanic languages on spelling and pronunciation in Gaul.
30. Wright (1982, p. 103).
31. Wright (1982, p. 114).
32. Bischoff (1990, pp. 83–111).
33. Wright (1982, p. 114).
34. Saenger (1990, p. 448).
35. Wright (1982, p. 114).
36. Keller (1978, p. 151).
37. Kontzi (1978, p. 408).
38. Brown (1994, p. 8).
39. Graff (1987, p. 40).
40. McKitterick (1989, p. 13).
41. Bullough (1991, pp. 131, 134).

42. Stock (1983, p. 16).
43. In an influential 1962 paper, Paul Baran of the RAND Corporation contrasted such a centralized network with two other configurations, namely, a decentralized and a distributed network. The principle concepts of this communication were later included in RAND Corporation Memorandum RM-3420-PR (Baran, 1964).
44. Heer (1975, p. 34).
45. Barraclough (1984a, p. 109).
46. For a map of Charlemagne's itinerary, see Glanz and Häusler (1993, p. 42).
47. Duckett (1951, p. 87).
48. Heer (1975, p. 39).
49. Reuter (1985, pp. 75–77).
50. Duckett (1951, p. 85).
51. Eginhard (1966, p. 41).
52. West (1899, pp. 42–43).
53. Duckett (1951, p. 106).
54. Heer (1975, p. 162).
55. Monk of St Gall (1966, p. 61).
56. Duckett (1951, p. 89).
57. Wright (1982, p. 108).
58. Wright (1982, p. 109).
59. Duckett (1951, pp. 98–103).
60. Heer (1975, p. 184).
61. Duckett (1951, pp. 111–112).
62. Duckett (1951, p. 122).
63. West (1899, p. 58).
64. Ganshof (1971, p. 125).
65. Heer (1975, p. 195).
66. Brown (1994, p. 33).
67. Bischoff (1990, p. 205).
68. Einhard (1970, p. 67).
69. Einhard (1970, pp. 64–67).
70. Heer (1975, p. 21).
71. Häusler (1993, p. 65).
72. West (1899, pp. 70–71).
73. Bischoff (1990, p. 112).
74. Bischoff (1990, p. 169).
75. Gaur (1984, p. 172).
76. Wright (1982, p. 115).
77. Ganz (1987, p. 33).
78. Ganz (1987, p. 35).
79. Ganz (1987, p. 33).
80. Wright (1982, p. 115).
81. McKitterick (1994, p. 222).
82. Bischoff (1990, p. 114).
83. Bischoff (1990, p. 114).
84. Bischoff (1990, p. 115).
85. Heer (1975, p. 198).
86. Brown (1994, p. 34).
87. West (1899, p. 73).
88. Almedingen (1968, pp. 153–154).
89. West (1899, p. 87).
90. Heer (1975, p. 227).
91. Nelson (1995, p. 118).
92. Reuter (1990).
93. Barraclough (1984a, p. 110).
94. Ganshof (1982, p. 39).

95. Ganshof (1982, p. 22).
96. Ganshof (1982, p. 29).
97. Ganshof (1982, p. 21).
98. Poly and Bournazel (1991, p. 379).
99. Duby (1974, p. 187).
100. Graff (1987, p. 62).
101. Bischoff (1990, pp. 114–115).
102. Bischoff (1990, p. 116).
103. Blumenthal (1988, pp. 12–13).
104. Blumenthal (1988, p. 12).
105. Bischoff (1990, p. 126).
106. Blumenthal (1988, p. 14).
107. Duby (1974, p. 229).
108. Ganshof (1982, p. 46).
109. Ganshof (1982, p. 70).
110. Ganshof (1982, p. 83).
111. Ganshof (1982, p. 86).
112. Vocke (1993, p. 143).

# 2. The ring of cities

In the last decades of the tenth century and the first decades of the eleventh, a profound transformation began to spread across Western Europe. The most visible indication of the change was that the minor nobility started to build castles, first of wood and later of stone. From there, they proceeded to dominate the peasants of the surrounding countryside, suppressing the previous distinction between free and servile status. Changes also took place within the family. In documents of the period, the surname or patronymic appeared for the first time in European history. Usually the name was taken from the family's principal estate.[1] At the top of the social pyramid, primogeniture became the norm for transfer of property from one generation to the next, younger sons having to accept careers as warriors or priests.

The new institution underlying this transformation is known as the *seigneurie banale* or feudal manor, and the social system itself is described as feudalism. Between the end of the invasions and the first decades of the new millennium, this form of organization replaced the previous patchwork of great estates and free landholdings between the Pyrenees and the Rhine in Western Europe.[2] In place of labor services, the feudal landholders collected rents for use of the new equipment they installed. Whatever their status, peasants were obliged to have their wheat ground in the lord's mill and bake their bread in the lord's oven.[3] In Picardy, where this transformation came earlier than in many other regions, payments in kind had virtually disappeared by the eleventh century.[4]

How may this transformation be explained? Such developments were only possible if the lord's estates were sufficiently well administered to generate the surplus that was required to maintain the castle and its personnel. Why was such administration possible now when it had not been before? One possible explanation was the emergence of a new group in European society, the *ministeriales*. Of servile birth, they were able to rise to positions of bailiffs or even knights. On them depended the success of the new economic system. In Germany, they appeared first on church estates, where during the tenth century they came to play a prominent role as administrators. Subsequently, in the eleventh century, German monarchs used this class to administer their own domains.[5] In France too, the *ministeriales* played prominent roles in the transformation in the rural sector. In Picardy, for example, every ecclesiastical manor was headed by a member of this class.[6]

How did the *ministeriales* emerge? Brian Stock has argued that there was a rebirth of literacy in the eleventh century as the ability to read and write gradually spread beyond the clergy. In the early decades of that century, he has pointed out, there appeared in the north-Italian cities a new class of official, the *iudex*, who was responsible for recording agreements in written form.[7] The result was the emergence of what might be called case law, with the outcomes of notable disputes being recorded to assist in later interpretation of the legal code.[8] Yet this development would have been meaningless had the lawyers of Pavia in the tenth century not drawn up the *Liber Papiensis*, a compilation of Lombard law along with modifications introduced by the Carolingians. In short, lay literacy can be pushed back at least into the tenth century.

Rosamond McKitterick has provided evidence from the lives of saints that in the last half of the ninth century it was not unusual for a boy of noble birth to receive a standard basic education. For example, both Odo of Cluny's father and his teacher seemed to have received such an education. Only when young Odo showed an incapacity for the martial arts was he given more advanced instruction.[9] It is plausible that on church estates such a basic education gradually came to be provided not only to the sons of nobles but also to the offspring of some of the servile class. If so, it was perhaps this extension of literacy into the upper levels of the lay population that explains the transformation in medieval society.

## THE PRIOR AND THE DUKE

When word of the ambitious Italian's criticism reached him, Duke William of Normandy, 26, exploded with rage. Several years earlier, William's marriage to Mathilda, daughter of the count of Flanders, had been disallowed by Pope Leo IX on grounds of consanguinity. The charge was clearly ridiculous, although William was ready to admit that he had not entirely respected the protocols of courtship in wooing his bride. Indeed, upon hearing that the young maid had dismissed him as a bastard, he had ridden to her father's castle in Lille, invaded her bedroom and dragged her around by the hair before galloping back home.[10] All the same, William told himself, there had been no violation of the church's rules.

Now, one of his own most able clerics, Lanfranc, 44, prior of the monastery of Bec, had dared join the critics of the marriage. The learned scholar from Pavia, who had originally trained as a lawyer, had undoubtedly decided to follow the papal directives in order to find favor within the church. However, William, his secular master, could not tolerate such open insubordination. To punish Lanfrac's abbey of Bec, the duke commanded his followers to burn one of its dependent farms. As for Lanfranc himself, William ordered that the dissenting prior be expelled from Normandy.

In the year 1054, William of Normandy was one of the mightiest warriors of his day. Five feet ten inches (178 cm) in height, he was much taller than the medieval soldiers he commanded. The power in his arms and shoulders enabled him to draw a heavy bow while riding a horse, controlling the animal with his thighs. He was merciless to those who stood in his way and violent in the sanctions he imposed. For poaching a deer in the royal forest, the penalty was blinding.[11] When in his harsh, rough voice he gave an order, his followers hastened to do his bidding. It was not long therefore before the buildings of the abbey's farm of Parque were ablaze.

Shortly thereafter, Lanfranc was riding a lame horse toward the duchy's borders, accompanied by a single servant, when he met the duke and his party. William at first refused to greet the Italian monk, but finally relented and motioned him to approach. Why was his command to leave not being obeyed, he asked? 'At thy order,' replied Lanfranc, 'I turn my steps from your duchy, hindered by this useless quadruped. Give me a better horse so that I may fulfill your order.' Charmed by the quick wit of the Italian, William laughed, and the two men were soon again on friendly terms with each other.[12]

William was understandably sensitive to criticism, for he faced a double dilemma. Within his own government, he had what is known as a problem of agency. He had to devise a mechanism to motivate the soldiers under him in order to keep his opponents in check. His victory over dissident Norman barons at Val ès Dunes seven years earlier had given him nominal control of a vast territory stretching from Picardy to Brittany. However, within the duchy, each of his unruly vassals considered himself the legitimate ruler of his own domain. Since the time of William's birth, the Norman vassals had been able to pass their land on to their own descendants. Indeed, they had documents to prove their rights.[13] Consequently, the duke had few possibilities of rewarding his followers by redistributing land, as his ancestors had done in the tenth century. Compensation for services rendered would have to come from current revenues. But to assure an efficient flow of tax receipts, William required a loyal corps of competent administrators.

William's second problem was one of legitimacy with regard not only to his lay subjects but also to the powerful Norman church and to external powers. Born out of wedlock to the previous duke and a Falaise undertaker's daughter, he was known to his contemporaries as William the Bastard. Now his own marriage had been judged illegal by the pope. His difficulties made him a tempting target for his feudal superior, King Henry I of France, and for his powerful neighbor to the southeast, Geoffroy II of Anjou. To keep them at bay would require a sustained effort with all of the resources at his command. Henry first tried to defeat William by sending an army to invade Normandy in February 1054 but was defeated at Mortemer. The king and Geoffroy would try again four years later.

Once assured of Lanfranc's complete loyalty, William had good reason to pardon him fully, because the Italian cleric offered the duke support on each of these fronts. At Bec, Lanfranc was winning a reputation as one of the leading scholars and teachers in Latin Christendom. He and the pupils he was attracting offered a potential source of administrative talent to the ducal government and to the Norman church. In addition, Lanfranc's Italian origins, his legal training and his authority within the monastic movement gave him ready access to the church and its leaders. The power behind the papal throne was another Italian, the deacon Hildebrand, who would himself be elected pope some 20 years later. Lanfranc was the ideal man for William to consult in order to shore up support in Rome.

The conflict with the papacy over William's marriage came to a head in 1059, when Pope Nicholas II imposed an interdict on the duchy. The dispensation of the sacraments would be suspended. It was Lanfranc who negotiated a settlement at the Rome Easter council of that year. As penance to earn papal recognition of their marriage, William and Mathilda would each found an abbey in William's new administrative center of Caen.[14] In 1063, Lanfranc was appointed abbot of the monastery of St Étienne in Caen. Four years later under his supervision, work was begun on a great church for the *Abbaye des Hommes*.

The construction lasted a decade. Finally, on 13 September 1077, in the presence of William and the ducal family, the new abbey church of St Étienne in Caen was consecrated. Two centuries later, the Benedictine monks of the monastery would enlarge the choir in the new Gothic style. However, the western facade, the nave and the transept remain today from the original Romanesque structure. The west front of the church stands at the end of a narrow street, dominating the neighboring buildings by its massive size. Approaching the church, one immediately notices several departures from the design of earlier Romanesque structures. Missing is the low porch that covered the entrance of previous churches. Instead, the Norman builders erected a white limestone facade block flanked by two corner towers that is at once harmonious and austere.[15] Above each of the doorways on the lower level and the windows on the two upper levels is the characteristic rounded Roman arch.

Inside, the Norman craftsmen prepared further surprises. Instead of the narrow, dark nave of earlier Romanesque churches, there is a vast wide space bathed in daylight from three levels of side windows. Looking up, one is amazed by the symmetric beauty of the sixpartite ribbed vaults high above that cover each pair of bays. The original builders prudently if unimaginatively closed the main part of the interior with a wooden roof when they completed the church over the decade from 1067 to 1077.[16] But early in the twelfth century, the Benedictine monks who administered the church decided that the risk of fire was sufficiently great that it was worth replacing the wood with stone. A new generation of Norman builders familiar with the latest construction techniques of northern Italy and the Loire valley proposed an innovative design to cover the immense span. In each pair of bays there would be ribs stretching out from the summit of the six side pillars and meeting in the center so as to support the weight of a stone vault. Since the upper-story walls on each side of the double bay no longer had to support the weight of the roof, they could be pierced with windows.

The Norman builders completed these renovations to St Étienne by 1115.[17] Three decades later, at St Denis, north of Paris, the round Roman arch in the ribbed vault would be replaced with the pointed arch – the final step in the development of a new style of architecture known as Gothic.

In the economic domain, the Normans were also quick to adopt the best available practices. They were at the forefront in northern Europe in introducing a monetary economy. Bishops and secular lords financed the construction of new towns with the revenues of tolls levied on trade. Caen's prosperity came in part from shipping grain from the flat plains in the Orme basin to distant urban markets such as Rouen.[18] That city in turn engaged in an active long-distance trade with Scandinavia.

The Normans were also innovators in military techniques. They were among the first to develop procedures for coordinating large groups of armored horsemen on the battlefield. Against disciplined infantry in formation, mounted knights could do no more than prod with their lances.[19] However, against a broken line or small groups of soldiers on foot, heavy cavalry was extremely effective. In addition, the Normans seem also to have introduced the crossbow into medieval warfare. Although its rate of fire was slower than that of the short bow, its quarrels were able to penetrate shields and armor.[20]

After a half millennium of declining skills in architecture, economic organization and warfare, Normandy in the eleventh century was suddenly at the forefront of a technological renaissance. How can this burst of innovation be explained?

## THE TURN OF THE MILLENNIUM

The eleventh century would bring together in violent confrontation two neighboring societies – Normandy and England – that had previously followed parallel paths with little interaction and even less conflict. Let us attempt to draw a picture of each land around the year 1000.

## Normandy

To understand better the situation in Normandy in the days before the reign of Duke William II (r. 1035–1087), we must go back over a hundred years. In the early tenth century, Scandinavian raiders established permanent settlements in the lower Seine valley. The weak Carolingian king of France, Charles the Simple, a great-great grandson of Charlemagne, did his best to defend his kingdom against Scandinavian pressure, employing a mixed strategy of attack and tribute. However, internal divisions weakened royal power. Some of his most powerful vassals, the Robertian lords of Neustria, ancestors of the Capetian dynasty, waged war against Carolingian forces.

With the defenders divided, the Viking commander, Rollo, was able to convince the leaders of France to recognize him as lord of the lower Seine basin. In recognition of this fait accompli, Charles the Simple formally ceded this territory to Rollo in 911. In return, Rollo agreed to become the king's vassal. Over the following decades, the Viking chieftain's descendants extended their power base to the west beyond the Seine basin. By the turn of the millennium, Normandy had expanded to include the valleys of the Dives and Orme Rivers, the Cotentin peninsula and the region around Avranches on the border of Brittany. The original settlements became known as Upper Normandy, the later as Lower Normandy.

By the year 1000, Normandy economically was still recovering from the destruction of the Viking invasions a century earlier. Politically, it was emerging as one of a number of territorial principalities competing for hegemony within the hexagon of present-day France. As in Flanders, Anjou, Blois and indeed the Ile de France, a powerful dynasty was attempting to consolidate its power. To the extent that the Norman dukes succeeded, they would inevitably come into conflict with their neighbors. The resulting regional wars would dominate political life in France until late in the reign of Philip Augustus (1179–1223).

At the beginning of the new millennium, Normandy had a population of perhaps 400 000.[21] The main center of Norman power was the city of Rouen, situated 75 miles (120 km) inland from the English Channel on the Seine. With 12 000 inhabitants, Rouen was a point of transshipment between ocean-going boats and smaller vessels traveling upriver to Paris and beyond. The city was the seat of an archbishopric whose boundaries coincided almost exactly with those of the duchy of Normandy. Cathedrals in the towns of Evreux, Lisieux, Sées, Bayeux, Coutances and Avranches all depended on the archdiocese of Rouen. One other important Norman site, as we have noted, is Caen, in lower Normandy near the mouth of the Orme River. Although it had been settled in Roman times, Caen was a small regional trading center, of considerably less importance than the neighboring cathedral town of Bayeux.[22]

The structure of government in Normandy had been carried over from Carolingian times. Normandy covered twelve *pagi*, local administrative units or counties into which the Carolingian Empire had been divided. In the year 1000, the ruler of this territory was William's grandfather Richard II, a descendant of Rollo, known as the Count of Rouen to those outside Normandy. In an effort to obtain recognition of his territorial claims, Richard was the first to attribute to himself the title of 'duke'.[23]

Landholding in Normandy at the turn of the millennium had not changed greatly from the Carolingian period. There were two basic types of tenure. One was the *alodium*, land that was held free of any military burden. It was family land that could be passed on from generation to generation. The other was the *beneficium*, land granted in exchange for some kind of service. In many cases, the beneficiary was a knight or soldier, but clerics, cooks and women could also hold *beneficia*. This second form of tenure involved a state of personal dependence of the landholder on his lord. Generally, it was not assumed to be hereditary. At this time, landowners were still known by their first names and their lineage rather than by the land they held.[24] With the breakdown of the Carolingian order, the complexity of power relationships among the landholding class increased. As we noted at the end of Chapter 1, vassals often held territories from two or more lords.[25] There thus arose the distinct possibility of conflicting loyalties if a dispute arose between two lords in the same region.

To complete our picture of Normandy at the end of the first millennium, let us consider the writing system. In the early ninth century, Normandy had been dotted with prosperous monasteries such as Fécamp, Jumièges and St Ouen in the region of Rouen and Mont St Michel in the west. Over the course of the ninth century, Viking invaders had pillaged and burned the monasteries and most of the churches of Normandy.[26] Under the patronage of the first dukes, there were modest attempts in the tenth century to restore monastic life at Jumièges and Fontanelles in the Seine valley, at Mont St Michel, and at St Ouen in Rouen. Nevertheless, in the year 1000, many of the monastic communities that had existed before the invasions had not been re-established.[27] Normandy still suffered from a severe shortage of clerics able to read and write.

**England**

Let us now jump across the English Channel to visit Normandy's closest overseas neighbor. England had suffered less permanent damage from the Viking raids of the ninth century. Although Scandinavians had settled in the northeastern region of the kingdom in the decades after 878, they had never succeeded in establishing a viable state there. By 918, the kings of Wessex had succeeded in incorporating the region the Scandinavians had settled – later known as the Danelaw – into their Anglo-Saxon kingdom.

In the year 1000, England was larger, richer and more advanced than Normandy. With a population between 1.5 and 2 million, the Anglo-Saxon kingdom including Wales was roughly four times as populous as the French duchy.[28] It was sufficiently wealthy to begin to attract raiders from Scandinavia once again. In 991, the English paid the Danes 10 000 pounds to stop them from pillaging.[29] In 994, the protection fee was raised to 14 000 pounds.[30] Yet even this sign of military weakness may be interpreted favorably. The *geld* paid to the Danes as tribute was raised by the first regular and permanent land tax in the West since the fall of Rome.[31]

The Anglo-Saxons had not neglected their Latin. The reforms to Medieval Latin introduced under Charlemagne reached England in the mid-tenth century. In 955, during a temporary reaction against monasticism, the English monk Dunstan had taken refuge at the Benedictine monastery of Blandinium in Ghent, which had adopted the reforms of Cluny. When he returned to England as Bishop of Winchester in 957, Dunstan introduced the strict Benedictine practices into English monastic life. Around 970, monks from Flanders and from Fleury in the Loire valley drew up a monastic code for English monks based on that of Cluny and written in the continental script.[32]

By the end of the first millennium, Latin scholarship in England nevertheless was in decline. Competition arose from writing in the language of the people. England at that time was the only non-Latin land in Western Christendom to have developed a writing system based on its spoken vernacular. A century earlier, Alfred the Great (r. 871–899) had promoted the use of written forms of the West Saxon dialect. He had ordered that historical documents in Latin from earlier periods be translated into Anglo-Saxon. In addition, he had begun the systematic registry of current events in a series of documents known as *The Anglo-Saxon Chronicle*. For the written form of Old English, the Anglo-Saxons used an insular script known as the Anglo-Saxon Pointed Minuscule.[33] In the late tenth century, Bishop Aelfric and Archbishop Wulfstan extended Alfred's initiative, insisting that the basic elements of the Catholic faith be made available to worshipers in their mother tongue.

At this moment, continental society was about to undergo rapid change. In cutting itself off in part from Medieval Latin, the main current by which these transformations were being diffused, England was becoming trapped in a cultural backwater. The consequences of this relative isolation for English society in the eleventh century would be dramatic.

## NORMANDY AND ENGLAND IN THE YEARS BEFORE 1066

The career of Lanfranc illustrates the influences that were transforming Western Europe during the half-century prior to 1066. The future Archbishop of Canterbury and Viceroy of England was born around 1010 in Pavia, the administrative center of the kingdom of Italy. Control of northern Italy was in the hands of the German emperors who had succeeded to the throne of Charlemagne's grandson, Louis the German. Lanfranc's father was a *iudex*, one of the judicial officials attached to the palace court who were called upon to certify the validity of legal transactions.[34] Lanfranc himself received a classical education and was trained in Roman law, possibly at Bologna. This was a period when Lombard law was being codified. Lanfranc mastered the new scholastic vocabulary for 'distinguishing, objecting and subsuming' that was being developed for use in rhetorical disputes.[35] He established himself in Pavia as a teacher and lawyer. Then around 1036, a year of strife between the German emperor and the Italian cities, he decided to leave Italy for France.[36]

Lanfranc's path from teaching law in Pavia to an eventual position of power within the Norman church was somewhat tortuous. He seems first to have studied in Chartres and then established himself as a teacher in western Normandy at Avranches, where he could remain in contact with the nearby abbey of Mont St Michel.[37] In 1042, he experienced an intense religious experience and decided to enter a new monastery that had been founded at Bec near Brionne in central Normandy. After three years of living in seclusion, Lanfranc became the prior of the monastery, responsible for its religious and administrative direction.

Lanfranc soon began teaching the young monks and local boys the elements of Latin and a knowledge of Benedictine rules. Within ten years, his fame as a teacher was such that he was attracting pupils from across Normandy, and even from Italy and Germany. For perhaps a decade in the 1050s, Lanfranc's school at Bec supplied the intelligentsia that were to run Norman society.[38] In addition, by the end of that decade, the Italian cleric himself had become a trusted adviser to Duke William on questions of both civil and religious administration within the duchy.

In the years before 1066, through people like Lanfranc, outside influences were increasingly penetrating into Norman society, integrating it into Western Europe. The question of property rights illustrates the differences between Normandy and England. When William's grandfather, Duke Richard II, died in 1026, he was succeeded by his eldest son, Richard III. After quelling a revolt by his younger brother Robert, Richard died the following year – possibly by poisoning. It was Robert who then inherited the duchy. He in turn died in 1035 while returning from a pilgrimage to Jerusalem, leaving as his heir his eight-year-old illegitimate son, William. The minority of the young duke saw further strife. Three of his guardians were killed and his tutor was also murdered. Order was restored only in 1047 when William at the age of 20 defeated a coalition of rebellious nobles at Val ès Dunes to the southeast of Caen.

In Normandy, during this period of instability, there occurred what David Bates has called a 'feast on church property'. [39] Initially, there was a wave of predation on the part of the lay nobility at the expense of the monasteries and cathedrals. In Upper Normandy, Goscelin, the Viscount of the Talou, seized estates that belonged to the monastery of Fécamp and the Rouen cathedral. Meanwhile in Lower Normandy, lands were taken from the abbey of Mont St Michel and the cathedrals of Bayeux and Coutances.[40] Then, when easily available church lands became scarce, local seigneurs began to fight among themselves over the remaining spoils. In Lower Normandy, the families of Humphrey de Veilles and Roger de Tosny came into collision as each attempted to expand at the other's expense.

Charlemagne, upon succeeding to the throne, had one by one eliminated the leaders of the quasi-autonomous 'tribal duchies' who posed a potential challenge to his centralized rule. He had deposed Chunoald II in Aquitaine, and the aristocracy of Alamannia and Tassilo in Bavaria, with a minimum of bloodshed.[41] Why could the ruler of Normandy not simply punish any potential vassal who threatened the property of a monastery or another vassal under the duke's protection?

Removal of a rebellious vassal was not as easy in eleventh-century Normandy as it had been under Charlemagne. Consider the following events. William's cousin, Guy of Brionne (also known as Guy of Burgundy), had been one of the leaders of the revolt against the young duke in 1047. Yet it took three years after Val ès Dunes for the ducal forces to dislodge him from his castle at Brionne on the Risle River southwest of Rouen.[42] Indeed it was perhaps during the prolonged siege that William first came to know and appreciate the intelligence of Lanfranc, prior of the neighboring monastery of Bec. Although Guy of Brionne was pardoned, he chose to leave the duchy. Nevertheless, William later returned the castle at Brionne and its dependencies to Guy's sons.[43]

In England, during the same period, there was no such weakening of the ruler's arbitrary power. The redistribution of property among the nobility remained a prerogative of royalty. Even a weak king such as Edward the Confessor was able to exile an important noble family – at least temporarily. He banished Godwin, Earl of Wessex, and his sons in 1051, for a relatively minor misdemeanor only to have them return in force the following year to reclaim their position. Similarly, in 1065, acting in the name of the feeble Edward, Godwin's eldest son Harold was able to strip his brother Tostig of the earldom of Northumbria. In 1066, power remained much more centralized in Anglo-Saxon than in Norman society.

**The Feudal Mutation**

The contrasting examples of Guy of Brionne and Tostig indicate that the profound changes taking place in the society of Normandy and other regions of continental northern Europe around the turn of the millennium failed to occur in England. As we saw in the introduction to this chapter, historical research over the past few decades has revealed the coincident appearance on the continent of three phenomena, namely castles, patronymics and heritable benefices. Let us first recall the changes and then speculate about what might have caused them to occur in Normandy but not in Britain. We will then be in a position to discuss the implications of these new social developments for relations of power and their economic effects.

A first change we noted was the appearance of castles. In Normandy, although some of these fortified residences were built of stone, often the technique consisted simply of a motte and bailey; that is, a wooden tower on a mound in a courtyard surrounded by a wooden palisade.[44] The techniques for building fortresses were well known in Antiquity. Under the Carolingians, fortification had been reserved for border areas such as Saxony in order to protect Frankish garrisons.[45] However, with the new millennium, there was a burst of construction of private castles across northwestern Europe in regions such as Burgundy, Flanders and Champagne. In Normandy, the building of castles on the borders of the duchy dates from the first quarter of the eleventh century. Duke Richard II of Normandy assigned these castles to counts who were his close relations. However, after his death in 1026, the original families continued to retain their tenure.[46] Then, in the 1030s and 1040s, came a second wave of castle building as many of the leading families fortified their own private residences in order to be able to withstand a siege by their territorial competitors.[47]

A second change, we have seen, was a modification of individual names by the addition of the surname or patronymic. The construction of castles coincided with a transformation in the structure of the family in northern Europe. One of the first regions to be affected appears to have been the Mâconnais, where the abbey of Cluny was located. Deeds from the Mâcon region in the tenth century made no mention of family surnames. However, over the first 35 years of the eleventh century, surnames began to appear. The use of the patronymic thereafter increased throughout the eleventh century. At first the custom was limited to the upper nobility, but gradually the castellans and lesser nobles followed suit.[48]

Family names were chosen from three different sources. In some cases, the name of a castle such as Montmerle or Sennecé was used. In other cases, a nickname describing individual members was chosen. For example, the lords of Uxelle were the Gros ('large') family. Although relatively few noble families had castles, all had estates. Accordingly, the most frequent category for the patronymic was the name of the family's most important estate.[49] In Normandy, the use of toponymics by the leading families began in the 1040s, when Beaumont, Montgommery, Montfort and Warenne are first mentioned in documents.[50]

The third change was in landholding practices. During the first half of the eleventh century, a major change in the conditions of tenure began to appear in Normandy. A charter to a vassal of the abbey of St Ouen of Rouen stipulated that a knight named Gonduin would be allowed to transmit a *beneficium* (or benefice) to his sons. They in turn would continue to do service to the monastery in place of their father. In short, the benefice was acquiring the characteristic of heritability previously reserved for free holdings. Gradually, the term *feudum* came to replace *beneficium* in order to indicate clearly the aspect of heritance.

At the same time, there were changes in customs of inheritance. In Normandy in the first decades of the eleventh century, it was common for all sons to share their father's property. However, in the 1040s there are signs of a new pattern emerging. William fitz Osbern received the bulk of the family estates while his brother emigrated to England.[51] Primogeniture would gradually prevail. By 1072, the first records of a new inheritance practice for feudal responsibilities appeared. One of several brothers was designated as responsible for the service due from a benefice.[52]

We should note that prior to 1066, England was virtually untouched by this feudal mutation. For much of the first half of the eleventh century, the kingdom's links with Scandinavia were as important as ties with the continent. In 1014, Danish conquerors seized the English throne. King Sweyn of Denmark and his son Cnut, allying themselves with the local family of Wulfnoth, *thegn* of Sussex and his son Godwin, were able to defeat the Saxon kings. In succession, Sweyn, Cnut and Cnut's sons Harald I and Harthacnut then occupied the English throne until 1042. There was, however, a crucial difference between the Scandinavians who took England and those who had captured Normandy a hundred years earlier. The early Vikings had been pagans who had burned the churches and monasteries of the lower Seine valley and slaughtered the priests and monks.[53] It took Normandy over a century to restore the human capital they destroyed. In contrast, Sweyn and his family were Christians who showed considerable respect for the church and its institutions.[54] Cnut was present at Rome in 1027 for the coronation of the emperor Conrad II.[55]

It was only in the 1050s during Godwin's exile that some of the continental changes began to seep into England. Edward the Confessor appointed his French-born nephew Ralph the Timid to a western earldom. Ralph made an initial start at castle building on the Welsh border.[56] He also began training his warriors to fight on horseback.[57] Nevertheless, these developments were exceptional. Ralf himself died in battle against the Welsh in 1057. Meanwhile, in inheritance customs, property in England continued to be divided among a man's sons.[58]

**The Revival of Standardized Latin**

The changes in social conventions in Normandy prior to 1066 followed a remarkable change in communications technologies. In 1001, Richard II, the Conqueror's grandfather, invited William of Volpiano to come to the duchy in order to restore the Benedictine tradition at the monastery of Fécamp, on the coast to the northwest of Rouen. William, one of the great reformers of the Cluniac house, and at that moment abbot of St Bénigne at Dijon, was reluctant. He replied that he believed the Normans to be more apt to destroy than to build the temples of the Lord.[59] Finally, however, he accepted the offer. Then, over the next few decades, he and the monks he brought with him from Burgundy to Fécamp trained a whole generation of Norman priests and officials.

In 1026, there were only six abbeys in Normandy – all founded by the dukes.[60] By 1070, there were 33 monasteries, most of which were founded by non-ducal aristocratic families.[61] In addition, during the first half of the eleventh century, there were many small colleges staffed by canons set up across Normandy. One measure of the impact of the output of trained scribes from these institutions is the number of charters issued to record grants or transfers of land. We have seen that there are few such documents from Normandy from the tenth century. However, from the eleventh century prior to 1066, there are some 230 ducal charters extant. In addition, there are many non-ducal charters.[62] These documents were not the product of a centralized bureaucracy; scribes working for the beneficiary prepared most of them. For example, the same type of handwriting is used in charters granting land from two different bishops to the monastery of St Ouen in the mid-eleventh century. Evidently scribes of the abbey's scriptorium prepared both documents in the 'house' style.[63]

The ducal government too benefited from the new flow of skilled manpower. As early as 1025, there are indications of systematic keeping of financial records by a chamber (*camera*) of the central government.[64] During the reign of William II, the Conqueror (1035–1087), there is the first evidence of taxes applied throughout the duchy. Oat production was taxed by a general levy. In addition, there were many tolls on traffic entering towns or crossing bridges.[65]

Prior to 1066, there was no corresponding penetration of Anglo-Saxon society by the new communications medium. Indeed, from the beginning of the millennium, observers have noted a decline in Anglo-Saxon scholarship. Very little original work was written in either Latin or English in the half-century preceding the conquest. By 1066, there was not even an adequate scriptorium capable of turning out good copies of borrowed manuscripts.[66]

It would appear that the Anglo-Saxon attempt to base the organization of a society on a written version of the vernacular was premature. In England outside of the southwest, the West Saxon dialect was not easily understood. Nor was there a standardized grammar or vocabulary. With the high cost of handwritten manuscripts, it had proved difficult to train a critical mass of adults to use the vernacular. The principal effects of the efforts to encourage Anglo-Saxon seem to have been negative, as competition from the vernacular hindered the learning and use of standardized Latin.[67] The resulting barrier to the flow of information between the continent and England would be one of the principal factors explaining the conquest of 1066.

## The Contractual Revolution

As long as a ruler could remove benefices easily, competition to secure his favor assured that there were strong incentives for his warrior followers to obey his commands. The house knights in turn could be used to apply the threat of force in order to assure compliance from the rest of the ruler's subjects. However, once a grant of land was recorded in a written charter, it became difficult for the lord to transfer it from one vassal to another without the first recipient's approval. Moreover, even after the original vassal's death, transfer of property by the ruler or his successor was in practice unfeasible if the heirs could produce a written document to prove their title. Over time, the situation could grow worse from the lord's point of view, since the rights of ownership implied by such documents provided an incentive for his tenants to fortify their residences. Then only a costly siege could remove the original recipient.

If William could not use the threat of land redistribution to convince his vassals to submit to his wishes, how could he hope to retain the lands that his military skills had brought under his control? The solution, he discovered, was a series of personal bonds with the most powerful landholding families. Historians such as David Douglas have noted that in his rise to power, William managed to obtain the support of the younger members of noble families.[68] He convinced them to join his battles against Geoffroy Martel and Henry I.

Instead of using land to elicit support, as his predecessors had done, William offered his family and followers both a share of political power and a flow of income from tax revenues. The duke's household grew considerably after Val ès Dunes in 1047. In addition to posts of chamberlain, butler and steward, there was a constable, a count of the palace and ducal chaplains. All of these posts were awarded to members of powerful landed families.[69]

The importance of personal bonds is also apparent when we examine local officials. As noted earlier, the counts who held the border castles during William's reign were the descendants of relatives of his grandfather. However, under William, they lost power to the *vicomtes*, who were responsible for tax collection and local administration in the twelve counties. Although these posts tended to be held by members of powerful landed families, there was considerable turnover.[70]

The question arose whether these officials were a new social class, members of families whose influence rose with that of the young duke. Were they examples of a new class of knights that according to Marc Bloch had seized power from the existing nobility?[71] The answer would seem to be negative. Although it is difficult to trace Norman lineages back beyond the early decades of the eleventh century, it would appear that, as elsewhere in northern Europe, there was a general continuity in the families that held power.[72]

How could a ruler deal with the possible confusion when a single person held benefices from different lords? In the 1050s, there was the first evidence in Normandy of attempts to establish precedence. A document of a grant to a church mentioned the donor's lord and his lord's lord.[73] In the next century, this practice of *liegeancy*, by which one lord would take precedence over all others, would become generalized across northern Europe.[74]

There occurred no such decentralizing contractual revolution in England prior to 1066. At any given time, there was a single person who controlled political power in the Anglo-Saxon kingdom. At the beginning of the century, it was the Anglo-Saxon king, Aethelred Unraed (nicknamed the Unready for his failure to halt raids by Danish armies). Under the Danes, it was also the king. Under Edward the Confessor, except for the brief period of Godwin's exile, the decision maker was the most powerful earl – either Godwin prior to his death in 1053 or Harold, his son, afterward. This person was responsible for hiring professional soldiers and finding the means to pay them. Provided they received their wages, the soldiers would fight without question.

Unfortunately for England, the application of this hierarchical command structure in an increasingly literate society proved inadequate as a means of defense. The semi-barbarian Danes conquered the English in 1016.[75] Over the following decades of Danish rule, the cost of both a professional army and a professional navy proved extremely onerous. Following the restoration of the Anglo-Saxon line, Edward the Confessor disbanded the English fleet in 1049 and canceled the *heregeld* used to finance it two years later. As a result, despite the defensive advantage conferred by England's island geography, foreign invaders from the continent would be able to conquer it for a second time within half a century.

## HASTINGS, 1066

It was late in the afternoon of 14 October 1066. The two exhausted armies had been fighting since nine o'clock that morning. Although each side had suffered heavy losses, the Saxon line on Senlac hill still held, having fended off three powerful attacks by the French. The day before, Harold, the Anglo-Saxon king, had hastened from London with only a part of his army, refusing to wait for the arrival of reinforcements from the northern earls. Nevertheless, he had brought a formidable force. With him had come some 2000 of Europe's finest infantry – the housecarls – professional soldiers loyal to their king. They were equipped with metal helmets, coats of mail, battle axes, swords, javelins and long, kite-shaped shields.[76] Backing them up were perhaps 6000 fighters of the traditional militia, the *fyrd*, armed with an assortment of missile weapons.[77] Although the Saxons had very few archers and no cavalry, as long as the shield wall remained intact, their hilltop position and projectile weapons made them virtually invincible.[78] Now, in anticipation of a final enemy assault, Harold ordered that the flanks be drawn in so as to fill the gaps in the line.

William, the Norman duke who commanded the invading army, could observe the battle's progress from the opposite hill. His 4000 infantry were inferior in quality to the housecarls, but he had brought with him over 2000 cavalry and 1000 archers. Some of these units of bowmen were equipped with the short bow, but others used the new crossbow, a weapon able to shoot metal quarrels that could penetrate both shields and armor.[79] As the fourth attack began, William noted that with the shortened enemy line, his cavalry for the first time was able to reach the summit of the ridge on the Saxon right. An experienced cavalry leader, he immediately ordered his mounted troops on the enemy's left to climb the hill to attack the other flank.[80]

Invested now on both flanks, the housecarls were gradually reduced in number until a group of French knights on horseback broke through to the Saxon rear. There they attacked and killed Harold. When words of the king's death reached the Saxon warriors, many fled, although some units of housecarls continued to resist for another two hours until darkness began to fall.[81] So ended the battle of Hastings.

**The Papal Banner**

Military historians have long questioned why Harold did not wait for reinforcements before setting out for Kent from London. Did he wish to protect his subjects on the southern coast from the pillaging French? Or did he perhaps wish to confront the Norman duke before William could be reinforced and establish a permanent beachhead on English soil? Neither of these explanations is entirely convincing. David Howarth has offered another possible reason for Harold's haste, one that involves the Italian monk, Lanfranc.[82]

William's pretension to the English throne was based on a promise supposedly made to him by Edward the Confessor, whose death early in 1066 had precipitated a competition for power in England. Also, Harold had allegedly sworn to support William's claim. However, there were no witnesses to support the first assertion and no documents to back up the second.[83] Nevertheless, Lanfranc, William's adviser and friend, found a persuasive way to convince both the French and the English that William's claim was justified.

Five years before the invasion of England, the College of Cardinals had elected one of Lanfranc's former students at Bec to be pope under the name of Alexander II. But Lanfranc's influence within the church did not stop there. The power behind the papal throne in the 1060s was Hildebrand (later Pope Gregory VII), an Italian cardinal whose position Lanfranc had successfully defended in 1063 during a debate over the doctrine of transubstantiation. Meanwhile, on the other side of the Channel, the English church was in Rome's bad graces for refusing to accept papal authority. The Archbishop of Canterbury was Stigand, an Anglo-Saxon ally of Harold's family who had been chosen while his Norman predecessor was still alive and who had received his pallium from an anti-pope. Moreover, the English church used the local vernacular instead of Latin in much of its documentation and in its pastoral work. Sure of support in Rome, Lanfranc suggested that William submit the dispute over the English succession to the pope.[84]

Thus it was that in the spring of 1066, a papal court decided to recognize William of Normandy as the rightful heir to the English crown. The pope sent the duke a papal banner, a ring and a relic of St Peter to carry on his expedition. It should be remembered that this event occurred 30 years before the first Crusade to Palestine. In effect, the battle for England had become a holy war, with the Normans as the instruments chosen by the pope to bring the wayward English church back to Rome. Those who died in the holy cause would be assured of salvation.

On landing in Kent, William had sent a monk to Harold in London with the offer that Harold either give up the throne or else meet William in single combat. On hearing the message, Harold is reported to have grown pale and ordered his army to prepare for combat. It is possible, as Howarth suggested, that Harold had just learned of the papal sanction given to his opponent, and wished to do battle before the news leaked out to his own troops.[85]

**Effects of the Norman Victory**

Perhaps the most visible effect on England of the Norman Conquest was the construction of castles and churches. Prior to the Norman invasion, residences of the nobility in England were not fortified. After the conquest, however, William kept a fifth of the kingdom for himself and ceded an additional quarter to his French followers. He replaced the 5000 Anglo-Saxon *thegns* by approximately 180 Norman barons. Since the Normans had good reason to wish to protect themselves from possible revolts by their subjects, there followed a surge of castle building. William himself began construction of the Tower of London and a number of other strategically placed royal castles, all built of stone. Although some of the great barons followed this example, most of their early castles were of the simple motte and bailey type.

William granted a quarter of the land he had conquered to the English church. In 1070, he had papal legates appoint Lanfranc as Archbishop of Canterbury. Gradually, as other English bishoprics and abbacies fell vacant, they too were filled with churchmen from Normandy. There followed a wave of church building as the immigrant clergy brought in Norman architects to design churches deemed fitting for their new functions. The cathedral at Canterbury had been destroyed by fire in 1067. Lanfranc supervised construction of a new, larger cathedral, built between 1070 and 1077 in Romanesque style along the lines of St Étienne, Caen. Durham cathedral, built between 1093 and 1133, was the first major church in England to be entirely stone vaulted. It was also one of the first churches in Europe to use ribbed vaulting, a technique that permitted thinner walls with larger windows.

The stone castles and churches along with the ambitious, aggressive men who occupied them, brought England a level of security she had never before experienced. Since 1066, England has never been successfully invaded. Moreover, with the exception of brief periods in the thirteenth, fifteenth and seventeenth centuries, England has also been at peace internally since the eleventh century. No other major European region has been so little disturbed by organized violence over the past millennium.

Another, although less visible, effect of the conquest was on the communications media. Under Norman rule, English as a written language virtually disappeared. In its place, the conquerors substituted Latin and French. Latin became the language of record in the government and the courts.[86] It was used to compile the great inventory of English fiscal and military resources, the Domesday book, undertaken in 1086 when William feared a Danish invasion. Norman French was the spoken language used by the nobility. Anglo-Norman was also used along with Latin for literature.

When written English finally re-emerged in the fourteenth century, it was greatly simplified grammatically, having lost the inflections it had inherited from its Germanic ancestors. Middle English was based on the Mercian dialect of the Midlands rather than the West Saxon dialect promoted by Alfred the Great. Old English word endings had been dropped in favor of prepositions such as *by*, *from* and *with*.[87] Most obvious perhaps were the many words of Latin and French origin that enriched English vocabulary. To take one example, in Old English, there was a single adjective, *kingly*, to indicate a characteristic of the king, formed by adding the suffix *-ly* to the noun *king*. By the late Middle Ages, three synonyms had come into the English language: *regal, royal* and *sovereign*.[88] The first of these new adjectives came from Latin, the latter two from French.

With the Norman takeover of the upper ranks of the English clergy, both the written language and the script used to inscribe it were brought into line with continental practice. In 1154, the monks who wrote *The Anglo-Saxon Chronicle*, a record of current events compiled over several centuries in Old English, finally abandoned their work.[89]

Toward the end of the twelfth century, an Englishman named Walter Map wrote a book entitled *De Nugis Curialium* (*Courtiers' Trifles*) describing life at the court of Henry II, the Conqueror's great-grandson. Written in Latin, the book mocked those who write in the vernacular as 'mummers in vulgar rhymes'.[90] The success of Map's book provides evidence that by the year 1200, there were a considerable number of English laymen who were able to read literary Latin. In developing their literary skills, they were imitating their French-born king, who also enjoyed private reading in Latin.[91]

In his study of the impact of Norman feudalism on England, Frank Barlow suggested that during the twelfth century, intellectual contact between scholars of different nationalities was 'standardizing European culture'.[92] While there is some truth to this statement, it is necessary to distinguish between two different dimensions of European culture. One dimension is the medium of communication. Here indeed there was standardization, with scholars using Medieval Latin written in a standardized script as a vehicular language to exchange their ideas.

In the other principal dimension of culture – the message being transmitted – movement was in the opposite direction, toward non-standardization. In the middle of the eleventh century, the church had been able to silence the French scholar, Berengar of Tours, who had suggested that transubstantiation, the transformation of bread and wine into the flesh and blood of Christ during the Catholic mass, should be treated symbolically. But by the end of the twelfth century, universities distinct from the Catholic Church had been founded in Paris, Oxford, Bologna and other centers. The ideas of scholars such as Peter Abelard, John of Salisbury, Maimonides and Averroës were being debated across Europe. Try as it might, the church was unable to stifle speculation.

Thus the real question about the year 1066 is not the impact of the Conquest on England but rather the effect of the integration of England upon Western culture. In ending England's isolation and integrating that land into continental developments, William of Normandy may have enabled the West to cross a critical-mass threshold. Within a century of William's death, the basic characteristics of Western civilization – standardized media and non-standardized messages – had been established. The rapid diffusion of information across a great mass of population made possible the ceaseless innovation that would henceforth characterize the West. While China, India and the Middle East were suffering from wave after wave of invasions, Western Europe became an impregnable fortress. Gradually it was developing the technologies that would allow it to achieve world dominance.

## THE FEUDAL CODE

### Medieval Urban Growth

Between the years 1000 and 1300, the population of Normandy's largest city, Rouen, expanded from 12 000 to 35 000. Over the same period, Caen grew from a small trading center into a city of 15 000 inhabitants. Across the English Channel, London too reached 35 000 in 1300. Meanwhile, the urban population of Latin Christendom as a whole tripled.[93] However, this growth did not occur through a uniform expansion of all cities but rather through a demographic decline of the largest urban centers accompanied by extremely rapid growth in many smaller towns.[94] In northern Europe, for example, the three largest cities in 1000 – the former Carolingian centers of Regensburg, Mainz and Laon – together lost residents. Meanwhile three smaller centers – Paris, Ghent and Cologne – increased their total population fourfold and overtook their rivals. Similarly, south of the Alps, two of the largest centers – Salerno and Rome – lost population. Their places were taken by Genoa and Milan, which also grew extremely rapidly.[95]

A striking feature of this reversal of fortune is that of the cities named above, those that were large in 1000 and subsequently declined were in the West's geographic center, a short distance from the central Rhine valley. As for the expanding cities, with the exception of Cologne, they lay in the periphery – a 500-mile-wide (800 km) ring whose inner edge was some 250 miles (400 km) from the central-German city of Mainz. In short, the rapid growth of Caen, Rouen and London was not exceptional. The same pattern was occurring across a broad arc of Western Europe in the first three centuries of the new millennium.

How can the rapid growth of these ring cities in the high Middle Ages be explained? The traditional answer to this question has been the rise of long-distance exchange. Henri Pirenne explained the growth of towns in the High Middle Ages by the expansion of inter-city trade.[96] But why did long-distance trade flows begin to increase around the turn of the millennium and not before? And why was the commercial expansion concentrated in the London–Sienna ring rather than more generally across Europe?

Recently, attention has focused on the institutions that permitted the rise of trade. It has been shown that the presence of a competitive political system dominated by merchants rather than by princes is a statistically significant factor in explaining urban demographic growth.[97] Douglass North explained economic growth in late medieval Europe by the development of institutions that protected property rights.[98] More recently, Avner Greif has shown theoretically and with historical examples why such institutions promoted exchange.[99] An example is the merchant guild that imposed sanctions on political leaders in order to prevent the arbitrary seizure of traders' assets.[100] However, merchant's associations existed across Europe in the High Middle Ages. Indeed, in northern Italy, even in the earlier Carolingian period, there were political groupings of townsmen that had attempted to oppose royal officials.[101] Why were some rulers during some periods in European history able to ignore or crush such associations while other rulers recognized their power?

## The Norman Example

At the beginning of this chapter, we saw how in Normandy early in the new millennium, Benedictine monks trained in the traditions of Cluny started a monastic revival at Fécamp that quickly spread to other sites across Normandy. Then in the second quarter of the eleventh century, powerful noble families also began to found monasteries. With access to their own scriptoria, able to replicate the principal institutions of Carolingian government, the castellans no longer needed to adhere to the policies of their lords. As the new millennium began, medieval governments therefore had a problem of agency – the subordinate did not necessarily act in accord with his lord's interest.

European political leaders in the eleventh century had another problem. They had usurped power by force from their Carolingian predecessors. In the case of William of Normandy, although his father had been the legitimate heir of one of these new families, his parents had not been married. As already noted, his government therefore suffered from a lack of legitimacy.

Duke William with his lay and clerical vassals solved these dilemmas by developing new codes of behavior. As we have already seen, William succeeded in building up personal attachments with members of leading families of the Norman nobility. In exchange for recognizing their fiefs as heritable property, William obtained a reliable military force trained and equipped with the latest technology. By associating them with his rule, he in effect shared the rents from efficient government.

In the decade of the 1050s, William also succeeded in establishing a personal bond with one of the most able of a new generation of clerics, Lanfranc, the prior of Bec, a lawyer trained in both Roman law and Catholic liturgy. In return for building two new monasteries and their churches at Caen, William through Lanfranc obtained Church recognition for his marriage.

The complementarity between the medieval church and the feudal state may be seen in the relationship between William and Lanfranc in the conquest of England. Lanfranc obtained papal backing for William's expedition. In return, once England had been conquered, William named Lanfranc as Archbishop of Canterbury. In 1075, a revolt against the Normans broke out in eastern England while William was absent on the continent. It was Lanfranc who coordinated the defence and imposed the sanctions once the uprising had been put down. He then wrote to William, 'Norwich castle had fallen and its defenders have sworn to leave England within forty days . . . By God's mercy, the clamor of war has entirely ceased on English soil'.[102] While William cooperated with the church, he refused to recognize papal sovereignty. In 1080, Pope Gregory VII wrote to William requesting that the customary payment from England to the papacy known as Peter's Pence be sent. In addition, he demanded that William recognize him as his sovereign lord. While William ordered that the payment be made, he refused to accept the status of papal vassal, arguing that there was no precedent for such a relationship.[103]

## The Implications for Europe

In the eleventh century, the diffusion of a standardized vehicular language among the lay nobility seems to have precipitated a change in the social organization in Western Europe. The earlier structure of command, with the ruler on top and his subjects below, had been carried over from the Roman Empire to that of Charlemagne. This vertical structure had now collapsed, as local rulers, both lay and religious, were able to replicate the system for storage and retrieval of written information previously accessible only to an emperor. In place of it, there arose circles of trust among small groups of clerics and bands of warriors and links between the two types of group. As literacy spread from the nobility to commoners, they too were able to form relations of confidence, punishing by exclusion those who failed to comply. The guilds formed by merchants and artisans are extensions of the codified behavior of the clergy and lay nobility.

With the Carolingian ruler's monopoly on property rights broken and political power distributed across decentralized networks linked by a standardized communications medium, the stage was set for Western Europe's great leap forward. One avenue of advance was to raise the yield from existing land. Surprisingly, there were no great technological discoveries in agriculture during the High Middle Ages. Rather, productivity was raised through the diffusion of a number of techniques that were already known at the time of Charlemagne. Under a new system of crop rotation, there were two sowings per year: wheat and rye were planted in the autumn, while oats and barley were sown in the spring.[104] Moreover, in the eleventh century, application of the collar harness permitted more efficient use of the ox's strength. During the next century, the horse was substituted for the ox in many places. It was also during the twelfth century that the metal-reinforced plow came into widespread use.[105]

Over the same period, from the tenth to the twelfth century, there was also a steady increase in the area under cultivation. In part, the expansion occurred as peasant communities extended the land under cultivation, but in addition, individual families moved to previously uncleared areas. Finally, feudal entrepreneurs organized new settlements on lands that had previously not been suitable for agriculture.[106] As a great landholder, the church itself often organized land clearance. Monasteries also served as subcontractors for lay lords, using their ties with other houses to attract colonists and raise capital, and sharing in the eventual profits.[107] The ties between the monasteries, whether formalized as in the case of Cluny and its daughter houses, or informal, as between Cluny and Fleury, were the channels by which information flowed across political boundaries.

The monasteries were not the only medieval institutions that formed human capital. As the Church gradually freed itself from secular overseers in the late tenth and eleventh centuries, its archbishops and bishops required literate scribes to administer their dioceses. Accordingly, there emerged schools attached to the urban cathedrals that began to complement the monasteries as centers of intellectual life.[108] One of the principal activities in these cathedral schools was the study of canon law, that is, regulations concerning the behavior of individuals and institutions within the Catholic Church. Late in the eleventh century, legal scholars in Bologna trained in the cathedral schools rediscovered Roman civil law and began teaching it to willing students. Out of the new legal school, there gradually developed two 'student universities' dedicated to a wide range of secular learning. A similar process occurred during the twelfth century in Paris, although there, the professors were clerics. Elsewhere, Montpellier and Oxford had established universities by the first decades of the thirteenth century.[109]

The development of a standardized medium for written and spoken communication across Western Europe made it possible for small states to acquire the administrative talent they required to function efficiently. As a result, there was competition among states. At the same time, the new communications technology permitted the formation of cultural institutions that spread across political boundaries. There thus appeared simultaneously the two conditions necessary for rapid innovation: first, the incentive to do things better, in order to stay ahead of competitors; and second, the ingredients for doing so, namely, easy access to the stock of information accumulated in the past.

Britain in the eleventh century would appear to have been held back by the inertia of a communications technology carried over from an earlier era. A rich, populous, advanced society, it was conquered by and subjected to a smaller state that shortly before had been considered poor and backward. The Norman Conquest imposed considerable suffering on many people and deprived many English nobles of their property. However, it resulted in the unhindered diffusion of a new communications technology that permitted accelerated innovation and economic growth. The ultimate beneficiaries were not just the English but rather the whole of Latin Christendom. The West had now attained a critical mass that would allow it to compete with the established civilizations of Eastern Europe and Asia.

Over the longer term, the Norman Conquest was perhaps the principal influence on the formation of the modern English language.[110] As a result of this venture, sanctioned by the papacy, there followed over two centuries in which Church-sponsored Latin and its French offshoot were the principal languages for written communication in England. Then, in the fourteenth century, a new English written language emerged. Over half the words now had Latin or French origins. In addition, compared to Old English, the new language's grammar had been radically simplified. Nouns were no longer inflected. Their gender was inferred from the meaning rather than signaled by accompanying articles or adjectives. A noun could become a verb and vice versa. Foreign words could be absorbed easily.[111] It would take another four centuries of evolution, but this transformed tongue would eventually displace both Latin and French to become the West's and the world's principal vehicular language.

## NOTES

1. Gies and Gies (1987, pp. 124–127).
2. Poly and Bournazel (1991, p. 370).
3. Poly and Bournazel (1991, p. 371).
4. Duby (1974, p. 222).
5. Barraclough (1984a, p. 81).
6. Duby (1974, p. 229).
7. Stock (1983, p. 41).
8. Gibson (1978, p. 6).
9. McKitterick (1989, pp. 217–218).
10. Slocombe (1961, p. 50).
11. Bates (2004, pp. 138–140).
12. Macdonald (1944, pp. 36–37).
13. Bates (1982, p. 126).
14. Bates (1982, p. 199).
15. Baylé (1997a, p. 20).
16. Conant (1966, p. 283).
17. Baylé (1997b, p. 59).
18. Bates (1982, p. 96).
19. Lemmon (1966, p. 108).
20. de Boüard (1984, p. 324).
21. Normandy today has about six per cent of France's population. Applying this percentage to the total population of 6.5 million from McEvedy and Jones (1979, p. 57), one obtains the estimate of 400 000.
22. Bates (1982, pp. 129–131).
23. Bates (1982, p. xiv).
24. Bates (1982, pp. 122–124).
25. Bates (1982, p. 52).
26. Brown (1984, p. 22).
27. Bates (1982, p. 31).
28. McEvedy and Jones (1979, p. 43), Maddison (2001, p. 241).
29. Loyn (1962, p. 311).
30. John (1996, pp. 144–145).
31. Loyn (1962, p. 305).
32. John (1996, p. 126).
33. Knight (1996, p. 318).
34. Gibson (1978, pp. 4–5).

35. Gibson (1978, p. 14).
36. Macdonald (1944, p. 8).
37. Gibson (1978, p. 20).
38. Gibson (1978, p. 38).
39. Bates (1982, p. 101).
40. Bates (1982, p. 100).
41. Collins (1998, pp. 38, 41, 88).
42. Gibson (1978, p. 31).
43. Gibson (1978, p. 31).
44. Bates (1982, p. 115).
45. Collins (1998, p. 53).
46. Bates (1982, p. 156).
47. Bates (1982, p. 114).
48. Gies and Gies (1987, p. 126).
49. Gies and Gies (1987, pp. 126–127).
50. Bates (1982, pp. 113–114).
51. Bates (1982, p. 119).
52. Bates (1982, p. 127).
53. Coupland (1995, p. 193).
54. John (1996, p. 145).
55. John (1996, p. 155).
56. Barlow (1972, pp. 61–62).
57. Barlow (1972, p. 68).
58. Loyn (1962, p. 185).
59. Brown (1984, pp. 25–26).
60. Bates (1982, p. 218).
61. Brown (1984, p. 26).
62. Bates (1982, p. xiii).
63. Bates (1982, p. 154).
64. Bates (1982, p. 154).
65. Bates (1982, p. 153).
66. Gibson (1978, p. 179).
67. Gibson (1978, p. 179).
68. Douglas (1966, p. 55).
69. Bates (1982, p. 155).
70. Bates (1982, pp. 156–157).
71. Bloch ([1939] 1994, pp. 452–454).
72. Bates (1982, pp. 106–111).
73. Bates (1982, p. 126).
74. Ganshof (1952, p. 93).
75. Schama (2000, p. 69).
76. Lemmon (1966, p. 92).
77. de Boüard (1984, p. 325).
78. Lemmon (1966, p. 93).
79. de Boüard (1984, pp. 323–324).
80. Lemmon (1966, p. 110).
81. Lemmon (1966, p. 111).
82. Howarth (1977, pp.100–102).
83. Howarth (1977, p. 99).
84. Howarth (1977, p. 100).
85. Howarth (1977, pp. 160–161).
86. Loyn (1962, p. 317).
87. McCrum *et al.* (1986, p. 78).
88. McCrum *et al.* (1986, p. 75).
89. McCrum *et al.* (1986, p. 74).
90. Clanchy (1979, pp. 157–158).

91. Clanchy (1979, p. 186).
92. Barlow (1972, p. 230).
93. From the Bairoch *et al.* (1988) estimates, the urban population of Western Europe was 1 432 000 in 1000 and 4 798 000 in 1300. Note that these figures exclude Palermo and Cordoba, for which the Bairoch estimates of 1000 seem to be exaggerated.
94. van Werveke (1971).
95. No data are available for Milan in 1000, but Genoa's population grew from 15 000 to 100 000 between 1000 and 1300 (Bairoch *et al.*, 1988).
96. Pirenne ([1927] 1971, pp. 62–75).
97. De Long and Schleifer (1993).
98. North and Thomas (1973), North (1981, 1990).
99. Greif (2000, 2003).
100. Greif, Milgrom and Weingast (1994).
101. Delogu (1995, p. 293).
102. Gibson (1978, p. 157).
103. Bates (2004, p. 218).
104. Duby (1974, pp. 189–190).
105. Duby (1974, pp. 191–193).
106. Duby (1974, pp. 199–208).
107. Duby (1974, pp. 207–208).
108. Reuter (1991, pp. 247–249).
109. Verger (1999, pp. 257–261).
110. McCrum *et al.* (1986, p. 73).
111. McCrum *et al.* (1986, p. 47).

# PART II

# The consensual revolution

# 3. The counter-attack of the clones

Across Western Europe by the mid-fifteenth century, thanks to the reforms initiated by the Anglo-Saxon churchman, Alcuin, both religious and secular literate elites were able to communicate in standardized Medieval Latin. However, this synthetic language, the mother tongue of no one, was too difficult to learn for the great majority of people. With only a thin layer of the population able to decipher written documents, the decoding of information had become expensive relative to the cost of storing it.

The solution was obvious, namely, to start publishing written communication in the vernacular tongues. However, since each region had its own dialect, there were not yet enough people able to read and write in any one spoken language to constitute a market for expensive manuscripts in the vernacular. The catch was that until someone discovered a way to teach literacy to a mass audience, such a market would never come into being.

## THE CARDINAL AND THE COIN-MAKER'S SON

The Turks are coming! In the spring of 1450, the Vatican officials could talk of little else. Cardinal Nicholas of Cusa, 49, was not surprised to learn the contents of the letter sent to Rome by the Latin ruler of Cyprus. The Catholic king of the small eastern-Mediterranean island was requesting urgent help in order to defend his realm against the Muslim threat. On the continent, Turkish armies now roamed at will around the great walls of Constantinople, the Byzantine port that controlled traffic between the Black Sea and the Mediterranean. If that city were to fall, Cyprus was certain to be one of the next targets. Yet the more the Catholic prelate reflected, the more he realized that this external challenge exposed an even graver internal crisis facing Christendom. The idealism and dedication of earlier generations of leaders had all but disappeared, to be replaced by selfishness and ignorance.

Several years earlier, the West seemed to have found a leader capable of stopping the Turkish advance in Eastern Europe. With funding from the papacy and Venice, the Hungarian general Janos Hunyadi had organized a great army comprising some 30 000 professional soldiers. Invading

Turkish-held territory in the Balkans, he had repeatedly been successful in battle. Then in 1444 at Varna on the Black Sea coast, reinforcements from Constantinople and Bulgaria failed to arrive, and naval support promised by the Venetians did not materialize. Deep in Muslim territory, the Crusaders were overwhelmed by the mighty army of Sultan Murad II. Four years later, in 1448, at the battle of Kosovo, the two commanders met again. Despite the Christians' use of German mercenaries with hand-held firearms, they suffered a second crushing defeat. The Turkish mounted *spahis* backed by deadly field artillery overwhelmed the Hungarian knights, leaving half of them dead on the battlefield.[1] Now there was no Christian force available to come to the aid of the beleaguered Byzantines. Although the Church had helped finance the Hungarian Crusaders, not a single secular ruler in the West had offered assistance.

## The Cardinal

Nicholas of Cusa was one of the rare Germans to be appointed cardinal in the Middle Ages. He was born in 1401, the son of a merchant boat owner in Cusa (or Kues), a small town on the Moselle River in northwestern Germany. Although Nicholas came from a middle-class background, because of his extraordinary intellectual abilities, from an early age he attracted the attention of powerful sponsors. However, he showed little aptitude for his father's profession. According to legend, his father once knocked him overboard because of his inability to handle an oar. The site where this humiliation occurred is still known as the *Schmeissgraben*, the 'Fling-moat'.[2]

Thanks to the intervention of Count Theodoric von Manterscheid, Nicholas was sent to Deventer in Holland to be educated by the Brethren of the Common Life (who later taught Erasmus). Subsequently, he studied liberal arts at the University of Heidelberg. He then went on to the University of Padua near Venice in northern Italy to study for a doctorate in church law.[3] In Padua, he met Cardinal Giuliano Cesarini, who was later president of the Council of Basel (1431–1437).[4] In 1425, back in Germany, Nicholas was appointed professor at the University of Cologne, where he specialized in canon law. In that city, the papal legate to Germany, Cardinal Giorgano Orsini, consulted the young lawyer on a legal matter and was so impressed that he hired him as his private secretary.[5]

While combing through the archives of the university and cathedral in Cologne, Nicholas came across a manuscript containing letters written by the popes to Charlemagne's predecessors some seven centuries earlier.[6] But the discovery that brought him fame on both sides of the Alps was a copy of a set of comedies dating from the second century BC, written by the

Roman playwright Plautus. Twelve of the plays were unknown when Nicholas brought them across the Alps to Cardinal Orsini in Rome in 1429.[7] From these works, Shakespeare borrowed the plot of *The Taming of the Shrew* and Molière the theme of *L'Avare*.[8]

Nicholas's great weakness was his tendency to sacrifice principles in order to please those in power. One of the greatest of medieval philosophers, he prepared a document for the Council of Basel, *De Concordontia Catholica*, which argued that supreme power resided in the church councils. According to this text, the pope was simply an administrator who executed the council's decisions. However, when Pope Eugene IV decided to move the council to Italy with the intention of bringing it under closer papal control, Nicholas supported the pontiff's decision.

**The Medium and the Message**

Nicholas of Cusa had been born into an era of intellectual freedom and exchange of ideas. In the twelfth century, the Arabs had introduced the production of paper, made from rags, into Spain. Europeans improved on the process by using animal glue to stiffen the surface so that one could write on both sides.[9] By the late fourteenth century there were paper factories in Italy, France and Germany producing to meet the growing demand from the universities and courts. However, all books were still written by hand. With circulation limited by the high cost of manuscripts, there was little need for formal censorship. As a result, in the first half of the fifteenth century, books and the ideas they contained circulated quite freely among the elite of Europe. The non-standardization of the message was a concept that Nicholas took for granted.

The problem of Christian society, Nicholas of Cusa felt, arose in the great gaps in awareness between the educated and the uneducated. The principal difficulty with the institutions of the Christian world, he believed, was the limited circulation of ideas beyond the universities. Most striking was the decadence of the church. Fewer than half the parish priests had studied theology. 'Much of the Christian religion has degenerated to an appearance', he would write in his 1453 work, *Visio Dei*.[10] Ideally, there should be some way of reproducing information cheaply so that all agents of the Church, down to the humblest parish priest, could be considered educated. Nicholas's predecessors had developed Medieval Latin as a medium for the exchange of information among people whose native languages differed. Now what was required was a means of diffusing this synthetic language broadly among the population of Europe, that is, a greater standardization of the medium of communication.

### The Coin-Maker's Son

In Mainz, the great cathedral city on the middle Rhine, 80 miles east of Cusa, there was another bright young German of about the same age as the canon lawyer. Johannes Gutenberg was the third child and second son of a patrician who had married a wealthy commoner. Gutenberg's father was a Companion of the Mint of Mainz, but his mother was the daughter of a mere shopkeeper. The young man was probably educated at a German University, possibly at Erfurt in Thuringia, where a certain Johannes de Altavilla was registered in 1418 and graduated in 1420. Altavilla is the latinized form of Eltville, a town on the Rhine where Gutenberg's mother had a country estate.[11] Because of his mother's common birth, however, Johannes was not eligible to become a Companion of the Mint.[12] He would have to find another outlet for his energies.

In 1424, Nicholas of Cusa was in Mainz for a court case. It was perhaps there that the two young men first met. Or possibly their paths crossed between 1429 and 1434, a period for which Gutenberg has left no trace. Albert Kapr suggested that Gutenberg may have been working in Basel and met Nicholas of Cusa during the Basel Council.[13] Or possibly the cardinal learned of Gutenberg's first successful experiments in Strasbourg during his travels in Germany in the years before 1448.

Nicholas de Cusa was one of the few scholars of his time who were capable of imagining the social impact of the revolutionary technology that Gutenberg was developing. It is not far-fetched to suggest that recalling these contacts in 1450, the cardinal realized that here lay the solution to the threat announced in the letter from the king of Cyprus. By allowing all Christians across Europe to read exactly the same texts, such a technology alone could bring about the unity required to restore the former glory of the Church.[14] Now he must return to Germany, in order both to encourage his former acquaintance and to begin the work of bringing people together in the lands most exposed to the Muslim menace. He would bring up the possibility of an extended tour of reform north of the Alps with the Holy Father at their next meeting.

## THE RENAISSANCE IN ROME

The direct superior of Cardinal Nicholas of Cusa also used the name of Nicholas, although he had been baptized Tommaso Parentucelli. Born in 1397 in Sarzana, a small town to the south-east of Genoa, Pope Nicholas V, like the cardinal, came from a family of moderate means. After his election three years earlier in 1447, he had chosen the name of his former patron, the Cardinal-Archbishop of Bologna, Niccolò Albergati. Now, with Europe gradually recovering from the disastrous plagues and violence of the fourteenth century, he found himself at the head of the Church, propelled into an unprecedented position of power and influence in many areas of human activity.

## Patron of the Arts

At the age of 53, Pope Nicholas V probably considered himself first and foremost a man of letters. As the late Cardinal Albergati's assistant for two decades, he had been able to indulge in his passion for book collecting. Now, one of his great projects as patron of the arts was to make this classical literature available to all. He brought scholars like Lorenzo Valla into the Vatican to translate the Greek classics into Latin. Thanks to these efforts, the historical studies of Herodotus and Thucydides would become accessible to succeeding generations of readers in the West. Similarly, the writings of Xenophon and Polybius were translated 'for the common convenience of the learned'. If any of the new generation of humanists declined his patronage, he advised them, 'Do not refuse; you will not always have a Nicholas among you'.[15]

Nicholas V had much less time to read these days, but he still took pleasure in admiring the handsome books he had collected, stamped with his own coat of arms. The glory of his reign would be the foundation of the Vatican library, a project that he was busy preparing. His agents were busy scouring the monasteries and episcopal palaces across Europe looking for forgotten manuscripts. Nicholas's collection would be the finest library of its time in the West: it is estimated that it contained approximately 1160 books.[16] (In comparison, the present Vatican library has over two million books.)

Another of Nicholas's projects in the artistic domain was to rebuild the Basilica of St Peter. The emperor Constantine had ordered construction of the present structure in the fourth century on the site where St Peter had been crucified. However, the old church was no longer large enough to hold the crowds that gathered on the great feast days and was badly in need of repair. In addition, its conception, with its low roof and dark interior, was obsolete when compared with the bright, spacious structures that Brunelleschi had recently designed for the Medicis in Florence. The Church must not be outshone by its bankers!

The pope was not simply the Bishop of Rome, its leader in spiritual matters. He was also in effect the first magistrate of the Eternal City, responsible for day-to-day administration of its bricks and mortar. In the millennium since the fall of the Roman Empire, the city's public works had been badly neglected. With the aqueducts in disrepair, Rome's citizens were forced to take their drinking water from wells or cisterns or, if they had no other means, from the muddy Tiber. Nicholas had the aqueducts restored to bring water to a public square, later known as the Trevi fountain. In addition, he had some fifty Roman churches repaired.

## First Among Equals

In addition to his spiritual duties, Nicholas V was also a secular ruler – of a middle power known as the Papal States. Although this territorial state paled in comparison to the great Roman Empire of classical times, Rome in the fifteenth century was still a capital. The Church controlled not only the land around Rome but also Umbria, Marche and a portion of the modern province of Emilia-Romagna to the northeast. Jostling the pope for precedence in northern Italy were Cosimo de Medici of Florence, Francesco Foscari, the doge of Venice, and Francesco Sforza, the new tyrant of Milan. Each of these rulers would be only too glad to expand his state's territory at the expense of the Church. Fortunately, the income the Church received from abroad enabled the pope hire the troops necessary to defend his lands.

Although the military resources of the Papal States were modest compared with those of the German Emperor or the kings of France, England, Aragon and Castile, the pope's moral authority allowed him to intervene as first among equals at the international diplomatic level. His network of superbly trained legates in the principal capitals of Europe gave him unparalleled access to information in an age where there were no newspapers, telegraphs or radios. He was currently using his influence in an attempt to arrange a settlement of the bitter war that France and England had been fighting with each other for over a century.

Nicholas had also soothed relations with the German Empire. Ever since the Investiture Crisis of the late eleventh century, the Papacy had experienced difficulties in its relations with the rulers of Germany. At issue was the right to appoint church officials. Most high ecclesiastic posts offered the holder a chance to tap into the flow of income the church received from tithes, rents on its properties and taxing and other privileges. As a result, the power to appoint conferred on the holder the opportunity to demand payment from potential candidates for these posts. The Council of Basel had insisted on its right to subject the pope to its decisions. The German Emperor Frederick III had initially supported the resolutions of the Council of Basel. But in 1448, Nicholas V had persuaded him to sign the Concordat of Vienna, by which he refused to recognize the priority of the council over the papacy.

Of course, there was the problem of the Turks. As leader of Christendom, Nicholas V was one of the few Christian rulers able to view Europe as a single entity whose very existence was threatened by the infidels. With their control over the trade by land between Anatolia and Europe, the Turks had a steady flow of income, but not enough to finance a major campaign against the West or to disturb the vital sea trade of the eastern Mediterranean. It was therefore essential to keep them from capturing Constantinople, the great port that controlled maritime traffic between the Mediterranean and the Black Sea. Unfortunately, the Turks had recently learned to master the new weapon of mass destruction, the cannon, powered by exploding powder and able to fire massive balls from a great distance.

The 46-year-old reigning Turkish sultan, Murad II, was apparently content to reign over the Balkans and Asia Minor from his capital at Edirne, near the present border of Turkey with Bulgaria. His siege of Constantinople in 1422 had been a failure. However, his 18-year-old son and designated successor Mehmed was reportedly eager to launch Turkish troops against the great double-walled fortress city and its few thousand defenders once again. Nicholas V had offered his help to Constantine XI, the Byzantine emperor who reigned over the decaying city. In addition, the pope was attempting to rouse the rulers of the Catholic states of Europe to aid their Orthodox colleague.

## The Successor of St Peter

Geopolitics was all well and good, but the pope knew that to finance his library, his urban reconstruction and his soldiers, he required a steady flow of gold and silver from the dioceses of Latin Christendom into the Church coffers. This flow in turn depended upon the unchallenged access of the Church to the hearts and minds of the faithful. Christianity had been weakened by the East–West schism that for centuries had divided the Catholic Church in Rome from the Orthodox Church in Constantinople. The Eastern Church allowed its priests to marry and used unleavened bread in the Eucharist. In addition, it refused a modification of the Nicene Creed implying that the Holy Spirit proceeds from the Son as well as the Father (the *Filioque* clause). All of these practices were contrary to the ritual of the Latin Church. In 1054, as a result of these differences, the Catholic Church had excommunicated the eastern patriarch, who had subsequently replied in kind to the pope.

The breach between the two churches had gradually widened. However, in 1430, when the Turks captured the Greek city of Salonika and massacred its population, both Catholics and Orthodox began to rethink their differences. In 1437, Nicholas of Cusa as papal legate persuaded the Eastern Emperor and the patriarch to come to a church council in Florence to discuss terms. Two years later, the union of Eastern and Western churches was announced. Yet no sooner had the eastern representatives returned to Constantinople than they renounced the accord. So matters stood in 1450. Nicholas V was prepared to offer military help, but only if the Byzantines could be more reasonable about church unity.

The authority of the Catholic Church had also been badly tarnished during what has become known as the Great Western Schism. For almost four decades between 1378 and 1417, there had been one pope in Rome and a second in Avignon in south-eastern France. By 1410 there was even a third pope in Bologna. The Council of Constance settled the problem in 1414 by deposing or forcing the resignation of all three, thereby allowing the election of a single pope, who thenceforth reigned from Rome. However, in 1439, the rump of the Council of Basel named the Count of Savoy as antipope Felix V. It had taken many months of negotiations before finally in 1449 Nicholas V persuaded this last of the antipopes to withdraw and accept a position as cardinal.

What Europe needed now, the pope felt, was a great outpouring of faith like that of the eleventh and early twelfth centuries, when thousands of new churches had been built and a great crusade had been launched against the Muslims. He realized that the situation in the mid-fifteenth century had evolved considerably from those far-off days. For one thing, the fraction of the population able to read and write had increased considerably. At the time of Pope Gregory VII, the great ally of William the Conqueror, literacy had been limited to a relatively small number of people trained in monasteries, convents or cathedral schools. How the situation had changed! Pope Nicholas V had been present in Florence during much of the period of the Church Council from 1439 to 1443. In that city there were numerous religious elementary and grammar schools. For older boys, alongside the cathedral school to teach canon law, there were specialized lay schools that offered notarial training and rhetoric.[17] Even in the towns of far-off England, there were parish schools and song and reading schools to provide the most elementary form of schooling. More formal ABC schools prepared children for entry into grammar schools.[18]

Another important difference between the eleventh and the fifteenth centuries was in the social position of those able to read and write. In the eleventh century, literacy had been confined principally to the clergy and to a small number of lay *ministeriales* trained in church schools. Now literacy was widespread among the lay nobility and the merchant classes of the towns and cities. In Florence, fully half of the children of school age were enrolled in elementary schools. Perhaps a third of the adult population was able to read.[19]

With the broadening of the reading public outside the institutions of the Church, there had come changes in the language of written communication. In the days of Gregory VII, Latin had held a virtual monopoly in written records. However, with the rise of the great ring of prosperous cities from southern England to northern Italy, there had arisen a great interest in poetry and prose written in the vernacular languages. In France, the *Roman de la Rose* by Guillaume de Lorris and Jean de Meun, in England the *Canterbury Tales* of Geoffrey Chaucer and in Florence *La Divina Commedia* by Dante Alighieri showed that the languages of everyday life were fitting vehicles for fine writing.

Unfortunately, not all change had been for the better. In the eleventh century, when the clergy had all taken vows of poverty, chastity and obedience, there was a spirit of cooperation among the *literati.* Gregory VII and his allies had been able to bend the proud German emperor, Henry IV, into doing penance in rags before the gates of the castle of Canossa. The flower of nobility had set off to reopen the holy city for Christian pilgrims. Today, however, how difficult it was to get people to cooperate with one another! At a time when Christianity was facing the greatest threat, Europe's princes were so preoccupied with territorial disputes among themselves that they were unwilling to commit resources to defending the eastern borders of the Church.

Some gesture on the part of the Church was called for. The Council of Florence had recently defined the nature of purgatory. According to this definition, purgatory offered the means of paying off the temporal punishment for sin. Prior to entering heaven, the soul must be purified by a temporal fire that was distinct from the eternal fire of hell. The idea of a celebration of atonement after every seven cycles of seven years is mentioned in the Old Testament (Leviticus 25: 8–55).[20] With the Western church reunited, it was the ideal time for a jubilee.

Nicholas V decided to restore the practice, begun in the fourteenth century, of celebrating a jubilee at the end of each half-century. All those who belonged to the Catholic Church would be offered a magnificent occasion to remit the terrible punishment of purgatory by worldly deeds. During the year 1450, the pope announced, there would be remissions and indulgences for sins. As for previous jubilees, those who were truly penitent and visited the Roman basilicas every day for a specified period would receive pardon for all of their sins. In addition, he authorized the issue of letters of indulgence. In payment of a fixed amount, the purchaser received a remission of the temporal punishment for sin, thereby reducing the time to be spent in purgatory. Vast crowds of pilgrims thronged to Rome to partake in the festivities. Unfortunately, some 200 people were trampled to death when panic broke out on the bridge of Sant' Angelo.[21] An outbreak of the plague even forced Nicholas V to leave Rome temporarily. Nevertheless, there was a new spirit of rejuvenation in Rome – the Renaissance.

With papal authority restored across Western Europe, it was time to reform the constituent churches. Nicholas of Cusa had requested that the pope send him to Germany. At the same time, Nicholas V would send John Capistran to Austria and Guillaume d'Estouteville to France. Then there was this Cyprus business. Unlike the perfidious Byzantines, the ruler of the island kingdom, John, of the French Lusignan family, was a faithful Catholic. A grant of aid to him would be a signal to the people of Constantinople that time was short and that they must return to the fold. The ideal support would be monetary assistance to finance the salaries of Christian mercenaries. Why not then allow another sale of letters of plenary indulgence? The king of Cyprus could appoint his agents.[22] It would be neither necessary nor expected that all of the funds raised make their way to the Cypriots. Some of the money could be used for the many other projects of the church. His legate, Nicholas of Cusa, could arrange for the letters to be copied and for their sale during his trip to Germany.

Maybe the cardinal might even make use of this wonderful new technology for copying manuscripts he had been hearing about. Provided that sufficient care was taken to control what was reproduced – particularly in the languages of the people – such an invention might permit a continuing renewal of the outpouring of faith witnessed during the jubilee.

## THE MIRACLE OF MAINZ

In a study of birth order and behavior, the historical sociologist Frank Sulloway has suggested that younger siblings feel a need to innovate in order to draw their parents' attention away from their older brothers and sisters.[23] Johannes Gutenberg was the youngest of three children. By age 35, however, he had done little to distinguish himself. He had no steady occupation, no wife or children and had yet to do anything very original. Since his father and uncle were Companions of the Mint in Mainz, he was familiar with the business of coin making.[24] He may even have earned a bit of money as a punch cutter.[25] Then in 1433, his mother's death brought him an annuity issued by the city of Strasbourg and the financial independence he had hitherto lacked. Packing his bags, he set out for Alsace, where he could be sure that the annuity was paid regularly, confident he could make his fortune. All he needed now was a product, the financing to develop it and, eventually, a market.

**The Product**

As a former university student, Gutenberg was well aware of the value of a book. A scribe working full time might be able to produce two pages of dense text per week. A Bible with almost 1300 pages might take two scribes five years to produce.[26] Alternative techniques such as wood-block printing (xylography) and copper-plate engraving (metallography) were simply too expensive for large amounts of text. In all Europe in the mid-fifteenth century, it is estimated that there were only about 30 000 books, most of them Bibles or religious commentaries.[27] Yet the potential demand from priests, students, teachers and an increasingly literate public was virtually inexhaustible, if only the cost could be brought down.

Gutenberg was familiar with the coin-maker's punch. It consisted of a handle and a shank with a raised letter engraved on the end. When struck with a hammer, the punch would leave an indentation in the mirror image of the letter in the coin-maker's mold. By pouring liquid metal into the mold, the mint worker could obtain a coin with a raised letter. Gutenberg's innovative idea was extremely simple. Could one not spread ink on such a punch and press it on to paper to print a copy of the letter? One would thereby obtain on paper the mirror image of the figure cut in relief on to the punch's head. Since the punch was metallic, it could produce many hundred copies of itself before wearing out. But where would one get a sufficient number of punches to produce entire pages of text? The Bible contained three million characters. It would take an army of skilled artisans working for years to produce the required number of characters.

Now the raised letter on a coin is in effect a clone of the original letter on the head of the coin-maker's punch. The obvious solution, Gutenberg realized, was to make an original punch engraved not with a letter of text but with its *mirror image* in relief, and then use the coin-maker's casting techniques to produce multiple clones of it. If one allowed for a shank to be attached to each letter, one could then fit a number of letters into a frame and use the resulting form to print, much as one would use a carved wooden block. Here was the basic idea. The difficulty came from the need to have shanks of varying widths to allow for the difference between, say, a 'w' and an 'i'. In addition, the letters would all have to be raised the same height above their shanks and the shanks must all be of the same length.[28] It took Gutenberg over ten years of experimentation in Strasbourg to perfect the details of the adjustable mold and the frame to hold the pieces of type it produced.

Although Gutenberg never married, he seems not to have been indifferent to women. In this respect as in most others, what little we know of him, we learn from court records. In 1436, a woman in Strasbourg, Elliwibel zur Yserin Thüre, took him to court, accusing him of breach of a promise to marry her daughter. As witness, she called a local shoemaker, a certain Claus Schott. Gutenberg scornfully called the witness, 'a miserable wretch who lives by cheating and lying'.[29] The original suit went no further, but Gutenberg had to pay a fine the following year when Schott sued him for defamation. Nevertheless, these legal developments were a victory for Gutenberg. Freed from the threat of marital entanglements, he could dedicate himself fully to solving his technical problems.

## The Financing

Once he had developed the process of printing with movable type, Gutenberg faced a second difficulty – the need for positive cash flow in order to stay afloat financially. Before he could publish his first book, he and his assistants would need to cut the dozens of punches required for the upper- and lower-case letters and punctuation of his texts. They must then use these punches to cast the many hundreds of thousands of cloned letters that the project would require. In addition, he would need to pay for paper, vellum, ink and other supplies, including those needed to manufacture a press to apply even pressure to sheets of paper or vellum. During the experimental phase in Strasbourg, Gutenberg was able to finance himself with the annuity payments along with income from teaching metalworking and profits from other small projects such as, perhaps, the sale of mirrors to pilgrims. But in 1442, he was forced to take out a loan for about 67 gulden (about $12 500 in present-day terms).[30]

In 1448, Gutenberg was back in his hometown of Mainz. One possible explanation for the move was that he needed new sources of venture capital. In that year, he borrowed 150 gulden from a cousin at five per cent interest.[31] However, Gutenberg's capital costs for the workshop he set up in the family house, the *Gutenberghof*, quickly ate up these funds. The following year, he borrowed 800 gulden from Johann Fust, a Mainz goldsmith and merchant, promising to pay six per cent interest. The modern equivalent of this sum would be about $150 000.[32] In case of default, Gutenberg's equipment could be seized as security for the loan. In addition, Gutenberg agreed to take on Fust's adopted son, Peter Schöffer, as his assistant.

Finally in 1452, Gutenberg had all of his equipment in place and his technique perfected. However, as he had still not received any income from his printing enterprise, he once more ran out of money. Reluctantly, Fust provided him with a second loan of 800 gulden. Gutenberg used the new funds to rent a house in Mainz – the *Helmsbergerhof* – where he set up a second workshop. While the first shop was preparing small printing jobs, the second would devote itself to a grand project that was to be Gutenberg's legacy to Western civilization.

**The Market**

Gutenberg's principal problem in the early 1450s was to find something printable that could be sold at a profit. Without a doubt, the most important market for books in the mid-fifteenth century was the Catholic Church. It alone had the wealth, the large numbers of educated readers and the set of common interests that could justify publication of multiple copies of multi-paged volumes. In 1449, Gutenberg had hoped that the authorization of a new missal for the churches dependent on the Mainz archbishopric would provide him with his first important printing order. However, there arose a dispute between the archbishop and the abbot who had been appointed by the pope to prepare the text of the missal. This project was postponed.

There was, however, a potentially even more lucrative project. In 1452, Nicholas of Cusa called representatives of the German Church to a synod to discuss reform. The delegates met first in Mainz and then in Cologne. Among the resolutions made by the 70 abbots who attended was the promise to obtain accurate editions of the Bible for their libraries.[33] Thanks to the cardinal's backing, Gutenberg could start preparing pages of text to be bound into books, confident that there would be a market.

Fortunately, while the massive project was being prepared, there were small printing jobs that could generate a bit of badly needed cash. In May 1452, Nicholas of Cusa instructed the prior of St Jacob's monastery in Mainz to prepare 2000 letters of indulgence for sale before the end of the month. It is possible that the sheets were printed by Gutenberg, but to date, no copy has been found. Then the pope's worst fears were realized. Mehmed II had become sultan upon his father's death. In 1453, under his command, the Turks conquered Constantinople, looting the city and killing many of its occupants. A new batch of letters of indulgence to help John of Cyprus could therefore be justified.

Produced between October 1454 and April 1455, these letters constitute the first articles printed with movable type in the West whose date is certain. The text is in Latin. The body of the text is printed in a *bâtarde* typeface that is very similar to the Caroline Minuscule characters standardized under Alcuin over six centuries earlier. Peter Schöffer, who had worked as a scribe in Paris before joining Gutenberg in Mainz, was probably responsible for designing and cutting the original punches.[34] It should perhaps be noted that very little of the money raised by these indulgences ever reached

John of Cyprus. Indeed, the Archbishop of Mainz siphoned off half of the revenues for his own use.[35]

The first printed *book* that can be dated for sure is the so-called Turkish Calendar published at the end of 1454.[36] It provides a schedule in German for the mobilization of Christian forces to meet the Turkish threat. Month by month over the coming year, the timetable is set out. In January the pope, in February the German emperor, in March the kings of the Balkan Peninsula, in April the other kings of Europe prepare, and so on, until at the end of 1455, all of the princes and towns of Europe are ready to wage war against the Muslims. However, in March of 1455, Nicholas V died and these plans came to nothing.

Probably at about the time of the calendar, Gutenberg's first workshop was printing copies of a Latin grammar known as the *Donatus*. In addition, during this period he managed to produce a small book in German, the *Sibylline Prophecies*, containing verses that told of future catastrophes under oppressive popes. The typeface used for these works is textura, a variant of the book hands known as Gothic that were developed from the twelfth century on by compressing horizontally the Caroline Minuscule so as to fit more letters on a page. The Gothic scripts with their thicker, angular characters became known as black-letter scripts, since they showed more black than white on the printed page.[37] Since this type was used for both the *Donatus* in Latin and the Turkish calendar – *Kalender* in German – it has become known as D-K type.

Meanwhile, in the *Helmsbergerhof*, Gutenberg's greatest creation was nearing completion. In October 1454, unbound 20-page sections of the Bible were on view in Frankfurt. Each page contained 42 lines of text in a beautiful Gothic script. This new typeface is now known as the B42 type. Probably Fust had taken this initiative to generate firm orders for the bound Bibles.[38]

In mid-1455, as the first of the 42-line Bibles were being completed, Gutenberg received what was undoubtedly the greatest shock of his life. He learned that his backer, Fust, was suing him to recover the amount of the two loans and accumulated interest – 2026 gulden in all. With all the loan proceeds invested in as yet unsold inventory and equipment, Gutenberg was helpless. The court judgment in November awarded the Helmsberg House workshop with the Bibles and printing equipment to Fust. Gutenberg was apparently allowed to keep the other workshop with the D-K type.[39] He was therefore able to continue printing over most of the following decade. Fust and his adopted son and future son-in-law Peter Schöffer published the Bible and went on to produce a beautiful psalter, each copy of which bore their logo.

Our two protagonists seem to have ended their careers relatively comfortably. Nicholas of Cusa spent his last years in Rome as a trusted adviser to the papacy, dying in 1464. Meanwhile, Gutenberg continued printing up until his death in 1468, although a war between rival claimants to the archbishopric in Mainz forced him to take up residence nearby in his mother's family town of Eltville.

For half a century, the effect of movable type on society was much as Nicholas of Cusa might have imagined. There was a gradual acceleration of printing. Some 1100 printers published about 26 550 editions of incunabula (defined as works printed before 1500, from the Latin word for cradle) – two-thirds of these in Germany and Italy.[40] Here was the miracle of Mainz. The humanist movement in European scholarship benefited considerably from the resulting fall in the cost of reproducing information, as classical Latin writings became readily available. Even the fall of Constantinople had positive effects. It led to the immigration of Byzantine scholars, who brought to Western Europe their knowledge of Greek classics, including more accurate versions of the New Testament. Above all, as Diarmaid MacCulloch had pointed out, the advent of printing gave scholars time to develop new ideas. Previously, they had been forced to spend most of their days copying information by hand. They were now able to devote their hours to thinking for themselves.[41]

Yet fifty years after its invention, this dramatic innovation had touched the lives of only a small percentage of Europe's population. The explanation is simple: 72 per cent of the titles published were in Latin, a language that few were able to read.[42] As for the vernacular, enterprising printers put out titles in the dialects of their regions, but since there were no standardized spellings or grammar, readership remained limited. In 1466, the first printed translation of the Bible in German was produced in Strasbourg by one of Gutenberg's former apprentices, Johann Mentelin.[43] A French printer who had also worked with Gutenberg, Nicolas Jenson, brought out the first printed Bible in Italian in Venice in 1471. Jenson also designed a new typeface known as Roman, intended to restore the classical tradition. In practice, his characters were modeled on the medieval script, Caroline Minuscule. His 1470 edition of Eusebius's fourth-century history of the Christian Church, *Historia Ecclesiastica*, marked the beginning of white-letter printing, so called because most of the page was left white.

Outside of Germany and Italy, the spread of printing in the vernacular was even less rapid. Thomas Caxton printed the first book in the English of London in Bruges in 1474. It was *The Recuyell of the Historyes of Troye*, his own translation of a French version of the Trojan Wars by Raoul Le Fèvre. However, early in the fifteenth century, Bishop Arundel had forbidden the translation of the Bible into the vernacular and banned the reading of Wycliff's existing English translation. It would take another fifty years after Caxton's first book before the first English version of the

New Testament, by William Tyndale, appeared in print. Even then, the copies had to be printed on the continent and smuggled into England. The French too were reluctant to allow translations of the Bible into the vernacular. Although a French New Testament appeared in 1474, the first complete version of the Bible in French was not published until 1530.

Despite the apparent social harmony of late medieval Europe, there was a fundamental conflict of interest in the position of the Catholic Church that remained unresolved. With its control of schools and universities, the Church was the manager of Europe's information system. At the same time, since the Church's doctrines encouraged people to give tithes and purchase indulgences, it stood to profit from the type of information that circulated. Inevitably, decision makers within the Church would be tempted to distort the flow of information so as to maximize this lucrative flow of income.

The fatal step came in 1515 when Pope Leo X promulgated the bull, *Inter Sollicitudines*. All printed works without exception were henceforth subject to censorship administered by the bishops. Any printer who defied canon law would be excommunicated and his books burned. A standardized medium would be allowed, but only to the extent that it diffused standardized information. The Catholic Church had begun its attack on the communications technology it had done so much to promote barely a half-century earlier. However, it seriously underestimated the power of Gutenberg's clones in the service of a determined revolutionary.

## THE VIEW FROM THE WARTBURG

The Wartburg Castle stands on a forested hill above the Thuringian town of Eisenach in central Germany. Today, you can walk up there from the train station in forty minutes. Once inside the stone ramparts, you can then visit the room where Martin Luther worked in seclusion for a year beginning in April 1521. You can even see the black spot on the wall where he is said to have thrown his inkpot at the devil. If you close your eyes briefly, you can imagine him sitting there, writing by candlelight to prepare the book that was to be as important for the West as the invention of movable type.

### The 95 Theses

Luther had visited Rome in 1510 and had been shocked by the worldly lives of the Roman clergy at that time. The current pope, Leo X, second son of the late Lorenzo the Magnificent, ruler of Florence, enjoyed a lifestyle that was without precedent in Western Europe. He maintained 683 servants, including his own musicians and theater company. In addition, he subsidized numerous humanist scholars, painters and composers; as a result, he was often in dire financial straits. When Albert of Brandenburg requested a papal dispensation in order to be allowed to occupy the German archbishopric of Mainz while still holding on to his current posts as Archbishop of Magdeburg and Bishop of Halberstadt, the pope accepted – provided that certain conditions were met. Albert would have to pay Rome the usual fee of 14 000 ducats for the archbishopric plus a special voluntary tax of 10 000 ducats.[44]

To help Albert finance this purchase, Leo X issued a papal bull permitting the sale of indulgences in the three German bishoprics. It was announced that the proceeds were to finance the construction of the new basilica of St Peter in Rome. It was understood, of course, that the pope would also have access to the funds for his own private purposes.[45] Albert then hired Johann Tetzel, a Dominican priest with ten years experience in the business, to sell the certificates. However, Luther's patron, the elector of Saxony, Frederick the Wise, forbade Tetzel to enter his territory. As head of the Wettin family, the elector was unwilling to help increase the wealth of the rival Hohenzollern dynasty to which the new archbishop belonged. Nevertheless, the bold Dominican with his cortege of valets, preceded by a servant bearing the papal bull on a red and gold cushion, stopped to preach at the principal churches of nearby Jüterborg and Zerbst in the archbishopric of Magdeburg. With a padlocked money chest waiting at his feet, he would cry,

> As soon as the coin in the coffer rings,
> the soul from purgatory springs.[46]

Inevitably, some of Luther's parishioners came to confess in Wittenberg bringing copies of Tetzel's printed letters of indulgence that they had bought in the neighboring towns. In 1517, Martin Luther was 34. He was the son of a miner who had risen from the peasantry into the middle class. For twelve years, Martin had been an Augustinian monk. He was a man quick to anger and tenacious in holding his position in debate. However, he also had an exceptional ability to explain his ideas simply by using examples and analogies that his audience could understand.[47] As professor of biblical theology at the University of Wittenberg, Luther had already preached against indulgences. What enraged him now was to come across a set of instructions for indulgence preachers that bore the coat of arms of the Archbishop of Magdeburg. Therein Albert promised complete forgiveness of all sins without the need for contrition or confession.

In response, Luther prepared 95 theses in Latin for academic debate. On All Saints' Eve, 31 October 1517, he posted them on the door of the castle church in Wittenberg – the bulletin board of the university professors. A few months previously, one of his colleagues had made public 52 theses on the same subject, criticizing the practice of indulgences, without provoking any reaction.[48] However, Luther sent copies to his archbishop and to different correspondents outside the university. As a result, although no one was willing to debate with him, the theses in Latin were quickly printed and became widely known by scholars and clerics in Germany.

What were the theses? Consider three that posed the greatest challenge to current practices of the clergy. Thesis 6 denied the Church's power to remit guilt for sin. 'The pope cannot remit any guilt, except by declaring that it has been remitted by God and by assenting to God's remission.' Thesis 36 went on to attack the specific use of indulgences by the Church. 'Every truly repentant Christian has a right to full remission of penalty and guilt, even without letters of pardon.' Finally, Luther in thesis 78 implied that the Bible was the ultimate reference for religious questions. 'The present pope, and any pope at all, has greater graces at his disposal [than to remit guilt]; to wit, the Gospel, powers, gifts of healing, etc., as it is written in I. Corinthians xii.'

It is evident that Luther was attacking not just the abusive use of indulgences for church financing, but rather the very basis of the Church's position in society. His theses denied the power of the pope to grant pardon, rejected the necessity of the believer to use the intermediary of the priesthood to obtain salvation and challenged the ultimate authority of the pope on questions of doctrine. In December, Archbishop Albert notified the curia in Rome of Luther's attack on indulgences, and Tetzel's order, the Dominicans, denounced Luther as a heretic. Could the Church with its great resources and backing from most secular rulers stamp out the flame of heresy before it spread? A century earlier, the criticisms of the Czech priest Jan Hus (which were similar to those of Luther) had been successfully contained and Hus burned as a heretic. What had worked once could be tried again.

## The Appeal to the German People

In that same month of December 1517, there was an unprecedented development that would prevent the Church from stifling the debate. Kaspar Nützel, a patrician in Nürnberg, translated the theses into German. Thanks to the printing press, and much to Luther's initial dismay, they now began to circulate widely among the laity.[49]

Luther was still hoping that he could find sufficient backing in the Church to push through a program of reform. In February 1518, he wrote in Latin *Resolutiones Disputationum de Indulgentiarum Virtute* to clarify his position to the clergy. The theses, he explained, were simply affirmations for debate. Nevertheless, he made every effort to support his arguments with reason and with biblical references, aware that his critics were beginning to call him a heretic. However, at the same time Tetzel, with the backing of the Dominican order, printed and distributed 106 theses that attacked Luther's position.[50] Tetzel bragged, 'I'll have the heretic burned within three weeks and send his ashes to heaven in a bathing cap'.[51]

Caught up in a swirl of controversy, Luther realized that he must explain himself to the lay public. At worst, if the Church refused to listen, he might convince Germany's secular lords to apply political pressure in support of reform. In March 1518, he published in German a *Sermon on Indulgences and Grace*, presenting the content of the theses in ordinary language. All that God required from sinners was sincere repentance. Indulgences were for people too lazy to do good works. He refrained from attacking the power of the pope directly.[52]

At first, it appeared that some sort of compromise could be arranged. The pope wished to remain on good terms with Luther's patron, Frederick the Wise, one of the electors who would choose the next German emperor. Leo X favored Frederick as successor to the ailing Maximilian I in order to limit the power of the house of Habsburg. Accordingly, Frederick was able to grant Luther a letter of safe conduct so that he might debate his ideas with other theologians.[53] On 4 and 5 January 1519, Luther met a papal legate and hammered out an agreement. First, both parties would refrain from speaking publicly of indulgences. Second, the pope would appoint a learned German bishop to specify which articles Luther would have to recant. Then, a week later, the German Emperor Maximilian died. The pope wrote to Luther through the elector offering him an audience in Rome.

When it became evident that Charles V, the Habsburg king of Spain, would be elected German emperor, the pope quickly realized that it was no longer in his interest to court the elector of Saxony. On 28 June 1519, Charles was elected with Frederick's support. Immediately, attacks on Luther began to appear in print again.

Luther replied in kind, keeping the printing presses of Wittenberg busy. There were three fundamental points on which Luther and the Catholic Church differed. Luther had already stated his disagreement in the 95 theses. In documents written in 1520, he set out clearly the basic principles of an alternative institution. The first issue concerned the authority of the pope on matters of church organization. In his address *To the Christian Nobility of the German Nation*, which appeared in print in August 1520, he expressed his belief that the secular authority had the right to intervene to institute reforms in the church. Payments of money to Rome should be stopped and the monasteries turned into educational institutions.

Evidently, Luther hoped that the new emperor, Charles V, would follow these recommendations.

The second dispute concerned the ultimate authority on questions of dogma. Since the eleventh century, the Church had maintained that there were seven sacraments, namely, baptism, penance, Eucharist, confirmation, matrimony, extreme unction and ordination. In his treatise, *On the Babylonian Captivity of the Church*, published in October 1520, Luther reduced these to three, arguing that there was biblical justification only for baptism, penance and the Lord's Supper. Marriage had always existed in human society. Confirmation, extreme unction and ordination were simply rites instituted by the medieval church. Implicitly, the Bible rather than the pope would henceforth be the source of Christian doctrine.

The third question concerned the Church's role in the individual's salvation. In October, Luther wrote a letter to the pope that included a tract he had prepared. The German version of this document was subsequently published under the title, *The Freedom of a Christian*. The central message is that the individual must justify himself to God by faith rather than by good works. 'This is that Christian liberty, our faith, which does not induce us to live in idleness or wickedness but makes the law and works unnecessary for any man's righteousness and salvation'.[54] A corollary of this position was that there was no possible justification for the remission of sin or punishment through a certificate issued by the Church.

A hundred years earlier, the conflagration could have been confined. However, thanks to the printing press, Luther's powerful arguments were reproduced by the thousands in the German language. As a result, he was supported by an ever-growing group of powerful supporters, most of whom had never met him personally.[55]

The final break was now inevitable. Late in October 1519, copies of a papal bull issued by Leo X in June reached Wittenberg. In this document, *Exsurge Domine* (Arise O Lord), not only did the pope excommunicate Luther, but also he ordered that all of Luther's works – even those not yet written – be burned. Anyone who defended him or promoted his writings would also be excommunicated. Shortly after, there came word of the first burnings of Luther's books in Louvain and Lüttich. On 10 December 1520, Luther replied in kind, inviting 'all friends of evangelical truth' to a ceremony outside the Elster gate of Wittenberg. There, on a fire that consumed books of canon law, Luther publicly threw a copy of the papal bull.[56]

## Literacy in the Vernacular

In April 1521, at the Imperial Diet in Worms, a cathedral city on the middle Rhine, the Habsburg Emperor Charles V added the ban of the Empire to that of the Church. So it was that Luther found himself 'kidnapped' by the knights of his protector Frederick the Wise and carried in secret to the Wartburg Castle. Looking out over the forested hills of Thuringia in central Germany, Luther realized that the Roman Church was not likely to change of its own accord. Accordingly, individual Christians must learn to take spiritual matters into their own hands. His principal activity over the following year, therefore, was to translate the New Testament from Greek into German with the help of his Wittenberg colleague and Greek scholar, Philipp Melanchthon. The new translation was first printed in Wittenberg in September 1522.[57] By 1525, there had been 14 authorized editions of this work – and 66 pirated editions.[58] (Luther's complete Bible in German would not be published until 1534.[59])

With the source material for his new church available in the vernacular, Luther's next task was to make sure that people could have access to it themselves without the intermediary of a trained priest. During the Middle Ages, most teaching – from the parish schools to the cathedral schools and the university – had been the responsibility of the Church. In Germany, only a small fraction of children of school age had been educated. In particular, the schooling of girls had often been neglected. Luther now proposed to strip the churches of their educational role and assign it to the state.[60] In 1524, he wrote a letter, 'To the Councilmen of All Cities in Germany That They Establish and Maintain Christian Schools'. He recommended that boys attend school for one to two hours a day and girls attend for at least an hour daily. The principal task of these new secular schools was to teach the gospel.[61]

Germany already had a system of Latin schools for the sons of the elite. As a result of Luther's efforts, there was a proliferation of new German-language schools in the Protestant areas of Germany during the sixteenth century. Schools were to be staffed by trained and licensed teachers. Teams of inspectors would examine the schools each month and test the pupils quarterly.[62] By mid-century, it was taken for granted that people from the aristocracy and the upper middle class would be literate in German. Among rural residents too, there was a rise in literacy rates. However, landless agricultural workers and unskilled manual workers were still generally illiterate.[63]

With the extension of literacy in the vernacular, there was a rising demand for literature printed in German. But since each region had its own dialect, German printers trying to maximize their readership had a difficult problem. Which vernacular should they choose? Until the 1530s, there was considerable variety, ranging from the Low German of the north to the High German of Nürnberg to the Alemannic of the southwest and Switzerland. More than anyone else, it was Luther who set the standard for future generations of Germans. He later explained that he had chosen the language of the Saxon chancery for his writings because it was the language 'used by every prince and king in Germany'.[64] In the key period from 1518 to 1524, he was the author of one out of three books sold in German. In the century after its first publication, 200 000 copies of Luther's Bible were printed in Wittenberg; in addition, numerous pirated editions were printed elsewhere. While Luther by no means can be said to have invented the modern German language, he and his printers tended to use a regularized vocabulary and spelling that had a great impact on subsequent German writing.[65]

Luther soon had strong personal reasons for desiring good schools in the Protestant states. In April 1523, he arranged for nine nuns to escape from a convent, smuggled in a wagon that transported barrels of herring. They arrived in Wittenberg with no belongings, looking to Luther for help. He arranged for one of the women, Katharina von Bora, to marry an associate, but the young man's family refused to let him wed a penniless runaway nun. When the woman refused another proposed match but said that she would be willing to marry Luther, the former monk began to take an interest in her. Finally, in June 1525, they were married – first in private, then in a large public ceremony – he at the age of 42 and she 26. The following year Katharina bore Luther the first of six children – three boys and three girls.[66] When a monk marries a nun to the general approval of society, it is evident that things are changing.

## THE DESTRUCTION OF MEDIEVAL EUROPE

Several decades ago, the French historian Georges Duby discovered a text written in about 1020 by Adalbéron, Bishop of Laon, France. The bishop observed that there were three orders of society: namely, those who pray (*orant*), those who fight (*pugnant*) and those who work (*laborant*). These three social groups were complementary, Adalbéron argued, since the efforts of each supported those of the others.[67] Until the early sixteenth century, the bishop's three orders had held together remarkably well. Latin Europe had managed to stop the Mongol invasions, drive the Muslims out of Spain and the Byzantines out of Italy. Divisions between the Church and the Empire, between rival popes and between the royal houses of England and Spain had been healed. Then, in the first half of the sixteenth century, the glue that had held the three orders together for half a millennium began to come unstuck.

### Those Who Pray

Luther died in bed of a heart attack in 1546 at the age of 62, but not before witnessing the first waves of social turmoil generated by the Reformation that he had launched. His excommunication for heresy by Leo X in 1519 triggered a major rupture in the solidarity of the first of the three groups. The German clergy were forced to take sides either for or against the reforms he began to institute with the support of Frederick the Wise in electoral Saxony.

The next major country whose clergy were affected by the turmoil was England. When the pope refused Henry VIII permission to divorce Catherine of Aragon so that he might marry her lady-in-waiting, Ann Boleyn, the king broke with Rome. In 1532, he compelled his subjects to acknowledge his position as head of the English church. The country's monasteries were then dissolved and members of the clergy who remained faithful to Rome were executed. Ann Boleyn soon shared their fate, accused unjustly of infidelity.

During the 1540s, the contagion spread to France following the publication in French of the writings of the reformer Jean Calvin. Despite royal persecution, the number of Protestants – or Huguenots, as they were known – increased rapidly, particularly in the Languedoc, Brittany and Normandy. A similar development occurred in the 1560s in the Low Countries after the translation of Calvin's *Institutes of the Christian Religion* into Dutch. In 1566, Protestant mobs pillaged churches including the Antwerp cathedral.

**Those Who Labor**

There had been peasant revolts during the Middle Ages, particularly in the fourteenth century following the Black Death. However, these disturbances were disorganized and had been quickly suppressed. In 1524, a much more serious uprising known as the Peasants' War began in central and southern Germany. The leaders of the revolt produced written programs of reform such as the *Twelve Articles of the Peasantry*. Taking their theme from a misreading of Luther's tract, *The Freedom of a Christian*, the peasants demanded an end to serfdom. Few secular rulers were sympathetic to these demands, mild though they were.

Unlike the medieval peasants, the rebels used organized military formations. The peasant armies were made up primarily of untrained farmers, but they also included many *Landsknechte*, troops experienced in fighting with handguns and pikes.[68] They attacked monasteries, castles and even towns. Finally, the soldiers of the princes confronted a large peasant army at Frankenhausen in Hesse in May 1525. In a one-sided victory of the nobility, large numbers of peasant troops were massacred. The peasant leaders were caught and executed.

## Those Who Fight

The principal armed conflicts of the Late Middle Ages in Western Europe had been disputes between sovereign states. For over a century after 1346, the monarchs of England and France had been at war with each another. The small states of Italy were also continually waging war among themselves. In Bohemia, the Hussite Wars between 1419 and 1436 pitched one ethnic group, the Czechs, against German imperial forces. Interstate rivalries also delayed the sending of a Catholic fleet to help defend Constantinople in 1453; it arrived after the city had fallen. During the last decades of the sixteenth century, Maximilian, the son of Emperor Frederick III, was engaged in continual campaigns to keep the French Valois out of Habsburg lands in the Low Countries and Burgundy.

The nature of warfare changed in the second quarter of the sixteenth century. For over a century thereafter, although there was continual tension between the Catholic rulers of Spain and France, the major conflicts in Western Europe would be wars of religion. In Germany, the Reformation set off a series of bitter clashes between Catholics and Protestants. In 1522, a group of imperial knights who had been influenced by Luther's writings attempted to take lands around Trier that belonged to the Church. Imperial and church forces soon routed them. Then in 1531, German princes who had converted to Lutheranism formed the Schmalkaldic league outside the institutions of the Empire. One by one, except for Bavaria, the other German cities and states followed their example. Finally, in 1547, the Emperor Charles V unleashed his troops; they defeated the Protestants at Mühlberg. Six years later, however, the princes got the better of an imperial army at Sievershausen. By the Peace of Augsburg of 1555, the emperor was forced to accept the principle, *Cuius regio euius religio* (He who rules over the land determines its religion).

During the second half of the sixteenth century, France and the Netherlands were also torn apart by religious violence. In France, a massacre of Calvinist Huguenots in 1572 triggered a series of wars between Protestants and Catholics. Religious peace could not be established until 1598, when King Henry IV, who was raised as a Protestant but converted to Catholicism, signed the Edict of Nantes granting Protestants the right to practice their religion. Meanwhile, in the Netherlands, the decision of Philip II of Spain (Charles V's son), to impose the Inquisition in order to stamp out Protestant dissent triggered a bitter war that would last for eight decades. The defeat of the Spanish Armada in 1588 occurred when Philip II attempted unsuccessfully to transport his Catholic army by sea from the Netherlands to conquer Protestant England. The stability of medieval society, with its three orders of those who fought, those who prayed and those who worked, had been destroyed.

In medieval Europe social equilibrium had depended upon differentiated ability to decode written information. At the top of the pyramid were the clergy and those they trained, literate in Latin. Then came the lay aristocracy and upper middle class, sufficiently literate to be able to perform their socially required functions but unable to mount a challenge to the Church's information monopoly. Finally there came the majority of the population, illiterate workers who were dependent on the first two orders for the salvation of their souls and for the protection of their lives and property. The printing of thousands of editions of Latin classics and other incunabula had not changed this basic structure. Prior to 1500, the Church had been justifiably confident of its capacity to destroy any outbreak of heresy.

Then in 1517, Martin Luther allied himself with Gutenberg's clones to begin a counter-attack on the Church. Luther's writings were disseminated across northern Europe thanks to the Reformation's promotion of education in the vernacular. By enabling ordinary townspeople to decode written information, they destroyed the Catholic Church's communications monopoly. As a result, there was no longer any need for a burdensome religious superstructure, since people could read the scriptures themselves. Nor was there any need to delegate decisions concerning the protection of property to a distant monarch. The contractual basis of medieval society had dissolved.

## NOTES

1. Eggenberger (1985, pp. 222–223).
2. Theosophy Trust (2006).
3. Joda (1977, p. 37).
4. Joda (1977, p. 38).
5. Man (2002, p. 83).
6. Joda (1977, p. 39).
7. Joda (1977, pp. 39–40).
8. Man (2002, p. 88).
9. Man (2002, p. 104).
10. Joda (1977, p. 44).
11. Man (2002, pp. 25, 41).
12. Man (2002, pp. 25–26, 44).
13. Kapr (1996, p. 62).
14. Presser (1967, p. 19).
15. Scannell (1911).
16. Boyle (1993).
17. Graff (1991, p. 77).
18. Graff (1991, p. 70).
19. Graff (1991, pp. 77–78).
20. Scannell (1911).

21. Scannell (1911).
22. Man (2002, p. 155).
23. Sulloway (1997).
24. Man (2002, p. 44).
25. Man (2002, p. 50).
26. Man (2002, pp. 89–90).
27. Did You Know (n.d.).
28. Man (2002, p. 133).
29. Man (2002, p. 59).
30. Man (2002, pp. 137, 149).
31. Man (2002, p. 142).
32. Man (2002, p. 149).
33. Man (2002, p. 152).
34. Kapr (1987, p. 191).
35. Kapr (1987, pp. 188–189).
36. Bechtel (1992, p. 340).
37. Lenhart (1935, p. 118).
38. Man (2002, p. 181).
39. Man (2002, pp. 189–190).
40. Japan (2004).
41. MacCulloch (2003, p. 71),
42. Japan (2004).
43. Man (2002, p. 218).
44. Gobry (1991, p. 97).
45. Loewenich (1986, p. 112).
46. Gobry (1991, p. 98), Loewenich (1986, p. 113).
47. Hail (1977, pp. 152–154).
48. Gobry (1991, p. 100).
49. Loewenich (1986, pp. 117–118).
50. Gobry (1991, p. 112).
51. Loewenich (1986, p. 117).
52. Lohse (1997, p. 145).
53. Loewenich (1986, p. 121).
54. Loewenich (1986, p. 184).
55. Marty (2004, p. 49).
56. Loewenich (1986, pp. 186–187).
57. Loewenich (1986, p. 210).
58. Wells (1985, p. 191).
59. Wells (1982, p. 191).
60. Holborn (1982, p. 188).
61. Loewenich (1986, pp. 243–245).
62. Graff (1991, p. 139).
63. Graff (1991, p. 142).
64. Loewenich (1986, p. 210).
65. Wells (1985, p. 192).
66. Loewenich (1986, pp. 279–285).
67. Duby (1978, p. 15).
68. Holborn (1982, p. 170).

# 4. King, lords and commons

During the second quarter of the sixteenth century, a breakdown in the internal cohesion of European society began to put Western civilization as a whole at risk. Internal divisions in Christianity between Catholics and Protestants gave the Turks the opportunity to expand westward. In 1520, Süleyman the Magnificent inherited the Ottoman throne and immediately began to apply pressure on Christian Europe. His victory at the battle of Mohacs in 1526 gave him control of Hungary. By the time of his death in 1566, the Turks also controlled North Africa and most of the Greek isles. Cyprus, whose defense had been used to justify the first order for printed documents, fell in 1571. The question was whether some alternative form of organization would emerge in the West in time to prevent its total collapse.

In the year 1604, the British Isles seemed an unlikely place for Gutenberg's remarkable invention to begin generating a new type of society. Together, the citizens of England, Scotland and Ireland – the three kingdoms over which King James I ruled – amounted to only a third the population of France or Germany. The British were not poor relative to the rest of Europe, but their per-capita income was nevertheless a third lower than that of the wealthy United Provinces across the North Sea.[1] Britain had missed out on the colonization of the New World and had failed to share in the prosperous trade with India and the Far East. To the extent that innovation requires the free circulation of ideas, Britain seemed an unlikely spot for an acceleration of technical progress. Although the Anglican Church had after a half-century of religious turmoil established its independence from Rome, its clergymen proved no more tolerant of dissent than their Catholic colleagues on the continent. Puritan leaders who wished to separate from the Church of England were arrested and thrown into the vilest of prisons for long periods.[2]

## IN SEARCH OF CONSENSUS

Hampton Court Palace lies west of London on the north shore of the Thames, 14 miles upriver from the smoke and dirt of the great city's heart. You can reach it by train after a half-hour's ride from Waterloo Station. The complex consists of two interlocking palaces: a majestic neoclassical pavilion designed by Christopher Wren for William and Mary in the late seventeenth century and an earlier Renaissance section built during the reign of Henry VIII. It was in the latter wing – the first you reach on entering the grounds today – that King James I early in 1604 brought together a number of church leaders and theologians. His goal was to discuss possible reforms to the Church of England. At the time, there was ice on the river and great fires were blazing in the fireplaces of the withdrawing room within the king's privy chamber.[3]

## The Bishops and Deans

Letters from the Privy Council had summoned the Archbishop of Canterbury, the primate of the English church, along with some of the leading bishops and the deans of some of the major cathedrals to meet the king at Hampton Court on Saturday, 14 January 1604.[4] Four leaders of the Puritan faction within the Church of England were also invited, but they were asked to retire before the king entered. On one side of the room sat the privy councillors, the great lords of the kingdom who were the king's principal political advisers. Opposite them were the bishops and deans, in their magnificent robes of black satin, silk scarves and four-cornered hats.[5]

James entered a little after eleven o'clock and took a seat on a velvet-covered chair at one end of the room.[6] He knew that there were many in England who objected to certain practices that their established church had retained from Catholicism. On his journey from Edinburgh across the English counties the previous year, he had received a document signed by a thousand ministers known as the Millenary Petition. The signatories objected to such ceremonial practices carried over from Catholicism as bowing at the name of Jesus, confirmation and signing with the cross during baptism. Another contentious issue was excommunication when imposed by lay officials rather than by church courts.[7] However, during his trip, James had also received the visit of Dr Thomas Neville, who had been sent by the Archbishop of Canterbury to plead with the king to retain the status quo.[8]

James saw himself as a peacemaker who could bridge the gap between these religious factions. As yet, however, there seemed to be little hope of compromise between those leading members of the clergy who desired no change and the Puritan reformers who sought to cleanse the church of papist practices. The difficulty was to reach a compromise without threatening his own position as head of state. The king had no desire to weaken the hierarchical structure of the English church, since he realized that the bishops were a strong source of support for the monarchy. Nevertheless, he had little sympathy for the intolerance that the English church leaders had shown for nonconformists.

John Whitgift, the 73-year-old Archbishop of Canterbury, presented the position of the established church, the practices of which had remained essentially unchanged for forty years. At his side was his deputy and designated successor, the Bishop of London, Richard Bancroft, 59. On their knees before their new sovereign, the bishops insisted that their institution was presently as near as possible to the perfect condition of the early Christian church. Skeptical, James with his heavy Scottish accent exclaimed, 'It was no reason that because a man has been sicke of the pox 40 years, therefore he should not be cured at length'.[9]

The discussion lasted for more than three hours.[10] Finally, after finishing his questioning, James concluded that 'excommunication for trifles' should be abolished. Moreover, the bishops would not be allowed to take important decisions concerning other people's fate arbitrarily without the advice of 'some grave men.'[11] The king also wished to make changes in the wording of the prayer book.[12] Satisfied with this meeting, the king announced that he would see the Puritan party on Monday.

## A King for all Seasons

At age 37, James was truly a king for all seasons. He was an amateur poet and an astute political writer who believed in the necessity of a strong monarchy. He was also a devoted father. Fifteen years earlier, he had married Anne of Denmark, by whom he had two surviving sons and a daughter. His advice to his elder son took the form of a book, *Basilikon Doron* (the Kingly Gift), that began with a sonnet.[13] Yet James was a practicing homosexual whose liaisons with royal favorites had been a source of gossip in European courts long before his voyage from Edinburgh to London the previous year. There was currently an epigram circulating: *Rex fuit Elizabeth: nunc est regina Jacobus* – 'Elizabeth was King: now James is Queen'.[14]

James was the only child of Mary Queen of Scots, by her second husband, Henry Stewart, Lord Darnley. In 1565, when the boy was eight months old, his father was assassinated. Shortly after, his mother was forced to abdicate, leaving one-year-old James as king of Scotland. Mary departed for England a year later, only to be imprisoned and subsequently executed. James had been baptized a Catholic but was raised in the Calvinist faith by a series of strict Presbyterian governors. During his childhood, the turbulent Scottish factions competed for control of the regency, but by 1586, at the age of 20, had James assumed control. One of his first measures was to arrange an alliance with his childless cousin Elizabeth. A non-negligible factor in this decision was James's awareness that his Tudor blood by the maternal grandmothers of both his parents made him next in line for the throne of his country's rich and powerful neighbor.

Now, in 1604, with the death of Elizabeth the previous spring, James had added England and Ireland to his Scottish inheritance. Curiously, each of his three realms had a different religion. He was all too familiar with the ascetic practices of his fellow Presbyterian Scots and the differences that separated them from the Catholics in his own country and Ireland. He was less familiar with the rituals of the English, who since the time of Henry VIII had deviated increasingly from the practices of Rome. His talk with the bishops and deans had exposed him to the conservative views of one faction. The next step was to meet the more moderate spokespeople of those who believed that the Church of England should be purified of unnecessary ritual – the Puritans.

**The Puritan Divines**

On Monday 16 January, four advocates of reform were ushered into the same room in Hampton Court to meet the king. The sovereign was accompanied by two bishops most vehemently opposed to the Puritans. The chief speaker for the opposition within the church was John Reynolds, 54, master of Corpus Christi College at Oxford. With him were Laurence Chaderton, 67, master of Emmanuel College at Cambridge and two other Puritan pastors. They addressed the king on their knees, with three requests for substantive change: 'That the doctrine of the Church might be preserved in purity, according to God's word. . . That the Church government might be sincerely ministered, according to God's word. [And] that the Book of Common Prayer might be fitted to more increase of piety.'[15]

James, who had often engaged in theological debate in Scotland, was familiar with all of the Calvinist criticisms of Catholic ritual. He was wise enough to reject any major revision of Church ceremonies, knowing that the only result would be acrimonious disagreement. However, he might well have accepted the second point on church administration had Reynolds not mentioned that each bishop should have a presbytery of ministers to advise him. Fearing that the Puritans might be advocating a decentralized system with quarreling committees, the king lashed out: 'If you aim at a Scots Presbytery, it agreeth as well with monarchie as God with the devil'.[16] He would not allow the existing system of bishops to be dismantled. 'No bishops', he insisted, 'no king.'[17]

During the discussion of the first point concerning doctrinal purity, Reynolds mentioned that the petitioning ministers desired 'one only translation of ye byble to be authenticall and read in ye church'. The Puritan divine was probably requesting royal approval for the translation he used himself, prepared by a group of Protestant exiles influenced by Jean Calvin and published in Geneva in the 1550s. However, James I threw the suggestion back with a totally different meaning, indicating his willingness to support a *new* translation of the Bible. The procedure he proposed was one of consensus building among English biblical scholars. In the words of Bishop Barlow:

> His Highness wished, that some especiall pains should be taken in that behalf for one vniforme translation . . . and this to be done by the best learned of both the Vniversities, after them to be reuiewed by the Bishops, and the chiefe learned of the Church; from them to be presented to the Priuy Councell; and lastly to be retified by his Royall authority; to be read in the whole Church, and no other.[18]

In the past, James I has often been portrayed as something of a failure as a king, both on the Scottish throne and on that of England. He has been seen as ineffective and pedantic as a ruler. His difficulties in coming to terms with a Parliament jealous of its rights have been interpreted as a precursor to the civil war that would cost his son his throne and his head. His obsession with the need for a strong monarchy has been viewed as a consequence of his own vanity.[19] However, recent studies have presented the king in a new light. In Scotland he had managed to establish religious peace without either war or mass executions of dissidents.[20] In England he viewed his role as similar – to establish a consensus as to political tolerance and the role of the monarchy.

Two days after meeting the Puritans, James met with the bishops to state clearly the conclusions of the conference. Although there were to be changes to the description of absolution and confirmation, most of the practices that the Puritans had criticized would remain. In particular, all ministers would be required to wear the square hat and the surplice, a knee-length outer vestment with long sleeves. However, the bishops were to be assisted by other members of the clergy in 'ordination, suspension and degrading' while only church courts were allowed to excommunicate. Finally, there was to be a uniform catechism and a new translation of the Bible. The task of organizing the translation would fall upon the shoulders of the Bishop of London, Richard Bancroft, who during Archbishop John Whitgift's last years was the de facto head of the Church of England.

## ENGLAND IN 1604

As a man to organize a procedure for reaching consensus on the wording of the Bible in English, it is hard to think of a less appropriate candidate than Richard Bancroft. His entire ecclesiastic career had been based on identifying and expelling from the church those who questioned its role as an intermediary in interpreting the scriptures. In 1589, as canon of

Westminster, he had preached a harsh attack on the Puritans. So vehement was his affirmation of the divine right of bishops to defend the faith that he had been identified as a possible threat to the crown. During the 1580s and 1590s, he succeeded in breaking up the groups of Separatists who met for service in private houses. Separatist leaders were imprisoned and many of them executed.[21]

In February 1604, a month after the Hampton Court conference, Archbishop of Canterbury John Whitgift died and Bancroft at 60 years of age was named to succeed him. One of the new primate's first assignments was to root out from the church those ministers who could not accept the conclusions of the Hampton Court Conference. Over the following year, it is estimated that about ninety non-conforming ministers were forced to resign. They comprised perhaps one per cent of the English clergy.[22]

Bancroft's differences with the leaders among the more moderate Puritans were not as great as might be imagined. He had been educated at Cambridge, where he had become friends with Laurence Chaderton, one of the puritan divines who had attended the conference at Hampton Court. The two were from Lancaster, where wrestling was a favorite sport. Even in their mature years, they enjoyed wrestling when they met.[23] Both men were from the minor gentry and had risen to their positions largely through their own merits.[24]

The king and the archbishop drew up guidelines for those who were to translate the Bible. There were already several Bibles that had been printed in English. Although the most popular was the Geneva version prepared by Calvinists, the Church used a translation made by 14 bishops that had first been published in 1568. Serious scholars attacked this official Bible for its inaccurate translations. Nevertheless, Rule 1 of King James's instructions stated that the Bishop's Bible, as it was called, was to be the default translation, to be altered as little as necessary.[25]

## The Evolution of the Vernacular

If we suddenly found ourselves projected back in time to the Globe Theatre in London in the year 1604, we might have some difficulty understanding what the actors were saying. As a reading of the plays of Shakespeare quickly reveals, English grammar at the beginning of the seventeenth century was different in many ways from the language that is spoken today. When addressing children and animals or people of a lower social status, people used the second-person pronoun *thou* rather than *you*. The informal *thou* was also used when lower status people talked among themselves. However, if someone of a lower status addressed a person of a higher status, the formal *you* was compulsory; the variant *ye* was also to be found.[26] Another difference was in pronouns: the third person possessive corresponding to *it* was *his*, as in the ghost's line from Hamlet, 'The glow-worm shows the matin to be near/And 'gins to pale *his* uneffectual fire'.[27]

It would not only be the grammar of the Shakespearean actors that would cause us confusion. The pronunciation of English was also noticeably different from that of today. In 1604, the word *bake* was pronounced identically to present-day *beck*, *meat* was pronounced to rhyme with today's *mate* and *cut* to rhyme with *put*. For over a century, a series of related changes known as the Great Vowel Shift had been occurring. The transformation would continue for another century.[28] In the spoken language there were also strong differences in dialects between regions. The London dialect's, 'I would eat more cheese if I had it', would be 'Ay sud eat mare cheese gin ay hadet' in northern England or 'Chud eat more cheese an chad it' in the west.[29]

Nevertheless, the written language had become standardized around the educated speech of London. As a result, the year of the Hampton Court conference, 1604, saw the publication of the first partial dictionary entirely in English. It defined about 2500 words that were difficult to understand. The author, Robert Cawdrey, took about half of his words from a Latin–English dictionary published in 1588 by Thomas Thomas and most of the rest from a list of words that were hard to spell brought out in 1596 by a schoolmaster, Edmund Coote.[30] Further editions of Cawdrey's dictionary were published in 1609, 1613 and 1617.

The success of the first English dictionary was a reflection of the growing numbers of people able to read. In 1500, only about 1 person in 20 had been literate. By 1600, roughly a fifth of the English population could read and write. Yet the new skills were spread unevenly among the population. As girls were still generally not taught to write, over 90 per cent of women were illiterate.[31] The degree of literacy also varied greatly across professions and consequently between town and country. Virtually all the gentry and the majority of urban tradesmen and small farmers could read and write, but agricultural laborers were mostly illiterate.[32]

Ethnically, apart from a Celtic fringe in Wales and Cornwall, England was quite homogeneous. There had been no major movements of population into the British Isles since the Norman invasion in the eleventh century. In 1290, under Edward I, England had been the first country in Christian Europe to expel its Jews.[33] None had been allowed to enter since. Nor were there any significant numbers of slaves. The main internal social divisions were a question of social status. The nobility and gentry had privileges that ordinary people could not obtain. Along with the wealthiest townspeople, they administered the country's system of justice. Although the magistrates received no pay, they were compensated by access to 'farms' – rights to certain government revenue sources – leases on Crown land, pensions, monopolies and government offices.

**King and Parliament**

Despite these class differences, England in 1604 was both prosperous and peaceful. Since the loss of Calais in 1558, England had held no overseas territories. Even Ireland, its one possession outside of Great Britain, was quiet. The Tyrone rebellion that had begun in 1594 and had received military support from Spain had been crushed a year previously. The king pardoned Hugh O'Neill, the leader of the Irish rebels, and allowed him to keep most of his lands. At James's request, a treaty to end over 15 years of war with Spain was being negotiated and would be signed in August 1604.[34]

One of the surprising features of English government early in the seventeenth century for the present-day observer was the wide-ranging power of the king. The sovereign could determine foreign and domestic policy. By custom, royal taxation was limited by a representative Parliament; however, the king could summon or dismiss the legislature whenever he chose. In addition, he could veto any bill passed by Parliament simply by refusing to sign it into law. Only in times of war was the legislature's fiscal constraint truly binding. At other times, the king's access to revenues from customary indirect taxes gave him substantial freedom. Indeed, during the largely peaceful 26-year interval from 1603 to 1629, Parliament was in session for only three years and four months.[35]

Parliament as a legislative assembly was unique to England. Called upon to authorize taxation, to pass legislation and offer advice, it was divided into two houses. The upper chamber, the House of Lords, was generally favorable to the monarchy. At the beginning of the reign of James I, it consisted of 55 lay peers along with 24 bishops and 2 archbishops. As for the lower chamber, the House of Commons, it comprised 475 members, four-fifths of them belonging to the landed gentry. The other 90 members were lawyers or merchants who represented the interests of the towns. Outside the towns, only those who held land with a rental value of at least 40 shillings a year could vote. In the boroughs, the right to vote varied, limited in some case to members of the corporation (the municipal council) but in others extended to all householders.[36] Many Members of Parliament were initially distrustful of the king because of his advocacy of monarchical power, but as he grew more conciliatory over the first two sessions, relations between king and commons improved.[37]

Active participation in political decisions was nevertheless restricted to a few hundred people at the most, if only because of the limited availability of information. From the beginning of the reign of James I, foreign news was available in *corantos*, news-sheets printed on the continent and imported into England. During the 1620s, such publications were printed in England. However, James I banned any publication of home news.[38] As a result, information about domestic public issues circulated mostly by word of mouth or by handwritten newsletters.[39]

Political harmony in England depended to a great extent on Parliament's reaction to the level of expenses of the sovereign and the methods used to finance them. On the expenditure side of the royal budget, the king was expected to pay not only for the cost of his household but also for the navy. In times of peace, there was no standing army; nor was there a police force. Toward the end of the reign of Elizabeth I, these ordinary expenditures had averaged about £300 000 annually.[40] In addition, there was interest on the accumulated debt of £400 000 resulting from the war with Spain and the revolt in Ireland to be financed at a rate of about ten per cent.[41]

To meet these costs, the king had the revenues from customs duties, the income from Crown lands and various feudal revenues. In 1604, the royal councilors succeeded in selling the right to collect most customs duties, collectively known as the Great Farm, to a group of merchants for £112 400 a year. The king however reserved the lucrative right to tax wine and currants separately. Among the feudal sources was the custom of 'purveyance', which allowed the king to purchase supplies for the royal household at low prices.[42] In addition, the income from the assets of heirs who were minors, known as 'wardship', was an important revenue source. Only about a third of the amount paid in rents by the lessees of the wards' lands actually reached the royal treasury.[43] Nevertheless, purveyance and wardship were worth on average about £200 000 a year to the Crown.[44] As for the accumulated debt, it had been largely covered by special parliamentary 'extraordinary' grants totaling £300 000.

It may be seen, then, that in 1604, there was a rough balance between the English king's income and his normal expenditures. If he wanted to spend a bit more on his household, he could always raise additional money by the sale of royal offices or Crown land. As long as the king and Parliament could agree on any major supplementary taxation should war occur, the system was remarkably efficient and effective for its time. As Francis Bacon exclaimed, 'The Englishman is most master of his own valuation and the least bitten of any nation in Europe'.[45]

## The Companies

With the royal budget in delicate balance, how was the new translation of the Bible to be financed? The king's councilors advised him that since this was a religious matter, it should be paid for out of the church's funds. Accordingly, in July 1604, the new Archbishop of Canterbury, Richard Bancroft, wrote to his bishops asking them to contribute to 'this most godly work'.[46]There is evidence that several of the bishops placed the members of the translation committee as prebendaries; that is, Anglican clerics receiving a stipend from church revenues.[47]

James envisaged the Bible translation as a joint work to be distilled from the individual efforts of a representative body of theologians. There would be six different companies, each assigned a particular section of the Bible. Every company would have eight members and a director. In comparison to previous efforts, it was to be a major undertaking, requiring over 50 experts. The first New Testament to be printed in English had been the work of a single man, William Tyndale. The Geneva Bible had been translated by a small group of Calvinist theologians. Even the hastily prepared Bishops' Bible had used only 14 bishops.[48] James wished to avoid missteps such as the Bishops' translation of 'Cast thy bread upon the waters', as 'Lay the bread upon wet faces'.[49]

The king and archbishop prepared 16 separate 'rules to be obserued in translation'.[50] The first rule stated that the translators were to follow the Bishops' Bible, altering it as little as possible. However, Rule 14 in effect nullified this constraint, stating that other English Bibles from the sixteenth century could be consulted. Further rules also aimed to avoid abrupt change in church practice: the commonly used names of biblical people and church institutions and the existing chapter divisions were to be retained. Consistency in quotations and terminology was to be maintained throughout the Old and New Testaments. Finally, the members of each company must first consult one another on their translations and then obtain the approval of the other companies for their completed work. It seemed like the ideal recipe for bureaucratic gruel.

## THE CREATION OF THE KING'S ENGLISH

In all, six companies of translators were set up, two at Westminster, two at Oxford and two at Cambridge. In accord with Rule 1, as a guide for the translators, some forty copies of the 1568 Bishops' Bible were printed and distributed unbound. However, it has been estimated that only eight per cent of the King James Bible was taken from this source.[51] Where did the rest come from? It has also been calculated that 94 per cent of the words in the New Testament are the same as in William Tyndale's 1534 edition.[52] In 1535, shortly before Tyndale's execution near Brussels, a complete Bible based on his work was published by Miles Coverdale in English. Was the

King James Bible then simply authorized plagiarism? To answer this question, it is helpful to compare the printed texts. First, though, let us look at perhaps the most important of the translators.

Responsibility for the first 12 books in the Old Testament was assigned to a team at Westminster directed by Lancelot Andrewes, 49, son of a master mariner in London. Both a scholar and churchman, Andrewes was not only the master of Pembroke College, Cambridge but also the Dean of Westminster Abbey. However, his weaknesses were all too human. Andrewes was also the vicar of St Giles Cripplegate, an old church just outside the city walls, in an area teeming with poor migrants to the city, many of them Irish. When plague struck London in the summer of 1603, St Giles Cripplegate was one of the parishes hardest hit. Some 70 per cent of its population perished, to be buried in mass graves. Yet Andrewes failed to visit his parish a single time during the months of the epidemic, preferring the abbey's 'pleasant retreat' at Chiswick on the Thames to the west of the city.[53]

Andrewes' great strength was his mastery of languages. There were the original Hebrew, Greek and Latin texts to be studied as well as previous translations into German, Italian, French and English. He was fluent in the three ancient tongues, along with 11 other languages.[54] Indeed, since he described his colleagues as negligent, it may well have been he who produced most of the translations of his team. The new translation was intended to be read aloud at Sunday church service; accordingly, the main criterion was whether it sounded right.

Here is Genesis chapter 1, verse 11 from Miles Coverdale's 1535 Bible, based on William Tyndale's translation.[55]

> And God sayde: let ye earth bringe forth grene grasse and herbe, that beareth sede: & frutefull trees, that maye beare frute, euery one after his kynde, hauynge their owne sede in them selues vpon the earth. And so it came to passe.

The Calvinist Geneva Bible of 1560 was as follows:

> Then God said, Let the earth bud foorth the bud of the herbe, that seedeth seede, the fruitfull tree, which beareth fruite according to his kinde, which hath his seede in it selfe vpon the earth. and it was so.

The 14 bishops in their 1568 edition borrowed heavily from the Geneva text:

> And God sayde: let the earth bryng foorth budde and hearbe apt to seede, and fruitfull trees yeeldyng fruite after his kynde, which hath seede in it selfe vpon the earth: and it was so.

In all three versions there are problems. Not only is the meaning not immediately clear, but also when one reads the passage aloud, the rhythm is broken and one's tongue trips over the superfluous syllables. Finally, here is Andrewes' contribution, in the King James version:

> And God said, Let the earth bring forth grass, the herb yielding seed, and the fruit tree yielding fruit after his kind, whose seed is in itself, upon the earth: and it was so.

The revised passage is limpid in its expression and gracious in its phrasing as it rises from the grass to the herb to the tree and then returns to the earth.

Meanwhile, the Puritans of the first Cambridge company were working on the next ten books of the Old Testament. Their senior translator was Laurence Chaderton, who was now approaching the age of 70. Yet his mind was still vigorous: he would outlive most of the other translators, dying in 1640 at the age of 103. Let us compare the translations of the last verse of the twenty-third psalm. The Tyndale–Coverdale version beseeches God to intervene:

> Oh let thy louynge kyndnes & mercy folowe me all the dayes off my life, that I maye dwell in the house off the LORDE for euer.

The Geneva Calvinists are more certain that they belong to the chosen. The wording is inelegant but clear:

> Doubtlesse kindnesse and mercie shall followe me all the dayes of my life, and I shall remaine a long season in the house of the Lord.

The bishops offer their listeners felicity and mercy, but for a period whose length is open to question:

> Truely felicitie and mercie shal folowe me all the dayes of my lyfe: and I wyll dwell in the house of God for a long tyme.

The Cambridge Puritans are as sure of their favored eternal fate as the followers of Calvin, but are much more in tune with the harmonious rhythms of the English language:

> Surely goodness and mercy shall follow me all the days of my life: and I will dwell in the house of the LORD for ever.

By 1607, the 50-odd translators had completed a first draft of the Bible. Since at least half of the translation was done by men like Chaderton who might be described as moderate Puritans, the King insisted on a thorough vetting of the text.[56] The next step, then, was to review what had been written to assure consistency. A committee of 12 made up of two translators from each company met at the Stationers' Hall in London. To evaluate a particular passage, the person most qualified was given the initial translation. He then read the text aloud while the other committee members followed along, some holding Greek or Latin Bibles, others consulting French, Spanish or Italian translations.[57] From notes that were taken, it would appear that most of the discussion was in Latin, the language of international scholarship. The final revision was then done by a committee of two made up of one of the translators and a second expert from outside the group.[58]

Adam Nicolson describes one incident in the revision process that suggests how British society was changing. Andrew Downes, approaching the age of 60 in 1607, was Regius Professor of Greek at Cambridge. He was an irascible preacher who had once stormed out of church when the congregation had jeered. In 1 Corinthians 10:11, Paul describes the past sins of the Jews, writing: 'Now all these things happened unto them for *ensamples*'. Downes insisted that the Greek word *typoi* be translated as 'types' or 'figures' to indicate that the Jews were condemned collectively to eternal damnation. The committee disagreed and settled on *ensamples*, indicating that the sins that Paul mentioned were meant simply as examples for illustrative purposes.[59]

One of King James's rules for the translators had been that margin notes were to be forbidden, unless necessary to explain translations from Hebrew or Greek.[60] He had wanted to avoid the criticisms of monarchy appearing in the margins of the Geneva Bible. Downes took advantage of this provision to insert a translators' note. When the Authorized Version of the Bible appeared in print, the Corinthians passage listing the sins of the Jews as *ensamples* contained the margin note 'Or, Types'.[61] English society had not yet reached a consensus on how rights and privileges were to be allocated.

A final text was ready to be printed in the spring of 1611, some seven years after the original Hampton Court conference.[62] It was published later that year by Robert Barker, 'Printer to the King's Most Excellent Majesty'. It was in folio; that is, a single sheet was folded so as to make two leaves or four large pages, each 10½ inches (27 cm) wide and 16½ inches (42 cm) long. Since some 20 000 copies of the new translation were required, it was printed in two separate issues that were not quite identical. In Ruth 3:15, there is a passage in which Boaz, Ruth's husband, gives her six measures of barley. One edition continues this account (incorrectly) with 'and hee went into the city' while the other reads (correctly) 'and she went into the city'. Inevitably, the former came to be known as the Great Hee Bible and the latter as the Great She Bible.[63]

There were other shortcomings in the King James Bible. A year after its appearance, a noted Hebrew scholar published a criticism of its translations of the Old Testament. And scholars today recognize that the New Testament was based on published Greek texts that even at the time were known to be of questionable accuracy.[64] As for its English, in 1611, it was already several decades out of date.

The 1500 pages of the first edition were printed in Gothic black letter in double columns. Although black letter can be read easily once one becomes accustomed to it, its characters take up more space than Roman type. Gothic letters had also been used for the Bishops' Bible that was authorized for reading aloud in church services. For private reading, however, the Geneva Bible had set the standard, using smaller Roman characters. Soon there was a demand for comparable versions of the new translation. In 1612, a handsome edition of the King James Bible was issued in Roman white-letter type. It was in quarto: each sheet was folded twice so as to make four leaves or eight smaller pages. In 1613, an even more compact octavo edition (with each sheet folded into eight leaves) was published in Roman type. Gradually, Roman replaced Gothic characters. By 1640, it was extremely rare for the Bible to be printed in black letter in English.[65]

Meanwhile, the King James translation was fighting for market share at the expense of earlier versions. Although in 1616, the king forbade the printing of the competing Geneva version, printers in the Netherlands continued to publish the earlier translation for sale in England well into the 1640s.[66] However, most new readers found the King James version to be superior. By mid-century, there were fewer and fewer still alive who had been raised on the Geneva translation. Over the next century and a half, there would be almost a thousand editions of the King James Bible.[67]

As the years passed, the translation by the six companies of scholars became a standard reference point for literary and poetic style. The rhythms of its text when read aloud have been an inspiration to many generations of writers and poets. Although there is no documentary proof that the king gave it his official sanction, it nevertheless came to be known as the Authorized Version. Indeed, for many English speakers, it came to be identified with the word of God. What, then, would happen if the acts of the king appeared to contradict the scriptures?

## NASEBY AND ALL THAT

It was early in the morning of 14 June 1645, 34 years after the first appearance of the King James Bible. The royal army was in battle formation on the crest of a hill some 50 miles (80 km) south of Nottingham when Prince

Rupert received a report from his scouts that the parliamentary army was withdrawing. By moving quickly now to catch the Roundheads out of formation, the royalists could make the most of their superiority in cavalry. King Charles I hesitated, reluctant to abandon the strong position that would favor his forces in an attack by the larger parliamentary army. Finally, recognizing the tactical brilliance of his 24-year-old nephew, the king yielded. However, later, as the king and his forces approached the village of Naseby, they found Thomas Fairfax's parliamentary army waiting for them, blocking the route back to the royalist capital at Oxford. Suddenly realizing their error, the royalists had no choice but to form up on the grassy ridge across from the enemy and prepare for battle.[68]

Thomas Fairfax knew that his force of 13 000 outnumbered the Royalists by almost two to one. However, many of his men were newly conscripted and inexperienced. Their nickname of 'Roundheads' originated possibly in the closely cropped haircuts preferred by many Puritans. On the advice of his cavalry commander, Oliver Cromwell, Fairfax had taken up a strong position on a hillside about a quarter mile (400 m) north of Naseby. To defend against a cavalry attack on his weak left flank, Fairfax disposed a regiment of dragoons – mounted infantry armed with muskets – to the left before his lines. Shortly before ten o'clock, he withdrew most of his troops back over the brow of the hill, out of sight of the enemy. Mistaking this maneuver for a retreat, the royalists began to advance. Fairfax then brought his men back over the hilltop.

The royalist infantry marched rapidly across Broad Moor and up the slopes to attack the Roundheads. By the middle decades of the seventeenth century, the heart of a European army was its regiments of musketeers, shooting deadly lead balls, ten to the pound, in a hail of fire that could destroy enemy cavalry or infantry. However, since the musketeers were vulnerable to attack by cavalry, their regiments were interspersed with units who carried 16-foot pikes tipped with steel points.[69] There was time for a single exchange of musket fire before the opposing lines came together in a 'push-of-pike'. Musketeers used their weapons as clubs. Despite the uphill advantage of the parliamentary army, its line was gradually forced back.

On the parliamentary left, Rupert's cavalry ran the gauntlet of fire from the parliamentary dragoons and then charged at Ireton's mounted defenders. The royalist horse styled themselves as 'Cavaliers', the name originating in the French word for a mounted knight, *chevalier*. Like the parliamentary cavalry, most carried a pair of muskets. Preferring to reserve their firearms for later pursuit, the horsemen would depend on their heavy-bladed broadswords in the initial charge.[70] The second line of Cavalier horse broke parliamentary resistance and many of the surviving Roundhead cavalry on the left fled the scene of battle.

Meanwhile, Cromwell's cavalry on the parliamentary right advanced in a disciplined charge to meet the attack of Marmaduke Langdale's Cavaliers. Cromwell's unit had earned the name Ironsides from the tight discipline their commander demanded, as firm as the iron breast and back-plate of their equipment. Outnumbering the Cavaliers opposite them, Cromwell's force was able to attack in a broader front. Just as Rupert's horsemen had driven the cavalry on the parliamentary left wing off the field, so were Cromwell's troopers on the parliamentary right able to rout the Cavalier force opposing them.

At this point, the fate of the battle hung in the balance. In the center, the royalist infantry continued to have the upper hand. Fairfax was sending in his last reserves of infantry in an attempt to stabilize the situation.[71] For both sides, it had become a situation of double or nothing. On the one hand, parliamentary defeat would fatally undermine the position of those reformers who desired to place constraints on the king's arbitrary powers. On the other hand, defeat of the king's forces would compel him to abandon the rights for which his ancestors had fought.

## Charles I

Charles I was born in 1600, the first year of the new century. He was two and a half years old in the spring of 1603 when his father left Edinburgh to take up the throne of England. Frail and suffering from a fever, the child was left behind in Scotland for a year until his parents were finally informed that he was well enough to travel.[72] Once in England, the young prince was placed in the care of one of the king's followers. He was late in learning to talk and always spoke with a stammer and a Scottish accent. A shy boy, he grew up in the shadow of his brother Henry, the Prince of Wales, who was six years older. At the age of five, he still had to be carried in the arms of an attendant.[73] Charles grew up to be shorter than he would have liked, not over five feet four (162 cm). However, he was a good student and quickly mastered Greek and Latin from his Scottish tutor. He also learned French, Italian and Spanish and developed a keen interest in theology.[74]

When his brother, Henry, died of typhoid fever in November 1612, Charles suddenly found himself compelled to play a role for which he was unprepared – heir to the throne.[75] Unsure of himself with people he did not know, he was attracted to outgoing men. At first Charles was jealous of his father's favorites, but at 18 he allowed himself to be charmed by the Duke of Buckingham. When his father convened Parliament in 1621, Charles frequently attended debates in the House of Lords and sometimes listened to speeches in the Commons.[76] Relations between James I and Parliament were often tense, but some basic rules had come to be accepted by both parties. In times of peace, the king was expected to live within his means, that is, to depend on customary sources of income such as customs duties and the sale of offices. Should he find himself with insufficient resources, he could request additional funds. James's first Parliament had granted him a special levy on trade by weight known as Tonnage and Poundage. When there was danger of war, the king was expected to call Parliament to seek the required financing. In 1624, for example, Buckingham as chief minister requested and received supplementary resources to fight Spain.

In 1625, the old monarch died and Charles succeeded to the throne. Unfortunately, the new king lacked his father's shrewd judgment in assessing how others would react to his actions. Instead he let himself be guided by arbitrary rules or concern for his honor. When the Commons refused to grant him Tonnage and Poundage unless he allowed impeachment proceedings against Buckingham, he dissolved Parliament. In the fall of 1626, Charles decided to send help to his uncle, the Lutheran king of Denmark, in the great struggle between Protestants and Catholics being waged on the continent. Rather than summon Parliament, he ordered that a forced loan be levied on the nobles and gentry. When some 70 gentlemen refused to pay, they were imprisoned without due cause.[77] However, such measures could not be repeated indefinitely. In 1627, Buckingham convinced the king to intervene in France to support the Huguenots of La Rochelle. In 1628, with wars against France and Spain plus support of Denmark to be financed, Charles had little choice but to summon Parliament.

Most Members of Parliament were willing to grant the king at least a part of the funds he requested. However, they sought assurance that their traditional liberties would be respected. In May 1628, Parliament passed the Petition of Right, forbidding arbitrary imprisonment, the imposed billeting of soldiers, martial law in peacetime and taxation without the approval of Parliament.[78] Charles signed the bill into law in order to secure passage of his supply bill.

When the next Parliament convened in January 1629, Buckingham had been assassinated by a disgruntled army officer. Meanwhile, Charles's bishops had angered the Puritans by adding a new preface to the Book of Common Prayer. Objecting to this increase in 'Popery' and 'superstitious ceremony', the members of the Commons refused to grant the king his customs duties.[79] Charles thereupon dissolved Parliament and hastily concluded peace with Spain and France.[80] For the next 11 years he ruled without Parliament, financing his increases in spending by generalizing a tax known as ship money that normally was limited to port cities in times of war.

## Cromwell

The years 1628 to 1630 were a watershed in British history. Before the crisis of the forced loan, the imprisonment of the 70 gentlemen and the bishops' preface to the Book of Common Prayer, most of Britain's leading citizens undoubtedly considered themselves to be loyal subjects of their king. Three years later, they were beginning to ask themselves whether their sovereign was truly a British citizen.

These years also marked a crisis in the life of Oliver Cromwell, a country squire from Huntingdon, some 70 miles (110 km) north of London, and a contemporary of Charles. In 1628, at 29 years of age, Cromwell was one of two representatives of Huntingdon elected to the House of Commons. Although he had been raised as a Calvinist and had briefly attended Sidney Sussex, a Puritan college at Cambridge, his behavior in Parliament on religious issues did not stand out from that of other members. However, while in London, he was treated for depression by a prominent physician.[81] In 1630, following a crushing defeat in local politics, he sold most of his property in Huntingdon and moved to nearby St Ives. There he temporarily moved down the social scale to become a yeoman farmer of rented land.[82]

At this point in Cromwell's life, there is evidence from his correspondence that he underwent an intense religious experience, becoming a fervent follower of Calvin. His writing and public speeches from this point suddenly became rich in images from the Bible.[83] As a child, Cromwell had undoubtedly been exposed to the Calvinist Geneva Bible. As an adult, however, he would be accustomed to read the new Authorized Version.[84] It was the one book that, along with a *History of the World* by Walter Raleigh, he recommended to his son, Richard.[85]

There is a story that as a boy, the boisterous young Oliver had given the future king Charles a bloody nose.[86] Cromwell's uncle, Sir Oliver Cromwell, after whom the younger man was named, had been an early supporter of James I. Oliver and Charles were about the same age (Oliver was born in 1599). They may well have met as boys at the estate of Sir Oliver near Huntingdon, where James was a frequent guest. Some three decades later, Oliver and Charles began a series of conflicts that would end with the execution of the king.

In 1636, Oliver Cromwell inherited freehold leases near Ely from his mother's childless brother and moved a short distance once again – this time back up the social scale.[87] During these years, many godly Protestants were beginning to fear that their king was a threat to both Protestantism and the English constitution.[88] Oliver chose this moment to intervene again in political life against the king and his allies. There is evidence that he went to court to support some farmers of Ely in their opposition to a royal project that would drain and privatize the marshy common land on which they grazed their animals.[89] As a result in part of the reputation he acquired over this issue, Cromwell was invited to stand for Cambridge in the forthcoming parliamentary elections.

Meanwhile Charles's decade of absolutist rule was coming to an end. In the spring of 1640, the king found that he needed additional resources to finance a war against Scotland. He had foolishly accepted a proposal by his Archbishop of Canterbury, William Laud, to impose Anglican ritual on the Scottish Presbyterians. When the Scots formed an army to resist these innovations, Charles had been forced to accept an uneasy peace. The Scottish Parliament then voted to abolish episcopacy within the Scottish church. Unable to accept this humiliation, the king now decided to raise an army to invade Scotland. At the king's bidding, the Short Parliament met on 13 April 1640 to consider a bill to finance this campaign. Instead of rallying behind the king, however, the Commons insisted first on addressing its grievances regarding the king's conduct over the past decade. On 5 May, the frustrated king dissolved Parliament.

Emboldened by this sign of English weakness, the Scots invaded England. They quickly captured the vital coal port of Newcastle and refused to withdraw until the English paid them compensation. In order to do so, Charles was forced to call Parliament once again. Over the following year and a half, the so-called Long Parliament, which would sit until 1653, forced a series of concessions from the king in return for financial support. Ship money was abolished; the king must call Parliament every three years; dissolution was possible only if a majority of its members agreed. From 1641 to 1643, censorship of the press was allowed to lapse. For the first time, the English could express themselves freely in print.[90]

Then in October 1641, a revolt against Protestant rule began in Ireland. Protestant refugees arriving in England brought reports of frightful massacres.[91] Clearly an army would have to be raised to restore order, but who should command it? Fearful of putting an army at the disposal of the king, Parliamentarians drew up a militia bill that would place the troops under parliamentary command. However, Charles drew the line at allowing Parliament to control the militia. When in January 1642 his attempt to arrest parliamentary leaders for treason failed, he fled the city and began to prepare for war.[92] In June, Parliament resubmitted the militia question as one of Nineteen Propositions. It now became clear that a break between the king and the legislature was inevitable.

Cromwell played no role in the Short Parliament. In the first year of the Long Parliament, he intervened, though not to great effect, as an ally of a middle group in the Commons around John Pym that sought to reform but not to overthrow the monarchy.[93] From the beginning of the Irish revolt, however, Cromwell played an active role in the debates on military issues. In November 1641, he moved that the earl of Essex be granted 'power to assemble at all times the trained bands of the kingdoms . . . for the defense thereof'. In January 1642, following the king's attempt to arrest Parliament's leaders, a motion by Cromwell led to the formation of a committee to put the kingdom into 'a posture of defense'. [94] Finally, in August, he left London to help prepare for the defense of his constituency of Cambridge. War began officially when the king raised his standard at Nottingham on 22 August 1642.

For most of the next two years, Cromwell was active in the defense of six parliamentary counties to the northeast of London that grouped themselves into the Eastern Association.[95] He began as a captain, organizing on his own initiative a cavalry troop of sixty men.[96] He then threw himself into the recruiting and training of additional units. By 1644, he had formed the Ironsides, a full double regiment of 14 troops, each with at least 80 men.[97] His repeated success in blocking royalist attempts to seize the wealthy territory of the Association led to his promotion to lieutenant-general. Meanwhile, Cromwell was also fully involved in the Long Parliament as a member of the powerful executive body, the Committee of Both Kingdoms.[98]

The parliamentary army surprised the royalists with a major victory at Marston Moor in July 1644. Cromwell played a key role in rallying his cavalry to support the beleaguered parliamentary infantry. However, by the end of the year, after royalist successes in the south and in Scotland, the war was still a stalemate. Despite an overall superiority in men and resources, the Roundhead armies were unable to overcome stubborn Cavalier resistance. A greater effort was necessary to assure the financing of soldiers' pay. And above all, those parliamentary commanders who were lukewarm in their pursuit of the royal armies would have to be replaced.

In the spring of 1645, Parliament introduced a series of reforms, creating what became known as the New Model Army. There were two major differences between this new force and the parliamentary armies that had plodded with mixed success through the first three years of the civil war. First, a new law, the Self-Denying Ordinance, forced sitting members of both houses of Parliament to choose between military command and parliamentary service. When these men resigned their military positions in order to retain their political influence, the army was stripped of most of its commanding officers. Many of these men favored a negotiated peace and had been hesitant in pursuing the royalists.[99] Second, pay for a new force of 22 000 men, most of them carried over from previous formations, was to be financed by regular assessments on the territories controlled by Parliament.

Since Parliament held the prosperous counties in the southeast and the rich city of London with its teeming population, it could afford to recruit and maintain a professional army.[100] In contrast, the royalist army, which held the poorer regions of the North, had an inadequate fiscal base. By 1645, royalist units were forced increasingly to live off the land, confiscating the goods of the regions through which they passed.[101]

## Endgame

It was perhaps the need to supplement their meager pay with the spoils of war that explains the undisciplined behavior of the royalist cavalry at Naseby on the morning of June 1645. It will be remembered that Rupert and his Cavaliers had driven the parliamentary left cavalry from the field. Then, instead of turning to attack the parliamentary foot, the royalist horse headed for the Roundhead baggage train. Meanwhile, Cromwell's confidence that God was on the side of Parliament remained unshaken.[102] He quickly redirected his victorious cavalry on the parliamentary right. Detaching a small force to deal with the broken cavalry units opposite him, he turned the bulk of his disciplined troops inward to attack the flank of the royalist infantry. At the same time, the parliamentary dragoons, mounted infantry, were attacking the opposite royalist flank.

Charles may often have lacked judgment, but he was no coward on the battlefield. Seeing his army destroyed before him, the king could not resist the temptation to make one last gamble. He led his Lifeguard forward in a final desperate charge. Only the intervention of his ally, the Earl of Carnwath, saved the king. Grabbing the bridle of the king's horse and cursing loudly, the Scot asked, 'Will you go upon your death in an instant?' and pulled the royal steed around. The Lifeguard thereupon abandoned the field with their king.[103]

At Naseby, Charles lost most of his foot and all of his artillery. Some 1000 of his trained infantrymen lay dead or dying on the battlefield and 5000 more were taken prisoner. The Roundhead cavalry slaughtered 100 Irish prisoners and slashed the faces of the women among the royalist camp followers in the belief that they were prostitutes.[104] Worst of all for the king, perhaps, one of the 200 baggage wagons captured by the parliamentary forces at Naseby contained the sovereign's personal correspondence. A month after the battle, Parliament published a selection of these papers under the title, *The King's Cabinet Opened.* They indicated that Charles had been planning to bring Catholic troops from France and Ireland to back his cause and had offered the Orkney and Shetland Isles to Sweden in return for military support. To a growing section of the British public, it became evident that the king could not be trusted.

Although Charles had lost on the battlefield, he still hoped to be able to restore his original position by exploiting divisions among his enemies. Parliament wanted to dismiss half of the army, but the soldiers wanted to be paid before being disbanded. In addition, the Scottish allies of the Roundheads were angry that Parliament would not respect an earlier agreement to establish a decentralized Presbyterian church in England.

Unfortunately for all, the king insisted on overplaying the few cards left in his hand. Instead of coming to terms with Parliament, he spent the next two years trying to play one party off against the other. In June 1646, with his hair and beard trimmed and disguised as a servant, Charles slipped through the parliamentary lines around Oxford and surrendered to the Scots who were besieging Newark.[105] In January 1647, the Scots turned Charles over to Parliament. Then in June of that year the king was kidnapped by the army. In November, Charles escaped, only to be recaptured on the Isle of Wight. In December he reached a secret agreement, an 'Engagement', with a group of conservative Scots to establish a Presbyterian system for three years. During the year 1648, there were scattered royalist uprisings and an invasion by a Scottish Engager army. All were put down by the New Model Army.

Finally, the army officers, those most affected by this turmoil, insisted that Charles be put on trial. The officers purged the Parliament of opponents to this measure. Its remaining members were known as the Rump Parliament. In January 1649, this body found Charles guilty of high treason. He was executed by decapitation on 30 January of that year. But would any other leader be capable of mastering a legislature suddenly aware of its sovereign power?

## THE EMERGING NATION

During the 11 years that followed the execution of Charles I, English society underwent a series of profound changes. For one thing, in place of a government based on the divine right of kings, it experimented with several forms of written contract between rulers and ruled. For another, during the 1650s, the English displayed a remarkable willingness to affirm their collective identity, supporting the army and navy in an unprecedented degree of assertion of their country's power. Finally, the country showed a greater willingness to tolerate diversity in ethnic orientation and religious affiliation. It would take several decades to work out the details of the new social and political structure. But by the turn of the century, the basic institutions of the English nation state would be in place.

**The Five Constitutions**

Between 1550 and 1660, England experienced no fewer than five new constitutions – three unwritten and two written. In March 1550, the Rump Parliament did away with the existing unwritten constitution by abolishing the monarchy and the House of Lords. It created a new state known as the Commonwealth with a unicameral legislature.[106] The Commons delegated executive power to Cromwell as chairman of a Council of State and appointed him to be Lord General, in command of the army.[107] However, over the following three years, the Rump Parliament did not prove sufficiently energetic in reforming the political system and collecting church tithes to satisfy Cromwell. In April 1653, he and the army marched on Westminster and dissolved Parliament. For five months thereafter, England was governed by a Nominated Parliament whose members were chosen by the army leaders. However, this second constitutional structure, known as the Barebones Parliament, proved too bitterly divided to make any headway in restructuring the government and administration of England. Its delegates passed a motion to abdicate in December 1653.

One of the army generals, John Lambert, then directed the drafting of England's first written constitution, the third constitution of the decade. Under the Instrument of Government, power was divided among a lord protector (Cromwell), a council of state nominated by him and a Parliament elected every three years. However, Cromwell proved too impatient and heavy-handed to respect the details of this new document. When a merchant refused to pay customs duties, arguing that the tariffs had not been authorized by Parliament, Cromwell ordered that he and his lawyers be jailed. Threatened with dismissal for sympathizing with them, the chief justice chose to resign his position. Increasingly, Cromwell's former republican backers charged him with tyranny.[108]

Ironically, many of Cromwell's troubles stemmed from his persistent refusal to accept the crown. There was a well-established body of English law concerning the powers assigned to the king but very little about those of a lord protector.[109] In February 1657, a group of civilians submitted a new constitutional document, the Humble Petition and Advice. It offered Cromwell the monarchy and called for the creation of an upper house nominated by him but approved by the Commons. Like the abolished House of Lords, the upper chamber would have the power to veto any legislation approved by the lower chamber. In June, Cromwell accepted this fourth constitution in a modified form, retaining the sections of the Petition creating the 'Other House' but refusing the monarchy. The following year, he died and was succeeded by his son,

Richard. In 1659, pressure from the army rank and file forced Richard to restore the Rump Parliament. When it assembled in May, it forced his resignation.

In November 1659, to protect itself from a coup by army officers under John Lambert, the Rump Parliament sought the help of General George Monck, who was stationed in Scotland. Monck and his troops intervened successfully but then insisted that those Members of Parliament purged in 1648 be readmitted. The restored Long Parliament then dissolved itself and called for new elections. When the new pro-royalist Convention Parliament assembled in April 1660, it declared that Charles II, the elder son of the deposed king, had been the rightful sovereign since his father's execution. Under this fifth new constitution of the decade, the traditional structure of king, lords and commons was restored.

**Other Revolutionary Changes**

One of the most important pieces of legislation passed by the Rump Parliament during the Commonwealth was the Navigation Act of 1651. William II, the stadtholder of The United Provinces, had married the eldest daughter of Charles I. He refused to recognize the Commonwealth and offered support to his brother-in-law, Charles II. In retaliation, the English Parliament passed an aggressive bill that threatened to cripple the Dutch carrying trade. It stipulated that imports between England, Ireland and English colonies could be carried only on English ships. Goods exchanged between England and any other country could travel on either English ships or those of the second country.

The wars of Charles I against Spain, France and Scotland had been to further the king's personal or dynastic interests. But the wars of the 1650s were fought to extend the power of the English nation. The Dutch War that began in 1652 was motivated primarily by economic considerations. Fighting broke out when a Dutch fleet in the Channel near Dover refused the customary salute of the English fleet's flag. The larger and more heavily armed English ships quickly got the better of the Dutch fleet and succeeded in disrupting vital Dutch commercial shipping. After two years, both sides were willing to make peace.

Another act of aggression – the seizure of Jamaica by an English naval and land force in 1655 – was motivated by Cromwell's Western Design to weaken Catholic Spain. This event triggered a war between England and Spain. In 1657, Cromwell decided to ally his country with France for a campaign against Spain in the Netherlands. For its part in the successful venture, England was rewarded with the port of Dunkirk, which was subsequently sold to Louis XIV.

England's Jews had been expelled under Edward I in 1290. Since the establishment of the Dutch Republic in 1579, however, England's Protestant neighbor had become the home for a prosperous Jewish community, most of them emigrants from Spain and Portugal and their descendants. In 1655, a Sephardi Jew named Menasseh ben Israel living in Amsterdam traveled to London in order to petition Cromwell to readmit Jews into England. Cromwell, who hoped to convert Jews to biblical Christianity, was favorable. Although the Protectorate Parliament refused Cromwell's request, from 1656 on it became possible for Jews to live openly in England for the first time in almost four centuries. In 1664, England's Jews were formally granted royal protection.

Under the Protectorate, tolerance was also shown to other religious groups. Catholics were allowed to celebrate mass in private or in the chapels of diplomats from Catholic countries.[110] Cromwell himself intervened on behalf of a Quaker accused of blasphemy. Although Cromwell's personal concern was to assure liberty of conscience for godly Christians, in practice his regime tolerated a wider diversity of religious views than did that of Charles I.[111] This increased tolerance was formalized in 1689 in the Toleration Act. Dissenting Protestants such as Baptists, Congregationalists and Quakers were allowed to set up their own schools and places of worship.

## On to Empire

In 1712, Jonathan Swift, an Anglo-Irish writer, wrote to the Tory first minister, Robert Harley, begging him to 'fix' the English language; that is, to make sure that accepted spelling and grammar were used. At the time, printers continued to use the long Germanic 's' and they were still capitalizing important nouns. Otherwise, today's reader is able to understand perfectly this English text written some 300 years ago. In short, over the century between the publishing of the King James Bible in 1611 and the prime of the author of *Gulliver's Travels*, present-day English had emerged.[112] By the early seventeenth century, moreover, over 40 per cent of the men and a quarter of the women in England were able to read and write.[113]

A number of other remarkable changes had occurred over the same interval. During the first half of the seventeenth century, English settlers had founded a number of small settlements in the New World. Five years before Swift's letter, the Scottish parliament had approved union with England to form the Kingdom of Great Britain. And at the time Swift was writing, negotiations were underway in Utrecht, in the Netherlands, to hammer out treaties between the belligerents in the War of the Spanish

Succession, namely, England and its allies on the one hand and France and Spain on the other. To England's existing bits of overseas territory would now be added Newfoundland, Nova Scotia, the Hudson's Bay basin, Gibraltar, Minorca and the island of St Kitt's.[114]

One of the most important factors behind the victory of the coalition led by England during the recent wars had been the country's ability to finance its military spending efficiently. Indirect taxes earmarked for loan repayment persuaded investors that government debt would be repaid on time.[115] The founding of the Bank of England in 1694 and the close relations between England and the Netherlands allowed almost a third of the country's wartime spending to be financed by loans raised on the markets of London and Amsterdam.[116] These new institutions allowed vast amounts of debt to be financed at rates between seven and eight per cent – considerably lower than the ten per cent James I had paid to his creditors for much smaller amounts.[117] The forced loans that had turned Parliament against Charles I were no longer necessary.

England at the beginning of the eighteenth century also had a new constitution. First Oliver Cromwell's son Richard in 1659 and then Charles I's second son James II in 1688 had angered powerful groups within English society by assuming excessive power. Each in turn was overthrown by a military coup that enjoyed wide popular support.[118] When the dust of marching troops had settled, the power of the monarchy had been sharply curtailed and that of Parliament and the independent judiciary enhanced. Although much of it was unwritten, the contract between ruler and ruled was not dissimilar to that of Cromwell's Protectorate. Under the Declaration of Rights of 1689, there would be no standing army in peacetime. Taxation had to be approved by Parliament, which was to be called annually. There could be no special courts or tribunals created by the sovereign.

By the early eighteenth century, England was one of the few states in Europe where information circulated freely. The country had enjoyed a brief period of a free press during the Civil War and initially during the Protectorate. Censorship was re-established first by Cromwell and then in 1662, by his successor, Charles II, under the Licensing Act. However, in 1695, seven years after the Glorious Revolution, Parliament decided to allow the Licensing Act to lapse.[119] Thereafter, except in times of war, England would have a free press. In 1702, the first daily newspaper in Britain, the *Daily Courant*, appeared. By 1710, there were 23 other papers appearing weekly, twice-weekly and thrice-weekly in London, and others just starting up in the provinces.[120]

Symbolic of the transformation in English society during the last half of the seventeenth century was the construction of a new cathedral designed by Sir Christopher Wren. Early in the morning of 2 September 1666, sparks from the oven of Charles II's baker had set fire to a nearby stack of firewood. Fanned by a strong wind, the flames quickly spread through the wooden buildings, most with thatched roofs. Five days later, roughly 80 per cent of the city of Shakespeare and James I had gone up in flames.[121] The stones of the medieval gothic cathedral of St Paul were said to have exploded from the heat. It took almost a decade before Christopher Wren was able to gain approval for the design of a new cathedral on the site of the old. For three decades, workers labored to build the massive stone church whose great dome rose to a height of 365 feet (108 meters). The construction of St Paul's cathedral was completed in 1708. By that date, around it was spread a new city, the capital of an empire that would soon span the world.

## NOTES

1. Maddison (2001, pp. 241, 264).
2. Nicolson (2003, p. 87).
3. Mathew (1967, p. 124), Nicolson (2003, p. 42).
4. Patterson (1997, p. 45).
5. Nicolson (2003, pp. 43, 48).
6. Ibid. (p. 48).
7. Lockyer (1989, p. 97).
8. Nicolson (2003, p. 11).
9. Nicolson (2003, p. 50).
10. Nicolson (2003, p. 52).
11. Lockyer (1989, p. 101).
12. Nicolson (2003, p. 52).
13. Ashley (1987, p. 21).
14. Norton (2006).
15. Lockyer (1989, p. 101).
16. Lockyer (1989, p. 102).
17. Nicolson (2003, p. 103).
18. Nicolson (2003, p. 59).
19. For traditional English assessments of James I, see Patterson (1997, p. 27, n.131).
20. Patterson (1997, p. 20).
21. Nicolson (2003, p. 46).
22. Lockyer (1989, p. 108).
23. Nicolson (2003, p. 46).
24. Nicolson (2003, p. 47).
25. Nicolson (2003, p. 73).
26. Barber (1993, p. 186).
27. Shakespeare (1602, Act I, Scene 5).
28. Fennell (2001, pp. 158–161).
29. Freeborn (1992, pp. 136–137).
30. Millward (1988, p. 207).
31. Graff (1991, p. 155), Cressy (1980, p. 177).
32. Graff (1991, p. 155).
33. Schama (2000, p. 195).
34. Patterson (1997, p. 53).

35. Houston (1973, p. 14).
36. Ibid.
37. Houston (1973, p. 41).
38. Bertrand (1969, p. 29).
39. Bertrand (1969, p. 27).
40. Houston (1973, p. 25).
41. Houston (1973, p. 26).
42. Houston (1973, p. 40).
43. Houston (1973, p. 17).
44. This was the amount initially agreed to by Parliament in 1610 in return for putting an end to wardship and purveyance (Houston, 1973, p. 43).
45. Houston (1973, p. 23).
46. Nicolson (2003, p. 67).
47. Nicolson (2003, p. 67).
48. Nicolson (2003, pp. 67–68).
49. Nicolson (2003, p. 73).
50. Nicolson (2003, p. 72).
51. Nicolson (2003, p. 73).
52. Nicolson (2003, p. 222).
53. Nicolson (2003, pp. 27–29).
54. MacGregor (1959, p. 165).
55. Greenslade (1963, p. 148).
56. Nicolson (2003, p. 121).
57. Nicolson (2003, p. 209).
58. MacGregor (1959, p. 158).
59. Nicolson (2003, pp. 212–213).
60. Greenslade (1963, p. 165).
61. Nicolson (2003, p. 213).
62. Nicolson (2003, p. 216).
63. MacGregor (1959, pp. 179–181).
64. Greenslade (1963, p. 167).
65. Black (1963, p. 455).
66. Nicolson (2003, p. 228), Black (1963, p. 454).
67. MacGregor (1959, p. 183).
68. Haythornthwaite ([1983] 1994, p. 107).
69. Haythornthwaite ([1983] 1994, pp. 29–30).
70. Haythornthwaite ([1983] 1994, pp. 49–52).
71. Plant (2006).
72. Gregg (1981, p. 12).
73. Schama (2001, p. 48).
74. Ashley (1987, p. 18).
75. Ashley (1987, p. 17).
76. Ashley (1987, pp. 22–23).
77. Lockyer (1989, p. 223).
78. Quintrell (1993, p. 39).
79. Gregg (1981, p. 185).
80. Gregg (1981, pp. 188, 197).
81. Morrill (1990, p. 35).
82. Morrill (1990, p. 33).
83. Morrill (1990, pp. 34, 38).
84. Ashley (1987, p. 33).
85. Davis (1990, p. 183).
86. Howell (1977, p. 6).
87. Morrill (1990, p. 22).
88. Coward (1991, p. 15).
89. Coward (1991, p. 9).

90. Bertrand (1969, p. 32).
91. Carlton (1983, p. 232).
92. Carlton (1983, p. 239).
93. Adamson (1990, pp. 51–52).
94. Adamson (1990, p. 54).
95. Ashley (1987, p. 85).
96. Woolrych (1990, p. 94).
97. Woolrych (1990, p. 95).
98. Woolrych (1990, p. 100).
99. Gentles (1998, p. 140).
100. Seel (1999, pp. 40–41).
101. Seel (1999, p. 35).
102. Davis (1990, p. 188).
103. Haythornthwaite ([1983] 1994, p. 110).
104. Carlton (1983, p. 287).
105. Gregg (1981, pp. 406–407).
106. Seel (1999, pp. 71–72).
107. Seel (1999, p. 74).
108. Seel (1999, p. 84).
109. Somerville (1990, p. 257).
110. Ashley (1987, p. 41).
111. Davis (1990, pp. 191–192).
112. Freeborn (1992, p. 180).
113. Cressy (1980, p. 177).
114. Ferguson (2004, p. 202).
115. North and Weingast (1989, p. 821).
116. Kennedy (1987, p. 81).
117. North and Weingast (1989, pp. 819, 823).
118. Speck (1988, pp. 241–242).
119. Bertrand (1969, p. 28).
120. Harris (1978, pp. 83–84).
121. AngliaCampus (2007).

# PART III

# The pre-emptive revolution

# 5. Printing with steam

By the beginning of the nineteenth century, thanks to the Bible in English, printed with cheap replicas of Gutenberg's wood-framed hand press, a majority of Britons could read and write. However, the overall literacy rate had barely budged now for over half a century. With books expensive and newspapers unable to print more than a few thousand copies a day of a given text, the high cost of transmitting information from producers to readers constituted a major bottleneck to the expansion of literacy.

A hefty increase in Stamp Duty imposed on newspapers by Prime Minister William Pitt the Younger to finance his wars with France had certainly not helped British publishers. Indeed, by 1803, *The Times* of London was on the verge of bankruptcy. Yet the paper's publisher, John Walter II, thought he saw a way out. One component of the stamp tax was levied on each printed sheet regardless of its size. If a means could be found to increase the size of each page, more advertisements could be crammed on a sheet for the same tax. Since the other component of the duty was based on the number of advertisements per issue rather than on the number of copies sold, there was a second potential way to increase profits. All that was required was to increase the number of copies of the same text printed each day. Surely it was possible to design a faster press! However, *The Times* with its middle- and upper-class readers was not the only publication that might benefit from such innovations. Others were thinking about how to reach an audience that was somewhat lower on the social scale.

## THE FOX AND THE PORCUPINE

Pall Mall, a fashionable street in London's west end, has been at the center of the city's political and social life for many years. It takes its name from the seventeenth-century game of palle maille, an early form of croquet played with mallets and ball in a long alley with an iron hoop at either end. Many of the city's famous men's clubs of today are the descendants of coffee houses that were set up on either side of this alley in the eighteenth century. By the turn of the nineteenth century, this street had become a center of the book trade.

The news in October 1801 that the government had begun peace talks came as a great relief to most of the people of London. After seven years of high prices and taxes caused by a desultory war against revolutionary France, life could at last return to normal. Merchants and householders lit their windows with candles to celebrate – and to signal their support for the Tory government. Providing an additional inducement to conform were the mobs of government clerks who roamed the streets smashing unlit windows. When they found the house of William Cobbett in Pall Mall dark, they broke the windowpanes and forced the door.[1] The 34-year-old publisher could only wait impatiently for his chance to strike back in print.

## The Porcupine

William Cobbett was a big man whose aggressive style of writing was well suited to his physique. He was over six feet tall (180 cm) at a time when the average male height was about five feet six inches (168 cm), with the broad shoulders of a farmer's son.[2] In his pamphlets and books, he was not shy about sharing his opinions with others. He hated Jews, blacks and democrats. Above all, he was sharply critical of France, England's 'natural enemy', and that country's Jacobin leaders.[3]

Cobbett was born on a farm in Surrey in 1767. At 17, he joined the army and was shipped off to New Brunswick. Subsequently, he taught French and published books and pamphlets in Philadelphia. Then in the summer of 1800, he returned to England with a reputation as an uncompromising journalist and a patriot. At that time, he met with the Tory prime minister, William Pitt, who offered him a position as editor of a pro-government daily.[4] Cobbett declined the offer, wishing to preserve his independence. Instead, he chose to set up his own daily paper, *The Porcupine*, that supported Pitt's government in its conduct of the war.[5] However, in February 1801, King George III forced Pitt to resign because he was opposed to the prime minister's plans for Catholic emancipation. The new Tory administration under Henry Addington decided to sue for peace. In December of that year, Cobbett's paper failed.

Fortunately, Cobbett retained the support of Pitt's former Minister of War, William Windham. In January 1802, with an advance of £600 from Windham and his associates, Cobbett launched a weekly, the *Political Register*. For over three decades Cobbett would continue to set forth his opinions in this paper and its successors. Two months later, England and France signed the Treaty of Amiens and peace returned to Europe. Cobbett criticized the treaty as a 'foolish and unnecessary capitulation'. As stubborn as ever, he left his windows unlit and the mob duly proceeded to smash them. This time, it required a troop of horse guards to break up the crowd of protesters before his house.[6]

## The Fox

The impact of the Peace of Amiens was not limited to a few broken windowpanes. It also meant a decline in the public's interest in current events and was consequently particularly unfavorable to the large daily newspapers dependent on the demand for the latest news. In January 1803, John Walter II took over as manager of a daily that his father and namesake had founded in 1785. Initially, the journal had been a sideline for the elder Walter's book-publishing firm and bore the name, *Daily Universal Register*. Three years later, Walter Senior had chosen a more streamlined name: *The Times*. By December 1792, the paper's audited circulation had reached an average of about 3000 copies a day – greater than that of any competitor.[7]

In 1799, the daily's managing editor had been jailed for his debts but had been allowed to return to work while released on parole. In return, *The Times* supported government policies favored by its editor's principal creditor.[8] That same year the paper lost its government subsidy of £300 a year, although it still held a government contract to print forms for the Customs office. Nevertheless, by early 1803, *The Times* stood on the verge of bankruptcy. Its circulation had fallen to well below 2000 per day.[9] At age 26, John Walter II faced the challenge of designing a new business strategy for his father's creation.

If Cobbett was the porcupine, a specialist in setting down his personal prejudices on paper and shooting them off as quills at his favorite targets, then John Walter II was the fox. Walter was a synthesizer, interested in all aspects of newspaper publishing, from the gathering of news, the sale of advertising space and the writing of editorials to the composition of the forms of characters and their reproduction in printing presses. A modest man, he drove his employees hard and willingly accepted the long hours required to put out London's foremost daily – or at least a newspaper that had once played that role.[10]

Consider how *The Times* was produced in 1803. It was printed on a single sheet of paper, folded once to create four pages, each four columns in width. The outer pages (one and four) with advertising copy were printed in an initial press run. The inner pages with the latest news and late advertising copy were then printed in a second run.[11]

The printing process itself had changed little in the 350 years since the days of Gutenberg. Type was set by hand into a wooden frame or form. The metal was then coated with ink by hand and covered with a blank page. This unit was then slid into a hand press where pressure was applied by a plate lowered on to the reverse side of the paper. With the wooden-framed press, two powerful strokes were necessary to lower the platen.[12] In this way, it was possible to produce 200–250 impressions per hour on one side of sheets of paper.[13] If the other side had been printed in advance, on a separate press, about 3000 copies could be produced in a twelve hour work day. In order to print more than this number of copies daily, it would be necessary to set up a duplicate type on another press. In short, the traditional printing process had the advantage that the initial investment to start up a new paper was low. However, the offsetting disadvantages were that the cost of each newspaper printed was high and that there was an effective ceiling to a paper's circulation.

## The Government and the Press

The great dilemma for the publisher was to determine his relationship with the government. Although in theory the press had been uncensored since 1695, in practice it was subject to considerable pressure by the administration in power or those seeking to replace it. We have seen that the Pitt government used direct subsidies to insure backing in the press for its legislation. Government departments could also withhold or place advertisements, thereby providing indirect subsidies.[14] If a publisher like Cobbett agreed to support a specific set of policies, he could often count on financial backing from the government or from a powerful political group. In return, however, the paper lost its independence and became identified as a mouthpiece for its backers. Alternatively, a publisher might refuse outside subsidies and attempt to survive on advertising and subscription revenues. In time of peace, when the demand for news was low, his newspaper would have difficulty covering its costs.

One of the principal costs to the publisher was the Newspaper Stamp Duty or stamp tax. This had first been applied to newspapers by a Tory government in 1712. Of course the tax brought in revenues but it also had the intended effect of limiting the number of publications.[15] The duty had two components. One was an advertising tax, set most recently (in 1789) at three shillings for each advertisement regardless of its length.[16] Advertising revenues were the principal source of income for a newspaper publisher. Since this part of the tax did not depend on the number of copies printed, it made it difficult for new periodicals to establish themselves legitimately.

The second part of the stamp duty was a tax that was applied to each printed sheet. In 1797, Pitt had raised this duty from 2 to 3½d per sheet. With *The Times* selling at 6d a copy, this tax amounted to over half the price of the newspaper to the buyer.[17] The Whig opposition accused the government of trying to put information beyond the reach of the majority of the population. Pitt blandly argued that if a man could not afford to pay 4d for a newspaper, he could convince three of his friends to join him, each subscribing a penny. At any rate, when the Whigs came into power briefly from 1806 to 1807, they left the tax intact.[18]

It is interesting to consider the effect of the stamp tax on publishers' incentives. The advertising tax made it profitable to increase circulation, since the newspaper could raise its advertising rates without being taxed on the additional revenue it earned thereby. As for the duty per printed sheet, it provided an inducement both to enlarge the size of the printed page and to search for ways of decreasing the unit cost of printing. Together, the two taxes provided a remarkable incentive to seek technologies that increased the economies of scale.

The principal advantage to the use of wood for the beams of the printing press was its low initial cost. Offsetting this feature, however, was the tendency of the wood to bend under pressure, the effect of which was to reduce the force that could be applied to the platen.[19] As a result, the printed surface was small and the quality of the printing variable. As for the use of human labor, once again it was the low initial cost of the machinery required to harness this force that was the main attraction. Such a press could be had in 1803 for about £60.[20] As long as newspaper press runs were under 3000 copies a day, and the demand for advertising remained moderate, this technology was very competitive. However, as the reading public grew there came a point at which it became desirable to increase the size of newspapers and the number of copies per issue.

The incentives to improve the productivity of Gutenberg's invention were strong. But were there entrepreneurs responsive to these possibilities? And was the rest of British society sufficiently willing to accept change to make innovation viable?

## THE ECONOMIC REVOLUTION

Around 1710, the year that St Paul's Cathedral was consecrated, there were two remarkable developments that over the following century were to transform virtually all aspects of British life, including the information sector. Although London continued to grow rapidly during the eighteenth century, growth was even more rapid in parts of the provinces, particularly in the Midlands to the northwest of the capital.

### Key Innovations

Abraham Darby was born in 1677 in Dudley, a small town about 10 miles (16 km) west of Birmingham. He was raised as a Quaker, a member of one of the most radical Puritan sects. After an apprenticeship to a maker of machinery for the milling industry, he set out for the Netherlands. There he observed how the Dutch were shaping brass into hollowware such as pots and pans. The War of the Spanish Succession had driven up the price of brass. Once back in England in the port city of Bristol, he therefore began to experiment with making such objects more cheaply by casting them from iron using sand molds.

Wartime demand had also raised the price of the charcoal used traditionally in the smelting of iron. Darby therefore decided to attempt to produce iron from coke, a product made from the distillation of plentiful coal of the area. To do so, he moved in 1709 to Coalbrookdale in Shropshire, a short distance northwest of his birthplace, where there were abundant deposits of hard coal. Shortly thereafter he succeeded in smelting marketable iron from coke. Using a blast furnace much larger than the usual charcoal-fired furnaces, he was able to produce large quantities of iron of sufficiently good quality that it could be used in the place of brass to cast inexpensive pots and pans.

The needs of war had driven up the price of yet another product, namely, the tin required for the production of bronze cannon. As a result, it became profitable to reactivate the ancient tin mines of Cornwall. However, because of wartime scarcities, it was expensive to purchase the horses needed to drive the pumps that evacuated water from the mines. Thomas Newcomen was a man fortunate to be in the right place at the right time. Born in 1667, he was raised as a Baptist, a member of another nonconformist Protestant sect. By profession he was a hardware merchant from Dartmouth in nearby Devonshire. Around 1705, he began to experiment to find a way of using steam to drive water pumps. Finally in 1710, he and his assistant Calley succeeded in using steam effectively to drive a pump at the Wheal Vor tin mine in Cornwall.[21]

It soon became evident that the inventions of Darby and Newcomen were highly complementary. Two years later, Newcomen installed a similar machine at a coal mine near Dudley Castle, some 30 miles from Coalbrookdale.[22] Meanwhile in the northeast, near Newcastle-upon-Tyne, there was a rich pit mine of coal that could not be worked because the water seepage exceeded the capacity of horse-driven pumps. A Newcomen engine was installed there in 1717–1718.[23] Since the 'fire-engine' allowed coal to be mined more cheaply, it contributed to a fall in the cost of the principal input in Darby's production process.

Of course, the lower the cost of the pumps to drain the coal mines, the more cheaply iron could be smelted. The initial cylinders for Newcomen engines had expensive brass cylinders. When Abraham Darby died in 1717, his son and namesake was only six years old. However, the father's firm, the

Coalbrookdale Company, lived on. The Coalbrookdale Company was the first to produce these cylinders from inexpensive iron.[24] Between 1722 and 1733, 23 iron cylinders for these engines were cast at Coalbrookdale.[25]

## Sources of Innovation

At the rate that innovations had been generated over the previous millennium, these three developments – the casting of complex shapes from iron, the production of iron from coke and the harnessing of steam to produce mechanical force – should have sufficed for the eighteenth century. However, they were but the first of over 60 significant innovations that historians have identified between 1700 and 1799.[26]

We have seen that these three technological developments all occurred in response to relative price changes caused by the War of the Spanish Succession. Was war then the cause of innovation? If so, then there should have been abundant innovations a century earlier, when all European states were caught up in the Thirty Years' War. However, there seem to have been few if any significant new technologies developed in Europe between 1618 and 1648. Or, if it was this particular war at the beginning of the eighteenth century that was the trigger of invention, then there should have been widespread attempts at innovation across Europe at that time. But England seems to have been the exception: there were no significant technological developments elsewhere between 1701 and 1714.

Indeed, the most difficult aspect of the eighteenth-century wave of inventions to explain is their geographical location. Over two-thirds of all the many successful new technologies that were introduced between 1700 and 1799 came from Britain.[27] High literacy was probably a necessary condition, but societies with even higher literacy rates – Germany, Sweden and the Netherlands – contributed very little in terms of innovation. France, which accounted for a fifth of the innovations, had a lower literacy rate than Britain.[28]

The timing of the innovations over the eighteenth century provides some indication of what the missing factor might be. In the seventeenth century, Britain had experienced civil war and the overthrow of two monarchs (three if Richard Cromwell is included) over the issue of responsible government. Union with Scotland in 1707 constituted the seal of recognition that a national state had been formed. British innovations were scattered over all the decades of the eighteenth century. However, almost all of the French innovations occurred in the last quarter-century, at a period when the French were gradually becoming conscious of their collective identity as a nation. Rousseau's *Du Contrat Social* was published in 1762. Similarly, the American innovations were developed over the final two decades of the century, following the Declaration of Independence of 1776.

In short, literacy combined with nationalist revolution would seem to be the twin prerequisites for sustained innovation.

## The Two Paces of Change

Although over the course of the eighteenth century, the British economy maintained the rapid pace at which it had been growing since the end of the Middle Ages, the country's political institutions could not keep pace. Consider first the economic changes. Between 1700 and 1800, Great Britain's population grew by over 60 per cent, from under 7 million in 1700 to almost 11 million in 1800. Political union with Ireland in 1801 added a further 5 million to the United Kingdom's total population.[29] Owing to rural–urban migration, it was in the cities rather than the countryside that demographic growth was most rapid. In 1800, London was Great Britain's (and Europe's) largest city. Its population had grown by two-thirds over the eighteenth century and was now approaching the one million mark. Although Edinburgh too had grown considerably, with 83 000 inhabitants in 1800, it had slipped from second place in 1700 into third place a century later. Meanwhile, Norwich, Bristol and Newcastle-upon-Tyne, cities that had been among the top five in 1700, had now been pushed out of the top ranks. Three upstart industrial towns in the Midlands, each of which had registered fewer than 10 000 inhabitants in 1700, had taken their places. Over the eighteenth century, Manchester, Liverpool and Birmingham had all increased their population tenfold and were now jostling Edinburgh for second place.[30]

The British in 1800 were not only more numerous than a century earlier; they were also more prosperous. Thanks to productivity increases in agriculture, industry and services, their average income had risen 30 per cent over the eighteenth century. With a per capita income approaching 2000 US dollars measured at today's prices, they now enjoyed the highest living standard in the world.[31]

There had been remarkable changes in transport and communications over the eighteenth century. Roads had improved considerably as turnpikes replaced poorly maintained parish roads. By 1770, there were more than 13 000 miles of turnpikes, operated by over 500 trusts. The new roads were of benefit not only for passengers but also for mail. From 1765, it cost only a penny to send a letter anywhere in the country. In 1784, the government introduced special red, maroon and black coaches with steel springs to carry the mail and paying passengers. Improved road surfaces made of crushed stone allowed the coaches to run in any weather. In 1700, it had taken two days to cross the country, from London to Bristol; by 1800, the time required to make this trip had fallen to twelve hours.[32]

Among the beneficiaries of the improved transport were the publishers of the London newspapers. In 1782, over three million copies of periodicals were sent by mail. There were by this date nine London dailies and over 60 other periodicals in England and Wales, most of them published in the provinces.[33] Altogether, data from the stamp duties show that there were over 14 million legitimate papers sold over the whole year in 1780, or roughly 1.5 periodicals per capita. By the turn of the century, the newspaper penetration ratio had changed very little.[34]

Nevertheless, in the latter part of the century, Britain crossed a crucial threshold. At the beginning of the eighteenth century, only a minority of both men and women had been able to read and write. By 1800, however, the overall literacy rate had risen over the 50 per cent mark. On average, in that year more than two out of five women and more than three out of five men were able to read and sign their names.[35] In England and Wales, out of a total population of over nine million, over three million of whom were adult males, there were then roughly two million men of voting age who were able to read and write.

However, only about one in four of these educated males was allowed to vote.[36] Britain's political institutions had failed to keep pace with the economic change. At the beginning of the nineteenth century, there were 658 seats in the House of Commons. Of these, 468 were filled by representatives from the cities and towns, each borough sending two Members of Parliament.[37] Since the constituency boundaries had changed little since the Middle Ages, there were many boroughs that had once been important towns but were now in decline. Each borough set its own rules for deciding who was eligible to vote, some giving the vote to members of the town council, others to all local tax payers. Some 40 per cent of the boroughs had fewer than 100 voters, while two-thirds had fewer than 500. For example, the borough of Dunwich in Suffolk had only 32 electors. Since voting took place in open hustings, it was possible for candidates to buy the voters in these 'rotten boroughs'.[38] Wealthy patrons were thereby able to control votes in Parliament.

The remaining 190 seats were filled by representatives of the countryside, two members from each county. In the counties, everyone who owned or rented land with an annual rent rated at 40 shillings was eligible. As a result, there was less possibility of corruption here, since the average county had over 3000 electors.[39]

As yet there were no organized political parties in Britain. However, during the last decades of the eighteenth century, there had emerged two groupings of politicians who tended to differ consistently on major issues.[40]

The designation 'Tory' was an Irish term meaning 'papist outlaw', that a century earlier had been applied to those who supported James II's claim to the throne despite his Catholic faith. The Tories tended to come from the country gentry; they favored the Anglican Church and resisted constitutional reform.

The term 'Whig' was short for Whiggamore, meaning a 'horse thief' and originally referred to Scottish Presbyterian rebels during the Second Civil War between king and parliament in 1648. Whigs tended to come from the landowning aristocracy and from the upper middle classes in the towns. This group favored religious toleration, including the granting of full rights to Catholics who had been forbidden to hold land, hold office or practice their religion freely since the sixteenth century. The Whigs also favored reform of the electoral system. However, the support of the king was necessary to form a government. Since George III was opposed to both Catholic emancipation and constitutional reform, the Whigs had been out of power virtually since his accession to the throne in 1760.

It has been estimated that in the first decades of the nineteenth century some 500 men selected the majority of the members of the House of Commons.[41] During a period of prolonged peace, this political system would not have been tolerated. However, in early 1803, Britain was preparing for its seventh major war with France since the Glorious Revolution of 1688.[42]

## BEYOND GUTENBERG

Like its predecessor, the Treaty of Aix-la-Chapelle of 1748, the Treaty of Amiens of 1802 failed to bring durable peace to Europe. Rather, the accord simply provided a short breathing period during which each side could prepare itself militarily for the inevitable struggle to come.

### War with France

The British had hoped that with the return of peace, their access to the trade of the continent would be restored and that the French would loosen their hold on their smaller neighbors. Instead, Napoleon kept the continental ports closed to British shipping while reinforcing French troops in the satellite states of the Netherlands, Switzerland and northern Italy.

The French army was three times larger and considerably more experienced than its British counterpart. However, to attack Britain directly, Napoleon needed to command the English Channel long enough to replicate the feat of William the Conqueror in transporting his troops to southern England. To do so, Napoleon planned to combine the French, Dutch and Spanish fleets and transport an army of 150 000 to Kent.[43] As the British government became aware of the military build-up in the Netherlands, it realized that these preparations must be disrupted. In April 1803, it issued an ultimatum demanding that the French withdraw their army from the Netherlands and grant Britain a long-term lease on the island of Malta. When Napoleon refused to negotiate, Britain declared war.[44]

The resumption of war implied a heavy burden for the British nation as a whole but it brought good news for the press. Once again, there was a strong demand for information that could only be provided by daily newspapers. With large enough circulation and advertising revenues, it might even be possible for publishers such as William Cobbett and John Walter II to free themselves from dependence on government funding and information from official sources. But could the higher demand be met without an exorbitant cost?

**The Stanhope Press**

After three and one-half centuries, the defects of the Gutenberg press were well known. The wooden frame was unstable. The size of the sheet it could print was limited. A great deal of effort was required to deliver the two pulls of the bar that lowered the paper on to the inked type a half page at a time and then return the bar to its original position.[45] The maximum size of sheet was only 30 by 20 inches (75 by 50 cm).[46] Since the printers applied ink by dabbing the form of type by hand with a leather ball coated with ink, the impression was rarely uniform.[47] Nevertheless, the device was inexpensive to build and when powered by a team of two to three strong pressmen, it could print a run of up to 2000 to 3000 copies for a daily newspaper at a moderate cost. Yet in the Age of Enlightenment, this technology constituted a stationary target for those who sought to better the world.

Charles Stanhope was the oldest surviving son of the second Earl Stanhope and the grandson of the chief minister of George I, the first Earl Stanhope. Educated in mathematics in Switzerland, Charles was elected a fellow of the Royal Society in 1772. When he succeeded to his father's peerage at the age of 33 in 1786, he decided to dedicate much of his income to the pursuit of liberty and scientific inquiry. He became chairman of the Revolution Society, a group that advocated parliamentary reform. In the 1790s, he also brought printers to the family estate at Chevening in Kent with the aim of improving the printing process. Out of these efforts came improvements to stereotyping, a procedure by which blocks of typographical characters are cloned from a mold into which hot metal is poured.

Another result of Stanhope's efforts was an all-metal press that corrected many of the shortcomings of the wooden press. The new device consisted of a massive frame of cast iron set on to a heavy wooden base. The platen holding the paper was lowered on to the inked type by an ingenious system of levers designed to apply great pressure at the moment of contact. As a result, a whole sheet could be printed in a single stroke. The rate of production remained about the same at 250 sheets an hour. However, considerably less effort was required on the part of the pressman.[48]

The Stanhope press was first invented about 1800, but the oldest surviving example, No. 5, dates from 1804.[49] Stanhope refused to patent the device. Instead, he made an arrangement with Robert Walker, a London ironsmith, to manufacture the press to his specifications.[50] After 1806, various improvements were made to strengthen the press and simplify its operation. Initially, the iron press sold for about three times the price of a wooden press. However, after competitors to Walker entered the market the price ratio fell to about two to one.[51]

One of the most important customers of the London pressmakers was John Walter II, publisher of *The Times*. He purchased a 'battalion' of Stanhope presses and set them to work in parallel, even though this procedure required duplicate typesetting.[52] The new presses allowed a sheet of 36 by 23½ inches (90 by 57 cm) to be worked; that is, a 40 per cent increase over the maximum permitted with the wooden press.[53] As a result, advertising revenues could be increased proportionally, while the stamp tax per copy remained unchanged.

With the resumption of war, Pitt returned to power in 1804. The following year, *The Times* came out against the Tory government and in support of the former prime minister, Addington, who accused the Pitt administration of financial irregularities in the administration of the navy. In reprisal, Pitt canceled a printing contract for the Customs Office that *The Times* had held since its founding. However, Walter now had sufficient revenues from advertising and increased circulation to be able to shrug off this blow. [54] Seeking an advantage over the competition, he engaged a fast sailing ship to bring the war news from France.[55] The gamble paid off when his paper was able to publish an account of the British victory at Trafalgar several days in advance of the official report by the navy. For the first time, the English press was freeing itself from government control.

Meanwhile William Cobbett too was liberating himself from constraints on his editorial independence. In 1805, he bought a house in Botley, Hampshire, 5 miles from Southampton, and began to devote his recreational hours to farming. The success of his newspaper enabled him to buy out several small farms in the neighborhood of Botley over the next few years.[56] Meanwhile, in his articles in the *Political Register*, he began to talk of the subjection of 'the common people' to those in power.[57] In 1806 he broke with his former patron, Windham, and began to attack the privileges of those in power. Writing on love of country, he wrote, 'amongst the mass of the people, freedom from oppression, and that happiness which arises from a comfortable subsistence, will always be the chief objects of attachment, and the principal motives of all the exertions which they make in defence of their country'.[58] Becoming a true radical, Cobbett even began to advocate the reform of Parliament.[59] However, major constitutional change would not be possible until the middle classes could be convinced that concessions were in their interest.

## The Steam Press

Parliamentary reform was far from the thoughts of a young Saxon printer as he contemplated emigrating to England. Friedrich Koenig was born in 1774 in Eisleben, Saxony, birthplace of the church reformer Martin Luther. After a secondary education at the local Gymnasium, he was bound as an apprentice for four years to a Leipzig printer. As a journeyman, he then moved from city to city, acquiring experience but taking time out for study at the University of Leipzig. Finally at age 30 he was back near his home, in Suhl, Thuringia, with an idea to improve Gutenberg's printing press. His machine had inking rollers and a mechanical process to remove the paper after impression. In Germany at that time, there was no supply of venture capital to finance the development of his project, in part because there was no patent law to protect inventors. However, in Britain, under the Statute of Monopolies passed under James I in 1623, the Parliament could grant 'letters patent' giving exclusive rights to an invention for a period of 14 years. So it was that Koenig found himself arriving at the docks of London in November 1806, possessing little other than a set of revolutionary ideas.[60]

It had now been almost a century since Newcomen's invention of the atmospheric steam engine but no one had yet been successful in using steam to power the printing process. John Walter II had consulted the great inventor Isambard Brunel on the matter, but the latter had given up after considerable fruitless effort. Walter then subsidized one of his employees, Thomas Martyn, at a cost of £1500, to develop a 'self-acting press', but again nothing came of these efforts.[61] Yet this was 'the discovery' that Koenig proposed to develop with the financial help of a London book printer, Thomas Bensley, under a contract drawn up in 1807. To assist with the construction of the machine, Koenig wrote to his friend Andreas Bauer in Stuttgart, who was trained as an engineer, and persuaded him to come to London.[62] In 1811 they managed to print a sheet of the *Annual Register* using what was essentially a steam-powered version of the Stanhope press to which a mechanical inking device had been added. Yet as long as the paper continued to be applied to the type by a flat platen, the rate of production was too low to justify the cost of the machine.

The breakthrough came when Koenig conceived a means of holding a sheet of paper on to a rotating hollow cylinder that would apply pressure evenly at its point of contact with the typeface.[63] Thereafter the rate of impression was limited only by the speed at which the cylinder could rotate. Koenig and his backers took out a series of patents between 1811 and 1814 to protect the invention as it evolved.[64]

When the first prototype of the new machine was ready, late in 1812, Koenig and Bensley invited the owners of several London newspapers to witness its operation. Although James Perry of the *Morning Chronicle* showed no interest, John Walter of *The Times* accepted the invitation. He was sufficiently impressed to order two machines, each with two cylinders so as to speed up the printing process. It took almost two years to build and install the first of the new presses secretly in a building adjacent to *The Times* office. On learning of these preparations, the newspaper's pressmen issued threats against the German inventor. Nevertheless, on the morning of 29 November 1814, Walter was able to announce to his assembled workers that 'The Times is already printed by steam!' Warning them against violence, he offered to continue their pay until they could find similar employment. An article that day in the first issue informed the reader that the new machine was able to print 1100 sheets in one hour.[65] Not only was the machine much faster than the manual press for high volumes but also it avoided costly duplicate composition.

Initially, diffusion of the new technology was very slow, in part because of the prohibitive cost. The double machine purchased by *The Times* cost £1400 – some 20 times the price of a Stanhope press. In addition, there was an annual fee of £350 while the patent lasted. In 1816, Bensley, the principal shareholder of Koenig's company and owner of a book printing firm, refused to allow manufacture of the new machines for his competitors. Discouraged, Koenig and Bauer returned to Germany in 1817, where they set up their own firm. By 1820, there were still only eight steam presses in England, all in London, and all but one used for newspapers.[66] Cobbett, like most publishers of books and small newspapers, continued to print on hand presses.[67]

## THE GREAT REFORM

As the Napoleonic Wars drew to a close, the British urban public began to be polarized into two groups – the respectable and the radical. In order to meet the housing demands of the former, the eminent architect and favorite of the regent, John Nash, drew up plans for a new development of streets and town houses around a green space in north London to be named Regent's Park. The Regency terraces were classical in inspiration, with tall, narrow windows, round-headed doorways and bow windows.

Among those for whom the houses were designed, the principal fear was that revolutionary sentiment might spread from the continent to England and Scotland. In 1812, skilled workers in the woolen industry who called themselves Luddites (after Ned Ludd, their probably mythical leader) smashed new machines that were taking away their jobs.[68] Although the authorities arrested the leaders of the revolts, sentencing them to be hanged or transported to Australia, the unrest among industrial and agricultural workers remained.

## Repression

The problem of social unrest, as seen by the Tory government of Lord Liverpool, was caused by writers in the radical press who were stirring up discontent. In 1810, the previous administration had tried to silence Willam Cobbett, publisher of the *Political Register*, by jailing him for sedition for two years after he wrote an article criticizing the use of German troops to quell unrest in an army unit that was demanding its back pay. However, Cobbett had continued to publish his paper from Newgate Prison. Soon after his release, he was criticizing the government for its repression of the Luddites, suggesting that it instead deal with unemployment and the high price of bread that were the underlying cause of the riots.[69] To many who supported the government, it was obvious that more extreme measures were necessary.

William Sheridan was a playwright, the author of *School for Scandal*. He was also a Whig Member of Parliament, very much concerned with defending press freedom. While Cobbett was in prison, the playwright observed during a parliamentary debate that there were three ways to destroy the liberty of the press: by excessive taxation, by oppressive legislation and by arbitrary arrest and trial.[70] A few years later, the end of the war caused hundreds of thousands of former soldiers and sailors to be dumped on to a depressed labor market. To keep a lid on expressions of discontent, the government began to apply the controls on Sheridan's list, one by one.

In June 1815, two weeks before the Battle of Waterloo, the Chancellor of the Exchequer announced new taxes on newspapers. The stamp tax on each newspaper was raised from 3½ to 4d, and the advertising tax on each item of publicity from 3s to 3s 6d.[71] The effect was further to limit access to information by the middle classes, since few families could afford to pay 7d a day for a newspaper.[72] At least one newspaper ceased production immediately; four others died over the next decade and a half, unable to cope with the new taxes.[73]

In 1816 and 1817, the industrial centers of Lancashire and Yorkshire were suffering from low wages, high unemployment and high food prices. Workers from the textile industry of Manchester organized a march on London to protest against government inactivity. It took a force of cavalry to halt their movement.[74] Part of the problem, it was felt, was with the 'pauper press'. Cobbett had not been deterred by the new taxes. In 1816, he began to publish the *Political Register* in a cheaper edition that sold for 2d instead of 1s.[75] He thus avoided the high stamp tax on newspapers, being subject to only a moderate tax of 3s on each edition of a pamphlet.[76] By 1817, the *Political Register* was selling up to 44 000 copies of each weekly edition.[77]

Since 1811, the prince regent, the future George IV, had reigned in place of his mentally ill father, George III. In January 1817, as the prince regent made his way to the opening of Parliament, his coach was attacked and its windows were broken, either by gunshots or stones. Henry Addington, now Lord Sidmouth, the home secretary, decided that something further must be done to quell the unrest. In March 1817, he introduced legislation to suspend the habeas corpus provision of the criminal code, thereby allowing arrest without trial for a period of a year.[78] He also addressed a Circular Letter to the country's magistrates telling them that they could arrest newspaper sellers unless they could produce a license. Several booksellers and newspaper peddlers who dared sell the *Political Register* and other radical publications were arrested under these provisions.[79] More generally, the repressive laws served as a warning to all publishers. Unwilling to face another long period in jail, Cobbett sailed to the United States with two of his sons in April 1817.[80]

## Thunder in the Center

Despite government efforts to stifle it, the movement for reform continued to gain momentum. Manchester was one of the new industrial cities that had no parliamentary representation. On 16 August 1819, the Manchester Patriotic Union organized a mass meeting at St Peter's Fields on the outskirts of the city. Over 50 000 people gathered peacefully to hear the orators who had been invited, among them Henry Hunt, a well-known radical. Also present was John Tyas, a reporter sent by *The Times*. On seeing Hunt arrive in an open landau, the local magistrates ordered the volunteer yeomanry cavalry to arrest him. Hunt duly surrendered. However, when the cavalry began to slash the flags of the demonstrators, brickbats were thrown at them. At that point, according to Tyas's report: 'the Manchester Yeomanry cavalry lost all command of temper . . . a man within five yards of us in another direction had his nose completely taken off by a blow of a sabre'.[81] In ten minutes of violence, 11 people were killed and 421 seriously wounded.[82]

Two years previously, John Walter II had decided that he could no longer manage his publishing firm and at the same time edit a daily newspaper. He had therefore appointed Thomas Barnes, a liberal journalist who had worked for *The Times* for several years, as editor. Barnes decided to focus on winning and holding a particular audience, setting as his objective the gaining of readership among 'the middle orders'.[83] It was Barnes who had sent Tyas to Manchester and published his report. And it was he who on 25 August printed an open letter from the radical MP Sir Francis Burdett to his constituents inviting them to a protest meeting over the Manchester massacre that was now being called 'Peterloo'.[84] The 'respectable' press was convincing its growing audience that reform was necessary.

The regime still had the third of Sheridan's arrows in its quiver, namely, oppressive legislation. During the last weeks of 1819, it passed the 'gagging bills', six Acts intended to further restrict radical political opposition.[85] Four of these acts were designed to suppress paramilitary and political activity, but two of them were aimed directly at the pauper press.[86] The Blasphemous and Seditious Libels Act permitted the authorities to seize all the copies of a libelous publication and banish the writer if he committed a second offense. In addition, the Newspaper Stamp Duties Act broadened the definition of newspaper to include for taxation regularly published pamphlets. Moreover, publishers had to pay a deposit of several hundred pounds. Cobbett had returned from America in November 1819, after habeas corpus was reinstated. However, the new press laws forced him to stop publication of the inexpensive version of his *Political Register*, whose sales consequently fell from the tens of thousands to the mere hundreds.[87] He himself was obliged to declare bankruptcy.

Although the British lower middle class and workers might no longer be able to afford a daily or even weekly paper, they were not necessarily cut off from information. When the newspaper men had finished delivering *The Times* to their subscribers, they supplemented their incomes by lending some 70 to 80 copies for a penny an hour.[88] People could also subscribe to reading rooms and coffee houses where a variety of newspapers could be read. On the average, a London paper might be read by 20 people.[89] An urban working man might pick up a newspaper to read on his Sunday visit to the barber shop.[90] Rural workers might hear the news read at a village alehouse even if they could not read themselves.[91] Another consequence of the gagging bills was a dramatic rise in circulation of the unstamped press.[92] By the early 1830s, there were over 550 unstamped papers appearing regularly.[93] For example, Henry Hetherington was publishing his *Penny Papers for the People* that sold for a penny a copy.[94]

## Reform

During the decade after Peterloo, *The Times* under the editorship of Thomas Barnes was committed to parliamentary reform. In January 1831, it published a lead editorial stating, 'Unless the people – the people everywhere – come forward and petition, ay, thunder for reform, it is they who abandon an honest ministry'.[95]

The harvests of 1829 and 1830 were poor, coming after unusually cold winters. Workers who could usually find jobs at harvest time suddenly found that they had been replaced by new threshing machines. Beginning in August 1830, farmers across southern and eastern England began to receive letters from a fictive 'Captain Swing', threatening reprisals unless they agreed to a minimum wage and ceased the use of threshing machinery. Rioting workers smashed agricultural machinery and set fire to haystacks and barns. Initially, local magistrates gave light sentences to the protesters.[96]

The summer of 1830 also saw the death of George IV and the succession of his brother, William IV. Because the Whig leader, Charles Grey, had opposed the late king's divorce, George IV had refused to ask him to form a government. However, the new monarch had no such aversion. When the Tories split over electoral reform, William IV agreed to give Grey and his followers a chance to form their first government in a quarter century.[97] Once in office, the new regime cracked down hard on the rural uprisings. By vigorous use of troops and the encouragement of harsh sentences, the new home secretary, Lord Melbourne, soon managed to restore order in the countryside. However, the Whig reformers had long been convinced that profound changes were necessary if social upheaval of the type experienced by France was to be avoided. One of Earl Grey's conditions in agreeing to lead the government was that the king accept a bill for parliamentary reform.[98]

The new prime minister assigned the task of drafting a reform bill to a committee of four Whig aristocrats led by John Russell. The third son of the Duke of Bedford, Russell had first been elected to the House of Commons in 1813 at the age of 21. In his first speech in 1817, the young aristocrat had opposed the Tory Habeas Corpus Act. During the 1820s he had become a fervent advocate of parliamentary reform. Working quickly,

Russell and his colleagues drafted a bill that he presented to Parliament on 1 March 1831. The proposals were much more drastic than had been expected and Russell immediately attracted a national audience. Under the proposed legislation, the rotten boroughs would disappear and 47 other boroughs with populations under 4000 would lose one of their two seats. London and the rural counties would get additional seats, while the industrial cities of Manchester, Leeds and Birmingham would be represented for the first time. In addition, the qualification for voting in the towns would be set at a uniform annual rent received or paid of £10 – a change that would allow an extra half million people to vote.[99]

The bill passed second reading in the Commons but became bogged down at the committee stage. When a Tory proposal to maintain the existing number of seats for England and Wales was approved by a narrow majority, the Whigs requested that Parliament be dissolved. In the ensuing elections of April 1831, many Tories who opposed electoral change were defeated. Not only London and other cities but also the rural ridings returned members committed to reform. A second reform bill was passed by the Commons in September by a majority of 109 votes, 345 to 236. However, despite the eloquent support of Earl Grey, the House of Lords defeated the bill on 8 October by 199 votes to 158.[100] When the news was announced, serious rioting broke out in London, Nottingham and Derby. In Bristol, 12 people died and 100 others were injured.[101]

While the Tories feared the consequences of any weakening of the political rights of property owners, the Whigs were convinced that Britain could avoid more radical change only by uniting the moderate groups in the society. In December 1831, the government introduced a third reform bill in the Commons, offering some concessions to the Lords. The new measure was carried by a majority of 162 votes.[102] Nevertheless, on 7 May 1832, the Lords approved by a majority of 35 votes (151 to 116) a procedural motion that would have split the reform bill into two parts. Earl Grey offered his resignation unless the king would accept the creation of at least 50 new peers favorable to reform.[103]

William IV accepted the resignation of the Whig cabinet and turned to the Tories, offering the Duke of Wellington the opportunity to form a new ministry committed to a more moderate reform package. However, Robert Peel, the leading reform Tory in the Commons refused to support Wellington's initiative. When the Duke informed the king that he was giving up his attempt to form a cabinet, the king had no further option. He summoned Grey and reluctantly produced the written promise to create additional peers if necessary. However, the king's secretary wrote to the bishops and the more moderate Tory peers, suggesting that if they stayed away from the House of Lords for the crucial vote, it would not be necessary for the king to dilute their power. So it was that on 4 June 1832, the Lords approved the reform bill by 106 to 22.[104]

## THE WATERSHED

In late summer of 1831, while the debate over reform was nearing its climax, a group of unemployed hand printers came to see William Cobbett. They requested that he cease to have his radical newspaper, the *Political Register*, printed on steam-powered presses. Although Cobbett had supported the Luddites some two decades earlier, he now brushed the press-men off. It was a purely technical matter that he left to his printer, he insisted. Besides, what were they doing walking the streets of London when there was work to be had harvesting crops?[105]

### Faster and Cheaper

In the years between the Napoleonic Wars and the Great Reform Bill, Cobbett like many other Britons had become accustomed to the permanence of technological change. It had taken 350 years after Gutenberg before the combined efforts of Stanhope and Koenig had revolutionized the printing industry in the years between 1804 and 1814. However, by the time that Koenig departed for Germany in 1817, new techniques in printing were being introduced continually.

Regarding the printing of newspapers, Koenig and his partner Bauer in 1817 succeeded in increasing the speed of the machine they built for *The Times* from 1000 to 1800 impressions per hour.[106] In 1823, John Walter II, publisher of *The Times*, accepted an offer from a London printer, Augustus Applegarth, to build an even faster machine in order to meet the increased circulation of the newspaper.[107] As installed in 1827, Applegarth's machine incorporated four cylinders, each holding a sheet of paper. The bed of type traveled back and forth, printing each of the sheets in its passage under the cylinders. This new machine was able to print 4200 impressions an hour.[108]

Like Gutenberg's press, the first powered printing machines printed on one side only. To print the reverse side, it was necessary to turn the pages and reload them. In 1816, Koenig and Bauer installed a new steam-driven machine that saved this extra labor and time for their partner, the book-printer Thomas Bensley. Known as a perfecting machine, it was able to print both sides of a sheet in a single pass. At 1000 two-sided sheets an hour, it increased the speed of book printing by a multiple of ten.[109] One disadvantage of both the Koenig and Applegarth presses was that the paper was held on to the cylinders by means of fragile tapes. In 1824, a

Scottish machinist working in London, David Napier, developed a perfecting machine that held sheets of paper on to a single cylinder by means of 'grippers' activated from within the cylinder.[110] In 1830, he introduced a double-cylinder machine with an output of 2000 perfected sheets an hour. With the simplified mechanism, production costs fell, although there was a substantial initial investment required. By the late 1830s, these Napier perfecting machines were selling for between £450 and £600 and could be driven either by steam or by hand. In short, scale economies had increased. In addition to printing books, the new machines proved ideal for weekly newspapers such as the *Illustrated London News*, founded in 1842.[111]

**The First True Political Parties**

As the debate over reform heated up in the press and among the public at the beginning of the 1830s, there was increasing pressure on Members of Parliament to commit themselves on the issues of the day. As a result, there occurred important changes in the organization of political groups in Britain. In March 1830, a group of Whig MPs in the Commons persuaded John Charles Spencer, the eldest son of the second Earl of Althorp, known as Lord Althorp, to lead their group in the Commons (Spencer was the elder brother of Princess Diana's great-great-grandfather). Soon almost all MPs opposed to the sitting Tory government of the Duke of Wellington expressed their support for Althorp, who became Chancellor of the Exchequer in Earl Grey's government after Wellington's fall.[112]

Once in opposition, the Tories, who had held power with few interruptions for almost five decades, were forced to redefine themselves as something other than the group who governed. Early in 1831, their refusal to accept the political reforms being drafted by Russell's committee brought them together as a 'loyal opposition' with a common goal.[113] A committee to coordinate parliamentary strategy was formed in a house on Charles Street – the 'Charles Street Gang'. During the electoral campaign of April 1831, the new organization allocated funds and constituencies to candidates. The following year, the Tories moved their activities to larger premises in Carlton Terrace, becoming the Carlton Club, the central organization of the party.

In 1834, the Whigs lost power briefly to a Tory minority government under Robert Peel. The reformers then saw their majority in the Commons reduced by 100 seats in the elections that Peel called in 1835. As a result, the Whigs too were forced to rethink their electoral strategy. In 1836, they founded the Reform Club to organize their party interests, opening the organization to the less extreme radical members of Parliament.[114] Both the Carlton Club and the Reform Club quickly developed decentralized party structures at the local level to contest elections in the new constituencies of the towns and counties.[115]

During the debates over reform in 1831 and 1832, the two parties had used the terms 'Liberal' and 'Conservative' to persuade the electorate in favor of their respective positions. To broaden the appeal of his party, Peel began using the word Conservative in place of Tory.[116] By the middle of the 1830s, these two labels were being used increasingly to identify the parties of the government and the opposition.[117]

## Social Reform

The program of the Liberal reformers involved much more than revising the British electoral system. In 1833, the government of Earl Grey passed three acts that signaled a willingness of the state to intervene to correct failures of markets. First came a bill that abolished slavery throughout the British Empire, offering slave owners £20 million in compensation. A second piece of legislation known as the Factory Act set a maximum working day of nine hours for children aged from nine to thirteen employed in the manufacture of textiles and twelve hours for those from thirteen to eighteen.[118]

The year 1833 also saw Parliament approve a grant of £20 000 to subsidize the construction of elementary schools administered by two voluntary educational societies.[119] After falling substantially over most of the eighteenth century, illiteracy had declined more slowly in the last decades of that century and the first decades of the nineteenth, particularly for women.[120] In 1832, a third of English men and half of the women were unable to sign their marriage certificates. However, over the next fifty years, thanks in part to state intervention, these rates fell by two-thirds.[121]

Under the Elizabethan Poor Law of 1601, responsibility for aiding the destitute was borne by the ratepayers of each parish. However, with rising rural poverty, the system was proving unbearably expensive, costing a total of £7 million in 1832.[122] A Royal Commission that reported in 1834 recommended centralizing the administration of the system and abolishing outdoor relief whereby the unemployed worked on the farms of the parish at a subsidized rate. Instead, there would be indoor relief in workhouses.

William Cobbett, publisher of the radical *Political Register*, had failed in earlier attempts to enter politics, but in the elections of December 1832, he succeeded in winning one of the two seats from the industrial town of Oldham. He was one of the bitterest opponents of the proposed Poor Law reform, describing it as 'a scheme for bringing every thing and every body within the control, the immediate control, of the kingly part of the government'.[123] He was joined in his dissent by John Walter and Thomas Barnes of *The Times*, who criticized the scheme as 'enormously expensive, degrading to the honest pauper and ruinous to fathers of families'.[124] Parliament passed the law nonetheless, but King William IV dismissed the reforming government under the new Whig leader, Lord Melbourne, because of its plans for church reform. The king called upon Robert Peel to form a minority Tory ministry. In April 1835, Peel finding himself unable to govern effectively, resigned and asked the king to call a general election.

When the Whigs under Melbourne returned to power in 1835, they were determined to take revenge on *The Times* for its opposition to their policies. They decided to amend the Newspaper Stamp Tax so that only smaller papers would benefit. However, Walter and Barnes succeeded in persuading the government to drop this part of the legislation. In 1836, the stamp tax was cut from 4d to 1d for all papers.

William Cobbett died in June 1835, but the radical tradition in British journalism that he had founded did not. Although his newspaper survived for only a short time under his son, the cut in the stamp duty made it possible for the workers to be represented by other legitimate publications. By the early 1840s, The Chartist weekly *Northern Star* was selling up to 36 000 copies an issue.[125]

Meanwhile, other newspapers also profited from the tax cut. The main Sunday papers that had boasted a circulation of 10 000–14 000 in 1821 were selling 20 000–55 000 copies by 1843. As for *The Times*, the tax cut greatly increased its profitability. John Walter II cut the price of a copy from 7d to 5d. By 1839, *The Times* was valued at over a half million pounds and could no longer be influenced by the offer or the withdrawal of the amounts of money the government had at its disposal.[126] Over the fifteen years that followed the reduction in the stamp duty, Walter's paper managed to capture all of the growth in circulation of London dailies, rising to a daily average of 38 000 in 1851.[127] John Walter II died in 1847, turning the paper over to his son, John Walter III. By the 1840s, the British press had at last established its full independence from the government in power. Thanks to its power, the process of pre-emptive social reform was now irreversible.

## NOTES

1. Sambrook (1973, p. 54).
2. Briggs (1967, p. 11).
3. Briggs (1967, pp. 17, 27), Sambrook (1973, pp. 48, 54).
4. Briggs (1967, p. 24).

5. Sambrook (1973, pp. 53–54).
6. Briggs (1967, p. 26).
7. Woods and Bishop (1985, p. 19).
8. Woods and Bishop (1985, p. 22).
9. Woods and Bishop (1985, p. 25).
10. Woods and Bishop (1985, p. 25).
11. Hutt (1973, p. 35).
12. Woods and Bishop (1985, p. 30).
13. Moran (1973, p. 53), Hutt (1973, p. 19).
14. Woods and Bishop (1985, p. 28).
15. Harris (1978, p. 84).
16. Woods and Bishop (1985, p. 18).
17. Woods and Bishop (1985, p. 19).
18. Aspinall ([1949] 1973, p. 9).
19. Moran (1973, pp. 53–54).
20. Moran (1973, p. 52).
21. Rolt and Allen (1977, p. 45).
22. Rolt and Allen (1977, pp. 46–48).
23. Rolt and Allen (1977, p. 64).
24. Mills (1983).
25. Rolt and Allen (1977, pp. 105–106).
26. Dudley (2008, Table 2).
27. Dudley (2008, Table 2).
28. Graff (1991, pp. 192–195).
29. Maddison (2001, p. 247).
30. Bairoch *et al.* (1988).
31. Maddison (2001, pp. 147).
32. Olsen (1999, pp. 179, 182–183).
33. Harris (1978, p. 87).
34. Asquith (1978, p. 100).
35. Cressy (1980, p. 177).
36. Brown (2000, p. 9).
37. Hollis (1996, p. 60).
38. Brown (2000, p. 9).
39. Brown (2000, p. 9).
40. O'Gorman (1982, p. ix).
41. Hollis (1996, p. 61).
42. Kennedy (1987, p. 126).
43. Christie (1982, p. 264).
44. Christie (1982, p. 260).
45. Moran (1973, p. 39).
46. Hutt (1973, p. 36).
47. Hutt (1973, p. 19).
48. Moran (1973, pp. 53–4).
49. Moran (1973, p. 51).
50. Moran (1973, p. 50).
51. Moran (1973, p. 52).
52. Moran (1973, p. 54).
53. Hutt (1973, p. 36).
54. Woods and Bishop (1985, p. 28).
55. Woods and Bishop (1985, p. 216).
56. Sambrook (1973, p. 59).
57. Briggs (1967, pp. 30–31).
58. Sambrook (1973, p. 57).
59. Briggs (1967, p. 30).
60. Smiles (1884).

61. Moran (1973, p. 106), Woods and Bishop (1985, p. 32).
62. Moran (1973, p. 105).
63. Moran (1973, p. 106).
64. Smiles (1884).
65. Smiles (1884).
66. Moran (1973, p. 124), Asquith (1978, p. 101).
67. Williams (1978, p. 47),
68. Brown (2000, p. 136).
69. Sambrook (1973, p. 77).
70. Aspinall ([1949] 1973, p. 37).
71. Aspinall ([1949] 1973, p. 19).
72. Aspinall ([1949] 1973, p. 23).
73. Aspinall ([1949] 1973, pp. 21, 23).
74. Briggs ([1959] 1965, p. 209).
75. Briggs (1967, p. 41).
76. Aspinall ([1949] 1973, p. 57).
77. Williams (1978, p. 46).
78. McCord (1991, pp. 14–15).
79. Aspinall ([1949] 1973, p. 49).
80. Briggs (1967, p. 43).
81. Woods and Bishop (1985, p. 45).
82. Schama (2002, p. 133).
83. Woods and Bishop (1985, p. 28).
84. Woods and Bishop (1985, p. 47).
85. Curran (1978, p. 53).
86. Aspinall ([1949] 1973, p. 58).
87. Sambrook (1973, p. 141).
88. Woods and Bishop (1985, p. 27).
89. Asquith (1978, pp. 100–101).
90. Williams (1978, p. 48).
91. Aspinall ([1949] 1973, p. 28).
92. Aspinall ([1949] 1973, p. 60).
93. Asquith (1978, p. 100).
94. Aspinall ([1949] 1973, p. 28).
95. Woods and Bishop (1985, p. 49).
96. Brown (2000, pp. 138–139).
97. Brown (2000, p. 49).
98. McCord (1991, p. 130).
99. Briggs ([1959] 1965, pp. 240–241).
100. Briggs ([1959] 1965, pp. 252–253).
101. McCord (1991, p. 129).
102. Briggs ([1959] 1965, p. 255).
103. Briggs ([1959] 1965, p. 256).
104. Briggs ([1959] 1965, p. 259).
105. Sambrook (1973, p. 166).
106. Moran (1973, pp. 125–127).
107. Moran (1973, p. 109).
108. Moran (1973, p. 129).
109. Moran (1973, p. 109).
110. Moran (1973, p. 131).
111. Moran (1973, p. 133).
112. O'Gorman (1982, p. 113).
113. O'Gorman (1982, p. 116).
114. Evans (1985, p. 42).
115. O'Gorman (1982, p. 118).
116. Brown (2000, p. 61).

117. O'Gorman (1982, p. 119).
118. Brown (2000, p. 54).
119. Briggs ([1959] 1965, p. 336).
120. Cressy (1980, p. 177).
121. Graff (1991, p. 314).
122. Briggs ([1959] 1965, p. 279).
123. Sambrook (1973, p. 182).
124. Woods and Bishop (1985, p. 54).
125. Asquith (1978, p. 100).
126. Aspinall ([1949] 1973, p. 373).
127. Asquith (1978, p. 100).

# 6. Instant information

From its inception, the American federation had been based on a consensus among the plantation owners of the South and the manufacturers, merchants and free farmers of the North that slavery was an acceptable practice. Implicitly, in return for the South's acceptance of tariff protection against imported manufactures, the North agreed not to interfere with the plantation economy's 'peculiar institution'. Nowhere in the Constitution of 1787 or in the Bill of Rights of 1791 are the words 'slave' or 'slavery' mentioned. However, under Article I, Section 2 of the Constitution, a state's representation in the House of Representatives is to be proportional to the number of free persons plus three-fifths of 'all other persons'. Implicitly, a black slave was worth only 60 per cent as much as a free white.

The initial goal of this interstate alliance had been to win independence from Britain. Subsequently, attention turned to expansion at the expense of the European colonial powers, with the benefits shared between slave and free societies. In Britain and its colonies, slavery was abolished by the reform Parliament of 1833, with slave owners receiving government compensation. However, in the southern United States, the institution of slavery continued to thrive, despite a ban on slave imports since 1808. Then in the 1830s came an invention that would expose the iniquities of slavery to those in the farthest corners of the republic, creating an unbridgeable gap between North and South.

## A PRESIDENTIAL AUDIENCE

The Washington Capitol, seat of the federal legislature of the United States, was built on a hill at the east end of a long strip called the Mall, on territory that the state of Maryland ceded to the federal government in 1790. Pierre L'Enfant, the French architect who planned the city, called the site 'a pedestal waiting for a monument'.[1] Originally the two wings of the Capitol were separate buildings, with the House of Representatives to the south and the Senate to the north. Built with Virginia sandstone, they were completed in 1811. However, during the War of 1812, they were set afire by the British. Charles Bullfinch, the Boston architect who directed the site's restoration after the war, added a central wing with a high wooden copper-covered dome that joined the two earlier structures. By the year 1838, the Capitol on its raised site was an impressive building.

The demonstration of the new invention was to take place in the premises of the House Commerce Committee in the south wing of the Washington Capitol on 21 February 1838. On the appointed day, a vigorous man with flowing hair stood at one end of the committee room. Before him on a table was the transmitting part of his invention, a wooden frame on which were attached a lever, two small cups of mercury and a 'port-rule' consisting of a rod fitted with eleven plates of metal type. The inventor was talking to an energetic younger balding man, explaining how the device worked. At the other end of the room, another young man was anxiously making adjustments to a complementary device, a 'register', made up of an electromagnet that caused a metal stylus to make marks on a roll of paper tape. Between the two instruments, running back and forth along the room, were several miles of insulated wire whose ends were connected to the devices.

The older man with the flowing grey hair was Samuel Morse, 46, a professor of art and design at New York University. He was six feet (183 cm) tall, slender and attractive. Morse had studied at the Royal Academy in London and is considered by some to be the finest portrait painter of his generation.[2] A widower with three children to support, he had been unable to finance himself by his art work and had all but abandoned painting. However, six years earlier, while returning to America aboard the packet ship *Sully* after studying art in France and Italy, he had heard a conversation about the newly discovered electromagnet. It occurred to him that if such a device could be operated from a distance, it might be used to transmit a coded message. All that was required was to attach the magnet to a pen or pencil that could make marks on a moving strip of paper when the electric circuit was opened and closed. Back in New York, he used a homemade battery and the parts of an old clock to build a crude working model of his idea.[3] A university colleague and professor of geology, Leonard Gale, aided him in designing the electric circuit.[4]

The younger bald man talking with Morse was the Commerce Committee Chairman, Francis Ormond Jonathan 'Fog' Smith, 31, a lawyer from Portland Maine. Ten years previously, Smith, as editor of the *Portland Eastern Argus*, had supported Andrew Jackson in his bid for the American presidency. When some older party leaders objected, Smith simply pushed them aside, thereby acquiring a reputation for ruthlessness. He was subsequently elected to the state Senate. He was now in his second term in the House of Representatives. Uncertain of re-election, he was on the alert for possible ways of making his fortune through the contacts he had made in politics. It occurred to him that Morse's telegraph might be just the opportunity he had been seeking.

Suddenly, the door opened and into the room walked the president of the United States, Martin Van Buren, accompanied by members of his cabinet. Barely five feet six inches (168 cm) tall, Van Buren was known as 'The Little Magician' for his skill as organizer of the popular party in the state of New York. Slim and impeccably dressed at age 57, he already had a long and active career in politics behind him. Ten years earlier, he had put together the northern half of the coalition that became the Democratic Party, with Andrew Jackson as its leader. He served as Jackson's first secretary of state and was rewarded for his loyalty by being named as vice president during Jackson's second term of office. Backed by Jackson, he won the Democratic nomination for the presidency in 1836. He then emerged as president when the opposition Whigs split their votes among three candidates.

As Van Buren approached, Morse invited him to suggest a short phrase suitable for transmission. The president whispered his proposal into Morse's ear and the art professor set about consulting a dictionary containing the numbers he had assigned to some 5000 commonly used words. Soon he was ready and began manipulating the 'port-rule' with its bars of type under the lever causing it to move up and down, thereby completing an electrical circuit for short and long periods. Simultaneously, the 'register' at the other end of the room began to move, embossing dots and lines on to the paper tape. When the transmission had ceased, Morse's assistant first translated the code into numbers and then set about looking up the numbers in his copy of the dictionary. When he had finished, he announced the message he had received, 'The enemy is near'. The smile on the president's face confirmed that there had been no error, and the other members of Van Buren's cabinet were equally impressed. As followers of former president Andrew Jackson, the Democratic leaders were proud to see that Americans could progress through their own skills and resources without the intervention of Europeans.

None of the spectators in the room realized that the success of the experiment owed as much to the efforts of the anxious assistant, Alfred Vail, as to those of the distinguished professor. The previous fall, Vail had been present when Samuel Morse had demonstrated his electromagnetic telegraph to colleagues and students at New York University. Vail, 29, had dropped out of divinity studies because of poor health and had met Morse at his boarding house. Morse's device failed to work, but impressed with the professor's powerful personality and by his innovative ideas, Vail offered his services. Three weeks later, Morse, Vail and Leonard Gale, professor of geology at New York University, drew up an agreement that assigned Morse a half interest and his two partners each a quarter interest in the telegraph. Alfred would build at his own expense a commercial model of the invention that could be shown to officials in Washington. All patents were to be taken out in the name of Morse alone and any new discoveries would be credited to the partners in proportion to their rights.

Alfred was one of two sons of Stephen Vail, a prosperous ironmaster in Speedwell, New Jersey, about 25 miles (40 km) west of New York City. The young man immediately began work on the top floor of a factory in Speedwell along with William Baxter, a young apprentice. Alfred's brother George was a silent partner. It soon became evident that Morse's design was impracticable. Working feverishly, Vail made the first of several important contributions to Morse's device. The pencil activated by the current failed to make a uniform set of marks. Vail, a skilled draftsman, designed a register in which a metal stylus when depressed by the passage of current through a magnet left an easily-read mark on a moving tape.

But could the telegraph actually be used to send messages from city to city? Congressman Smith was sufficiently confident that he offered his financial and political backing to Morse. In return, Morse agreed to restructure his partnership so as to give Smith a one-quarter share.[5] Smith then backed a bill that would pay Morse $30 000 to subsidize the construction of a line from Washington to Baltimore. It should be noted that the congressman neglected to mention that he was one of the principals in the venture. The partners hoped that the Post Office would agree to run the telegraph as a public service. Unfortunately, not all members of Congress were as impressed as the president and Congressman Smith had been. Cave Johnson, a Democrat Representative from Tennessee, commented that the proposed appropriation should be divided between experiments in mesmerism and 'that other absurdity'.[6] To make matters worse, Van Buren's term of office coincided with the most severe recession the young republic had known. With revenues from public land sales drying up, the federal budget sank into deficit. The combination of public skepticism and fiscal crisis was enough to cripple Smith's proposal. The bill was defeated.

Nevertheless, Morse remained optimistic. He had already filed for an American patent. With Smith's financial support he made plans for a trip to Europe to apply for British and French rights. In May 1838, he and 'Fog' Smith sailed from New York. However, the British refused Morse's request for a patent on the flimsy pretext that the device had already been described in print in America. And although he was granted a patent in France, the title was of little use since it would lapse unless a line was built within two years. Neither the French private sector nor the public sector proved willing to finance such a project. While in Paris, Morse did meet Louis Daguerre, inventor of photography, and arranged to take this new technology back to the United States.

In May 1839 Morse sailed, penniless, back to the United States. A portrait of the inventor was one of the first photographs taken in the United States.[7] However, Morse was still no nearer his goal of marketing the telegraph device he had invented with Alfred Vail. Fortunately, there was still the American patent application and his partner, Smith, still had the contacts he had built up in Washington.

The America to which Morse returned had changed considerably from the thirteen states that had separated from Britain some sixty years earlier. Although most Americans were probably not aware of it, their Union had coalesced into two very distinct societies, one based on voluntary association and the other on the exploitation of an easily identified minority by an uneasy majority. One of the most articulate witnesses of the striking differences between North and South was a young man from the east shore of the Chesapeake Bay in Maryland.

## BLACK AND WHITE

On the morning of 3 September 1838, some six months after Morse's presidential presentation, a young man slipped on to a crowded railroad car just as it was pulling out of the Baltimore station. Dressed in the clothing of the merchant marine, he could easily have been a sailor returning to his ship in a northern port after visiting his home. Because the young man was black, however, the conductor asked him for his freedom papers. Frederick Bailey replied that he never took this precious document to sea with him. Instead he pulled out a paper which stated that he was a free American sailor. After giving the document a cursory examination, the conductor smiled, collected the fare and passed on. His heart beating rapidly, the young black man put away his borrowed papers and began to count the minutes that remained until he reached freedom in Pennsylvania.

### Frederick Bailey

In 1837, the rapid growth that the American economy had experienced over the half-century since independence had abruptly stopped. Banks collapsed, prices fell sharply and hundreds of thousands were thrown out of work.[8] Yet already the beginnings of another great wave of expansion were emerging. The first railway lines were being built and the powered printing machinery that had spurred the Great Reform in Britain was beginning to be used in the United States. The one dark cloud on the horizon for the young republic was the issue of slavery.

Frederick Bailey was 20 years old, although only his late white master (and possibly his father), Aaron Anthony, had noted his date of birth in 1818. Before his departure for the north, Frederick had been living with a Baltimore shipyard manager, Hugh Auld, who was the brother of his legal owner. When Frederick was eight, Auld's wife Sophia had started to teach him to read. The young boy had proved to be a rapid learner, but when Sophia told her husband of her efforts, Auld was furious. He informed her that in Maryland, it was illegal to teach a slave to read. While Auld was mistaken – there was no such law in Maryland – the lessons stopped. Nevertheless, the boy managed to learn the alphabet on his own with a grammar book that had belonged to his master's son. By the age of 14, Frederick had taught himself to write and to do simple arithmetic.[9]

At about that time, he heard his young white friends reciting passages from a book of famous speeches, *The Columbian Orator*, first published by Caleb Bingham in 1797. The book was reprinted and used in schools throughout the nineteenth century. In one of the essays, 'Dialogue between a Master and a Slave', a master chides a slave who has run away for a second time, accusing him of ingratitude since he has been well treated. The slave replies, 'What have you done, what can you do for me, that will compensate for the liberty that has been taken away?'[10] Frederick was able to buy a second-hand copy of the book and soon memorized the entire passage.

By 1838, the boy had grown into a man, six feet tall, strong and healthy. His master, Auld, eager to supplement his own meager income, hired the young slave out to a shipyard as a caulker (a worker who sealed the joints between wooden planks). There one day he was savagely beaten by young white apprentices who disliked having a black man in their midst. Many other workers had observed the attack, but when Frederick's master attempted to prosecute the youths, he found no witnesses who were willing to testify. Under a Maryland law that dated from colonial times, a black person's testimony could not be used against a white person.[11] Frustrated, Auld found Frederick a job at the yard where he himself worked as foreman.

As for Frederick, although he was not mistreated by his master, he greatly resented having to surrender all of his weekly pay to someone else. In addition, he had come to know a young free black woman who worked as a servant for a wealthy Baltimore family and the two had become engaged. In the spring of 1838, realizing that he needed more resources if he were to marry, Frederick proposed an arrangement with his master. Instead of being obliged to feed and clothe him, Auld would allow the slave to support himself. In return, the young man would pay his master a fixed weekly sum of three dollars. However, one weekend that summer, Frederick was two days late in bringing his payment. His master angrily canceled the agreement.

Realizing that as a slave he had no possibility to better his condition, the young man resolved to try to escape to the North. Three weeks later, with money advanced by his fiancée and identity papers and a sailor's outfit borrowed from a friend who was a retired merchant sailor, Frederick set out for Philadelphia.[12] There he caught another train to carry him farther north. He arrived in New York at one o'clock on the morning of 4 September 1838, with little money, no friends and no job. For the moment, he was free, but at any time under the Fugitive Slave Law of 1793, he could be captured by a slave hunter and forcibly returned to his owner.

## Martin Van Buren

New York was the home state of President Van Buren, who was born in 1782 in the town of Kinderhook, in the Hudson River valley 130 miles (200 km) north of the great port city. He was the son of a prosperous tavern keeper who kept slaves. Indeed when Martin was young, he himself owned a slave named Tom. Although in 1799 New York had passed a law that emancipated children born to slaves, it was only in 1827 that the last slaves in the state were freed. In any case, north of the Mason–Dixon Line that separated Maryland from Pennsylvania, slaves had always been few in number, most of them working as domestic servants. In the 1830s the great majority of black people in the United States lived in the South, where they constituted almost half the population. Over 90 per cent of them were slaves.[13]

Like many other residents of the North, Van Buren accepted slavery as a necessity in order to hold the union together. As a candidate in the period before the 1836 elections, he openly recognized the validity of the Missouri Compromise of 1820. In that year, Congress had approved the entry of Missouri into the union as the twelfth slave state while at the same time allowing Maine to enter as the twelfth free state. Thus the crucial balance between representatives of slave and free states in the Senate was maintained. At the same time, the law stipulated that with the exception of Missouri itself, the southern boundary of that state would henceforth be the northern limit for slavery in the territories west of the Mississippi. As the 1836 campaign proceeded, Van Buren assured southern voters that he supported slavery in those states where it already existed, including the District of Columbia, and that he opposed abolitionism.

Once installed as president, Van Buren had to decide what to do about Texas. When Mexico won its independence from Spain in 1821, its territory included a broad band of land stretching from the western boundary of Louisiana to the Pacific coast. Since the early 1820s, settlers from the southern states had been moving into this territory, many of them with their slaves. In 1835, the American settlers in Texas – the eastern section of this vast region – revolted against Mexico. They managed to defeat a Mexican army at San Jacinto in 1836 and declared themselves an independent country. Texas then applied for admission to the United States. Since the entry of Texas as a slave state would upset the balance between slave and free states (now at thirteen apiece with the recent admission of Arkansas and Michigan), Van Buren refused to approve it.

## Transportation

For most Americans in 1838, Texas was a distant land. The rail link between Baltimore and Wilmington that allowed Frederick Bailey to escape from slavery in September of that year had been completed only the previous year.[14] By the beginning of 1838, fewer than 1500 miles (2400 km) of track had been laid. This track represented less than one per cent of the total rail network that would be in place by the end of the nineteenth century. Although most of the new lines were in the north-east, the longest line was in the south.[15] The 136 miles (218 km) of track of the Carolina Canal and Rail Road Company linked the cotton port of Charleston to the town of Hamburg and intermediate points in the interior.[16]

As yet, the new means of transport had had little impact on the lives of most Americans. The 1830 census shows that the great majority of people still lived in villages or on farms and plantations. In that year, only eight per cent of the population of 13 million resided in towns of 5000 or more.[17] People did not move very far or very often over their lifetimes. For the great majority who did not live close to the new rail lines, transport between distant points was both expensive and time-consuming. Along the coasts or inland on the major rivers, one could travel by steamboat. Linking the river systems, there was a network of newly constructed canals on which passengers could travel by horse-drawn boat at a leisurely 4 miles an hour.[18] In the interior, away from water, travel was by road at about the same speed of 3 to 4 miles an hour.[19]

## Communication

The ten million white Americans in 1830 were possibly the most literate people in the world. American reformers established publicly financed schools modeled on British examples. Unlike the British, however, Americans extended education to all free children. As a result, by the second quarter of the nineteenth century, some 90 per cent of the white population were able to read and write.[20] The main pockets of illiteracy among whites were in rural regions of the South. In Connecticut, only 0.3

per cent of people of European descent were illiterate; in North Carolina, the corresponding figure was 28 per cent.[21]

Most Americans in the 1830s knew little of the world beyond their own county. For slaves, information about the outside world was particularly difficult to obtain. When Frederick Bailey first contemplated running away, at the age of 18, he did not know that there was a state of New York or a state of Massachusetts where slavery was illegal.[22] In the 1830s, the two and one-half million black Americans undoubtedly had the lowest literacy rate of any large group in Western Europe or North America. Early in the country's history, religious or charitable groups had attempted to provide schooling for slaves. Then in 1822, a freed slave named Denmark Vesey planned a revolt by thousands of slaves in the region of Charleston. The city was to be burned and its white inhabitants killed. However, plans for the revolt were discovered and 35 men including Vesey were arrested, tried and hanged. Vesey was inspired by passages from the Old Testament describing how Yahweh had commanded the Israelites to kill the people of Canaan. After this incident, many southern states passed legislation that prohibited the education of slaves. It is estimated that only about five per cent of slaves were able to read.[23]

Although almost all white Americans were literate, the quantity and the quality of reading matter available to them in the 1830s were limited. Newspaper editors tended to wait for the news to come to them, either from copies of the foreign press, from letters or from travelers. Accordingly, the content of newspapers tended to reflect, more than anything else, the opinions of their publishers. In New York State, for example, James Gordon Bennett, publisher of the New York *Herald*, favored the Democratic party.[24] In the state capital, Thurlow Weed, founder of the *Albany Evening Journal*, backed the opposition Whigs.

Prior to 1850, the average circulation of American daily newspapers was under 1000 copies. In the early 1830s, there were about 200 daily papers, all printed on hand presses.[25] In 1835, Benjamin Day's New York *Sun* was the first American paper to begin printing on a steam press. Instead of political issues, his paper concentrated on sensational reports of local violence and crime.

In the presidential campaign of 1840, there was very little to distinguish the two main parties. The Democrats nominated Martin Van Buren, the incumbent. The Whigs, a coalition of local interest groups, differed little in policy from their opponents. Instead, they decided to focus on personality. They nominated William Henry Harrison, 67, who almost four decades earlier had defeated an Indian alliance under Tecumseh at the battle of Tippecanoe, Indiana. When the Democrats criticized Harrison's drinking, the Whigs portrayed Van Buren as an aristocratic dandy who drank from a silver cup. In contrast, they posed Harrison in front of a log cabin with a barrel of cider. As his running mate, the Whigs chose John Tyler of Virginia. The Whigs won with the slogan, 'Tippecanoe and Tyler too'. The participation rate in the election was 80 per cent, an all-time high. Harrison died a month after his inauguration, to be succeeded by Tyler.

Frederick Bailey quickly learned that New York City was a dangerous place for escaped slaves since slave catchers kept a watch on boarding houses where blacks stayed. Fortunately, he discovered that there were people trying to help runaways. David Ruggles, a member of the New York Vigilance Committee took Frederick in and arranged for his fiancée Anna to come north. Ruggles then suggested that the young man take up a job as a caulker in the shipbuilding town of New Bedford, Massachusetts. There Frederick changed his last name to Douglass after James Douglas, the principal character in Sir Walter Scott's poem, *The Lady of the Lake*.

In August 1841, almost three years after his escape from Maryland, Frederick Douglass was invited to attend the annual meeting of the Massachusetts branch of the American Anti-Slavery Society in Nantucket. Founded by William Lloyd Garrison, the group attempted to persuade people to abandon slavery through public lectures and through their newspaper, *The Liberator*. A pacifist, Garrison opposed slave uprisings. He also forbade his followers to use the political system since, as we have already noted, the American constitution implicitly recognized slavery.

After a long evening with many speakers, Douglass finally summoned the courage to speak. He stammered confusedly at first, but once he started telling his story the words began to flow. The New England audience sat spellbound as he described his experience growing up under slavery and how he had finally run away. After hearing Douglass speak, Garrison rose and asked his audience whether such a man should be sent back to bondage. The assembly rose, crying, 'No! No! No!' Shortly thereafter, Garrison offered Frederick a position as a lecturer traveling with other anti-slavery speakers to raise money for his cause.

For the next four years, Douglass would be on the lecture circuit with Garrison and his associates. Although a vociferous minority of Northerners was opposed to slavery, the vast majority either approved of it or passively accepted its presence in the South. As long as most residents of the North lived in small isolated agricultural communities, there was little likelihood that this situation would change.

## WHAT HATH GOD WROUGHT!

In 1840 Samuel Morse's luck finally turned. Back in the United States once again, he was awarded an American patent in June of that year. All that remained was to convince Congress to grant him the required subsidy. The Whigs who controlled the Congress elected in the fall drew much of their support from the wealthier landowners and businessmen, both in the North and the South. Accordingly, they were more favorable to subsidizing internal improvements than the Democrats had been. Morse was helped by a letter of support from the distinguished scientist Joseph Henry of the College of New Jersey (now Princeton University) and by the contacts of his associate, former congressman F.O.J. 'Fog' Smith. Finally, the House approved the project in February 1843. The Senate passed the bill on 3 March of that year. The same day President Tyler signed the bill into law, authorizing $30 000 to be spent to construct a 41-mile (66 km) line between Washington and Baltimore.

With this infusion of funds, Morse was able to reactivate his partnership with F.O.J. Smith and Alfred Vail.[26] Morse insisted that the line be buried in underground pipes. Smith contracted a young engineer, Ezra Cornell, to carry out the digging with a machine that Cornell had invented.[27] However, after 9 miles (15 km) of wire and pipe had been laid and $23 000 spent, it was discovered that the insulation was faulty. Morse had been so involved in his financial and political problems that he had paid little attention to the technical feasibility of his project.

**Vail's Contributions**

The telegraph system that Samuel Morse had demonstrated to President Van Buren and Congressman Smith in 1838 had several important defects. Perhaps most serious was the necessity of two separate codes, one attributing a number between one and 5000 to each commonly used word from a standard dictionary, and the second consisting of combinations of long and short impulses that permitted the digits of the given number to be transmitted electronically. Aside from the high risk of error with two separate translations, the system did not offer a practical means of sending proper nouns, such as the names of people, towns and firms.

Actually, at the time of the Washington demonstration in 1838, Samuel Morse and Alfred Vail had already discovered a solution to this problem. Shortly after the development of the register (the receiving device that embossed long and short marks on paper) by Vail, the two partners conceived a means of eliminating the first step in Morse's original coding system.[28] Combinations of dots and dashes could be used directly to represent letters of the alphabet.[29] There would be no need to translate words into numbers. The most frequently used letters would have the shortest codes; for example 'e' was a single dot, while 'k' was dash-dot-dash.[30] To estimate the relative need to transmit each letter, according to one account,

Alfred made a trip to the office of the local newspaper in nearby Morristown, New Jersey. The size of the compositor's type cases showed the frequency of use of each letter in the English language.[31]

It was Vail who later found the most practical means of sending the signals over a long distance. He learned that Cooke and Wheatstone, the English inventors of a similar electric telegraph, had begun using wires hung from posts instead of buried lines. Accordingly, Morse and his partners switched to stringing the wire on poles along the track of the Baltimore and Ohio Railroad. As construction progressed, Vail followed the workers with a transmitter and register, communicating with Morse in Washington periodically to verify that the line was functioning.

Yet another problem with Morse's original system was that his port-rule transmitter, by which bumps on pieces of metal type caused an electric contact to be closed and opened, was extremely cumbersome and slow. To replace it, Vail developed a device that worked, as he described it, 'in much the same manner as a key closes a door'. By simply pressing on a lever, the operator closed an electric circuit. A spring caused the circuit of this telegraph key to reopen when pressure was released. By holding the circuit for a short or long interval, one could send a dot or a dash. Vail's register at the other end of the line provided a permanent record of the coded message, but he quickly discovered that an experienced operator could learn to translate the incoming code by ear.

On 24 May 1844, there was a formal ceremony in the chamber of the Supreme Court in Washington to celebrate the opening of the first American telegraph line. Annie Elsworth, daughter of the patent commissioner, chose a biblical passage from Numbers 23, 'What hath God wrought!' Morse tapped the symbols on his key. Meanwhile, in Baltimore, Vail recognized the letters being embossed virtually simultaneously on to his tape drive. He then removed the wedge from his key and tapped the message back to Morse.[32] The quotation was appropriate because none of those participating could possibly conceive of the social impact of instantly available information.

## An Emerging Network

Two days after the first formal message, the Democratic National Convention met in Baltimore to choose the party's candidates for the forthcoming presidential election. The delegates chose a dark-horse candidate, James Polk, former speaker of the house and governor of Tennessee, on the ninth ballot. They then approved Silas Wright, a senator from New York, for the vice-presidency. However, only a few minutes later the delegates were amazed to receive a telegraphed message from Wright, who declined the nomination. Suspecting a hoax, the disbelieving convention sent a committee to Washington to confirm the message. There the committee members learned that Wright had indeed declined, preferring to run as candidate for governor in his home state. They duly wired their report back to Baltimore and the convention subsequently chose another running mate for Polk.[33]

Despite the publicity given to this event, interest in the telegraph for commercial purposes was initially disappointing. Morse, Gale and Vail hoped to sell the rights to the telegraph system to the Post Office. But the conditions that the government offered proved unacceptable to their partner, 'Fog' Smith, who wanted the lucrative rights to any construction contracts. When Congress adjourned in 1844 without settling the question, the partners turned to the private sector. Morse and his two closest allies entered into an agreement with Amos Kendall, the former postmaster general. In May 1845, Kendall organized the Magnetic Telegraph Company to build a line from Washington to New York. Later in the year, under an agreement with Kendall, Smith formed his own company, the New York & Boston Telegraph Association, to build lines from New York into New England.[34] By the end of 1846, the lines reached from Washington to Boston.

Once this initial section had been completed, the pace of construction accelerated as other groups formed to build lines using patent rights purchased from Morse's group. John Butterfield of Utica built a line from New York to Albany and Buffalo by the end of 1846. Henry O'Rielly built lines to Cincinnati, Louisville and St Louis in 1847. And a group headed by Amos Kendall completed a line from Washington to New Orleans through Richmond, Charleston, Montgomery and Mobile by the end of 1848.[35] Still other lines were built using competing technologies.

By 1851, there were over 50 different telegraph companies with 25 000 miles (40 000 km) of lines functioning in the United States, 80 per cent of them using the Morse technology.[36] In that year Hiram Sibley and Samuel L. Selden of Rochester, New York founded the New York and Mississippi Valley Printing Telegraph Company to exploit the rights to an alternative technology developed by Royal E. House of Vermont. Their firm soon began to take over competing firms in the Midwest. In 1854, the Supreme Court upheld Morse's patents on the telegraph, forcing all firms to pay him royalties. The Rochester firm converted to the Morse technology and two years later changed its name to the Western Union Telegraph Company. Similar consolidation occurred elsewhere. Morse's Magnetic Telegraph Company was merged into the American Telegraph Company in 1859.[37] By 1861, there were six large regional systems cooperating with one another and with the remaining small companies.[38]

## The Demand for News

Apart from local events, most of the news reported by American newspapers in 1845 was days or weeks old. In that year, a regular steamer service began between Liverpool and Boston.[39] An enterprising information gatherer, Daniel Craig, arranged to board the ship with carrier pigeons when it stopped in Halifax. Then as the ship approached Boston, he would release the pigeons laden with news from the porthole of his cabin. The local papers that had contracted for his services received the latest news from England hours before the ship docked. Even so it took from ten days to two weeks for news from Europe to reach the east coast.[40]

A dramatic change in the public's demand for news occurred during the Mexican War. Under the Missouri Compromise of 1820, slavery in the northwestern territories acquired under the Louisiana Purchase was forbidden north of the southern border of Missouri. Therefore the only way for southern slave owners to increase the territory open to them was through expansion into the southwest. Beyond Louisiana was the independent republic of Texas and further lay Mexican territory through to California. During the 1844 presidential election campaign, Polk proposed annexation not only of Texas but also of Oregon. He found strong support in both North and South and was able to win a close election. However, before he could take office, the outgoing president, John Tyler, a slave owner from Virginia, staged a fait accompli. On 1 March 1844, he was able to sign a joint resolution of the House and Senate admitting Texas to the Union. Immediately, Mexico broke off relations with the US. In July, a Texas convention duly voted to join the Union.

In that same month, an American journalist, John O'Sullivan, published an editorial in the *United States Magazine and Democratic Review* proclaiming that it was the 'manifest destiny' of the United States to expand its territory across the continent. With strong popular support for expansion, Polk in the fall of 1845 sent a representative to Mexico to negotiate the purchase of California and New Mexico. However, the Mexican government refused to receive him. To increase the pressure on the Mexicans, Polk ordered an American expeditionary force under Zachary Taylor to move into territory disputed by Texas and Mexico between the Nueces River and the Rio Grande farther south. Texas was then admitted to the Union in December 1845. In the spring of 1846, shortly after a Mexican declaration of defensive war, there was a skirmish between Mexican and American forces. Polk submitted a declaration of war which Congress approved by a large majority.

During the course of 1846, Taylor's forces fought and routed the Mexicans in a series of battles along the Rio Grande. In 1847, General

Winfield Scott opened up a second front, staging an amphibious landing on the Gulf coast and capturing the city of Veracruz. Scott then led his army inland toward Mexico City. One of the key battles was at Cerro Gordo, 55 miles (88 km) from the coast, where the Mexican commander, Antonio López de Santa Anna, had established a strong position blocking a pass through the mountains. A young captain of engineers, Robert E. Lee, discovered a trail to the enemy's rear, enabling the Americans to destroy the Mexican artillery positions. Second Lieutenant Ulysses S. Grant also participated in the battle and was later commended by Lee in one of his reports.[41]

With the outbreak of war with Mexico in April 1846, there was a sudden demand for rapid news from the areas of fighting along the Rio Grande. Regular mail from New Orleans to New York took seven days. Could the press reduce this time? The New York *Sun* and the Charleston *Courier* arranged a pony express costing $750 a trip to connect with the telegraph at Richmond, Virginia. Using a similar system, the Philadelphia *Ledger* and the Baltimore *Sun* managed to cut 30 hours from the mail's time.[42] In the first two weeks of 1848, when Congress was debating the terms of a treaty with Mexico, the New York *Herald* and its correspondents sent 79 000 words by telegraph, at a cost of $2381. Although other newspapers shared part of this amount, two-thirds of it was absorbed entirely by the *Herald*.[43]

By the spring of 1848, the Mexican War was over. Defeated along their northern border and with their capital under American occupation, the Mexican leaders were forced to come to terms. In return for 15 million dollars, Mexico ceded virtually all the territory comprising the present states of California, Arizona, New Mexico, Utah and Texas. During the war, the American press had learned that the public had a voracious appetite for detailed reports of distant conflicts that concerned them directly. They quickly found that the paper which was first to print the news sold the most copies. Fortunately, there were many other stories developing to hold their interest. In that year political revolution was spreading across continental Europe, a US presidential election lay ahead and gold had been discovered in California.

Newspaper publishers had also learned how costly the gathering of news was, even when two papers shared the expense. Typically it might cost $0.25 – a quarter of a man's daily wage – to send ten words by telegraph over a distance of 100 miles.[44] In May 1848, at the invitation of David Hale of the *Journal of Commerce*, the publishers of New York's six major newspapers met in the offices of the New York *Sun*. Hale reminded them of the cost and difficulties of obtaining news by telegraph. For example, to receive reports from Washington, all papers relied on the single line of the

Magnetic Telephone Company which reached only to the New Jersey shore of the Hudson River. There the operator read the dispatches aloud to each paper's representative while eavesdroppers listened in. Hale proposed that each of the six papers contribute to a general fund that would finance the coverage of news stories from around the world for their mutual benefit.

Shortly after this meeting, the group arranged for news from incoming ships to be telegraphed from Boston along the line of F. O. J. Smith.[45] The following month, the papers also jointly chartered a steamer christened the *Newsboy* to meet the ships arriving in New York harbor from Europe. In both cases, a single dispatch would be shared by all members.[46] As similar groups were subsequently formed by newspapers in New England and the Middle Atlantic states, the New York group in 1858 identified itself with the designation, New York Associated Press.[47]

Over the decades between 1830 and 1860 there was phenomenal growth in the sales of American newspapers. In 1833, no American paper had a circulation greater than 5000. However, by 1860, the New York *Herald* was selling 77 000 copies a day – more than any other daily in the world.[48] Between 1850 and 1860, the total circulation of American dailies doubled, reaching 1.5 million copies a day.[49]

The stability that the American federation had enjoyed over its first six decades was based on a fundamental asymmetry of information. In the early 1830s, few southern blacks knew that north of the Mason–Dixon Line there was an alternative society where all people were equal before the law. And few northern whites were aware of the degrading conditions endured by southern slaves. By the early 1850s, however, with the growth of newspaper circulation and the extension of telegraph lines, this asymmetry was rapidly disappearing. The effects of this information restructuring on American society would be profound.

## THE DISINTEGRATION OF CONSENSUS

The note said, 'Two weary people here; need transportation in the morning'. It was brought to the Porter house in Rochester by one of Frederick Douglass's children and signed, 'D.F.', the father's inverted initials. Samuel Porter, a wealthy businessman and abolitionist, immediately understood that two escaped slaves were staying at the Douglass house, some 2 miles (3 km) south of town. At dawn the next day, he sent a wagon to carry the refugees to the town's port on the Genesee River. From there, they were taken by boat across Lake Ontario to Canada and freedom. In the British Empire, slavery had been abolished two decades earlier, but in 1852 the institution was more heavily protected by American law in the

United States than ever before. Those like Douglass and Porter who supported the Underground Railroad, helping runaway slaves to escape, did so at considerable risk to their own well-being.

## The *North Star*

Seven years earlier, in 1845, Frederick Douglass had published a written version of his fiery autobiographical lectures under the title, *Narrative of the Life of Frederick Douglass*. The book was an immediate best-seller on both sides of the Atlantic. Within five years, 30 000 copies had been sold.[50] However, Douglass learned that because of his new fame, he was in danger of being captured and sent back to Maryland as a slave.[51] The book's success in Britain suggested to Garrison and the leaders of the American Anti-Slavery Society that it was time to send Douglass abroad. For almost two years, from the fall of 1845 until the spring of 1847, Douglass was away from the United States, in England, Scotland and Ireland, lecturing to raise money for the abolition of slavery. During his stay abroad, Douglass made new friends in England who arranged for the purchase of his freedom. They also raised £500 to help him start a newspaper expressing the point of view of blacks.[52]

In the fall of 1847, Garrison learned that Douglass was moving to Rochester in order to launch his own newspaper. Garrison wished his protégé well in a *Liberator* message, but announced regretfully that the latter's position as a lecturer for the Society was being terminated.[53] Fortunately, Douglass's move to upper New York State received the support of Gerritt Smith, a wealthy philanthropist living in Peterboro, just outside Syracuse.[54] Douglass and two associates were able to publish the first issue of the *North Star* on 3 December 1847.[55] The masthead announced, 'The object of the North Star will be to attack slavery in all its forms and aspects'.[56] Although subscription receipts barely covered printing costs, Douglass was able to finance it from private donations and from his income as a public speaker.

Thanks to the telegraph and railroad, an editorial writer in a small town in upstate New York could now be as well informed on the great issues of the day as a decision maker in Washington. Douglass used his new platform to comment on the news as it affected the cause of abolition. As a result of the Mexican War, the United States had acquired vast new territories south of the southern border of Missouri. The great question was whether slavery would be allowed in the new states to be formed there. Southerners were angry when it was proposed that California and New Mexico be admitted immediately, as most of their residents favored free soil. To compensate them, Henry Clay, one of the promoters of the Missouri Compromise of

1820, proposed a new law to reinforce the old Fugitive Slave Act of 1793. Under the former Act, states were not obliged to enforce the return of runaway slaves. Every year, some 200 to 300 slaves were now escaping to the North.[57] However, under the new bill, passed by Congress in the fall of 1850, a new federal officer was created, a 'federal commissioner', who could decide whether an alleged fugitive should be sent back. Moreover, northern citizens could be deputized to help capture such fugitives. 'Under this law', criticized Douglass, 'the oaths of any two villains (the capturer and the claimant) are sufficient to confine a free man to slavery for life.'[58]

It was becoming clear to Douglass that the growing number of people opposed to slavery should act through the American political system to bring about a peaceful solution to the problem. In the spring of 1851, he therefore broke rank with his mentor, William Garrison. An article in the *North Star* announced a change of opinion to a position favoring the American constitution. Douglass argued that this document should be made consistent with its preamble and 'wielded in behalf of emancipation'.[59] He merged his *North Star* with an abolitionist paper of Gerrit Smith to form a new weekly, *Frederick Douglass' Paper*.

For the first few years, under the Whigs, the new Fugitive Slave Law was enforced sparingly and opposition to it gradually died down. Then in 1854, the new Democratic administration of Franklin Pierce started to apply the law with great vigor. A case that infuriated many moderates in the North involved Anthony Burns, a slave who worked in Richmond, Virginia. In March 1854, Burns boarded a ship and fled to Boston. However, his owner intercepted a letter from Burns to his brother back in Virginia and traveled to Boston to claim his property. When Burns was arrested, an abolitionist mob attempted to break into the courthouse where he was being held. The administration was forced to call in the marines to assist the federal marshals. Burns was tried and shipped back to Virginia on a federal ship. It may have cost the government as much as $100 000 to apply the law in this single case.[60]

## Bleeding Kansas

Not all northerners were opposed to the extension of slavery. In 1854, Senator Stephen Douglas, a Democrat from Illinois, submitted a bill to organize the territory immediately to the west of Missouri into two new states, Kansas in the south and Nebraska to the north. Although both lay to the north of the southern border of Missouri, slavery would be allowed if their residents by 'popular sovereignty' so decided. On 30 May, a coalition of Democrats and Whigs from the South backed by northern Democrats approved the legislation.

Senator Douglas's immediate intention was to promote a railroad from Chicago to the west coast. However, the effect of his measure was to destroy the two-party system that had existed since the 1820s. The Whig party broke apart, while many northern Democrats opposed to the extension of slavery also abandoned their party. Over the next two years, northern dissidents from both parties came together to form a new grouping, the Republican Party, that was opposed to the extension of slavery. A prominent organizer of the new party in his home state of Illinois was Abraham Lincoln, a successful lawyer and former Whig member of Congress.

Meanwhile, free-soil and proslavery settlers were rushing into Kansas, where abolitionist groups from the East helped finance antislavery communities in Topeka and Lawrence. At the same time, proslavery settlements sprang up at Atchison and Leavenworth. In March 1855, on the eve of elections for a territorial legislature, groups of heavily armed 'Border Ruffians' rode into the territory from neighboring Missouri. Few of them were slave owners, but they had no desire to have free blacks or abolitionists as neighbors. They stuffed ballot boxes and intimidated those opposed to slavery, preventing them from voting. Although there were only 2905 registered voters, 6307 ballots were cast.[61] As a result, proslavery representatives dominated the new legislature at Pawnee. Later in the year, free-soil forces in turn elected their own legislature at Topeka. Only a minority of the free-soilers supported abolition; however, they feared that the extension of slavery would deprive white settlers of homesteads.

On 21 May 1856, a posse of proslavery men, many from Missouri, entered the town of Lawrence with orders to arrest the leaders of the free-soil government. They proceeded to burn the town's hotel, loot several houses and destroy two newspaper offices. Three days later, a band of free-soilers led by John Brown, a fervent 56-year-old abolitionist from Connecticut, launched a reprisal attack. They raided three cabins in a community of proslavery settlers at Pottawatomie Creek and killed five men. Brown's men slaughtered four of their victims with swords in order to avoid alerting the other residents by a discharge of firearms.[62]

There followed some four months of guerrilla warfare between proslavery and antislavery forces in eastern Kansas in which some 55 people died, including one of John Brown's sons.[63] It took the arrival of a new governor in September and additional federal troops to restore order. After several proslavery constitutions were rejected by the US Congress, a free-state constitution was finally approved by a state convention in 1859. However, southern representatives in the US Senate blocked the admission of the state into the Union.

John Brown remained convinced that violence was justified to bring an end to slavery. In December 1856 and again in January 1858, he visited the house of Frederick Douglass in Rochester to persuade him to support his projects.[64] Brown planned to set up a separate state in the mountains of western Virginia where fugitive slaves could find refuge. From there, he would attack slaveholders. By the early fall of 1859, however, these plans had changed. Brown was then living outside Chambersburg, Pennsylvania, directly north of the federal arsenal at Harpers Ferry, Virginia. Douglass, visiting him there at Brown's request, learned that Brown planned to raid the arsenal and use its arms to equip a slave uprising. Dismayed, Douglass warned Brown that he would be 'going into a perfect steel trap, and that once in he would not get out alive'.[65]

Despite Douglass's refusal to support him, Brown launched his raid on Harpers Ferry on the night of 16 October 1859. His little band of five blacks and 17 whites captured the arsenal and a nearby rifle factory. However, early the next day, they were surrounded by the local militia. Marines under the command of Colonel Robert E. Lee arrived later in the day and stormed the fire engine house where the raiders had barricaded themselves. When the fighting was over, ten men of Brown's group, including two of his sons, were dead. Brown was arrested, tried for treason and convicted. On his way to the scaffold, he warned his countrymen that he was 'certain that the crimes of this guilty land will never be purged but with blood'.[66]

A year after the Harpers Ferry Raid, in November 1860, Abraham Lincoln, the candidate of the antislavery Republican Party, was elected president of the United States. Although the Republicans had promised to respect slavery where it already existed, in December, a South Carolina state convention voted to secede from the union. By February, six other southern states had joined South Carolina to form the Confederate States of America. Meanwhile, supplies were running out in the federal fort of Fort Sumter on an island that controlled access to the key cotton port of Charleston.

Lincoln was faced with a dilemma. Thanks in part to the development of the press, Northerners and Southerners now realized that their societies were distinct and incompatible. Compromise was unacceptable to both. If the president did nothing, there was the risk that North Carolina and the slave-owning Border States – Virginia, Tennessee, Kentucky, Missouri, Maryland and Delaware – would join the Confederacy. Together, these states would form a dangerous rival power to the free states of the North. If, however, the federal government moved to defend Fort Sumter, there would almost certainly be war, with the North viewed as the aggressor. As a result, Lincoln could easily lose the support not only of the Border States but also of the European powers and large numbers of Northerners.

There was a third possibility. If the North moved to send food to the besieged fort and the Confederacy blocked the relieving fleet, the South would be seen as the aggressor. Most of the Border States would hesitate to rebel. The North, with its great resources, could not lose a vigorously prosecuted attack on the seceding states. Once the war had been brought to a quick end, slavery could be abolished with compensation to the former owners, as in Britain in 1833. Resupplying Fort Sumter was therefore a pre-emptive strategy to take the initiative away from the Confederacy while bringing an end to slavery in the only way feasible.

Against the advice of his commander-in-chief and the majority of his cabinet, Lincoln decided to send a relief expedition by sea to supply the federal fort.[67] On 12 April 1861, shortly before the supply fleet was due to reach the fort, Confederate guns opened fire. Under a withering fire, the fort was forced to surrender the following day. When Lincoln called for volunteers to preserve the Union, four other states including Virginia joined the Confederacy. The Civil War had begun.

## THE PURSUIT OF PRE-EMPTION

The Washington Capitol had been transformed since the presidency of Martin Van Buren. In order to provide offices for the representatives of the new states that had entered the Union since the 1830s, both the north and south wings of the great building had been extended. In keeping with the enlarged structure, it had been decided to replace the old wooden dome with a larger stone and cast-iron crown topped with a bronze Statue of Freedom. However, when war broke out, the project was only partially completed. By the evening of 30 August 1862, revisions to the dome to accommodate the heavy 20 foot (6 m) statue had still not been completed.[68]

Earlier that evening President Lincoln had joined his war secretary Edwin Stanton and his pretty wife for supper at their home. On his way back to the White House, Lincoln dropped by the War Department to get the latest news from the front. He had spent most of the two preceding days in the Department's telegraph office, following the reports as they arrived and were decoded.[69] It was a room that he knew well, since he had also spent many hours in July of that year working in the quiet of the cipher office to prepare a draft proclamation of emancipation. For months he had been under pressure from northern leaders, including Frederick Douglass, the black orator, Horace Greeley, publisher of the New York *Tribune*, and Salmon Chase, his own Treasury secretary, to free the slaves in the rebelling states.[70] All that he needed now in order to announce his decision was a military victory that would convince anti-abolitionists in the Border States that it was in their interest to remain in the Union.

Lincoln was having problems in bringing the great resource advantage of the North to bear on the rebellious southern states. West of the Appalachians, the war was going well for the Union. General Ulysses S. Grant had succeeded in capturing two forts commanding the Tennessee and Cumberland Rivers and in fighting the Confederates to a draw at Shiloh, Tennessee. However, in the East, there were continual problems coordinating the movements of two armies sent to converge on the rebel capital of Richmond, Virginia. Most recently, McClellan's lethargy in withdrawing the Army of the Potomac from the James River peninsula left Pope's new Army of Virginia to the north of the Confederate capital temporarily exposed to attack from the entire force of Confederate commander General Robert Lee. Indeed, only four days earlier, Thomas 'Stonewall' Jackson's Confederate corps had penetrated behind Pope's line to destroy the federal supply base at Manassas. Now the two armies were engaged in a mortal struggle that would be known as the Second Battle of Bull Run.

Shortly before eight pm, Lincoln received news: there had been a disastrous Union defeat. As a result, the remains of Pope's army would be forced to retreat to the fortresses around Washington. With the Union on the defensive, emancipation would have to be postponed. And the way now lay open for Lee to attack the North.

## Antietam Creek

From the outset of the war, the North had been forced to adopt an offensive strategy in order to coerce the South back into the Union. Operating on external lines, Lincoln's generals had attempted to isolate the south from the rest of the world. They had then attempted gradually to weaken the seceding states by blockading southern ports and capturing key positions along their border. The northern press had dubbed this approach the Anaconda Plan.[71] In contrast, the South, with less territory and less manpower than the North, had prudently adopted a defensive strategy. For a year and a half, Confederate commanders had shifted their troops along internal lines as required to meet uncoordinated attacks from the North. While the southern strategy had thus far been highly successful, it was coming under increasing criticism as the conflict dragged on. So far, almost all of the major battles in the war had been fought on southern territory, with the result that northern Virginia had been badly ravaged by armies on both sides. Moreover, with fewer resources, the South had little hope of winning a war of attrition. A Richmond newspaper noted that one fourth of the Southern soldiers were barefooted and half were 'as ragged as scarecrows'.[72]

In early September 1862, Lee therefore decided to gamble by going on the offensive. He would invade the North, allowing his army to live off the land for a month in the rich farming country of southern Pennsylvania. Crossing through Maryland, he hoped to be able to recruit southern sympathizers. In addition, he reasoned, a southern victory on northern soil might lead European powers to recognize the Confederacy diplomatically. Dividing his army of 55 000 in two, he sent one corps across the Potomac into Maryland while a second corps secured his supply lines to the south by attacking Harpers Ferry on the Virginia side of the river.[73] Meanwhile, Lincoln had appointed McClellan to command a reunited Army of the Potomac. With 80 000 troops under him, he was guardedly searching for Lee. Then on 13 September, two federal soldiers found a copy of Lee's marching orders wrapped around three cigars near Frederick, Maryland.[74] Suddenly, McClellan possessed the information required to defeat the southern army decisively. Lee's two corps, separated by some 20 miles, could be destroyed.

Instead of reacting immediately, McClellan waited for 18 hours in order to draw up detailed battle plans.[75] On 15 September, units of Union troops came across the bulk of Lee's army camped at Sharpsburg, Maryland, between the Potomac and one of its small subsidiaries, the Antietam Creek. However, it was not until two days later, on 17 September, that McClellan was at last ready to attack. During the interval, Lee was able to bring up many of the units that had been besieging Harpers Ferry. With the two sides evenly matched in fighting capacity, the ensuing battle saw the bloodiest day of fighting in US military history. A total of 5000 soldiers were killed, 18 000 wounded and 2000 missing.[76] Although these losses were evenly divided between the two armies, the smaller southern army suffered proportionately more. The Army of Northern Virginia could only limp back across the Potomac to lick its wounds. Lee had gambled and lost, but McLellan's hesitancy to pursue undoubtedly postponed Confederate defeat by many months.

## Emancipation

Emancipation of slaves in the southern states had been unthinkable as federal government policy on 4 March 1861, when Abraham Lincoln took office. In his inaugural address, he had assured Southerners that he would respect their property rights, including, implicitly, the right to own slaves. He even announced his endorsement of the Fugitive Slave Law.[77] However, he also declared that the Union was indestructible, that secession was illegal and that he would enforce the constitution.[78]

Once war had broken out, the situation concerning slavery changed. For many northern members of the Union Congress, slaves in the seceding states must be considered the property of the enemy and therefore subject to possible seizure. In the First Confiscation Act of August 1861, Congress voted to free slaves whose owners had been using them in the Confederate war effort. In practice, the law proved virtually impossible to enforce.[79] The Second Confiscation Act of July 1862 declared free the slaves of those who participated in the rebellion. However, without presidential enforcement, it too would have little effect.[80] One congressional measure that did have effect was the immediate abolition of slavery in the District of Columbia in April 1862. Slave owners would be compensated, and a colonization fund was set up to assist those blacks who desired to settle outside the United States.

The changing attitude of the president and Congress to slavery reflected a shift in the views of millions of readers of the press. This new political force – public opinion – expressed itself principally through newspaper editorials and letters to the editor. Although the Democratic newspapers such as James Gordon Bennett's New York *Herald* generally supported the president's war effort, they were opposed to emancipation.[81] Many of their readers feared the consequences of allowing millions of freed blacks to compete for jobs held by whites. Most Republican editors, such as the New York *Tribune*'s Horace Greeley, had initially agreed that the purpose of the war was not to eliminate slavery. However, by the summer of 1862, their opinion was changing. Greeley published an open letter to the president, 'The Prayer of Twenty Millions', calling for an immediate end to slavery.[82] As for Frederick Douglass, in his new publication, *Douglass's Monthly*, he had been sharply critical of Lincoln for enforcing the Fugitive Slave Law. He also insisted that blacks be allowed to enlist. Addressing a largely black audience early in 1862, he had called for striking the rebels 'with the iron hand of the black man'.[83]

McClellan's qualified victory at Antietam gave Lincoln the occasion for which he had been waiting. On 22 September 1862, he used his powers as commander in chief to issue a Preliminary Emancipation Proclamation. The following 1 January, said the declaration, the slaves in any territory occupied by the armies of the rebellious states would be forever free. However, in any state willing to abolish slavery, slave owners would be compensated. The announcement carefully omitted emancipation of slaves in the Border States and in parts of the Confederate States occupied by Union armies.[84] In the fall congressional elections, although the Democrats made considerable gains in the House of Representatives, the Republicans maintained their control of Congress. Lincoln could finally dismiss McClellan as commanding general for his failure to attack Lee's army.

When no southern state offered to come to terms, Lincoln proceeded with the Emancipation Proclamation as scheduled on 1 January 1863.

Although most editorialists were unenthusiastic, liberal newspapers such as *Harper's Weekly* applauded the Proclamation.[85] As Lincoln later remarked, 'it is the central act of my administration, and the great event of the nineteenth century'.[86] On the day of the Proclamation, there were celebrations by blacks in cities across the north and in southern towns occupied by Union armies. A new clause that had not been in the Preliminary Proclamation was a promise to recruit freed slaves into the armed forces of the Union. In May 1864, the War Department set up a bureau to form 138 infantry regiments that were known as the United States Colored Troops.[87]

## External Lines

As 1864 – a year of presidential elections – opened, Abraham Lincoln was deeply worried. Not since Andrew Jackson in 1832 had a sitting president been re-elected. Even Republican Party supporters were asking why, after almost three years of bitter fighting, the 20 million citizens of the North had not been able to defeat the five million whites of the South.[88] Many northern Democrats were opposed to emancipation. Among these anti-Republican Copperheads – so called for the pennies many wore around their necks to protest federal banking policy – were Samuel Morse and his partner in the development of the telegraph, F.O.J. 'Fog' Smith.

There was a great demand for news from the various fronts. The largest newspaper, the New York *Herald*, had over 30 reporters in the field with Union armies, sending reports by telegraph from distant battle sites.[89] During the previous year, the Union war effort in the East had stagnated. A second invasion of the North by Lee had been blocked at Gettysburg, Pennsylvania, but Union armies had failed in their pursuit and the Confederate army of Northern Virginia was still intact as a formidable fighting force. Admittedly, the Union had been quite successful in the West. Under Ulysses S. Grant, the border cities of Vicksburg on the Mississippi River and Chattanooga on the Tennessee River had fallen.

There were rumors now that both the Democrats and Lincoln's own Republicans were courting the North's most successful general as their presidential candidate. It took a letter from General Grant assuring the president that he had no presidential ambitions before Lincoln finally appointed him to be commanding general of the Union armies in March 1864. From the moment Grant assumed supreme command, it became obvious that his strategy differed radically from that of his predecessors. Unlike Scott and Halleck, he refused to take an office in Washington where he would be cut off from developments in the field. He set up camp in Virginia with the Union's largest force, the Army of the Potomac. Yet contrary to McClellan, he refused to concern himself with the day-to-day administration of the military force he accompanied. Instead, he delegated this arduous task to George Meade, the victor at Gettysburg. While overseeing Meade, Grant concentrated on coordinating the movements of over a half million men in uniform scattered across half a continent.[90]

The key to Grant's new approach was his mastery of the latest developments in telegraph technology. From Washington, his predecessors had attempted to communicate with scattered field commanders over non-insulated wire strung on overhead posts. Because of the difficulty of building such lines rapidly, there were invariably delays in transmitting messages from the end of the line to wherever the field commander happened to be. As regards communication on the battlefield itself, commanders such as McClellan relied on signal flags to keep in touch with their subordinates.[91] However, this technique did not work properly in darkness, fog or in thickly wooded areas.

Accompanying Grant as the Army of the Potomac moved south across Virginia was a curious horse-drawn wagon containing a large galvanic battery divided into sections.[92] From this wagon, mules carrying reels of wire insulated with gutta-percha (rubber) laid telegraph lines quickly on the ground and then rewound them as necessary. There was a link from Grant's headquarters to each corps commander in the Army of the Potomac. In addition, Grant maintained a constant telegraph link with the commander of each of the other dispersed union armies.[93] To operate this network, Grant relied on a team of 30 telegraph clerks. Messages were coded so that they could not be understood even if they were intercepted.

The main explanation for the Confederacy's success to date had been the ability of its military leaders to take advantage of inside lines. With a compact territory to defend, first Beauregard and then Lee had been able to shift units back and forth as needed to meet uncoordinated Union attacks. In the spring and summer of 1864, Grant proceeded to nullify this strategy, using the telegraph to coordinate simultaneous attacks on the South along *external* lines.[94] While pinning Lee's army down in the defense of the Confederate capital of Richmond, he delegated Sherman to attack Georgia from Tennessee. Then in August, he directed Sheridan to destroy the Confederacy's food production in the Shenandoah Valley of western Virginia. Atlanta fell and burned on 1 September, and the Shenandoah was taken by October.

These victories undermined the peace platform of the Democratic candidate, the cashiered Union General George McClellan. In the elections of November 1864, Lincoln won an overwhelming victory, taking 55 per cent of the popular vote. The following spring, Grant finally broke through Lee's defenses at the rail center of Petersburg, south of Richmond. The Confederate commander surrendered at Appomattox Court House on 9 April 1865. Unfortunately, many Southerners refused to accept the judgment of the battlefield. Five days later, a fervent anti-abolitionist assassinated Lincoln as he sat enjoying a play. With the conclusion of the Civil War, the long campaign to abolish slavery in the United States gradually drew to an end. Maryland had become the first of the Border States to emancipate its slaves when a new state constitution took effect on 1 November 1864. Missouri followed suit in January 1865. It took an amendment to the federal constitution to force Delaware and Kentucky to free their few remaining slaves.[95] The Thirteenth Amendment, approved in December 1865, abolished slavery throughout the United States. Yet it would take another century before blacks in the South were finally granted the same political and civil rights as whites.

The return of peace also allowed the consolidation of the major telegraph lines to continue. In June 1866, the American Telegraph Company was merged into the Western Union Telegraph Company.[96] By January of the following year, Western Union owned or operated virtually all the network of telegraph lines in the United States.[97] Meanwhile, the successful completion of a transatlantic cable in July 1866 allowed information to flow virtually instantly between Europe and a vast, unified American network.

Lincoln was no longer there to witness the results, but his policy of preemption in attempting to supply Fort Sumter had ultimately been a success. The Confederacy had been forced to fire the first shot, thereby uniting the population of the North as well as foreign opinion against it. By preventing the Border States other than Virginia from seceding, Lincoln had not merely prevented the expansion of slavery but had succeeded in erasing the pernicious institution entirely from American soil.

## NOTES

1. Library of Congress (1995).
2. Kloss (1988, p. 11).
3. Cavanaugh *et al.* (1981).
4. Mabee (1943, pp. 189–192).
5. Gaffney (1979, p. 218).
6. Cavanaugh *et al.* (1981).
7. Edited Appletons Encyclopedia (1981).
8. Nash *et al.* (1986, p. 413).
9. Preston (1985, p. 96).
10. Bingham ([1797] 1997).
11. Preston (1985, p. 145).
12. Preston (1985, p. 154).
13. Nash *et al.* (1986, p. 292).
14. Preston (1985, p. 152).

15. United States Bureau of the Census (1977, Series Q321).
16. Modelski (1984).
17. United States Bureau of the Census (1977, Series A2, A58–A65).
18. Nash *et al.* (1986, p. 337).
19. Nash *et al.* (1986, p. 280).
20. Graff (1991, p. 342).
21. Graff (1991, p. 343).
22. Douglass ([1855] 1987, p. 172).
23. Graff (1991, p. 361).
24. Stephens (n.d.).
25. United States Bureau of the Census (1977, Series R246, R247).
26. A fourth partner, Leonard Gale, professor of geology at New York University, dropped out in 1845.
27. Calvert (2004).
28. Mabee (1943, pp. 203–206).
29. Pope (1888, p. 937).
30. Mabee (1943, p. 202).
31. McEwen (1997).
32. Mabee (1943).
33. Rosewater (1930, p. 35)
34. Gaffney (1979, pp. 391–396).
35. Calvert (2004).
36. Ibid.
37. Reid ([1879] 1974, p. 141).
38. Harding and Oswald (2001).
39. Rosewater (1930, p. 28).
40. Rosewater (1930, p. 33).
41. McPherson (1988, p. 5).
42. Rosewater (1930, p. 34).
43. Rosewater (1930, p. 52).
44. Calvert (2004).
45. Rosewater (1930, pp. 64–65).
46. Rosewater (1930, p. 67–68).
47. Desmond (1978, p. 143).
48. Mott (1962, p. 303).
49. United States Bureau of the Census (1977, Series R246, R247).
50. McFeely (1991, pp. 115–117).
51. Douglass ([1855] 1987, p. 221).
52. McFeely (1991, pp. 143–147).
53. McFeely (1991, p. 149).
54. McFeely (1991, pp. 150–151).
55. McFeely (1991, p. 153).
56. Fassett (2003).
57. Folsom (n.d.).
58. Spartacus (n.d.).
59. McFeely (1991, p. 169).
60. Folsom (n.d.).
61. Public Broadcasting Service (n.d.).
62. Cutler (n.d.).
63. Public Broadcasting Service (n.d.).
64. McFeely (1991, pp. 190–192).
65. McFeely (1991, p. 196).
66. West Virginia Archives and History (2007).
67. Johnson (1997, p. 460).
68. Architect of the Capitol (n.d.).
69. Donald (1995, p. 370).

70. Donald (1995, pp. 363–364).
71. McPherson (1988, pp. 333–334).
72. Eicher (2001, p. 339).
73. Eicher (2001, pp. 337–339).
74. McPherson (1988, p. 537).
75. McPherson (1988, p. 537).
76. Eicher (2001, p. 363).
77. Guelzo (2004, p. 27).
78. Donald (1995, p. 283).
79. Guelzo (2004, p. 42).
80. Guelzo (2004, pp. 112–113).
81. Mott (1962, pp. 351–352).
82. Guelzo (2004, p. 133).
83. McFeely (1991, p. 213).
84. Guelzo (2004, p. 154).
85. Guelzo (2004, p. 187).
86. Guelzo (2004, pp. 185–186).
87. Guelzo (2004, pp. 217–218).
88. Donald (1995, p. 477).
89. Mott (1962, p. 332).
90. Eicher (2001, p. 659).
91. Cornell University Library (2002a).
92. Cornell University Library (2002b).
93. Smith (2001, p. 318).
94. McPherson (1988, p. 722).
95. Guelzo (2004, p. 230).
96. Reid ([1879] 1974, p. 526).
97. Reid ([1879] 1974, p. 503).

# PART IV

# The prescriptive revolution

# 7. The circulation war

In the last decade of the nineteenth century, the major European powers were at peace, calmly digesting the chunks of Asia and Africa they had carved up among themselves. So far, the United States had politely restrained itself from attempting to build an overseas empire. Instead, the main goal of its foreign policy had been to keep Europe out of the Western Hemisphere.

Meanwhile, a series of innovations was transforming the publishing industry. The web-fed rotary press, stereotypy, the linotype machine, the electric motor and paper from wood pulp had dramatically reduced the cost of producing an additional copy of a printed page. Together, these improvements had also greatly increased the initial investment required to launch a daily newspaper. As a result, a newspaper publisher needed to be able to sell hundreds of thousands of copies each day to be able to turn a profit. But how could such publications possibly attract the required number of new readers at a time when most men and women lacked the patience to break into walls of dense text describing complex political, economic and social issues?

## SHAPING THE PUBLIC'S TASTES

The American steamer *Olivette* had just left Havana harbor and the passengers were sitting at their dinner tables. Richard Harding Davis, reporter for the *New York Journal*, began a conversation with Señorita Clemencia Arango, a well-dressed young woman who described the humiliations to which she and two other young women had just been subjected. She related to the American journalist that the Spanish authorities had ordered her to leave Cuba because her brother was a revolutionary. On the day of her departure, detectives had come to her house, forced her to undress and searched her for messages to the revolutionary junta in Florida. An hour later, she and the two other young women were again forced to remove their shoes and stockings during a search in the customs house. Then, when they were already on the American ship, Spanish officials had come aboard and demanded a cabin where the young women were stripped and searched yet again. Davis had just spent a month in Cuba recording the suffering of the island's women and children at the hands of Spanish authorities. But, as he reported in his dispatch of 10 February 1897 from Tampa, nothing had shocked him as much as this barbaric treatment of innocent young women on a ship flying the American flag.[1]

The latest phase of Cuba's struggle for independence from Spain had begun some two years earlier, in February 1895, with the publication of the declaration *Independencia o Muerte* (Independence or Death). The exiled poet and patriot, José Martí, had organized an invasion and uprising in the east of the island. He and the military leader, Máximo Gomez, then landed with several hundred soldiers on the southern coast on 11 April. Although Martí was killed in a skirmish a few weeks later, the rebels were at first quite successful. Using guerrilla tactics, they attacked the Spanish and then melted back into the local population. But in 1896, Spain transferred command of the colony to the hardnosed General Valeriano Weyler, backed up by 50 000 soldiers transported from the mother country.[2] For his ruthless suppression of opponents during an earlier phase of the Cuban independence movement, Weyler had earned the nickname *El Carnicero*, the Butcher.[3] In an attempt to deprive the rebels of support from the population, the new Spanish governor forced some 300 000 people, mostly women and children, into '*reconcentración* camps' that became notorious for their horrid conditions of hunger and disease. After two years, the struggle had become a war of attrition, with the Spanish commanding the towns and the rebels the countryside. Meanwhile, tens of thousands were dead and the island's plantation economy was in ruins.[4]

The Cuban independence movement had strong support in the United States. From the beginning of the insurrection, the press associations had sent representatives to Havana and Santiago, the two main cities. The *New York Journal* was but one of several large dailies that had their own correspondents covering the conflict.[5] Americans were shocked by the brutality of 'Butcher' Weyler, as he became known in the popular press. Sympathetic to the plight of the Cubans, many Americans participated in Cuba rallies that raised funds and food for the suffering population. Americans also had material reasons to favor the movement for *Cuba libre*. They had invested heavily in the island's mines, plantations and sugar mills. By the mid-1890s, nine-tenths of Cuba's production of raw sugar was being sold to American refineries. In addition, the United States had replaced Spain as Cuba's principal supplier of imports.[6]

A war of a different sort was being waged on the sidewalks of New York between two of that city's newspapers, Joseph Pulitzer's *World* and William Randolph Hearst's *Journal*. Pulitzer's leading correspondent in Cuba in 1896 was James Creelman, who began reporting on the insurrection with a vivid account of the execution of political prisoners by the Spanish. He subsequently sent a report on the execution of 33 noncombatants by the authorities in a farming district close to Havana. The victims had been hastily buried, their hands tied behind their backs.[7] Shortly after this report was published, General Weyler had Creelman expelled from Cuba. Meanwhile back in New York, Creelmans's vivid writing had not gone unnoticed. Toward the end of 1896, anxious to improve his international reporting, Hearst hired Creelman away from the *World* to be the Madrid correspondent of the *Journal*.

It was Creelman who in his 1901 memoirs described one of the most famous stories to come out of the Cuban conflict. Hearst hired a two-man team, writer Richard Harding Davis and artist Frederic Remington, to accompany the rebels. However, after bad weather thwarted an attempt to land the men in the insurgents' territory from Hearst's yacht, the *Vamoose*, Davis and Remington made the trip to Havana on a regular passenger ship. Davis received a pass from General Weyler allowing him to report on the situation in western Cuba, distant from the areas of fighting. However, Remington found little outlet for his artistic skills. According to Creelman, Remington wired back to New York, 'Everything is quiet. There is no trouble. There will be no war. I wish to return.' Hearst replied, 'Please remain. You furnish the pictures and I'll furnish the war'.[8] Although there is no concrete evidence that such a telegraphic exchange actually took place, Hearst was sufficiently successful in promoting his own image that succeeding generations believed Creelman's account.[9] For the moment, Remington stayed in Havana.

Who was William Randolph Hearst? At age 34, with the wealth of a co-founder of the Anaconda Mining Company behind him, he was one of America's most eligible bachelors. He was tall, slender with light-brown hair parted in the middle and metallic blue-green eyes that stared severely at the world around him.[10] Fresh out of college, he had made a name for himself as the innovative publisher of the San Francisco *Examiner*. Now he was also the owner of the *New York Journal* and was determined to make it the best-selling paper in the United States.

William's father, George Hearst, was a veteran miner who had made a fortune in the gold fields of Nevada in the late 1850s and then married a schoolteacher 20 years younger than himself. The couple's only child, Willie, born in 1863, was a big, healthy boy who was shuttled from school to school in San Francisco as the family's wealth fluctuated.[11] After years of rising and falling fortunes, Hearst senior struck it rich again in the silver and copper fields of the Dakotas and Montana, where he was a founding partner of the Anaconda Mining Company. There was now plenty of money to enroll the young man in an eastern prep school and to pay a tutor to assure his admission to Harvard.

By his junior year at Harvard, William was showing more interest in the theaters and restaurants of Boston and New York than in his studies. More than anything else, however, it was running a newspaper that attracted him. He was elected business manager of the *Lampoon* and was able to increase its circulation by 50 per cent. At the same time, by increasing its advertising revenue, he succeeded in transforming a deficit of $200 to a surplus of $650. Nevertheless, when he failed to show up for his final examinations in political economy, history and chemistry, he was asked to leave the university.[12] Intervention by William's mother obtained a reprieve. However, the young man spent the following year not in Cambridge studying for final exams but in New York observing the world of newspaper publishing. He was particularly fascinated by the methods used by Joseph Pulitzer as publisher of the city's most successful newspaper, the *World*.

Several years earlier, William's father had purchased the *Examiner* of San Francisco – the only Democratic newspaper in that city – in order to win support in a planned future campaign for governor or senator. Although the paper consistently lost money, it did help George Hearst to be appointed to the United States Senate when the Democrats gained control of the California upper house in the 1886 elections.[13] On 4 March 1887, the day that George Hearst was sworn in as senator, his son's name, W.R. Hearst, first appeared in print as the *Examiner*'s publisher. Nevertheless, when the senator died four years later, he left not a cent to his son.[14] For years, Will would be dependent upon his mother both for an allowance and for venture capital to be invested into his business projects.

In the fall of 1895, Will Hearst decided to try his hand in New York. He persuaded his mother to lend him some $400 000 – enough money to buy a paper in the American metropolis and to bring it up to his standards. His choice was the *Morning Journal*, a money-losing daily with a circulation of under 10 000. He then set about trying to overtake the city's largest paper, Joseph Pulitzer's *World*, with its circulation of 250 000.[15] Hiring the best journalists and supporting their stories with illustrations by the best artists was expensive but Hearst was willing to pay the price in order to build circulation. The challenge was to discover what subjects could attract New York readers.

New York's journalism community expected Hearst to fail.[16] Indeed, after more than a year, the paper was still losing money. However, his preparations made, Hearst was now ready for an experiment. Davis's dispatch on the strip search of Señorita Clemencia Arango on board the *Olivette* provided the ideal opportunity to explore the public's journalistic tastes. On 12 February 1897, the *Journal* published the report on its first page under screaming headlines, 'Does Our Flag Shield Women? Indignities Practiced by Spanish Officials on Board American Vessels'. When the reader turned to page two, there was a five-column drawing by Frederic Remington displaying a naked young woman being examined in a ship's cabin by three leering, clothed Spanish officials.

The reaction of the American public to the story and picture was both immediate and emotional. The Spanish consulate in New York was stoned and a reader from the South wrote that General Weyler should be lynched. Clergymen attacked 'bestial Spanish defilers of womanhood'. Little notice was taken when the rival paper, the *World*, revealed that Miss Arango had been searched by a female officer rather than by three men.[17] For Hearst, success in journalism was measured in terms of circulation. The *World* had announced an average circulation for 1896 of 743 000. In February 1897, Hearst was able to assert in print that the *Journal* was now selling 750 000 copies a day.[18] The challenge for him now was to maintain this remarkable level of circulation on a day-to-day basis. To do so, he must keep one step ahead of his principal competitor, the idiosyncratic publisher of the *New York World*, who was also closely following events in Cuba.

## THE NEW JOURNALISM

In the spring of 1897, Joseph Pulitzer, age 50, the owner and publisher of the *New York World*, had been virtually blind for eight years. To maintain contact with the details of his publishing kingdom and to keep up to date on world events, he was forced to rely on oral summaries prepared by a staff of six secretaries.[19] In addition, Pulitzer had become hypersensitive to sound. He was obliged to eat alone so that the noise of a dinner companion's utensils would not upset him. During the winter of 1896–1897, even the bells in the yacht basin at Monte Carlo were too jarring for his nerves. He could not relax until he found a hotel to his liking on an isolated peninsula just inside the French border.[20] Although he was well aware of his own handicaps, Pulitzer found himself unable to delegate authority. Constantly on the move between the French Riviera and homes in Maine, Georgia, and New Jersey, he insisted on interfering in the day-to-day work of his hired managers.[21]

From the latest cables he had received, Pulitzer now felt that he had good reason to intervene. Arthur Brisbane, the brilliant young editor he had appointed to run the Sunday *New York World*, had overstepped the bounds of his authority. Brisbane had been very successful with his Christmas number, selling 623 000 copies. But now he had expanded the headlines of the weekly supplement to fill the width of the page. Clubhouse committees and Sunday-school workers were writing to protest against the new type of journalism Brisbane had championed, with its crime stories, freaks and scantily dressed women.[22] In addition, Brisbane had dared to write his own editorial column. Pulitzer cabled from abroad, 'Stop column, don't want independent editorial opinions in my newspapers'.[23]

But these were minor irritations. Pulitzer's big problem was William Randolph Hearst and the family fortune that allowed the younger man to violate the accepted rules of business behavior. Pulitzer had learned that Hearst earned an income of $100 000 a year from the San Francisco *Examiner*, but was losing that amount a *month* with the *Journal*. Only his mother's generosity in spending her inherited wealth kept Hearst afloat. Not content with undercutting Pulitzer in price and upstaging him with bold journalism, Hearst had dared to hire many of the *World*'s top staff. As the *Journal*'s circulation began to pull ahead of that of the *World*, Pulitzer knew it was time to sail back to the United States.

## The Second Industrial Revolution

America in the last decades of the nineteenth century was on the move. A second industrial revolution based on steel, chemicals, steam and, most recently, electricity had completely transformed the landscape since the end of the Civil War. Thanks to the railway, what had formerly been a land of isolated farms and agricultural villages was becoming a network of densely populated industrial cities. In 1870, only 25 per cent of the population lived in the cities and towns. But as the end of the century neared, the urbanization rate was approaching 40 per cent.[24] In many cities, the majority of the residents were foreign-born. Between 1860 and 1900, 14 million immigrants came to America seeking better lives for themselves.[25] By 1890, the United States, with its 63 million residents, was more populous than any of the other major industrial powers.[26] In Europe, only the Russian Empire surpassed it in population. America was also well on its way to becoming the world's most prosperous nation, as it caught up with and pulled ahead of the United Kingdom in per-capita income.[27]

The millions of active participants in this new urban, industrial economy demanded information. With near universal literacy, except for blacks and Native Americans, Americans needed to know the prices of basic commodities, manufactured goods and financial instruments.[28] They also wanted to be informed about the latest events in distant places. And they wanted to be told about themselves, entertained and diverted with news of who was doing what and going where in their own city. Joseph Pulitzer was one of the first to perceive and to attempt to satisfy these demands.

## The World of Joseph Pulitzer

Pulitzer had worked his way to the top the hard way. He was born in Hungary in 1847, the second son of a prosperous Hungarian Jewish grain merchant who had married an Austrian Christian beauty. At age 17, despite his weak eyes and frail physique, Joseph left Hungary, having been recruited to fight for the Union in the American Civil War. But on his arrival in Boston harbor in September 1864, he had slipped into the chilly water and swum ashore, preferring to enlist on his own terms.[29] After serving briefly in the cavalry, he had been released at the war's end and then made his way west toward St Louis. He arrived there in October 1865, without an overcoat, penniless and hungry. A series of odd jobs kept him from starving while he learned to read and write English and studied for the bar.

Since Pulitzer could speak and write German fluently, in 1868 he was offered a job as a reporter with the local German-language paper, the *Westliche Post*. With his tall, thin frame, his thick-lensed spectacles and his pointed chin and its tuft of red whiskers, 'Joey' was the butt of jokes by reporters for the English-language press. However, by working tirelessly from ten o'clock in the morning until two early the following day, he was soon unearthing stories that his rivals had missed.[30] Over the next several years, he managed to be elected to the Missouri legislature, then to buy two newspapers and sell them at a profit. He was admitted to the bar in the District of Columbia in 1877.[31]

Pulitzer's big chance came back in St Louis, in December 1878, when the sheriff auctioned off a bankrupt newspaper, the *Dispatch*, on the city's Court House steps. Calculating that he would need at least $2700 for the initial operation costs, Pulitzer figured he could afford a bid of $2500 along with acceptance of debts of $30 000. The creditors agreed to these terms. Although a competing group arrived a few minutes later with a higher bid, they were too late. Two days later, the editor of a rival newspaper, the *Post* agreed to merge with Pulitzer's paper in order to get access to the latter's Associated Press wire-service link.

The St Louis *Post-Dispatch* made money from its first weeks. Pulitzer's guiding principles were simple. First, he would feature hard-hitting investigative journalism, fighting corruption wherever he found it. Second, he would appeal to a mass audience, courting readers who supported the Democratic Party. In place of the stodgy editorials of his competitors, he would provide them with a rich variety of news and entertainment.[32] Finally, he would publish a product of quality that appealed to both the mind and the eye. He was an excellent judge of ability and soon recruited top reporters and writers, including the talented John A. Cockerill, a former drummer boy in the Civil War.[33] Within three years, thanks to annual profits of over $40 000, Pulitzer was able to purchase two new rotaries from the firm of the late Richard Hoe to replace the rickety flat-bed press that had come with the *Dispatch*.[34]

In the spring of 1883, Pulitzer was passing through New York City on his way to Europe when he heard that the financier Jay Gould wished to sell a money-losing newspaper, the *New York World*. With a circulation of 20 000, Gould's two-cent paper lagged far behind the *Sun* which was also priced at two cents.[35] The most profitable of New York dailies at that time was the *Herald*, which sold for three cents. Although Pulitzer paid the enormous price of $346 000, his new daily financed itself from the outset. The immigrant publisher simply applied the principles of the New Journalism he had developed in St Louis: crusades exposing corruption and incompetence, 'human-interest' stories and lively writing.[36] When the paper's circulation doubled in four months, the *Herald* tried to compete by cutting its price to two cents.[37] However, the *World*'s circulation continued to rise. By 1892, its morning and evening editions together were selling 374 000 copies and the Sunday edition 250 000 copies.[38] Its 20-storey building overlooking City Hall was the highest in the world when it opened in 1890.[39]

## The New Imperialism

As publisher of his adopted country's largest newspaper, Pulitzer felt a responsibility to guide the direction of foreign policy. Before the 1890s, Americans had not been greatly concerned with what was going on in the rest of the world. Of course, the Munroe Doctrine of 1823 was still in force, stating American opposition to further colonization of the Americas by European powers. However, it also stated that the United States would stay neutral in European wars. Even with regard to the Western hemisphere, American administrations and Congresses had been hesitant to intervene. For 20 years Venezuela had been pleading in vain with the United States to support it in a dispute with Great Britain over its boundary with British Guiana. Meanwhile, the British were busily settling the disputed territory.

Finally, in 1895 the Democratic president Grover Cleveland decided to make a stand. Pointing out that Britain had refused to accept arbitration over the question, he asked Congress for the authority to appoint an American commission to determine the border unilaterally along with the power to enforce its findings. The British, for their part, announced that they refused to accept the Monroe doctrine. Suddenly there was talk of war between the two powers. At this point, Joseph Pulitzer jumped into the debate with a series of editorials criticizing the president's aggressive position and urging restraint on both sides.[40] Thanks in part to such cool-headed pressure from the press, the administration softened its position and a compromise was arranged. The British agreed to accept the findings of an American commission.

By 1897, the scramble for the remaining non-colonized territories in Africa was heating up. The British were pushing up the Nile into the Sudan from their protectorate in Egypt. They envisioned a railroad from Cape Town to Cairo. Meanwhile, the French had sent an expedition east from their territories in West Africa. They wanted to link the Red Sea and the Indian Ocean with their principal African colonies. Each country saw Africa as an outlet for its investments and a market for its products.

Suddenly, American business leaders too began to express concern about markets for *their* industrial production. Until the 1890s, US imports and exports had been in relative balance. But in the 1890s a massive trade surplus opened up. US exports in 1895 were 17 per cent greater than imports and the gap was steadily widening.[41] Increasingly, American manufacturers looked at the heavily populated countries of Latin American and Asia as potential markets for their surplus production.[42] They were concerned that the Cuban conflict had reduced their country's trade with that island from $100 million to a tenth of that amount.[43]

In the summer of 1897, Pulitzer was locked into a ferocious circulation battle with William Randolph Hearst. Seeing how readers had reacted to the news coming out of Cuba, Pulitzer admitted that he rather liked the idea of American involvement in a war. He favored one that was not too big – just large enough to give his circulation figures a boost.[44] As it turned out, his rival William Randolph Hearst would provide him with a war both in the Caribbean and on the streets of New York.

## MANUFACTURING THE NEWS

One hot day in late July 1897, two reporters of Hearst's *New York Journal* and a British colleague were at Havana's Casa de Recojidas prison following a lead concerning the Cuban war of independence. To their surprise, they noticed a beautiful girl who was being held captive with 'women of the lowest type'.[45] Upon inquiry, they learned that the young woman was Evangelina Cosio y Cisneros, the 17-year-old niece of an imprisoned leader of the revolutionary movement. According to the Spanish regime, Señorita Cosio had attempted to lure the Spanish military governor of the Isle of Pines prison, Colonel José Berriz, into a trap, where he was beaten by three prisoners.[46] However, the young woman asserted that the colonel had tried to attack her innocence and that the prisoners had merely attempted to rescue her. The two American reporters quickly telegraphed the girl's story to their New York office.

When the reporters' dispatch portraying the plight of Miss Cisneros (as she was to be known in the U.S.) reached the *Journal*'s offices in New York, William Randolph Hearst immediately took charge of the newsroom. As the paper's publisher, he saw a way of pulling ahead in the current circulation battle with his rival, Joseph Pulitzer of the *World*. Hearst began issuing orders. A petition must be sent to the Queen Regent of Spain asking her to pardon the girl. Copies of the petition must be sent to each of the *Journal*'s 200 correspondents across America, who would ask the leading women of America to sign. Hearst himself contacted Mrs McKinley, the president's wife, asking her to add her signature in order to save the girl, 'almost a child, sick, defenseless, and in prison'.[47] Women by the hundreds of thousands responded to Hearst's plea and many of their replies were duly published in the *Journal*.

## Hearst in San Francisco

Why was Hearst so committed to a story that was all but ignored by the other major papers? To answer this question, we must go back to San Francisco a decade earlier. In the spring of 1887, young Will Hearst at age 23 became editor of his father's paper, the *Examiner*. At the moment Will took the paper over, it had a circulation of 15 000 and was losing money. Its principal competitor, the profitable Republican *Chronicle*, had a circulation of about 37 500.[48] Fixing the market leader as his target, Hearst began to apply the principles that he had learned from observing Joseph Pulitzer in New York while supposedly cramming for exams at Harvard.

In place of the boring local political news presented by his rival, Hearst featured hard-punching investigative journalism. His first major crime story, prominently displayed on the front page, was about a band of San Francisco thugs who murdered people to collect their insurance.[49] He attacked corruption in all its forms, whether bribery of local police and politicians, jury tampering or prison administration. Like Pulitzer, Hearst aimed at a mass audience and therefore supported the Democratic Party. To appeal to the city's growing immigrant population, he featured international news obtained by telegraph from the New York *Herald*. Finally, like Pulitzer, Hearst insisted on a top-quality product. He hired a new team of reporters, cartoonists and illustrators. He expanded the paper from six to ten pages.[50] Two years earlier, as a student writing to his father, Will Hearst had been sharply critical of the quality of the type, the typesetting and the newsprint used by the *Examiner*.[51] Now installed as editor of the paper, he persuaded his father to purchase two new web presses from Hoe and Company. Will also installed several of the new linotype machines that permitted rapid setting of entire lines of freshly-cast type.[52]

But Hearst went beyond the conservative style and content of his mentor, Pulitzer, to innovate on his own accord. In the decades after the Civil War, newspapers presented each story in single columns of type, with a multi-decker headline at the top of the lead column.[53] Hearst began to change the look of the *Examiner*, constantly experimenting with the layout of the front page. He introduced banner headlines that stretched across several columns. They were accompanied by large drawings designed to attract the potential reader's attention.[54] In addition, he changed the way stories were covered. David Nasaw tells of Hearst's reaction to a fire that destroyed the Hotel Del Monte in Monterey in April 1887. Hearst immediately rented a train car to carry *Examiner* writers and artists to the site of the disaster. They produced a special edition of 14 pages of interviews with victims, a description of the smoldering site and the plans for rebuilding. Each article was presented as a quickly paced, highly colored short story.[55] Indeed, the newspaper's coverage of the event was itself one of the featured stories.[56] In effect, Hearst was manufacturing his own news.

By 1890, the *Examiner* had caught up with the *Chronicle* in circulation and was turning a profit.[57] Three years later, its circulation had jumped to almost 60 000.[58] But San Francisco at that time had a population of only 300 000. Hearst calculated that there were much greater profits to be earned by applying his innovations in a larger market.

## New Printing Technologies

Hearst's arrival as editor of the San Francisco *Examiner* coincided with a period of rapid technological innovation in the printing industry. In the late 1850s, most of the large American newspapers used type-revolving cylindrical presses that printed on individual sheets of newspaper. Type was set by hand, character by character. To use an additional press for the same publication, the type had to be set a second time. Most papers had four pages of unrelieved type in narrow columns.[59] The paper itself was made from rag fibers and was expensive, costing 7.5 cents a pound in 1861. The paper with the largest circulation at the beginning of that year was the New York *Herald*, with a circulation of 77 000.[60]

One area of change was in the making of newsprint. In 1863, near Philadelphia, Hugh Burgess and a partner established the first successful mill that made paper from wood chips. By the late 1880s, wood pulp had replaced four-fifths of the rag pulp in newsprint. Over the same period, the introduction of larger, faster Fourdrinier paper-making machines made it practical to produce newsprint in rolls. In this process, liquid pulp was poured on to a moving mesh belt and then dried and pressed by heavy rollers. As a result, the price of newspaper fell to three cents a pound in 1892.[61] By 1897, increased competition and improved technology had driven the price down to 1.8 cents a pound.[62]

Another area of progress was in the printing presses themselves. In 1861, R. Hoe and Company introduced a rotary press that used curved stereotyped plates.[63] To produce one of these plates, a printer pressed a whole page of type into a paste which he allowed to dry. By pouring lead alloy into the resulting mold, he could make as many copies as he desired of the original type. He could then print multiple runs of the same text simultaneously without resetting the type. In 1871, R. Hoe and Company brought out a rotary press that perfected, that is, it printed on both sides of a sheet at the same time. It was fed from a roll in a continuous sheet known as the 'web'.[64] A later version, the 'sextuple press' of 1889, turned out six four-page sheets simultaneously from three rolls. It could print 24 000 papers of 24 pages per hour.[65] The addition of a 'folder' made it possible to cut and fold 24-page newspapers at press speed.[66]

A final area of innovation was in the reproduction of drawings. The zincography process, developed in France in 1859, began to be used in American papers in the 1870s.[67] The artist's sketch on translucent paper was placed on a varnish-coated zinc plate that had been specially treated. The plate was then placed in sunlight that hardened the varnish wherever it was exposed to light. Next, the printer applied acid that etched into the surface of the metal where the varnish had not been hardened. When the rest of the varnish was subsequently removed with benzene, the areas of the surface that had not been etched by acid would repel ink, while the etched parts would hold it and could transfer it to paper. It now became possible to reproduce drawings cheaply.

Although these innovations considerably reduced the cost of preparing an extra newspaper of a given size and quality, they also greatly increased the initial capital that was required to start a paper. A single Hoe press could cost as much as $80 000.[68] In addition, a new entrant to a big-city market would require a staff of journalists, illustrators, editors, pressmen and deliverymen, whose annual salaries would run into the hundreds of thousands of dollars. In short, the innovations since the start of the Civil War had greatly increased the scale economies of newspaper publishing. To make a profit, the press entrepreneur would have to attract readers who previously would not have bought a paper. Fortunately, this was a period of growing population with rapidly rising purchasing power. For the first time in history, near universal literacy allowed virtually all men, women and even children access to the newspaper. All that was required was a way to attract them to the new medium.

## Yellow Journalism

After his father's death in 1891, William Randolph Hearst began to examine the possibilities of breaking into the newspaper market of New York City with its 1.5 million inhabitants.[69] As mentioned earlier in the chapter, in October 1895, with money borrowed from his mother, he bought the *Morning Journal* and proceeded to apply the techniques that had been so successful with the San Francisco *Examiner*.[70]

Hearst's first problem was personnel. He quickly telegraphed to San Francisco to summon the *Examiner*'s best reporters, illustrators and sports writers east.[71] Hearst knew that almost half Pulitzer's profits came from the Sunday *World*, whose conception was the responsibility of Morrill Goddard, 31, an energetic Dartmouth graduate. Goddard had introduced pseudo-scientific articles and sex scandals involving chorus girls in their underwear. The Sunday World was the first paper to introduce a color comic – 'The Yellow Kid', by R.F. Outcault.[72] Hearst invited Goddard to meet him in the New York offices of the San Francisco *Examiner*, which happened to be in the *World* Building.[73] When Goddard hesitated to accept Hearst's offer because he did not wish to leave the team he had built up, Hearst promptly hired the whole staff of the Sunday *World*. However, the following day, when Pulitzer upped the ante, the Sunday *World* staff returned. Then, 24 hours later, Hearst with a new offer hired Goddard and his team a second and final time to put out the Sunday *Journal*. Pulitzer promptly canceled the *Examiner*'s lease and hired a new cartoonist to draw a competing Yellow Kid comic.[74] As a result, the other New York papers soon began referring to the Pulitzer and Hearst papers as the 'yellow press'.[75]

What exactly was Yellow Journalism? As Frank Luther Mott has explained, there were several characteristics that distinguished this new approach to selling newspapers. One feature was the banner headline, while a second was the abundant use of pictures. A third feature was the faking of interviews and stories, and a final aspect was the creation of sympathy for the 'underdog'.[76]

A good example of Yellow Journalism is the manner in which Hearst used the story of Evangelina Cisneros to maintain the circulation of his papers, day after day, month after month. Although the public's concern for the young Cuban woman had died down by the end of August 1897, Hearst realized that the melodramatic story still had great potential. A little more than two months later, on 8 October, banner headlines in the *Journal* announced that Evangelina had escaped from prison. The next day, readers learned that she was on her way to the United States. There followed a story written by 'Charles Duval' describing how he had rescued Miss Cisneros and arranged for her to leave Cuba. Duval, *Journal* readers subsequently learned, was a pseudonym for broad-shouldered *Journal* reporter Karl Decker, who had used a ladder to reach the young woman's cell, had cut the bars and then whisked her on board a passenger ship bound for the United States, dressed as a young sailor.[77] (Actually, Decker had simply used

Hearst's money to bribe the prison guards.[78]) In New York, Hearst arranged a room for her at the Waldorf. Then dressed in the long white robe of a princess, she was paraded through Manhattan. In Washington, she was received at the White House by President McKinley.[79] Her fictionalized biography ran for three months in the Sunday *Journal*.[80]

In the Evangelina Cisneros story, Hearst had found a formula for selling an unprecedented number of newspapers. A paper must attract the public's attention with screaming headlines, it must provide abundant pictures, and there must be an item of human interest to which ordinary people can relate. If such stories could not be found through investigative journalism, then they must be manufactured. An opportunity to improve Hearst's ability to do so came in November 1897, when Pulitzer suspended his innovative young editor, Arthur Brisbane, for daring to sign his name to an editorial in the evening *World*. The next day Hearst hired Brisbane to edit his *Evening Journal* with the right to his own byline.[81] Hearst had made his preparations for combat. Let the fighting begin!

## THE SPLENDID LITTLE WAR

On 16 February 1898, William Randolph Hearst, 34, was awakened by his butler, who informed him that the office wanted to talk with him. When Hearst telephoned the *Journal* headquarters, he was told that the American battleship *Maine* had blown up the previous evening in Havana harbor. The story had been put on the first page of the morning *Journal*. 'Have you put anything else on the front page?' Hearst wanted to know. 'Only the other big news', his editor replied. 'There is not any other big news', Hearst decreed. 'Please spread the story all over the page. This means war.'[82]

A month earlier, on 12 January 1898, street disturbances by pro- and anti-Spanish demonstrators in the streets of Havana had briefly threatened the lives and property of Americans in that city. In response, the US administration had arranged an exchange of courtesy calls by American and Spanish warships. While a Spanish vessel visited east coast ports, the battleship Maine would be sent to Cuba. Accordingly, on the morning of 25 January, the 6700-ton American vessel with her crew of 355 sailed into Havana harbor and anchored at a mooring buoy designated by the Spanish officials.[83] Over the following three weeks, officers were allowed ashore, but to avoid any incidents with the local population, enlisted men were confined to the ship.[84]

Shortly after 9:10 on the evening of 15 February 1898, a series of explosions tore open the hull of the *Maine*, setting the big ship afire. Despite the efforts of crews of boats from nearby ships, 260 men were killed. The battleship itself quickly sank, leaving only the top of a mast and twisted bits of superstructure to be seen above the water the next morning. In his report, the ship's captain, Charles Sigsbee, recommended that no judgment of criminality be made until after an examination of the evidence.[85] The navy quickly appointed a court of inquiry to examine the destruction of the battleship.

## The *Journal* Declares War

Meanwhile, the New York press was unwilling to await the results of the inquiry. Reports on the morning after the explosion limited themselves to the few facts that were known. However, on the following day, an early edition of Hearst's *Journal* bore the headline, 'Destruction of the Warship *Maine* was the Work of an Enemy'. Below was a drawing of the Maine anchored above a submarine mine. Although the lead article reported that no one thought that the Spanish authorities were responsible, the caption under the picture stated that the Spaniards had deliberately anchored the Maine over a harbor mine.[86]

Hearst immediately hired yachts to send dozens of correspondents to report on the situation in Cuba. On 18 February, the *Journal*'s headline shouted, 'REMEMBER THE *MAINE*! TO HELL WITH SPAIN!'[87] Every day for a week, the paper offered eight pages of illustrations, articles and editorials covering the crisis and its aftermath. On 24 February, front-page illustrations pictured 'The Journal's War fleet' of three boats along with portrait drawings of its correspondents and artists. The next day, one of the paper's headings proclaimed, 'Wherever Americans Gather, the Word "War" Awakens Wild Enthusiasm'.[88] Pulitzer's *World* and the other major New York papers simply did not have the financial resources to compete with this coverage. Together, the morning and evening editions of the *Journal* were now selling over a million copies a day.[89] At about this time, the term jingoism, meaning blind patriotism, entered the American vocabulary.[90]

The president, William McKinley, a mild-mannered former governor of Ohio who disliked conflict of any kind, tried to resist the popular pressure for war. However, the Spanish government refused to make any concessions, accusing the United States of fomenting insurrection in Cuba.[91] A Republican, McKinley has been called the first modern president.[92] Instead of criss-crossing the country during his 1896 campaign, he had stayed at home in Canton, Ohio, and let representatives of the new mass-circulation press act as intermediaries between himself and the electorate. His platform, promising economic prosperity behind protective tariffs and calling for Cuban independence, won the approval of a decisive majority of voters.

A day before taking office in March 1897, McKinley had confided to his predecessor, Grover Cleveland, that he wanted above all to avert a war with Spain over Cuba. However, eleven months later, a week before the sinking of the *Maine*, the *Journal* published a stolen letter written by the Spanish minister in Washington to a friend in Spain that described McKinley as 'weak and a bidder for the admiration of the crowd'.[93] Despite loud American public protests against this insult, the president failed to react to resolve the conflict. Finally, on 6 March, three weeks after the *Maine*'s destruction, McKinley felt forced to ask Congress to approve an emergency appropriation, in the words of a motion the president himself prepared, 'For the national defense, fifty million dollars'.[94]

Meanwhile the court of inquiry was writing up its report. Somehow, the Associated Press obtained a copy of the finished document before the president sent it to Congress on 28 March. The morning papers that day summarized the main findings, along with the conclusion that, 'the *Maine* was destroyed by the explosion of a submarine mine which caused the partial explosion of two or more of her forward magazines'.[95] The following day, the *Journal* published interviews with congressmen who supported the cause of independence for Cuba. The headline read 'Armed Intervention at Once!'[96]

McKinley, anticipating that the public reaction to the court's finding would be explosive, sent a stiff note to Spain. He offered his intervention to mediate the Cuban dispute, stipulating three conditions that must first be accepted. The Spaniards must grant an immediate armistice, they must repeal the *reconcentración* policy, and they must offer the Cubans 'full self-government'. Finally, if there were no agreement by 1 October, the president would assume the role of 'final arbiter'.[97] On 30 March, the Spanish governor in Cuba unilaterally put an end to the concentration camps.[98] Then on 10 April, the Spanish announced an unconditional armistice.[99] They would also accept 'self-government', although it must not diminish the powers reserved to Spain.

As far as members of the American Congress were concerned, it was a case of too little too late. War was now inevitable. Realizing that if he did not intervene as commander in chief, Congress would declare war on its own, McKinley requested authority to deal with the Cuban problem. On 19 April, Congress passed a resolution granting the president the power to intervene militarily if Spain refused to grant independence to Cuba. An amendment by a liberal senator stipulated that the United States did not seek sovereignty over Cuba. The next morning, McKinley signed the joint resolution and began plans for a naval blockade of the island and a call for 125 000 volunteers for the army.[100] Spain reacted by breaking off diplomatic relations and preparing for war.[101]

## The Battle of Manila Bay

On the afternoon of Friday 25 March, a month before the war broke out, the navy secretary, John Davis Long, had decided to leave his office early to get some badly needed rest. He turned the department over to his young, aggressive assistant secretary, Theodore Roosevelt. Taking advantage of Long's absence, Roosevelt sent 'secret and confidential' instructions to Commodore George Dewey, the commander of the Asiatic Squadron. The squadron was to be concentrated at Hong Kong with its coal bunkers full. In the event of war, Dewey was to assure that the Spanish Asian fleet did not leave the Asian coast and then begin offensive operations in the Philippines.[102]

Philippine nationalists were not opposed to Spain but rather to the Catholic Church, which owned vast tracts of land and urban properties and exploited its tenants mercilessly. In 1896, when the poet José Rizal protested against this inequity, he was charged with treason, arrested and executed by a firing squad. Open revolt then broke out on the island of Luzon under the leadership of a 29-year-old street fighter, Emilio Aguinaldo. The following year, the Spanish offered exile for the rebels and reforms that were never put into effect. As war between the US and Spain became likely, there were initial contacts between the American authorities and Aguinaldo, first in Hong Kong and then in Singapore. The rebel leaders were asked to fight Spain in return for assurances of political freedom if the Spanish were defeated. Although there was no written commitment, Dewey agreed to joint military action with Aguinaldo.[103]

When war broke out, Dewey had more pressing concerns than cooperating with a few young guerrilla soldiers. The Spanish Asian squadron consisted of three obsolete cruisers, the *Reina Cristina*, the *Don Juan de Austria* and the leaky *Castilla*, along with two gunboats and a dispatch vessel.[104] They were no match for the modern fast vessels in Dewey's squadron, the four cruisers, *Olympia*, *Baltimore*, *Boston* and *Raleigh* and two gunboats, the *Concord* and *Petrel*. However, all of Dewey's vessels were unarmored.[105] Properly commanded, under the protection of shore batteries, the Spanish ships could pose a serious threat to the American squadron.

On arriving off the coast of Luzon, Dewey first searched Subite Bay to the north of Manila but found no Spanish boats. Then in the dead of night, he and his fleet slipped past the coastal batteries and entered Manila Bay, a vast protected inlet some 20 miles (30 km) wide and 12 miles (20 km) long. When dawn arrived, Dewey found the Spanish ships strung out in a line at the far end of the bay defending the naval base of Cavite, to the south of the city. The Spanish commander, Admiral Patricio Montojo, had anchored his fleet in shallow water, hoping that if the ships were sunk, the crews could be saved.

With shells from coastal batteries and the enemy vessels falling around them, the American ships steamed toward the stationary Spanish ships at high speed. Finally with the range down to 5500 yards (5 km), Dewey gave the order to the captain of his flagship, the *Olympia*, 'You may fire when ready, Gridley'. Over the next two hours, the Americans made four passes, their heavy guns and precise firing completely destroying the Spanish squadron. Meanwhile, the opposing ships and shore batteries scored few hits against the Americans. Indeed, not a single American sailor was killed in the battle.[106] Dewey then silenced the shore batteries by sending word that he would bombard the city if the Spaniards fired upon his ships. With the surrender of the troops holding the Cavite naval base, his victory was complete.

Because the Spanish governor refused to let Dewey use the Manila–Hong Kong cable, the American commander ordered one of his captains to pull it up and cut it.[107] Thus it was not until six days later, when an American ship sent by Dewey arrived in Hong Kong, that the rest of the world finally learned of the Spanish defeat. In Washington, Theodore Roosevelt was leaning over the shoulder of the cipher clerk as the message came in. He was the first to break the news to the 50 anxiously waiting journalists.[108]

## El Caney and San Juan Hill

On that same day, 7 May 1898, a Spanish expeditionary fleet under Admiral Pascual Cervera was en route from the Cape Verde Islands to the Caribbean. Cervera hoped to obtain coal for his ships in Martinique and then proceed on to San Juan, Puerto Rico, in order to protect that island from possible American invasion. However, the news he obtained on reaching Martinique was all bad. Not only was there no coal to be had, but also the Americans had been victorious at Manila Bay and were now patrolling before San Juan. In addition, the American cruiser *Harvard*, on the other side of Martinique, was surely now aware of his fleet's presence. He decided to take his ships on to the safe harbor at Santiago in southeastern Cuba.[109]

The southeast coast of Cuba runs almost due east–west for 250 miles (400 km), with Santiago half way along and Guantánamo Bay some 70 miles (110 km) further east. The American navy had sent a flying squadron under Commodore Winfield Scott Schley to search for Cervera's fleet. It was with great delight that Schley and his men spotted the black-hulled *Cristobal Colón* and the *Almirante Oquendo* in Santiago harbor on 29 May. Turning to the Associated Press reporter attached to the fleet, Schley declared, 'We've got them now, Graham, and they'll never go home'.[110] In his haste to protect his ships, Cervera had overlooked the difficulty of supporting Santiago militarily by land. Only the roughest of roads through mountainous jungle connected the port with the other main towns on the island.[111] Although the Spanish ships were protected from seaward threats, they could be flushed out by a land attack.

On 14 June, a flotilla of 29 American transports carrying 17 000 men, 1000 horses and 1300 mules left Tampa bound for Santiago de Cuba. Instead of landing directly near the mouth of Santiago harbor, the army commander, General William Shafter, chose to disembark at the village of Daiquirí, 18 miles (30 km) to the east. Unfortunately, the landing possibilities there were limited to a high metal dock unsuitable for small boats, a shaky wooden pier and an open beach. Moreover, as the rainy season began, the narrow *camino real* that led through the jungle to Santiago quickly became a huge gutter of 'liquid mud a foot deep'.[112] Although the landings began on 23 June, it took another week before enough men and equipment had been brought ashore to permit the army to prepare an attack on the approaches to the port city.[113] It had proved impossible to land heavy artillery; consequently, the attacking troops had only light field guns.[114]

While the American troops in their wool uniforms were struggling in the heat and humidity, William Randolph Hearst was sailing toward Cuba in the *Sylvia*, a freighter he had chartered from the Baltimore Fruit Company. The ship carried food, darkrooms, medical supplies and a plentiful supply of ice. Among the group Hearst brought with him were reporter James Creelman, photographer J.C. Hemment and two chorus-girl sisters, Millicent and Anita Willson.[115]

Santiago was defended by 12 000 men under General Arsenio Linares. The Spanish commander had fortified the eastward approaches along the San Juan Heights and Kettle Hill with rows of trenches reinforced by blockhouses. Backing up his riflemen were two modern Krupp field guns.[116] To the northeast, additional fortifications at the village of El Caney controlled the road coming from the town of Guantánamo. On the morning of 1 June, some 6000 American troops attacked El Caney, but were stopped by vigorous fire from trenches before a stone fort. At this crucial moment, the *Journal* reporter James Creelman led a successful attack on the fort, taking the surviving defenders prisoner. However, before he could return to write his story, Creelman was shot through the shoulder.[117] He was lying in great pain awaiting medical aid, when he felt a hand on his forehead. It was Hearst leaning over him wearing a straw hat, a revolver at his waist, and a pencil and pad ready to take the reporter's story. 'I'm sorry you're hurt,' Hearst consoled him, 'but wasn't it a splendid fight? We must beat every paper in the world.'[118]

Meanwhile, the former assistant Navy secretary, Theodore Roosevelt, now a volunteer lieutenant colonel, was leading a charge of his volunteer cavalry regiment up first Kettle Hill and then San Juan Hill. Although

Roosevelt was mounted, his men were on foot. Since the Americans had little protection against the entrenched Spanish riflemen and artillery, Roosevelt soon realized that the best tactic was a frontal assault. Along with other American companies whose commanders had made the same decision, the Roughriders overran the Spanish lines. As they reached the crest of San Juan heights, they saw the town and port of Santiago before them.

**The Battle of Santiago Bay**

In Santiago harbor, Admiral Cervera had four cruisers – his flagship, the *Infanta Maria Teresa*, along with the *Almirante Oquendo*, the *Cristobal Colón* and the *Vizcaya* – and two destroyers. The Spanish captain general back in Havana, General Ramón Blanco, was loath to see these ships scuttled or destroyed by land-based artillery. Late on 1 July, the day of the capture of the San Juan heights, he therefore ordered Cervera to attempt to break out at the first opportunity. Cervera decided that he would try to ram one of the battleships with his flagship, thereby allowing the three other cruisers to escape. It was a desperate maneuver: the admiral calculated that he was outgunned four to one.[119]

In the early dawn of Sunday 3 July, observers on the American battleship *Iowa* saw six columns of smoke rising into the morning sky behind the hills that blocked their view of Santiago harbor. After checking for himself, Captain 'Fighting Bob' Evans gave the order to hoist signal No. 250, 'Enemy's ships escaping'. To the west of his ship were the new armored cruiser *Brooklyn* and the old battleship *Texas*. To the east were the battleship *Oregon*, then Admiral William Sampson's flagship, the armored cruiser *New York*, and finally, the battleship *Indiana*.[120]

At 9:30 a.m., the Spanish battle line began to emerge from the harbor and turn to the west. Immediately, the American ships commenced firing. Within two minutes of rounding the point, the *Infanta Maria Teresa* was already badly damaged by shells from the *Brooklyn*. An hour later, Cervera managed to beach his flagship shortly before her magazines exploded. One by one, her sister ships were attacked by the American fleet and suffered a similar fate. The last was the *Cristobal Colón*, which failed to escape the pursuing *Brooklyn*, *Oregon* and *Texas*. At 1:00 p.m., she was run aground 50 miles (80 km) west of Santiago. Like the battle of Manila Bay two months earlier, the battle of Santiago Bay had been extremely one-sided. Most of the poorly-aimed Spanish shells passed over their targets. On the American ships, only one man was killed.[121]

Although Hearst was not present for the naval battle, he was on board the *Sylvia* the next day, 4 July, to describe the string of wrecks on the beaches to the west of Santiago. First was the *Vizcaya*, lying on her side with 'gaping wounds' in her hull. Further along the shore, he took his ship's lifeboat to examine the blackened wreck of the *Oquendo*. Next, he found the remains of the *Infante Maria Teresa* still smoking. On the beach nearby, he spotted some 20 blackened survivors who waved a handkerchief in a gesture of surrender. Hearst took them on board his own ship, gave them food and clothes and delivered them to the navy on the armed liner *Harvard*.[122] On board a second liner, the *St Louis*, Hearst was able to interview Admiral Cervera in his white uniform, his trousers 'very damp from wading ashore'.[123] Then Hearst set sail for Jamaica in order to telegraph his story back to New York.

With their fleet destroyed, the Spanish had little reason to continue to defend the port of Santiago. Meanwhile, the American besieging army was losing more casualties to malaria than to the enemy's arms.[124] On 17 July, both parties were relieved to sign a capitulation agreement under which the Spanish forces would march out of Santiago 'with the honors of war'. The United States would transport back to Spain those soldiers who so desired.[125] As the US Ambassador to Britain, John Hay, observed shortly thereafter in a letter to Theodore Roosevelt, it had been a 'splendid little war'.[126] For Joseph Pulitzer, however, the war had not been so splendid. Hearst's *Journal* had reported that an Austrian artilleryman, Colonel Reflipe W. Thenuz, had been killed during the fighting around Santiago. When the *World* repeated the story through 20 editions with its own dateline, the *Journal* then revealed that the incident was its own invention. Rearranged, the letters of the man's name became, 'We pilfer the news'.[127]

Commercially, for New York's two leading newspapers, it was turning out to be a nice little war. Circulations had risen dramatically. Although the results had yet to show up in the form of increased profits owing to the costs of covering a distant conflict, there was clearly a mass market to be exploited in coming years. For the country as a whole, there was an equally remarkable effect. American armed forces were achieving worldwide recognition and fame at a moderate cost. Their victories were propelling their country into the top ranks of world powers. However, for the first time, the United States was faced with the dilemma of how to deal with distant territories that its armies had conquered.

## THE IRRESISTIBILITY OF EMPIRE

The procedure for the surrender of the Philippines' capital, Manila, had been arranged through the intermediation of the Belgian consul. The Spanish insisted on a show of force by both sides, so that the honor of their army could be upheld. But there was perhaps an additional reason for the detailed surrender script, namely, that the Spanish had no desire to be captured by the Philippine insurgents.[128] The latter had made a fearsome reputation for themselves by boiling captured Portuguese friars in oil or roasting them over fires.[129] In May, the Americans had brought the rebel leader, Emilio Aguinaldo, back from exile in Singapore, and since then the rebels had played a major role in capturing the area around Manila.[130] Now as word came that the Spanish were surrendering, the insurgents began advancing with their flag from the suburb of Paco toward the inner city. However, before they could reach the citadel they found their way blocked by several regiments of tall Americans. The American commanding officer insisted that the insurgents give way. But the rebel commander refused to withdraw, insisting that his troops be allowed into the city.[131] On each side, the tension mounted.

## The Battle of Manila

America's first fateful step on the road to empire had been taken three months earlier, on 13 May 1898 – six days after news of Dewey's victory at Manila Bay reached Washington. With the Spanish Pacific squadron destroyed, American dominance in the waters around Cuba was assured. Accordingly, there remained no reason for American forces to remain in the Philippines unless a permanent conquest of territory was intended. But if the United States were to take advantage of its stunning naval victory, how much territory should it acquire? Would it be sufficient to capture Manila Bay as a naval base or should the whole island chain be taken? The president asked General Wesley Merritt for an estimate of the number of men required to constitute an expedition to the Philippines. Merritt suggested a force of 14 000 men. Their chief objective would be to capture and hold Manila harbor.[132]

Accordingly, on 25 May, a first contingent of 2500 men under Brigadier General Thomas Anderson sailed from San Francisco bound for Manila. The troop transports were joined at Honolulu by the cruiser *Charleston*. On 20 June, the expedition arrived at Guam, midway between the Hawaiian Islands and the Philippines.[133] Since the small Spanish force there had no means of resistance, it quickly surrendered to the Americans, who desired to use the island as a coaling base. Here, then, was the first American colony. Upon reaching the Philippines, Anderson's contingent disembarked at the Cavite naval base south of Manila on 30 June. A second contingent of 3500 men under General Francis Greene arrived on 17 July.[134] By 31 July, General Merritt and a third contingent of 5000 men under General Arthur MacArthur, father of Douglas MacArthur, had arrived.[135]

During the month between the departures of Anderson and Merritt, the US game plan had changed. Merritt's orders stated that the objective of the expeditionary force was now to take not just Manila but the Philippine archipelago as a whole.[136]

At 9:30 a.m. on the morning of 13 August 1898, the American flagship *Olympia* opened the shelling of the Spanish fort of San Antonio de Abad, which defended the southern approaches to Manila. American army artillery on land soon joined in the firing. Then after a half hour of shelling, American infantry under Brigadier General Francis Greene charged the fort. Meeting little resistance, they moved quickly on through the outer suburbs toward the walled inner city. The Spanish defenders retreated rapidly before them, until finally the Americans found themselves blocked by the massive ramparts of the citadel. There tied to a corner of the grey walls they saw a large white sheet.[137] Meanwhile, a second force of American infantry under General MacArthur advancing farther inland found the going much more difficult. The Americans encountered heavy firing from the retreating Spanish. However, the attackers eventually realized that the shooting was not directed primarily at them but rather at the Philippine insurgents on their flank who were moving toward the citadel with them.[138]

General Greene met his Spanish counterparts in the citadel to examine the proposed terms of surrender. Then, leaving the details for General Merritt, who was on his way, Greene returned to his soldiers outside the ramparts. He led his force toward the Pasig River bridges that controlled the access to Manila from the east. These were the American troops that the insurgents encountered as they advanced to take control of the citadel. Greene had strict orders not to let the rebels enter the city. How could the impasse be resolved? Greene remembered the techniques for dealing with urban mobs. 'Port arms', he called and then wheeled his companies from column into line position. The burly Nebraskans then simply pushed the rebels into the fields beside the road.[139]

## Puerto Rico

While General Merritt had been assembling his expeditionary force in Manila, back in the Caribbean another expeditionary force under General Nelson Miles left newly captured Santiago de Cuba. Sailing east past Hispaniola, the ships headed for Puerto Rico. After the bitter fighting around Santiago de Cuba, the Americans were confident that their campaign to take the island of Puerto Rico would be a cakewalk. There was no longer any Spanish naval force to threaten their invasion, and the presence of the American fleet meant that the local garrison was cut off from outside supplies of food and munitions. The first American forces landed at the small south-shore port of Guánica on the morning of 25 July 1898.[140] Two days later, the threat of naval bombardment forced the surrender of the larger port of Ponce 25 miles (40 km) to the east. A third port, Arroyo, still further east, fell on 2 August. Miles then sent four columns north to converge on the capital, San Juan.[141] At several points on their overland route, the Americans encountered determined resistance. However, on 13 August, before any serious fighting could occur, the American commanders received telegrams from their superiors. 'The President directs all military operations against the enemy to be suspended.' Peace negotiations between the United States and Spain were under way and an initial protocol had been signed on 12 August.[142]

Back in New York, by the last months of the Spanish–American War, the *Journal*'s various editions were selling a total of 1.5 million copies a day – substantially more than the number sold by the *World*.[143] Hearst had defeated Pulitzer in the circulation war. It had cost $8 million, but his papers would soon be profitable.[144] He had succeeded in building up a readership that was now accustomed to a bold, new form of journalism. Blaring headlines, lavish illustrations and personalized writing for a mass audience were to remain permanent features of American journalism over the following century. However, the genie was now out of the bottle. Once aware of its collective power, this audience would no longer be content to let its elected representatives decide for it.

**Annexation?**

At the outset of the war, President McKinley had no interest in acquiring additional territory for his country by conquest. At most, he agreed with Secretary of State William Day, he would be happy with a 'hitching post' for the navy and American traders in the Far East.[145] After Dewey's great victory in Manila Bay, however, many Americans began to realize that their country too might acquire an empire.

McKinley, vowing that he would not be overtaken again by public opinion, reacted accordingly. On 3 June, when he first specified terms that the United States would find acceptable for ending the hostilities, he stated three conditions. First Spain must evacuate its troops from Cuba; second, instead of reparations, Spain must cede Puerto Rico to the United States; third, in the Pacific, America would retain possession of a port in the Philippines and an island between the Philippines and Hawaii as a coaling station.[146] Then, on 28 July, with American troops in possession of Guam and about to attack both Puerto Rico and Manila, McKinley further specified that his country would probably retain Guam and Manila Bay.

The fate of the rest of the Philippines would be determined by negotiations between the two countries.[147] Two weeks later, on 12 August, the Spanish government, aware that its soldiers in Cuba, Puerto Rico and the Philippines were in effect American hostages, signed an armistice accepting these terms.

As the summer progressed, McKinley agonized over what to do with the Philippines. A devout Methodist, he admitted that he often fell to his knees praying for guidance.[148] Militarily, he was told, it made little sense to seize part of the Philippines while leaving the other great powers to squabble over the rest. There was also a strong ethical argument for annexation. Clergymen declared that the United States had a civilizing mission to bring humanity along the road to 'freedom and progress'.[149] As in the decision to go to war, however, the deciding factor was probably public opinion as expressed on the streets and in the press. A close acquaintance observed that the 'President's ear was so close to the ground that it was full of grasshoppers'.[150] An opinion poll in August revealed that 43 per cent of Americans favored keeping the Philippines, only 25 per cent were against and the rest were undecided.[151] The following month, the *Literary Digest* printed a list of 84 major newspapers, including the *World* and the *Journal*, that favored annexing the Philippines.[152]

On 16 September 1898, as the American mission was about to leave for the Paris peace conference, McKinley instructed its members to demand full sovereignty over the Philippines.[153] Two weeks later Felipe Agoncillo, one of the closest advisers of Aguinaldo, arrived in Washington to remind the president of the commitments made to the insurgents by American representatives, including Dewey, prior to American landings. Agoncillo insisted that the Filipinos had been promised independence in exchange for their military support. However, McKinley was not to be moved. He offered no reply and ordered that Agoncillo be barred from the Paris conference room.[154]

Finally, on 31 October, the American government announced that it desired to annex all of the Philippines. It offered Spain $20 million to compensate it for the improvements it had made on the islands.[155] Realizing that the Americans were unwilling to budge from this final offer, and unable to contemplate a renewal of the war, the Spanish had little choice but to accept. The peace treaty was signed on 10 December 1898.

On the night of 4–5 February 1899, shortly before the US Senate was to vote on the treaty, there was an incident near a bridge over the San Juan River in the Manila suburb of Santa Mesa. An American patrol encountered three Filipino soldiers in the no-man's land between the two lines of troops. Private William Grayson ordered the Filipinos to halt. When the rebels refused to withdraw, Grayson fired, killing one of the Filipinos. Immediately, fighting broke out between the two former allies.[156] The incident was enough to tip the balance back in Washington. In the subsequent Senate vote on 6 February, there were 57 in favor and 27 against the treaty – sufficient to assure the two-thirds majority required for passage.[157]

Over the next two years, some 200 000 American soldiers gradually ground down the regular units of Filipino troops. Aguinaldo was captured in March 1901 and persuaded to swear allegiance to the United States. However, it took another year of bitter warfare before the islands could be considered pacified. The guerrillas in southern Luzon were defeated only when the military regime applied a policy similar to that used by General Weyler in Cuba. It herded the civilian population into 'protection zones' and proceeded to destroy both property and bands of guerrillas in sweeps outside these areas. Although many civilians died through disease in their allotted zones, the war was brought to an end by June 1902.[158] Over the three years of the Philippine–American War, 4200 Americans were killed – twice the number of American deaths in the Spanish–American War.[159]

Meanwhile, on 6 September 1901, President McKinley was shot by an anarchist while he visited an exposition in Buffalo. He died a week later in hospital. Ten years later, in 1911, the wreck of the USS *Maine* was carefully examined by a second navy commission. Again the conclusion was that the battleship had been blown up by a mine.[160] However, in 1976, Admiral Hyman Rickover organized a new investigation. The experts he consulted concluded that the initial explosion had probably resulted from spontaneous combustion in the ship's coal bunker that caused the adjacent six-inch shell magazine to explode.[161]

Once again, we see the unintended consequences of an innovation in communications. William McKinley was the first president to rely primarily on the new mass-circulation newspapers to address the American people. However, since he himself did not have the charisma required to hold the media's attention for long, in doing so, he lost the chief executive's traditional capacity to direct government policy. Unwilling to channel popular opinion in a consistent fashion during the critical period that followed the *Maine* explosion, he found himself swept along by a tide of irresistible pressure from circulation-maximizing newspaper publishers. Hearst, Pulitzer and their competitors were interested primarily in capturing enough advertising revenue to finance their massive investments in journalists and printing equipment. Meanwhile, despite their president's own pacifist intentions, Americans suddenly found themselves quite pleased to be ruling over an empire. The consequences of this change in political behavior would be felt through most of the twentieth century.

# NOTES

1. Brown (1967, pp. 80–81)
2. Nash *et al.* (1986, p. 670).
3. Werstein (1966, p. 18).
4. Hernandez (2002).
5. Brown (1967, p. 8).
6. Hernandez (2002).
7. Brown (1967, p. 37).
8. Brown (1967, p. 78).
9. Nasaw (2000, p. 128).
10. Nasaw (2000, pp. 92, 99).
11. Nasaw (2000, pp. 13–21).
12. Nasaw (2000, p. 48).
13. Nasaw (2000, p. 61).
14. Nasaw (2000, p. 89).
15. Nasaw (2000, pp. 96–98).
16. Nasaw (2000, p. 98).
17. Werstein (1966, p. 20), Brown (1967, p. 82).
18. Swanberg (1967, p. 231).
19. Mott (1962, p. 440).
20. Seitz (1924, p. 228).
21. Nasaw (2000, p. 105).
22. Swanberg (1967, p. 216).
23. BookRags.com (2007).
24. Nash *et al.* (1986, p. 601).
25. Nash *et al.* (1986, p. 603).
26. United States Bureau of the Census (1977, Series A 2).
27. Maddison (2001, p. 264).
28. Graff (1987, p. 376).
29. Seitz (1924, p. 42).
30. Seitz (1924, p. 59).
31. Barrett (1941, p. 45).
32. Brown (1967, p. 11).
33. Swanberg (1967, p. 52).
34. Seitz (1924, p. 108).
35. Mott (1962, p. 435),
36. Mott (1962, p. 434),
37. Seitz (1924, p. 145).
38. Mott (1962, p. 435),
39. Swanberg (1967, p. 162).
40. Seitz (1924, pp. 202–203).
41. United States Bureau of the Census (1977, Series U 187, U 188).
42. Nash *et al.* (1986, p. 666).
43. Swanberg (1967, p. 234).
44. Seitz (1924, p. 238).
45. Giessel (n.d.).
46. Swanberg (1967, p. 236).
47. Nasaw (2000, pp. 128–129).
48. Nasaw (2000, p. 69).
49. Nasaw (2000, p. 77).
50. Nasaw (2000, p. 70).
51. Nasaw (2000, p. 55).
52. Nasaw (2000, p. 81).
53. Hutt (1973, p. 78).

54. Nasaw (2000, p. 75).
55. Nasaw (2000, p. 78).
56. Nasaw (2000, p. 75).
57. Nasaw (2000, p. 80).
58. Mott (1962, p. 475).
59. Mott (1962, pp. 396–397).
60. Mott (1962, p. 403).
61. Mott (1962, p. 498).
62. Mott (1962, p. 601).
63. Mott (1962, p. 401).
64. Ibid.
65. Mott (1962, p. 498).
66. Mott (1962, p. 497).
67. Mott (1962, p. 501).
68. Mott (1962, p. 498).
69. United States Bureau of the Census (1998).
70. Nasaw (2000, p. 98).
71. Nasaw (2000, p. 99).
72. Swanberg (1967, p. 206).
73. Seitz (1924, p. 211).
74. Seitz (1924, p. 212), Swanberg (1967, p. 207).
75. Mott (1962, p. 526).
76. Mott (1962, p. 539).
77. Giessel (n.d.).
78. Swanberg (1967, pp. 238–239).
79. Nasaw (2000, p. 129).
80. Swanberg (1967, p. 239).
81. Swanberg (1967, p. 241).
82. Nasaw (2000, pp. 130–131).
83. Musicant (1998, pp. 116, 140).
84. Musicant (1998, p. 128).
85. Musicant (1998, p. 141).
86. Brown (1967, p. 123).
87. Musicant (1998, p. 144).
88. Brown (1967, p. 130).
89. Nasaw (2000, p. 131).
90. Johnson (1997, p. 612).
91. Musicant (1998, pp. 152, 156).
92. Nash *et al.* (1986, p. 655).
93. Musicant (1998, p. 132).
94. Musicant (1998, p. 158).
95. Brown (1967, p. 143).
96. Brown (1967, p. 145).
97. Musicant (1998, p. 173).
98. Musicant (1998, p. 177).
99. Musicant (1998, p. 183).
100. Brown (1967, pp. 148–149).
101. Musicant (1998, p. 189).
102. Musicant (1998, pp. 153–154).
103. Musicant (1998, pp. 196–198).
104. Musicant (1998, p. 209).
105. Musicant (1998, p. 555).
106. Musicant (1998, p. 209).
107. Musicant (1998, p. 230).
108. Musicant (1998, p. 233).
109. Musicant (1998, pp. 279, 291–294).

110. Musicant (1998, pp. 326–327).
111. Musicant (1998, p. 371).
112. Brown (1967, p. 325).
113. Brown (1967, pp. 302, 336).
114. Musicant (1998, p. 394).
115. Hearst would marry Millicent in 1903.
116. Musicant (1998, p. 401).
117. Brown (1967, p. 347).
118. Nasaw (2000, pp. 138–139).
119. Musicant (1998, p. 435).
120. Musicant (1998, p. 443).
121. Musicant (1998, p. 464).
122. Nasaw (2000, p. 140).
123. Brown (1967, p. 390).
124. Musicant (1998, p. 488).
125. Musicant (1998, pp. 497–498).
126. Stenzel (2006).
127. Nasaw (2000, p. 134), Swanberg (1967, pp. 251–252).
128. Musicant (1998, p. 569).
129. Musicant (1998, p. 196).
130. Musicant (1998, pp. 547, 551).
131. Musicant (1998, p. 578).
132. Musicant (1998, p. 544).
133. Ibid.
134. Musicant (1998, p. 565).
135. Musicant (1998, p. 567).
136. Ibid.
137. Musicant (1998, pp. 576–577).
138. Musicant (1998, p. 578).
139. Ibid.
140. Musicant (1998, p. 529).
141. Musicant (1998, pp. 533–534).
142. Musicant (1998, p. 537).
143. Mott (1962, p. 537).
144. Swanberg (1967, p. 207).
145. Musicant (1998, p. 590).
146. Musicant (1998, p. 587).
147. Musicant (1998, p. 592).
148. Musicant (1998, p. 600).
149. Musicant (1998, p. 603).
150. Musicant (1998, p. 615).
151. Ibid.
152. O'Toole (1984, p. 384).
153. Musicant (1998, p. 604).
154. Musicant (1998, pp. 605–606).
155. Musicant (1998, pp. 616, 637).
156. Linn (2000, pp. 45–46).
157. Musicant (1998, p. 629).
158. Linn (2000, pp. 302–304).
159. Nash *et al.* (1986, pp. 659–660).
160. O'Toole (1984, p. 397).
161. O'Toole (1984, p. 400).

# 8. The self-fulfilling prophecy

In the United Kingdom during the last decades of the nineteenth century, government expenditures averaged around ten per cent of the country's total income. The situation was similar in other Western democracies, where in times of peace, most voters were reluctant to accept the taxes that would be required to exceed this level.[1] To date, the extension of voting rights to urban workers had not been followed by income redistribution via government taxes and expenditures.

Since the Combination Act of 1825, workers in Britain had been allowed to form trade unions to bargain over working conditions and wages. But because obstruction and intimidation were forbidden, the courts were given considerable leeway to punish those who organized work stoppages. Workers who attempted to arrange a strike could be prosecuted for restrictive trades practices. During the 1830s and 1840s, owing to divisions among the workers, first Robert Owen and then the Chartists had failed in organizing large number of laborers. It was not until 1851 that the first successful union, the Amalgamated Society of Engineers, representing steam engine operators, machinists and other skilled mechanical workers, was established.

More recently, in 1871, Gladstone's Liberal government had exempted unions from laws prohibiting the restraint of trade. And in 1875, Disraeli's Conservative majority had approved the Conspiracy and Protection of Property Act allowing unions to organize strikes and to picket peacefully during industrial conflicts. As a result, by the 1890s, a number of successful unions had been organized. All functioned relatively peacefully within the rules set up by Parliament. Would the labor movement dare to go beyond the negotiation of wages in individual firms and attempt to improve the conditions of workers and their families in the country as a whole? And if so, what other parallel changes might occur?

## THE CARRIAGE AND FOUR

William Kennedy Jones was gazing down into London's Tudor Street from the offices of the *Star* one morning in the summer of 1894. Below him, across the street, a stylish carriage pulled by a team of four horses stopped at the offices of the weekly paper, *Answers*. Out jumped a young man of about his own age in top hat and morning coat, accompanied by a well-dressed young woman. Asking his office mates who the couple were, Jones was told, 'Alfred Harmsworth and his wife'. The elegant pair made a vivid impression on Jones.

As the hardened assistant editor of a money-losing daily paper, Kennedy Jones was looking about for new opportunities. He and a partner decided to secure an option to purchase another troubled daily, the *Evening News and Post*, and then set about finding financial backing for their venture. A few days before their option was to expire, a colleague mentioned Harmsworth's name, adding that the publishing house across the street was making profits of over £40 000 a year.[2] When Jones approached Alfred Harmsworth and his brother Harold, they were not particularly keen to purchase a nearly bankrupt daily which, its sellers insisted, must remain loyal to the Conservative Party. Nevertheless, they finally agreed to underwrite a bid. For £25 000, the Harmsworths and their new partners succeeded in obtaining the *Evening News*, its plant and equipment. However, when Alfred Harmsworth subsequently went to Coutts' Bank to sell some securities in order to finance his purchase, the manager cautioned him that there were few more certain ways to lose money than by operating a daily newspaper. Nevertheless, Alfred, aged 29, with no experience of running a daily, blithely disregarded the warning and signed away his assets.[3]

## Alfred Harmsworth

Who was this young Alfred Harmsworth and why was he so confident that he could succeed where others had failed? Some three decades earlier, his father, a schoolmaster from London also named Alfred Harmsworth, had obtained a teaching post at a military school in Dublin. There the elder Harmsworth married a young Protestant woman who in 1865 bore him a boy. When young Alfred was two, the family moved back to London so that his father could complete his training for the Bar. Unfortunately, Alfred senior's income as a barrister was never quite sufficient to finance both the needs of his growing family and his consumption of alcohol. The couple eventually had 14 children, three of whom died as infants. There were frequent periods when their mother put the youngest children to bed wrapped in newspapers to keep them warm.[4]

Young Alfred was never a very serious student, but at age 15 he became the successful manager of a new magazine that he convinced his school to publish. He himself wrote most of the copy, touching on a variety of subjects, including school gossip, his own poetry and a proposal for a committee of boys to handle school discipline.[5] Driven by a desire to get ahead, he also set up his own business producing 'Tonks's Pills – Cure All Ills' that he distributed to local shops.[6]

By age 16, Alfred realized that his greatest goal in life was to succeed in journalism and accordingly quit school. Shortly afterward, he answered a personal advertisement in *The Times* and was offered a position of traveling companion for a young aristocrat, E.V.R. Powys, 27, who was about to set off to the continent. Harmsworth proved an excellent fellow traveler, thoughtful and intelligent. Indeed, at Aix les Bains, a French admiral complimented his patron: 'Si votre jeune ami est un modèle de la jeunesse anglaise, je vous félicite de tout mon coeur, c'est un charmant garçon, d'une intelligence surprenante'.[7]

Back in London, Alfred began to submit articles to magazines published for young readers. At age 18, he often earned £3 a week by his freelance writing.[8] However, there also came depressing periods when editors refused to accept his submissions. On one such day, he and a friend visited George Newnes, an untidy man with a black and white streaked beard who published a weekly magazine called *Tit-bits*, and who reportedly paid a guinea a column. Newnes specialized in short self-improvement articles that offered the reader interesting information on a wide variety of topics not readily found elsewhere. Inspired by this encounter, Harmsworth was soon a regular contributor, writing on 'Some Curious Butterflies', 'How Fortunes are Made' and 'Newspaper Special Editions'.

At the precocious age of 20, Alfred applied for and was appointed to the position of editor of a weekly for cyclists, *Bicycling News*, published in Coventry by a small magazine chain. There he introduced a series of innovations that attracted new readers – articles cut into short paragraphs, features for women and items about photography. He had grown into an attractive young man, above average height, five feet eight inches (173 cm) tall, with straight, light-colored hair, a pleasing oval face, and bright eyes.[9] In April 1888, he married Mary Milner, a young woman he had known from childhood.

Recalling his meeting with Newnes, Alfred had begun to ask himself whether he could not launch a paper similar to *Tit-bits*. He put his ideas together in a folder labeled in capital letters, SCHEMO MAGNIFICO.[10] It called for not one paper but a whole series of publications. To start, there was a projected weekly that would answer questions submitted by its readers but would carry no advertisements. Since most of the 22 previous attempts to imitate *Tit-bits*' success had quickly failed, Alfred's principal difficulty was in getting financial backing.[11] After several unsuccessful attempts, he was introduced to Alexander Spink Beaumont, a retired soldier who had married a wealthy woman 14 years his senior. The

Beaumonts were persuaded to put two successive instalments of £1000 into Alfred's firm.[12]

The first issue of *Answers to Correspondents* (later shortened to *Answers*), a 16-page publication printed on cream-colored paper, was offered to the public for a penny a copy on 16 June 1888. The paper's stated goal was to educate the readers on a variety of subjects. Accordingly, there were articles entitled, 'What the Queen Eats', 'Narrow Escapes from Being Buried Alive' and 'Why Jews Don't Ride Bicycles'.[13] Almost all the articles in these early editions were written by Harmsworth himself, who recycled many of the items he had written as a freelancer.[14] He quickly adjusted the paper's approach as he struggled to keep revenues ahead of costs, beginning to accept advertisements, adding an orange cover and introducing serial stories.[15] His most successful idea was to purchase the rights to a puzzle in which seven colored balls in a glass-covered box had to be jiggled so as to spell out ANSWERS. The paper organized *Answers* puzzle clubs in cities throughout the UK. In June 1889, when Alfred's brother Harold quit his civil service job to become the *Answers* business manager, circulation climbed to 45 000 copies a week.[16] The paper quickly began to churn out a rising stream of profits. The following year, the Harmsworths launched two new weeklies – *Comic Cuts* and *Illustrated Chips* – that published collections of jokes.

Although an outwardly calm man with a quiet voice, Alfred also had a cruel side to his character. It is said that in the bathroom of his country house at Broadstairs on the coast in Kent, there was an aquarium with two compartments. In one were goldfish, in the other a pike. Occasionally, he would lift the glass partition between the two sections and observe the outcome.[17]

## Winning the Evening Market

By the summer of 1894, Alfred Harmsworth at 29 was the head of a prosperous publishing house with a stable of periodicals whose total circulation had reached 1.5 million copies a week.[18] With his newly acquired wealth, came a desire to enter politics. What better way was there to put his name before the public than as publisher of a daily newspaper? Alfred's political ambitions help explain the Harmsworths' purchase of *Evening News and Post*, described above. However, Harold insisted that the paper be expected to contribute its share to the profits of the firm. For many an evening that fall, therefore, the two brothers and Kennedy Jones met under the broken skylight of the top floor of the *News* building trying to devise a strategy to resuscitate their new patient.[19]

A first step was to cut costs. With the financial security of the magazine firm's profits to support him, Harold was able to beat down the prices of the newsprint suppliers. In addition, the technical side of the newspaper must function smoothly. Here the experience of Kennedy Jones was invaluable. New type was purchased to change the look of the paper. Above all, new readers must be courted and won over. It was Alfred who adapted the lessons he had learned in magazine publishing to the production of a daily newspaper. On the first day, the paper's name was shortened to *The Evening News*. Its position would be Conservative, it would 'preach the gospel of loyalty to the Empire' and it would be 'sympathetic towards Labour'.[20] Gone were the dreary political commentaries occupying whole columns. In their place were short articles broken up into easily read paragraphs.

It was as though Alfred could slip into the minds of his potential readers, discovering what each most enjoyed and needed. To hold the attention of the male readers, he introduced a sort of football pool. Readers were invited to predict the winning football teams, sending a stamp with each prediction in the hope of winning a £5 prize. For female readers, there was a women's column (later expanded into a women's page) that became a standard feature. Plentiful maps were added to illustrate the main stories. And every day there was a fresh short story.[21]

## The Bottom Line

In 1894, at the moment that the Harmsworths entered the daily newspaper field, London had nine evening papers, five selling for a penny and four others, including the *Evening News*, priced at a halfpenny. Their circulation ran far behind that of the large morning papers. Most were losing money. The *Evening News* was selling 100 000 copies a day, but in its last week before its sale to the Harmsworths, it had showed a loss of £100.

The financial controls introduced by Harold had an immediate effect on the bottom line of the *Evening News*. In the Harmsworths' first week, the paper made a profit of £7; by the third week the profits had climbed to £50.[22] How was it possible to make a profit on a newspaper that sold for only a halfpenny? The answer was through a new type of advertising. With Britain's rising prosperity there was a vast potential market for standardized consumer goods such as Lipton's tea, Epps Cocoa and Hudson's soap. The manufacturers of these products found that large circulation newspapers were the most efficient way to reach this market. As more readers began buying the paper, Harold was able to raise the advertising rates to £40 a half-page.[23]

This financial success was of course possible only if the paper was able to capture the attention of large numbers of readers. Although explicit reference to sex was prohibited by the Victorian moral code, Albert discovered that the description of violence, playing on readers' unconscious fears, was a sure way to boost circulation. In late September, a police hunt for the murderer of a young woman captured the headlines for several days until a suspect, James Canham Read, was arrested. Sensing that the case would attract great attention, Alfred, accompanied by the author of several books on crime, visited Read's cell in Chelmsford prison in Essex. He then alerted Kennedy Jones to the importance of the coming trial.

**An Untapped Market**

Having turned around the *Evening News*, Alfred turned to his next projects. For one thing, the term of office of the present Conservative government was drawing to an end. Soon there would be a general election. With an important newspaper behind him, Harmsworth would surely have a good chance of winning a seat for the Conservatives. A more long-term interest was the morning newspaper market. In the UK, the total circulation of morning newspapers was considerably greater than that of evening papers. The success of the *Evening News* suggested that there might be a market in Britain for one or more new dailies, distributed in the morning and oriented to the interests of those who read *Answers*.

In early October 1894, Alfred Harmsworth left for a trip to Paris. In addition to his visits in the city and outings to the theater, he was interested in the local market for newspapers. He had several meetings with Hippolyte-Auguste Marinoni, inventor and manufacturer of rotary color printing presses. In 1890, Marinoni had launched *Le Petit Journal*. At the time of Alfred's visit, the four-page paper had a circulation of 630 000 – a figure greater than that of all the London evening papers together.[24] Before leaving Paris, Alfred learned that his latest venture was not doing badly. On the last day of the Read trial, the *Evening News* had sold 390 000 copies.[25] By the end of its first six months, the renamed daily would be selling a comfortable 160 000 copies a day and earning £1000 a month in profits.[26] However, the purchase of this paper was merely the first step in Alfred's plan to remodel the newspaper industry in Britain.

Two days after his return to London, Alfred dined with Cecil Rhodes and his associate, Leander Starr Jameson. Harmsworth was so captivated by Rhodes's vision of empire that three weeks later he made a speech defending the adventurer's ambitious vision with 'unqualified admiration'.[27] Over the following two decades, this fiery mixture of mass journalism and expansionist imperialism would push Britain and its European neighbors ever closer to war.

As a wealthy publisher without family backing and personal charisma, Alfred now realized that he could probably best contribute to the Empire by supporting it in his publications. To do so effectively, he would have to find a way to capture a sufficiently large share of the morning newspaper market to complement his successful afternoon *Evening Post*. Meanwhile, as the year 1894 drew to a close, a charming young man with a famous name but no money was also wondering how best to get ahead in life. Over the next quarter-century, the careers of Alfred Harmsworth and this articulate descendant of the Duke of Marlborough would often intersect.

## ETERNAL SUNSHINE

It is difficult today to imagine that the Winston Churchill of the famous bulldog jowls was once a slim young man. But a photo taken early in 1895 shows him at age 20. He is a bit below average height – five feet six and one-half (169 cm) tall – with wavy brown hair, in the gold-braided uniform of a second lieutenant in the Fourth Hussars, a British cavalry regiment. He faces the camera proudly, his hand on his sword hilt, confident that he can meet any challenges that life will throw at him.[28] His father, Lord Randolph Churchill, had considered him not bright enough to study law and had sent him to study at the Royal Military Academy Sandhurst.[29] To the family's surprise, Winston did well, graduating eighth in a class of 150 in December 1894. Shortly thereafter, his father died from the effects of syphilis.[30] The Hussars were slated to leave the following year for an eight- to nine-year posting in India.[31] First, however, Winston had time to visit America and to report on the growing insurrection in Cuba for the British press.

As the example of Winston Churchill illustrates, the late nineteenth century was a time of exceptional opportunity in the United Kingdom. By European standards, British society was surprisingly open to men of talent, whatever their family or ethnic background. Moreover, the country had been spared the bitter class conflicts that divided the emerging industrial societies on the continent. And its vast empire offered a variety of possible careers for ambitious young men.

### Open to Success

Two years before his death, Lord Randolph had taken young Winston to meet 'Natty', Lord Nathan Mayer Rothschild, at Tring, the Jewish family's country seat. The head of the Jewish banking family in Britain had been appointed to the House of Lords in 1884 and had been a close adviser of Winston's father in 1886–1887, when the latter had been Chancellor of the Exchequer. Lord Rothschild was now accepted almost as a member of minor royalty by the English aristocracy.[32] The Rothschilds had raised the funds that allowed Britain to purchase control of the Suez Canal in 1875.

More recently, Lord Rothschild had helped to fund Cecil Rhodes's British South Africa Company, modeled after the East India Company, to exploit the resources of South Africa's interior. When Lord Randolph Churchill died, it was later revealed, he owed £66 000 to Rothschild's bank.[33]

Since 1858, Jews in England had enjoyed full political rights. Benjamin Disraeli, born of Jewish parents and baptized a Christian, had twice been prime minister. However, not all Jews in England were as fortunate as Disraeli and the Rothschilds. There were no restrictions limiting immigration into the United Kingdom. Accordingly, after the pogroms that broke out in Russia following the assassination of Tsar Alexander II in 1881, waves of Jewish immigrants began to arrive in English ports. During the 1880s and 1890s, an average of 1000 East European Jews landed in Britain every year. Many settled in East London, finding jobs in tailoring or shoe making. When the English used the term 'aliens', they were generally referring to these impoverished Jewish immigrants.[34]

In 1884, a reporter from *The Lancet*, the journal of the British Medical Council, investigated the sweatshops of East London. He found dreadful conditions: often eight or ten workers crowded into a tiny overheated room with an overflowing toilet – a sanitary situation made considerably worse by the use of urine in the glazing of cheap textiles. At this time, there was high unemployment in British manufacturing, particularly in those industries that employed unskilled and semi-skilled workers. In response, some voices called for restrictions on alien immigration. However, in a report published in 1889, a committee of the House of Lords found that the problems in the sweating system had been greatly exaggerated. It recommended against imposing restrictions on the entry of aliens. As the Jewish trade unionist Joseph Finn later argued, the presence of the immigrant workers created jobs in sectors that supplied the sweatshops with cloth and other inputs.[35] In addition, as a representative of the London wholesalers observed, the system generated substantial export receipts for the British economy.

### Social Harmony

On his return from the United States in 1896, young Winston Churchill wrote to one of his new American friends about the nature of government: 'The duty of governments is to be first of all practical. I am for makeshifts and expediency. I would like to make the people who live on this world at the same time as I do better fed and happier generally.'[36] In short, society's leaders, among whom he of course included himself, should be prepared to make concessions as necessary to assure a minimum of well-being for their fellow citizens.

Support for such reforming ideas was limited. In 1869, union representatives from the principal industrial cities and towns had met in the first Trades Union Congress. Two years later the delegates voted to establish a parliamentary committee that would apply pressure on Members of Parliament. These political activities were carried out within the existing two-party structure. In 1893, Keir Hardie, a Scottish miner who had been elected to the Commons as an independent, called worker representatives to a conference in Bradford, Yorkshire. There they founded the Independent Labour Party, vowing to support independent candidates. Their members were pledged to work for 'the collective ownership and control of production, distribution and exchange'.[37] In the 1895 elections, the new party managed to field 28 candidates. However, all, including Hardie himself, were defeated. Lord Salisbury's coalition of Conservatives and Liberal Unionists (so called because they opposed Irish Home Rule) won a large majority.

One radical Liberal member who survived the rout was an eloquent young lawyer from Wales. Twelve years older than Churchill, David Lloyd George was short, sturdy, good looking, and a ferocious debater.[38] After witnessing the electoral defeat of fellow Welsh nationalists at the hands of Conservatives, Lloyd George decided to devote himself to social reform within the Liberal Party rather than to Welsh autonomy.[39]

**Imperial Equilibrium**

Winston Churchill and his regiment left by ship for their new posting in India in September 1896. With the Royal Navy commanding the seas, only a moderate land force was required to protect the homeland. Indeed, over 60 per cent of the British army's 300 000 soldiers were stationed on the Indian subcontinent.[40] As a second lieutenant, Churchill would earn £300 a year, or twice what he would have received on home duty. On arriving in Bombay, he and his unit departed by train for Bangalore in the cool southern highlands.

The scramble for territory on the part of the European powers during the last decades of the nineteenth century has been described as the 'New Imperialism'. However, until the final years of the century, there was arguably nothing particularly new about this latest wave of conquest. During the seventeenth and eighteenth centuries, the British, the Dutch and the French had conquered territory to the limits that were economically feasible under the technology of sail, musket and pen on paper. They had seized the higher-yielding lands in the Americas and south Asia. Then, after 1870, the development of the steamship, the Maxim gun and the telegraph rendered profitable marginal lands that had previously been considered uneconomical.[41] Africa in particular was now up for grabs.

By 1895, the British controlled the most populous areas in West Africa along with Egypt and extensive territories in East Africa. With the exception of two small Boer republics, the Empire also included much of the land stretching north from the Cape of Good Hope into central Africa. Cost–benefit calculations show that the British were earning a normal profit on their investments.[42]

Inevitably, expansion by the British frustrated the projects of their European neighbors. In Africa, the principal competitors were the French, who dominated the Mediterranean coast from their colonies of Algeria and Tunisia. They were pushing west into Morocco and toward the Nile from territories along the Atlantic coast. In the Middle East, the Russians were the main competitors, striving to reach Constantinople through the Balkans and to the borders of India through Persia. In 1892, these two rivals of Britain signed a military alliance, each promising to support the other if it was attacked by a third party.

During the first two decades after 1871, Britain's implicit ally, both in reining in the Russians in the Balkans and in assuring a balance among the main European powers elsewhere, was the reunited German Empire. In 1878, Bismarck had brokered a conference in Berlin to deal with the Balkans. Again in 1884, the great powers met in the German capital to set out rules for the division of Africa. Britain and Germany had traded territory in 1890, the British ceding the North Sea island of Heligoland to Germany in exchange for Zanzibar. Thus far, however, Britain had refrained from entering any sort of permanent alliance with a foreign power. Salisbury, who had been foreign minister from 1886 to 1892, preferred to maintain his country's 'splendid isolation'.

**The Portsmouth Campaign**

In 1895, when his government of Liberals and Irish nationalists lost a vote in the House of Commons, Lord Rosebery asked the Queen to issue a writ for parliamentary elections. Alfred Harmsworth accepted the Unionist (that is, Conservative and anti-Home Rule Liberal) nomination to stand as a candidate in the two-member constituency of Plymouth. His first step was to buy the local Conservative newspaper, the *Evening Mail*. Then he hired a songwriter to compose a patriotic song to be performed in the local music hall. However, Alfred quickly discovered that he did not have a voice strong enough to command the attention of a large audience. Then, just before the vote, the local dockers heard an Anglican priest warn them against splitting their ballots. Despite the tide running in favor of the Conservatives in the nation as a whole, a local current swept both Liberal candidates ahead of Harmsworth and his fellow Tory.[43]

Several months later, Harmsworth changed the name of the Portsmouth paper to the *Southern Daily Mail* and lightened the content as he had done with the *Evening News*. One of his ideas was to run a serial story on an invasion of Portsmouth by an unnamed foreign army. Posters around the city displayed wave after wave of foreign soldiers attacking the Town Hall. The viewer was left to decide whether the invaders were French, Russian or German. However, readers along the south coast in the summer of 1895 seemed uninterested in a story about war, preferring the local welcoming festivities for a visiting Italian naval squadron. The circulation of the Portsmouth daily stagnated.[44]

At the urging of their Scottish partner, Kennedy Jones (K.J.), the Harmsworth brothers purchased a paper in Scotland, the *Glasgow Mail and Record*, renaming it the *Glasgow Daily Record*. For an investment of £7000 they were able to launch a halfpenny daily in Scotland's largest city. K.J.'s idea was to dispatch news reports by telegraph from London to a series of regional papers such as those in Portsmouth and Glasgow. Once again, the partners' vision proved incomplete and the paper failed to turn a profit in its first year. Yet there was perhaps a lesson to be learned. If the concept of a decentralized network had proved faulty, might the converse idea of a centralized system consisting of a paper printed in London and delivered early across the country not be worth trying?[45] To do so, it was first necessary to break into the London morning market, by far the most important selling place for British daily newspapers.

## A MIGHTY MEDIUM

The beginning of 1896 saw the emergence of an issue that had the potential to attract millions of new readers to the daily press. When slavery was abolished in the British Empire in 1833, many Dutch-speaking families in the Cape Colony left for the interior in a movement that was later known as the Great Trek. The British recognized the independence of the new Boer republics of the Transvaal and the Orange Free State in 1854. However, with the discovery of diamonds in the Transvaal in 1867 and gold in 1886, many in Britain and the Cape began to regret this decision. Not only had many British *uitlanders* been denied the vote by the Boers, but also British developers such as Cecil Rhodes, the wealthy prime minister of the Cape Colony, desired to integrate the resources of the two Boer republics into the Empire.

In December 1895, Rhodes's associate, Leander Starr Jameson (or 'Doctor Jim' as he was known) led an unauthorized cavalry expedition of 600 men from British territory into the Transvaal. Jameson and Rhodes had hoped that the raid would provoke an uprising of foreigners living in the Boer republics. However, Jameson and his men were disavowed by the British government. The raiders were quickly defeated, and Jameson and his surviving followers imprisoned. The raid caused considerable resentment in Germany, where most people sympathized with the Dutch-speaking Boers. The German government deliberately created a diplomatic incident when it sent a telegram signed by Kaiser William II to the Transvaal president, Paul Kruger, congratulating him on defeating the raiders. However, in a subsequent letter to his grandmother, Queen Victoria, the Kaiser explained that he had not intended any hostility toward Britain.[46] Salisbury decided to let the matter drop. But Alfred Harmsworth would not.

## Literacy

Who were the new readers that Harmsworth wished to seduce? If the new publications that the Harmsworths had launched since 1888 had been surprisingly successful, it was because the brothers happened to be in the right place at the right time with a new idea. Even 30 years earlier, their accomplishments in building a mass market in journalism would have been unthinkable. At the time of Alfred's birth, in 1865, one out of four newly wedded men had been unable to sign the marriage register. The reading skills of brides were even lower: one in three was illiterate.[47] Among the adult population as a whole, the rate of illiteracy stood at around 30 per cent. For purposes of comparison, in Germany, the Netherlands and Scandinavia, the adult illiteracy rate was under 20 per cent.[48] Even among those in Britain who could read, however, low real wages and salaries meant that prior to the 1890s, the potential market for popular newspapers was quite limited.

One of the priorities for William Gladstone's Liberal government, which had taken office in 1868, was to close the literacy gap between England and the rest of northern Europe. The 1870 Education Act divided the country into some 2500 school districts, each of which was to have an elected school board. Should the voluntary societies not be providing sufficient schools, the Act called for the establishment of publicly financed elementary schools to be paid for by taxes on property owners. Ten years later, in 1880, the Liberal government decided that there were enough school places to make attendance for children compulsory.

With free universal compulsory education, rates of illiteracy began to fall rapidly, particularly for women. By 1895, illiteracy rates for newly married men and women were virtually equal, at about four per cent. Britain was rapidly approaching a situation in which all those of working age were able to read and write.

## Democracy

With the vast majority of the population able to understand written messages, it was only natural for them to wish to participate in political decisions. Under the conditions of the Great Reform Act of 1832, only one man in five in Britain had been granted the right to vote. During the last half of the nineteenth century, there was therefore great public pressure to extend the franchise. In France, universal male suffrage had been introduced after the revolution of 1848, briefly curtailed and then restored by Napoleon III for the 1851 plebiscite that granted him dictatorial powers. In Germany, Bismarck had given all men the vote under the constitution that established the North German Confederation in 1867. With the adherence of the four southern states in 1871, universal male suffrage was applied to the whole German Reich.

It was Disraeli, briefly serving as prime minister in 1867, who convinced the Conservative Party's leaders that they should avoid being labeled as reactionaries by approving a new Reform Act. In the towns, all male householders and men paying at least £10 for unfurnished rooms were given the vote. In 1884, Gladstone extended this measure to the rural constituencies. As a result, by 1895, about two-thirds of all men had the right to vote.

Here, then, for Alfred Harmsworth was a great mass of recently enfranchised young voters, able to read and write, and anxious to improve their own living and employment conditions. As a group, they needed information. While they desired to be entertained, they were also eager to learn about the complex issues of foreign affairs and economic policy. But the information must be presented simply in short blocks that were easy to understand. For the generation of their parents, disenfranchised and often illiterate, the bounds to political behavior had been narrow: one left the important decisions to the educated elite. But the new generation had to decide how best to use the power to vote that was now in their hands. Harmsworth sensed that in helping them answer this question he could bring about the 'Schemo magnifico' he had dreamed of some eight years earlier.

## The Daily Mail

It was after midnight on the morning of 4 May 1896. As he watched the pressmen readying the three powerful new rotaries, Alfred Harmsworth cut the tension with a remark to Kennedy Jones, 'Bankruptcy or Berkeley Square!' (referring to the fashionable restaurant and hotel district in London's Mayfair).[49] He had invested £100 000 and untold hours in preparation for this moment.[50] At 1:20 a.m., the giant machines finally throbbed into action, churning out the first edition of a new London morning paper, the *Daily Mail*. Harmsworth wrote his signature on the first copy ceremoniously and sent it off by messenger to his mother's house. Then, having signed another 100 copies for his employees, he retired to the nearby Salisbury Hotel to get some much-needed sleep.[51]

Harmsworth had made his first visit to the United States in 1894.[52] There he had talked with New York newspaper owners and visited printing plants.[53] As he prepared to launch his new morning daily, he weighed these American impressions against those gained over the intervening months as publisher of the *Evening News*. What he must find was a way to innovate journalistically without shocking the British reader. Between February and May 1896, he had some 65 different experimental issues of the new paper prepared. Reporters were assigned stories that only their colleagues would read. In New York and Paris, local offices were set up and a cable news service established. Printers were trained to set up copy on the new linotype machines. Above all, editors and sub-editors were taught to keep their text as clear and simple as possible, eliminating excess words and phrases. Harmsworth himself supervised the composition of each page. Now, across London and southeastern England, billboards in searing yellow on a blue background screamed out DAILY MAIL.[54]

The front page of the first edition bore the new paper's name in large black gothic characters along with the slogan, 'A penny newspaper for one halfpenny'. As with other British papers, the rest of the first page was covered with small classified advertisements. Turning to the back page, the reader found more substantial advertisements for such products as Dr Tibbles' Vi-Cocoa, Bovril and Erard Pianos. Inside, however, was a journalistic innovation: sections with the headings 'The Daily Magazine' and 'Women's Realm', that is, features designed to attract those who would normally not buy a newspaper. An editorial criticized the new speed limits for motors cars – 3 miles (5 km) per hour. And above all, there was the news of the day, in short articles broken up into easily read paragraphs. There had been atrocities in the Cuban revolutionary war, an assassination in Persia and a murder in Reading. And in far-off southern Africa, Rhodes's British South Africa Police were using artillery and Maxim guns against black tribesmen armed with spears near the town of Bulawayo.

At the time, London's leading morning newspaper was the *Daily Telegraph*, with a circulation of 300 000.[55] How would the London public react to its latest daily? At lunchtime, young Winston Churchill, soon to leave for India, noted the presence of Harmsworth at Londonderry House, where a small party was celebrating the publisher's latest success. Harmsworth's realistic guess at the circulation for the day had been 100 000; he had hoped for 150 000. In fact, 390 000 copies of the new paper were sold. Lord Salisbury commented that it was merely a newspaper 'produced by office boys for office boys', Nevertheless, the 30-year-old office boy Alfred Harmsworth was about to shake up British society with his revolutionary new communications medium.[56]

## The Diamond Jubilee

A year after the launching of the *Daily Mail*, on 20 June 1897, the British Empire celebrated 60 years of Victoria's reign. The Queen, 78, rode through the streets of London in an open landau to St Paul's Cathedral. Because she was unable to walk up the steps, a brief thanksgiving service was held outside the massive church.[57] Accompanying her on the 6-mile (10-km) drive in a separate carriage was her German grandson, the Kaiser's brother. At several points during the procession, the German representatives were booed. When the parade halted briefly, there was a cry from the crowd in a cockney accent, 'There's a post office round the corner, if you want to send any more telegrams'.

When Alfred Harmsworth heard of this incident, he was surely delighted. He himself had viewed the Queen and the long parade of soldiers accompanying her from a room overlooking St James Street, across from the royal palace. He then hurried away to oversee the printing of a special edition of his new paper, the *Daily Mail*, printed in golden ink. Over the year since its first edition, the halfpenny daily had been warning its readers about the German threat. 'The keynote to modern Germany is militarism', they were told. The world was endangered by 'the inherent brutality of the German character, which the saving grace of art and music has never destroyed'.[58]

Six days after the London parade, the Prince of Wales, his sister the Dowager Empress of Germany and other foreign guests were in Portsmouth for a review of the fleet. Stretched out in the Solent between the mainland and the Isle of Wight were 165 warships of the British Navy.[59] Farthest away from Portsmouth was the pride of the fleet, the 11 new battleships of the *Royal Sovereign* and *Majestic* classes, with no equivalent elsewhere for speed, armor and firepower. As the mother of the German Kaiser boarded the royal yacht *Victoria and Albert*, the gold and black German imperial flag was run up the masthead.[60]

During the summer of 1897, Alfred Harmsworth delivered a speech to the shareholders of his newspaper company. 'We are Unionist and Imperialist', he declared, adding that he and his papers stood for 'the unwritten alliance of the English-speaking peoples'.[61] In case some thought him guilty of jingoism, he explained: 'It is possible that we suffer from the arrogance of youth, that of the strongest combination of newspapers in the United Kingdom, if not in the world'.[62]

Meanwhile, he cautioned his readers to be ever-vigilant against the German threat. In September 1897, the *Daily Mail* began a series of 16 articles, entitled 'Under the Iron Heel'. The dispatches from Germany were written by George Steevens, a young Oxford graduate with a vivid, energetic style. On his return, Steevens was certain 'that Germany will keep her hands free to deal with us. Let us make no mistake about it. For the next ten years fix your eyes very hard upon Germany.'

It did not take long to confirm Harmsworth's intuition that the fear of Germany was a rich vein to be exploited in order to drive up circulation. In the fall of 1897, the new German naval secretary, Alfred von Tirpitz, presented to the Reichstag a plan for building a German fleet capable of defending his country's ports and shipping. The naval bill called for the construction of 19 battleships over a five-year period.[63] Implicitly, Tirpitz's project was directed against Britain.

Two years later, in October 1899, war broke out between the Boer Republics and Britain. Chamberlain's militant intransigence in demanding voting rights for *uitlander* provoked the Afrikaners into a series of attacks on British army bases on their borders. Meanwhile, thanks to interest in events in South Africa, by the century's end, the circulation of the *Daily Mail* had reached 700 000. It would soon pass the million mark.[64]

Many Germans, including the Kaiser, would have liked to intervene to aid the Boers, but Germany as yet had virtually no navy to back up its position. Tirpitz took advantage of the tension to have the Reichstag approve a second naval bill that would double the proposed German fleet. Of course, because of its geographic position, bottled up in the Baltic and the North Sea, Germany could never hope to seriously challenge British naval dominance. However, the narrowing of the gap between the two fleets was a source of growing anxiety in Britain. Although the naval construction was a source of pride in Germany, its military leaders knew that the country's real source of strength was its army. Allied with Austria, the Germans on land were more than a match for the new alliance of Russia and France. It followed that as long as Britain maintained its splendid isolation, there would be peace in Europe.

Nevertheless, in 1900, before the end of the Boer War, Harmsworth was predicting a war with Germany. 'Tomorrow may be the day of world-wide conflict', asserted the *Daily Mail*. 'Britain must be ready.'[65] It is difficult to explain Harmsworth's dislike of Germans. Two of his mother's sisters had married Germans, but their relations with the Harmsworth family were extremely cordial. One of the uncles insisted on treating the children to ginger beer at the local pub whenever he visited.[66] Yet when Alfred visited Germany for the first time in 1902, he felt that 'a daemonic force was rising in Europe'.[67]

There were indeed revolutionary changes occurring in European society. But they were not limited to Germany. In Britain, Alfred Harmsworth and Winston Churchill were at the center of a series of momentous events that occurred during the year 1904.

## THE TURNING POINT

Late in the afternoon of 29 March 1904, Winston Churchill, the Conservative member for Oldham, a Lancashire mill town, rose from the back benches on the government side of the House of Commons to speak. Immediately, Arthur Balfour, the Unionist leader and prime minister, stood and left the House. When Churchill objected, the rest of the cabinet and most of the remaining Unionist members followed. It was a critical moment. In the early years of the twentieth century, Britain's position was to all appearances little different from that which it had enjoyed throughout the nineteenth century. The country had no alliances with continental powers, it placed no limits to immigration from outside the empire, and the central government made little effort to redistribute income from rich to poor or to insure its population against economic hardship. Yet all of this was about to change, for the division that had emerged between Churchill and the leaders of his party was symptomatic of a profound crisis facing the nation as a whole.

Churchill had returned from military service in India and Africa in the spring of 1899 having lived enough frontier adventures at this point in his life to fill three best-selling books. However, his new fame was not sufficient to win him a seat as a Conservative candidate. In a June by-election in the Lancashire constituency of Oldham, he lost by a small margin. Then in October, with fighting about to break out in South Africa, he received a message from Alfred Harmsworth offering him an assignment to cover the campaign for the *Daily Mail*. However, Churchill, who had recently reported on Africa for Oliver Borthwick's *Morning Post*, politely declined in order to continue writing for the latter paper. In return, he would be compensated by an unprecedented salary of £250 a month plus expenses and copyright protection.

In late November, the English press reported that Churchill had been captured by the Boers and thrown into a prison camp. Then three weeks later came the astounding news that he had escaped and made it overland to Portuguese East Africa. Returning to the front, he managed to obtain a commission as a lieutenant while still writing for the *Morning Post*. There followed six months of combat before Pretoria was finally taken and the Boer field army defeated. Guerrilla fighting would continue for two years, until the Afrikaners finally accepted Chamberlain's demand for unconditional surrender. Meanwhile, Churchill decided that it was time to return to England. Shortly after his arrival, Parliament was dissolved to make way for what became known as the Khaki election because so many voters were wearing the new brown uniform of the British army. On 1 October, Churchill was elected by a margin of 22 votes as the Conservative member for Oldham.[68]

In 1902, Churchill met Alfred Harmsworth for the first time at the home of Lord Rosebery, the former Liberal prime minister. Although the newspaper man was nine years older than the politician, the two men got along well. Each respected the independence of mind and driving ambition of the other. It was this unwillingness of both men to be bound by conventional restraints that would disrupt the social and political equilibrium in that fateful year of 1904.

**The Diplomatic Revolution**

On 7 April 1904, two weeks after the government benches had emptied while Churchill was speaking, the foreign secretary, Lord Lansdowne, announced to the House an important diplomatic initiative. Britain and France had reached an agreement to settle their outstanding colonial disputes. For Lansdowne, the accord was simply a means of removing some of the minor irritants in his country's colonial policy. However, the signing of the bilateral agreement marked the beginning of a rapprochement between the two powers that would soon have major military and diplomatic consequences.

For most of the preceding eight years, foreign policy had been in the hands of the powerful colonial secretary, Joseph Chamberlain. He had realized that there were two alternatives for Britain, one implying a continuation of the current policy of free trade and occasional intervention to assure a balance of power in Europe, and the other consisting of a tightening of economic links within the Empire along with treaties to protect against possible aggression by its enemies. Perceiving France and Russia as the British Empire's principal opponents, Chamberlain had on three occasions between 1898 and 1901 tried to arrange a purely defensive alliance with their common enemy, Germany.

Although the Germans at first professed interest in such a pact, they subsequently set unacceptable conditions for an agreement. Britain would have to formally join the Triple Alliance with Austria and Italy. Britain refused to be constrained in this way. Then one day, in a moment of exasperation toward the end of the Boer War, Chamberlain lashed out at the press for its criticisms of British conduct with regard to the Boers. He declared that

British policy in South Africa was little different from Prussia's conduct in the Austro-Prussian War. Infuriated, the German government demanded an apology. Chamberlain refused and instead broke off negotiations with Germany. As an alternative means of applying pressure on Russia, he arranged a defensive treaty with Japan that was signed on 30 January 1902.

The other plank of Chamberlain's foreign policy was to replace free trade by imperial protection. No major country other than Britain was naïve enough to leave its agriculture and industry unprotected. In 1902, he advocated a tariff on imports of foreign wheat and manufactures accompanied by preferential rates for the Empire. Because the cautious Balfour hesitated to give unconditional support for such protectionist policies, Chamberlain in September 1903 resigned from the cabinet. He then set off on a campaign of speech making around the country to raise popular support for Imperial Preference.

One of Chamberlain's bitterest opponents on imperial protection sat not with the Liberal opposition but on the governing coalition's back benches. In May 1903, Winston Churchill delivered a passionate speech in favor of free trade. Should a European war break out, he argued, the United States would be more willing to help Britain if she remained an open market for American food exports.[69] Alfred Harmsworth feared that such tariffs would unduly raise the prices of foodstuffs and reluctantly refused support for tariff reform in his papers.[70]

Meanwhile, Chamberlain's former cabinet colleagues were pursuing a totally different strategy that saw a more limited place for the Empire in the British economy and a more active political role for Britain in the concert of nations. Some 45 000 men had lost their lives during the Boer War and as a result the popularity of imperialism had fallen.[71] There was also a personal dimension to the change. In 1900, Lord Lansdowne had replaced the ailing Salisbury as foreign secretary in the Unionist government. The new secretary's mother was French; in fact, she was the granddaughter of one of Napoleon's generals. Seeking to take advantage of this cultural tie, the French foreign secretary, Théophile Delcassé, instructed his ambassador in London to approach Lansdowne regarding the settlement of colonial conflicts between the two rivals. Nothing concrete came of these contacts until after the resignation of Chamberlain in the fall of 1903. Serious negotiations began in January 1904 and were rapidly concluded despite the outbreak of war between the principal allies of the two nations. On 8 February 1904, the Japanese navy launched a surprise attack against Russia's Pacific squadron in the harbor of Port Arthur, in distant Manchuria. Nevertheless, two months later, the Anglo–French agreement was signed. The treaty touched on matters concerning overseas territories from Newfoundland to Madagascar, but the essential concessions saw

France agreeing to give Britain a free hand in Egypt in return for the right to intervene in Morocco.[72]

### The Road to Socialism

On 22 April 1904, Winston Churchill rose to speak to the House of Commons on labor policy. He had learned to prepare his speeches meticulously, writing biting text to attack his opponents and then learning it by heart. For the past two years he had found himself increasingly at odds with his own party policy concerning the rights of trade unions. The pressure on him from his Conservative colleagues was intense. Once again he now deviated from party policy, insisting that workers have the right to organize trade unions without the risk of being sued by their employers. Then, in the middle of his address, his mind suddenly went blank. He fumbled for notes in his pockets but of course, as was his practice, he had none. In despair, he sat down, his head between his hands.[73]

Four years earlier, in February 1900, Keir Hardie, the Scottish miner who led the Independent Labour Party, had summoned those who favored the rights of workers to a conference in London's Memorial Hall. On the agenda was the formation of a political organization to further the interests of labor. Among those who answered Hardie's call were the major unions making up the Trades Union Congress, socialist intellectuals of the Fabian Society, and Marxists from the Social Democratic Federation. The delegates agreed to set up a political group – the Labour Representation Committee (LRC) – that would be independent of the two major political parties. The new organization would support candidates pledged to favor the rights of workers.

By the time of the 1900 Khaki election, held only seven months after this meeting, the LRC had not yet been able to organize an effective campaign in the principal industrial regions. As a result, only two Labour MPs were elected. Then in August 1901, members of the Amalgamated Society of Railway Servants set up picket lines in support of their strike against the Taff Vale Railway in South Wales. Although the strike was quickly settled, the firm sued the union for its lost income. A judge declared in favor of the employer – a decision subsequently upheld by the House of Lords. This judgment in effect vitiated the strike as a weapon in labor disputes.

Many members of the British electorate found the Taff Vale decision to be highly unfair to workers. In by-elections in 1902 and 1903, several constituencies returned candidates of the LRC. Seeing the rising support for workers' representatives, the Liberal opposition proposed a strategic alliance with the labor group. Under the pact between the LRC secretary and the Liberal whip, it was agreed that in specific constituencies the Liberals and Labour would not oppose each other in order to avoid splitting the reformist vote.

## The Aliens Bill of 1904

On 30 May 1904, five weeks after his breakdown in the House, Winston Churchill sent to the *Manchester Guardian* and *The Times* copies of a letter addressed to a leader of the Manchester Jewish community. In his text, Churchill vigorously attacked the Aliens Bill, a proposal to restrict immigration into Britain. 'The whole bill', he wrote, 'looks like an attempt on the part of the Government to gratify a small but noisy section of their own supporters . . . by dealing harshly with a number of unfortunate aliens who have no votes.'[74]

Until the turn of the century, Britain had somehow managed to absorb its Jewish immigration. However, on Easter Sunday, 19 April 1903, in Kishinev, the capital of Bessarabia, the first pogrom of the twentieth century broke out. Mobs pillaged Jewish neighborhoods for two days, setting fire to 1500 homes, killing 45 Jews and wounding an additional 600.[75] Although these attacks were not officially approved by the Tsarist government, it made no attempt to punish local officials who condoned the violence. The indirect result of this and subsequent pogroms was a new wave of Jewish immigration that washed up on the shores of Britain as well as other states in Western Europe.

Arthur Balfour, who had succeeded his uncle the earl of Salisbury as prime minister in 1902, was deeply concerned by the arrival of these destitute refugees. His government had introduced the proposed legislation that Churchill was criticizing two months earlier as the second part of a two-pronged attack by the Balfour government on what many considered to be the 'Jewish Problem'.[76] In 1903, Joseph Chamberlain had initiated the other part of the government's new immigration policy by offering to settle Jewish immigrants in what is today Kenya.[77] That same year, a Royal Commission was set up to examine the impact of immigration into Britain. It made a number of recommendations to restrict the flow of undesirable aliens that were subsequently incorporated into the 1904 Aliens Bill. The most contentious clause would allow immigration officers to prohibit without appeal the landing of any alien of 'notoriously bad character'.[78]

Alfred Harmsworth was not prepared to overlook this new invasion of Britain. Like Balfour, he was disturbed by the tendency of Britain's Jews to cluster into exclusive communities, refusing to assimilate into the modern state. In addition, he felt threatened by the rising influence of Jews in the world economy.[79] Editorials in his newspapers supported the government's proposed Aliens Bill and criticized the Jewish community for its opposition to immigration restrictions.[80]

Although Churchill found himself on the other side of the fence from Harmsworth on the immigration issue, his intervention against the Aliens Bill was not entirely altruistic. In December 1903, the local Conservative Party leadership in Oldham Riding had informed Churchill that it would not support him in the next elections.[81] However, in early April 1904, he learned that the Liberal Party Association in northeast Manchester would be very pleased to have him as a candidate. This constituency had an important Jewish population.[82]

## The End of an Era

On 31 May 1904, the day after Churchill's letter to *The Times*, came the beginning of the end for Balfour's government. When Parliament resumed its sitting after the recess for Whitsun, Winston Churchill brought to a head the tension over imperial commercial policy, immigration law and social programs within the Conservative–Unionist coalition. Sensing that the opposition Liberals would be eventually carried to power over the free trade issue and more comfortable with their social policies than with those of the Conservatives, he decided to cross the floor of the House. The new seat Churchill chose was to the left of the Speaker, next to the up-and-coming Liberal orator from Wales, David Lloyd George. The fiery Welshman had been criticized by the Liberal leadership for his opposition to the Boer War but was now recognized as one of the party's key figures.

Over the year and a half that followed Churchill's switch of party, the momentous changes in orientation that had begun during the first few months of 1904 would continue. The shift in focus from the Empire to Europe, the question of alien immigration and the issue of social inequality would command increasing attention in Britain. Three weeks after Churchill's departure to the Liberal benches, the Unionist Government began detailed discussion of its 1904 Aliens Bill. However, after two months of slow progress, thanks in part to the obstruction of Churchill, Balfour was forced temporarily to abandon this legislation. When the bill was reintroduced in 1905, the 'notoriously bad character' provision had been removed. Nevertheless, the new bill required each alien immigrant to have £5 to support himself, along with an additional £2 for each dependent. As Liberal opposition to the measure had died down, the new law was approved in August 1905.

Meanwhile, the diplomatic revolution continued. On 27 May 1905, the Russian Baltic fleet, sent to relieve the siege of Port Arthur over seven months earlier, finally reached waters off Korea. During its long voyage, the

Japanese navy had destroyed the Russian Pacific fleet which the Baltic fleet had been sent to rescue, and the Japanese army had captured the Russian strongpoints of Port Arthur and Mukden. To reach safety in the nearest Russian port (Vladivostok), the Russian fleet had to pass through the Strait of Tsushima separating Korea and Japan. There, in a two-day battle, the slow Russian ships with their poorly trained crews were set upon by a faster, better-trained and more heavily armed Japanese fleet. In two days of battle, the Russian squadron was destroyed: two-thirds of the Russian ships were sunk and four others captured. These Russian defeats on land and at sea dramatically upset the balance of power in Europe. For Britain, the alliance of Russia and France was all but removed as a serious threat for the foreseeable future. If Britain could no longer consider Russia a potential enemy, why could she not be an ally?

By the fall of 1905, Arthur Balfour realized that his divided MPs could no longer be held together. On 5 December, he submitted his resignation as prime minister. One of his last acts before withdrawing was to name Alfred Harmsworth to the House of Lords as Lord Northcliffe. Parliament was dissolved and elections scheduled for the beginning of the new year. King Edward VII, who had succeeded to the throne in 1901, invited the Liberal leader in the Commons, Henry Campbell-Bannerman, to form a new government. Campbell-Bannerman accepted, naming David Lloyd George as the new president of the Board of Trade, responsible for economic policy, and Winston Churchill, just 31, as under-secretary for the colonies.[83] The new foreign secretary was Sir Edward Grey. On 13 December 1905, two days after assuming office, Grey received the Russian ambassador, Count Beckendorff. Just as the previous secretary had reached an agreement with France, Grey confided, so also the new administration desired to settle its differences with Russia.[84]

Meanwhile the German General Staff too had concluded that Russia's defeat by Japan combined with the earlier *Entente Cordiale* between France and Britain had profound implications for the balance of power in Europe. Germany had previously been confident of obtaining an alliance with Britain on its own terms. Instead, there was now a distinct possibility that Britain would ally itself militarily with France and a weakened Russia. Germany suddenly found itself threatened on land and at sea by a potential alliance of the three other powerful states in Europe. Germany's best chance, if war on these terms became a strong possibility, was a pre-emptive strike before its enemies' manpower and material advantage became too great. In December 1905, the German army chief of staff, Alfred von Schlieffen, began circulating a plan calling for a lightning attack on northern France through Belgium and Luxembourg to capture Paris before Britain and Russia could mobilize their forces.

During the British election campaign over the following two months, the pressure for social reform was strong. With the Unionists split over the issue of free trade, it had long been clear that the new government would be Liberal. But how committed was the party of Campbell-Bannerman to social change? During the campaign, David Lloyd George promised that the law concerning trade unions would be revised. He also mentioned the need to consider the welfare of the aged.[85] In February 1906, when the last of the votes had been counted, the Liberals had won a landslide victory, with a majority of 84 seats over all of the other members combined. The LRC, renamed the Labour Party, had 29 seats and independent union members a further 24 seats.[86]

While the Liberals promised social reform, it was by no means clear that their control of the House of Commons would allow them to carry out their proposed legislative program. The House of Lords was dominated by Conservative peers – whether from old families, as in the case of Lord Lansdowne, or newly minted, as in the case of Lord Northcliffe – who had no desire to abandon laissez faire. The stage was set for another showdown between reformers and conservatives. Once again, the press would play a key role.

## A WILLINGNESS TO SACRIFICE

Early in 1908, Alfred Harmsworth, now Lord Northcliffe, learned that the owners of *The Times* had begun negotiations to sell their paper to one of Northcliffe's rivals, Arthur Pearson, founder of the upstart *Daily Express*.[87] There were rumors that Pearson planned to sack *The Times*'s manager, Moberly Bell. With its circulation fallen to 38 000, *The Times* was in considerable financial difficulty, a victim of its own failure to modernize its printing machinery and organizational structure.

Northcliffe was approaching the height of his power. The original firm that he and his brother Harold had founded almost 20 years earlier had been reorganized in 1901 as the Amalgamated Press. It was one of the world's largest publishers of periodicals.[88] In 1903 the brothers had launched *The Daily Mirror* as 'the First Daily Paper for Gentlewomen'.[89] After initially losing £100 000, this startup had been remodeled in 1904 as the first illustrated tabloid. A runaway success in its new format, the *Mirror*'s circulation was now approaching that of the *Daily Mail*. In April 1905, the latter had been folded with the *Evening News* into a new firm, Associated Newspapers Limited.[90] Together, the Harmsworth daily newspapers accounted for almost 40 per cent of the total circulation of London's weekday press.[91]

In 1905, Harmsworth had purchased a Sunday paper of political opinion, *The Observer*.[92] All that was missing in his crown was the prestigious and politically influential jewel of British newspapers, *The Times*. Ten years earlier, and again in 1901, Northcliffe had expressed an interest in Printing House Square, but his approaches had been rebuffed by the Walter family who owned the paper.[93] Now he decided to make its aging manager, Moberly Bell, 60, an offer that could not be refused. 'I am going to buy *The Times*', he told Bell. 'With your help, if you will give it to me. In spite of you, if you don't.'[94] Bell would die at his desk of a heart attack three years later under the strain of working for Northcliffe. But it was Bell who persuaded the Walters to accept Northcliffe's offer of £320 000 in March 1908.[95]

Could the takeover that allowed Northcliffe to dominate the British press have been stopped? The answer is: probably not. British anti-trust legislation was relatively weak. Generally, the country relied on free trade to keep large corporations from abusing their market power. In sectors such as steel and salt, this policy worked quite well.[96] But in the newspaper publishing industry, imports could not compete successfully with local products. The Liberals were by no means eager to see *The Times* in the hands of Northcliffe, who generally supported the Unionist opposition. However, an attempt by Campbell-Bannerman to organize a competing offer failed when the prime minister's health suddenly deteriorated.[97] The two pro-German ministers in the cabinet who were opposed to rearmament, Lloyd George and Churchill, were successively presidents of the Board of Trade in 1908. Since this post was concerned with the regulation of both labor and trade and industry, they could conceivably have intervened. However, they chose not to do so, perhaps because they were distracted by the deteriorating health of the prime minister and its implications for their own careers.

Ownership of *The Times* along with his other papers and magazines gave Northcliffe, 42, direct access to all strata of British society. He could now devote himself to promoting the causes that he felt were most important. Three issues were of particular concern to him. One was the wide gap between the interests of politicians and those of the middle-class readers of his papers. Another was the disturbance to traditional British values that arose from the mass of alien immigrants and the growing power of the wealthy Jews who supported them. Finally, there was the threat to the British Empire from the armament and naval construction under way in Germany.

### The Birth of the Welfare State

On 3 August 1909, Northcliffe was in the peer's gallery of the House of Commons when he met his younger brother Cecil, MP for Droitwich, who invited him to the members' tea room. There a friend of David Lloyd George spotted Northcliffe and asked if he would like to come to the office of the chancellor of the exchequer, who was 'keen' to meet him.[98] Northcliffe had been sharply critical of Lloyd George for favoring social programs over naval spending. Nevertheless, he agreed, and for more than an hour the two talked privately. The minister revealed the details of amendments to his so-called People's Budget that he was to present the following day, trying to convince the press baron to support him. Northcliffe came away 'delighted in Ll. G.'s splendid imprudence'.[99]

In the spring of the preceding year, the elderly Henry Campbell-Bannerman had resigned from his position as prime minister after suffering two heart attacks.[100] In the new cabinet formed in April 1908, Lloyd George had been named chancellor of the exchequer and Churchill moved up to a cabinet position as president of the Board of Trade. Before assuming his new post of prime minister, the outgoing chancellor of the exchequer, Herbert Asquith, had placed in his budget an entry for expenditures on old age pensions. Single people 70 or over would receive five shillings a week, those married slightly less. However, Asquith had provided no means of financing this measure, as his successor David Lloyd George quickly discovered. To put even this modest pension scheme into effect would leave a gaping revenue shortfall of almost £5m. Nevertheless, with the support of Winston Churchill, Lloyd George resolved to finance the pensions – in part by trimming military expenditures.[101]

These plans were disrupted when the first lord of the admiralty insisted on beginning construction of eight new battleships to meet the threat from German naval construction. Britain and Germany were caught up in a naval arms race to build heavily armored, turbine-powered battleships modeled on Britain's new *Dreadnought*.[102] Although Lloyd George and Churchill attempted to cut this spending, they were unsuccessful. It would thus be necessary to finance both guns and butter, with the projected deficit jumping to £16m. On 29 April 1909, Lloyd George presented his People's Budget, involving a massive increase in taxation. Income taxes, death duties, licensing fees, land taxes and excise taxes on alcohol and tobacco would all rise sharply, so that instead of a deficit there would be a modest surplus.

Although the Northcliffe dailies were at first sharply critical of the Budget, after their owner's August meeting with Lloyd George, their tone softened. Northcliffe himself visited the *Daily Mail* one summer Sunday afternoon for its editorial session. On being told by one of his editors that the Budget enjoyed wide popular support, Northcliffe simply said, 'Well, say so, say so'.[103] Much to the annoyance of the Unionist opposition, the *Daily Mail* and *The Times* softened their attacks on Lloyd George.[104]

Nevertheless, the House of Lords voted down the Budget in November 1909 – the first time that the Lords had blocked a money bill since the advent of the Glorious Revolution of 1688. Parliament was dissolved and a general election was called for 8 January 1910. When the results came in, they showed that the Liberals' margin over the Conservatives and Liberal Unionists had been cut from 143 seats to just one seat. Nevertheless, Asquith's party could continue to govern since it had the support of the 82 Irish Nationalist and 40 Labour MPs.[105] In April 1910, unwilling to oppose the wishes of the electorate, the Lords finally passed the People's Budget.[106] For Lloyd George and Churchill, it was a major victory. But Northcliffe could justifiably feel that his change in stance in supporting the Budget had probably made the difference between victory and defeat for the government on this issue.

In March 1910, Prime Minister Asquith introduced a parliamentary reform bill that would remove the power of the Lords to control financial legislation or to block other bills for more than three sessions of Parliament. In addition, the maximum length of Parliament was fixed at five years. Edward VII, who was opposed to this measure, died on 6 May and was succeeded by his son George V. The new king reluctantly agreed to the creation of enough peers to pass the parliamentary reform bill. When new elections in December 1910 yielded virtually the same result as the previous January, many Lords reluctantly yielded. Finally, on 10 August 1911, Conservative amendments that would have killed the Reform Bill were defeated in the Lords by a narrow margin.[107] The constitutional crisis was over. Four months later, a National Insurance Bill that covered both sickness and unemployment insurance reached the Statute Book.[108]

## The Internal Threat

On 3 January 1911, Winston Churchill was in his bathtub when he was summoned to the telephone, 'dripping wet and shrouded in a towel'. The police had been informed that a gang of Latvian Jewish anarchists, responsible for the murders of three policemen a few weeks earlier, were holed up in a house at 100 Sidney Street in London's East End. When Churchill arrived on the scene, he learned that the criminals were heavily armed and had already shot one policeman. While he was discussing with senior officers how to take the house by storm, witnesses observed smoke coming out of one of the rooftop windows. The fire brigade insisted that the fire must be put out, but Churchill stopped them. After the house had burned for an hour, Churchill waved and water was sprayed on the house. Upon entering the house, Churchill and the police found only charred bodies.[109]

Churchill's relations with Britain's Jewish community were ambiguous, depending in part on his political interests of the moment. In 1908, he had been appointed president of the Board of Trade, with responsibility for labor legislation. At the time, it was still the custom for new ministers to resign their seats and stand again in a by-election. To his surprise, he was defeated in Manchester – in part because many Jewish voters felt that the Liberal administration had been too rigid in applying the 1905 Aliens Act. It is estimated that the Act cut Jewish immigration by about one-third between 1905 and 1914.[110] Fortunately for Churchill, he was soon offered a new seat – Dundee in Scotland – in a constituency with few Jewish voters.[111] By June 1910, freed of the need to represent Jewish interests, he was no longer criticizing the Aliens Act. Rather, he declared that it had 'taken its place in the legislative and administrative machinery of this country'.[112]

Meanwhile many British Gentile voters were crying that the 1905 Act had failed 'in protecting Britain against undermining criminal influences'.[113] Two months after the siege of Sidney Street, in March 1911, *The Times*, now an obedient member of the Northcliffe stable, described the effect of Jewish immigration on East London in a feature article entitled 'The New Ghetto':

> The overwhelming majority of the alien newcomers are Jewish, and from one-half to two-thirds of them are from Russia. [Alien immigration] enlists the wealth, the religious zeal, and the business skill of the Anglo-Jewish community in raising them. But the Judaism of the people also adds to the problem. They are knit together by a common speech of varying dialects – Yiddish – and by a common racialism. The mutual helpfulness of the sons of Israel tends to make the East-End immigrants an exclusive caste. The alien Jews give employment to people of their own faith . . . they live together, they gradually oust the Englishman, be he shopowner, fellow-workman, or business competitor.

In April, Churchill introduced a bill to strengthen the powers of the police to monitor such aliens already living in Britain, but the proposed legislation died on the order book for lack of time.[114]

During these years before 1914, novels began to appear in Britain describing events in a future war with Germany. In A.J. Dawson's *The Message* (1907), the principal danger comes not from the German military, but from a fifth column of a quarter-million German sympathizers living within British society. In reality, the number of German-born residents of the United Kingdom was small. However, there were hundreds of thousands of others who spoke German dialects, namely, the Jewish immigrants from Eastern Europe. Similarly, William Le Queux in *Spies of the Kaiser*, published in 1909, revealed that there were documents proving the existence of a secret network of German spies who watched Britain's coasts and worked to steal plans of airplanes and battleships. In fact, no such documents existed.[115] The 1913 novel by Saki (Hector Hugh Munro), *When William Came: A Story of London under the Hohenzollerns*, describes a conquered Britain run by Bohemians, petty bureaucrats and the 'ubiquitous' Jews.[116] Ironically, in this way, immigrants fleeing persecution in Russia may have helped trigger British animosity not toward Russia but toward its principal military opponent.

## The External Threat

On the afternoon of 25 July 1911, six months after the Sidney Street siege, Churchill was walking with Lloyd George by the fountains of Buckingham Palace when a messenger ran up to summon the chancellor to the office of the foreign secretary. Accompanying his colleague, Churchill learned from Grey that the Royal Navy was on high alert because of the danger of war with Germany.[117] Northcliffe's *The Times* had reported that the German high seas fleet had left port and disappeared into the 'desolate wastes of the North Sea'.[118] Two days later, at a garden party in London, Churchill learned while chatting with the chief commissioner of police that as home minister he was responsible, through the Metropolitan Police, for guarding the supplies of cordite for the navy. Cordite is an explosive invented in 1889 that is used in artillery shells. Churchill immediately left the party to arrange for a company of infantry to protect each naval magazine. In the spring, he had written to the king, encouraging him to be conciliatory in his relations with the German Kaiser.[119] But now he was sufficiently aroused about the danger of war with Germany that he sat down to prepare a memorandum for his cabinet colleagues about the strategic implications for Britain of war on the continent.

Some four weeks earlier, on 1 July, a small, lightly armed German gunboat, the *Panther*, had anchored off the port of Agadir in southern Morocco. The German government had insisted that the boat was simply protecting the property of German firms that had been threatened by hostile tribes in the area. Over the following two weeks, however, it gradually became clear to the French ambassador in Berlin that the Germans wanted a piece of the Moroccan coast. The French refused, offering instead territory in the Congo.[120]

Lloyd George and Churchill had visited Germany separately in 1908. Both were impressed by German social legislation set up two decades earlier under Bismarck. Upon his return, Lloyd George was anxious to promote an improvement in relations between Germany and his own country. Churchill too sought to minimize the possibility of conflict between the two countries, declaring, 'Although there may be snapping and snarling in the newspapers and in the London press, these two great peoples have nothing to fight about, have no prize to fight for, and have no place to fight in'.[121]

Northcliffe could not agree. That same year, he instructed one of his journalists to prepare a memorandum, 'Why England Believes that Germany is Making War Preparations'.[122] The subject of Germany was probably on the agenda in March 1909, when Northcliffe invited Churchill and his new wife, Clementine, to lunch at the elegant Regency house with its bay windows that he had rented on St James's Place, opposite Green Park. In May 1909, Northcliffe too traveled to Germany. While there, he affirmed to a German news agency that there was 'no antipathy towards Germans in England or toward Englishmen in Germany'. Nevertheless, he wrote to a *Daily Mail* journalist, 'Every one of the new factory chimneys is a gun pointed at England'. In December of that year, the *Daily Mail* published a series of articles by the socialist journalist, Robert Blatchford. 'The Germans are making gigantic preparations to destroy the British Empire', Blatchford wrote, and 'to force German dictatorship upon the whole of Europe'.[123]

In Britain, the *Panther*'s arrival in Agadir a year and a half later raised fears that Germany was seeking to establish a naval port on the Atlantic coast of Morocco. Such a base could easily threaten Britain's sea links to southern Africa. On 4 July 1911, the foreign secretary, Sir Edward Grey, visited the German ambassador to inquire about Germany's intentions. When after 17 days, British diplomatic inquiries elicited no reply or clarification from Berlin, the hot-tempered David Lloyd George, chancellor of the exchequer, decided that he had had enough. On the evening of 21 July, he rose to speak before the bankers of the City of London. After talking of his last budget and the government's efforts to reduce inequality, he picked up a piece of paper on which was written a statement he had drawn up with Grey. If Britain were treated as if she were of no account where her interests were vitally concerned, he read, 'peace at that price would be a humiliation intolerable for a great country like ours to endure'.[124]

The German government had been ready to go to war with France over Morocco. When confronted with the British government's resolute support of its ally, however, the Germans blinked. They agreed to accept territorial compensation elsewhere in Africa in return for recognizing the rights of the French over Morocco. After long weeks of negotiation, the Germans finally accepted a slice of the French Congo to add to their own territory in Cameroon.

Lloyd George was not the only British minister whose attitude to Germany changed after the Agadir incident. On 23 August 1911, Churchill presented a memorandum to the Imperial Defence Committee that predicted the likely pattern of a coming war. He foresaw that Germany and Austria would attack Russia and France, the troops of which would be pushed back to defend Paris. To prevent the fall of France, Britain would immediately have to send an expeditionary force of 100 000 across the

Channel, with a further 100 000 men arriving from India within 40 days.[125] In addition, he became convinced that it was always in Britain's interest to support the second-strongest nation on the Continent – under present circumstances, France. In September, Churchill was appointed to the post of first lord of the admiralty.

To what extent was Lord Northcliffe responsible for the about-face of these two key formerly pro-German ministers? One man had managed to obtain control of the most important British magazines and newspapers at a time when they were the only source of information and opinion for most voters and indeed most decision makers. Both Churchill and Lloyd George cultivated a relationship with Lord Northcliffe because support from his newspapers was important for their careers and the success of the policies they favored. It is clear that the Agadir incident of 1911 was critical in converting these two pro-German doves in the British cabinet into committed anti-German hawks. During the days in which Churchill and Lloyd George changed their opinion concerning Germany, their primary information came from *The Times*. On 21 August 1911, this paper revealed not only the harsh demands the Germans were making on France but also the sailing of the German High Seas Fleet into the North Sea.[126]

Meanwhile, Northcliffe's health had deteriorated. In 1910, he had what appears to have been a serious bout of depression.[127] There is speculation that the recurring periods of illness that afflicted him for the remaining twelve years of his life were due to syphilis.[128] He was out of the country on a trip to North America with his wife in August of that year when his Irish mistress gave birth to the first of three illegitimate children.[129] The boy was named Alfred.

## 3 August 1914

Monday, 3 August 1914 was a civic holiday in Britain. Under a bright blue sky, crowds jammed the streets of central London from Trafalgar Square to the Parliament buildings. There had been plans for a massive antiwar demonstration the previous day at Trafalgar Square. Now, however, thousands were crying for their government to defend neutral Belgium by declaring war on Germany. Many in the throng were waving small Union Jacks that vendors were selling by the hundred. Young English men were even making an effort to sing the *Marseillaise*.[130]

Eight days earlier, on Sunday 26 July, Russia had begun pre-mobilization measures along its borders with Austria-Hungary and Germany. Military leave was canceled and rail lines near the borders were cleared to permit movement of military trains. Immediately Germany and Austria detected the change and demanded that Russia back down. The crisis that had begun the previous month, when a Bosnian Serb had assassinated the heir to the Austrian throne, now began to accelerate. After Serbia failed to satisfy all points in an Austrian ultimatum delivered the preceding week, Austria declared war on Serbia on Tuesday, 28 July. On Wednesday, 29 July, the Russians began partial mobilization against the Austrians alone. On Thursday, 30 July, the tsar authorized general mobilization against both the Germans and the Austrians. Two days later, on Saturday, 1 August, Germany and Austria began their own full mobilizations. When Russia refused an ultimatum to demobilize, Germany declared war on her that same day.[131] Under the Schlieffen plan, war with Russia meant that Germany must first attack France through Belgium and Luxembourg. The machinery of war whose operation Churchill had predicted three years earlier was about to swing into action.

The question for the British was under what conditions, if any, their country should participate in a war on the continent. While Lord Rothschild was doing everything possible to avert conflict, Northcliffe at *The Times* on 27 July was calling for Britain to participate in the coming conflict.[132] At a meeting with his financial editor, he agreed that Rothschild's efforts were 'a dirty German-Jewish international financial attempt to bully us into advocating neutrality'.[133]

Three-quarters of the sitting members of the governing Liberal party were against intervention.[134] Nevertheless, at a cabinet meeting on Sunday afternoon 2 August, Northcliffe's converts, Lloyd George and Churchill, along with Grey and Asquith, managed to convince the reticent majority of their ministerial colleagues that if Belgian neutrality were violated, their country should go to war. Two days later, on Tuesday 4 August, Germany invaded Belgium. The following day, a committee of the British cabinet duly decided to send the six divisions of the British Expeditionary Force to France immediately.[135]

At the outset of the war, Britain had a small professional army of only a quarter of a million men – that is, roughly one-third the size of the conscript armies of France and Germany.[136] During the following month, however, a further half-million Britons would volunteer for armed service. They would be joined by two million other military volunteers before conscription was introduced in January 1916. Over 700 000 British soldiers would be killed before the war finally ended in November 1918.[137] Never before in their history had the British been so willing to sacrifice themselves for their country.[138]

After the Great War, the Allies divided Germany's small colonial territory among themselves. However, the British Empire itself had been mortally wounded by the enormous losses of manpower and material it had suffered. Unable to retain its vast territories either by consent or by constraint, it would be forced gradually to spin off its holdings. Alfred Harmsworth, Lord Northcliffe, would not live to see its decline. After suffering a nervous breakdown, he died of heart failure in London on 14 August 1922, at the age of 57.[139] Nevertheless, the three great themes that had marked his career during the immediate prewar decade – anti-Semitism, the threat of Germany and support for social-welfare legislation – would continue to dominate world history for another tumultuous quarter-century.

## NOTES

1. Dudley and Witt (2004).
2. Pound and Harmsworth (1959, pp. 170–171).
3. Pound and Harmsworth (1959, p. 172).
4. Taylor (1996, p. 3).
5. Pound and Harmsworth (1959, pp. 37–39).
6. Pound and Harmsworth (1959, p. 40).
7. Pound and Harmsworth (1959, p. 43).
8. Pound and Harmsworth (1959, p. 46).
9. Pound and Harmsworth (1959, pp. 77, 189).
10. Pound and Harmsworth (1959, p. 73).
11. Bourne (1990, p. 16).
12. Pound and Harmsworth (1959, pp. 74, 78).
13. Pound and Harmsworth (1959, p. 82).
14. Bourne (1990, p. 16).
15. Bourne (1990, pp. 16–17).
16. Bourne (1990, p. 17).
17. Ferris (1971, pp. 57–58).
18. Pound and Harmsworth (1959, p. 148).
19. Pound and Harmsworth (1959, p. 172).
20. Ibid.
21. Pound and Harmsworth (1959, p. 175).
22. Pound and Harmsworth (1959, p. 173).
23. Pound and Harmsworth (1959, p. 175).
24. Ibid.
25. Pound and Harmsworth (1959, p. 177).
26. Pound and Harmsworth (1959, p. 178).
27. Ibid.
28. Jenkins (2001, p. 234).
29. Jenkins (2001, pp. 19–20).
30. Cannadine (1993, p. 12).
31. Churchill (1966, p. 280).
32. Churchill (1966, p. 284).
33. Cohen (2004, p. 44).
34. Kershen (2005, p. 13).
35. Kershen (2005, pp. 14–17).
36. Churchill (1966, p. 280).
37. Craig (1989, p. 293).
38. Rowland (1976, pp. 2, 23).
39. Rowland (1976, pp. 114–115).
40. Ferguson (2004, p. 143).

41. Ferguson (2004, pp. 137–142, 188).
42. O'Brien (1988).
43. Pound and Harmsworth (1959, pp. 180–186).
44. Pound and Harmsworth (1959, p. 182).
45. Pound and Harmsworth (1959, p. 188).
46. Massie (1991, pp. 227–228).
47. Graff (1991, p. 314).
48. Cipolla (1969, p. 113).
49. Pound and Harmsworth (1959, p. 193).
50. Pound and Harmsworth (1959, p. 206).
51. Pound and Harmsworth (1959, p. 194).
52. Pound and Harmsworth (1959, pp. 161–162).
53. Fyfe (1930, p. 66).
54. Pound and Harmsworth (1959, pp. 194–197).
55. Cranfield (1978, p. 216).
56. Bertrand (1969, p. 125).
57. United Kingdom (n.d.).
58. Pound and Harmsworth (1959, p. 232).
59. Massie (1991, p. xvii).
60. Massie (1991, p. xxvi).
61. Pound and Harmsworth (1959, p. 231).
62. Pound and Harmsworth (1959, p. 231).
63. Massie (1991, p. 172).
64. Hutt (1973, p. 73).
65. Pound and Harmsworth (1959, p. 252).
66. Pound and Harmsworth (1959, p. 27).
67. Pound and Harmsworth (1959, p. 272).
68. Manchester (1983, p. 330).
69. Manchester (1983, p. 353).
70. Pound and Harmsworth (1959, pp. 289–290).
71. Ferguson (2004, p. 229).
72. Massie (1991, p. 348).
73. Manchester (1983, pp. 362–363).
74. Cohen (2004, pp. 21–22).
75. Encyclopedia Britannica (2004).
76. Cohen (2004, p. 15).
77. Cohen (2004, p. 25).
78. Cohen (2004, p. 18).
79. Fyfe (1930, p. 158).
80. Pound and Harmsworth (1959, p. 352).
81. Manchester (1983, p. 358).
82. Cohen (2004, p. 21).
83. Jenkins (2001, p. 104).
84. Massie (1991, p. 597).
85. Rowland (1976, p. 184).
86. Craig (1989, p. 295).
87. Pound and Harmsworth (1959, p. 323).
88. Taylor (1996, p. 86).
89. Hutt (1973, p. 87).
90. Pound and Harmsworth (1959, p. 290).
91. Lee (1976, p. 293).
92. Pound and Harmsworth (1959, p. 291).
93. Pound and Harmsworth (1959, pp. 240, 271).
94. Taylor (1996, p. 91).
95. Taylor (1996, p. 91).
96. Dillard (1967, pp. 401–402).

97. Koss (1984, p. 90).
98. Pound and Harmsworth (1959, p. 376).
99. Pound and Harmsworth (1959, p. 377).
100. Rowland (1976, pp. 199–200).
101. Rowland (1976, p. 202).
102. Massie (1991, pp. 482–486).
103. Fyfe (1930, pp. 165–166).
104. Koss (1984, pp. 115–117).
105. Rowland (1976, p. 223).
106. Rowland (1976, p. 235).
107. Rowland (1976, pp. 234, 248).
108. Rowland (1976, p. 259).
109. Manchester (1983, pp. 418–420).
110. Rubinstein (2004, p. 225).
111. Cohen (2004, p. 38).
112. Cohen (2004, p. 39).
113. Ibid.
114. Cohen (2004, p. 41).
115. Woods (n.d.).
116. Ferguson (1999, p. 3).
117. Massie (1991, p. 735).
118. Ibid.
119. Manchester (1983, p. 426).
120. Massie (1991, pp. 726–729).
121. Craig (1993, p. 24).
122. Pound and Harmsworth (1959, p. 331).
123. Taylor (1996, p. 141).
124. Rowland (1976, p. 250).
125. Manchester (1983, pp. 428–429).
126. Massie (1991, pp. 731, 735).
127. Ferris (1971, p. 167).
128. Ferris (1971, p. 170).
129. Ferris (1971, p. 169).
130. Massie (1991, p. 902).
131. Stevenson (2004, p. 23).
132. Ferguson (1999, p. 217).
133. Pound and Harmsworth (1959, p. 462).
134. Stevenson (2004, p. 30).
135. Stevenson (2004, pp. 29, 164).
136. Ferguson (1999, p. 92).
137. Ferguson (1999, p. 295).
138. Stevenson (2004, p. 164), Rowland (1976, p. 328).
139. Taylor (1996, pp. 219, 363).

# PART V

# Another contractual revolution

# 9. The decentralization of desire

By the late 1950s, economic progress in the West faced a seemingly insuperable constraint. Thanks to the telex system – an extension of the telegraph – information could now be transmitted around the world automatically at the speed of light. Furthermore, with literacy rates approaching 100 per cent in Europe and its offshoots, virtually everyone was able to decode the simple Roman characters standardized by the Anglo-Saxon cleric, Alcuin, over a millennium earlier. However, because of the high cost of storing information in multiple copies, the headquarters of governmental and private organizations were drowning in seas of paper. Decision making had to be concentrated near these central information stocks and could not easily be delegated to those closer to the real problems that inevitably arose.

Ironically, electronic computers spewing out page after page of detailed information had merely exacerbated this storage problem. Since only the largest organizations could afford the high fixed cost of mainframes, their use had further increased the optimal concentration of power. The one exception to date was military technology, where the United States with its decentralized decision structure, had always been able to keep a step ahead of its highly centralized rival, the Soviet Union. Then came an event that shocked the world.

## SOUNDS FROM SPACE

The signals came from a 184-pound sphere the size of a basketball that was rotating the earth every hour and a half.[1] Around the world, radio stations rebroadcast the characteristic 'beep, beep, beep' from the earth's first artificial satellite. The intention of the project was to mark the International Geophysical Year that had begun the previous 1 July. But the signals from space were not the outcome of the Vanguard civilian research program that the United States had announced with great fanfare. Rather, Sputnik I had been blasted into orbit by the Soviets on the tip of a powerful new military rocket designed to transport a thermonuclear warhead between continents.

That evening, Friday 4 October 1957, the newly designated US defense secretary, Neil McElroy, 52, was in Huntsville, Alabama visiting the army's

Redstone missile arsenal. At six feet four (193 cm), the former president of the soap manufacturer, Procter and Gamble, was a big man and a man in a hurry. He was on a tour of military bases in preparation for his confirmation hearings before the Senate. Although he had made his way to the top of the corporate ladder by his expertise in marketing soap on radio and television, McElroy, a Harvard MBA, was a firm believer in the need for unfettered research. Indeed, he had been talking to Wernher von Braun, the emigré German physicist who had headed Germany's V-2 research program, when reporters rushed up to inform him about Sputnik I.

Four weeks later came the second shock. The Soviet Union announced that the same type of rocket had successfully launched another satellite, Sputnik II, into space. This time, the payload was a half ton, and the satellite carried a live dog, Laika ('Barker' in Russian), a mongrel female found on the streets of Moscow. Although the Russians had made no provision for the return of their space capsule, they did provide food and water for the dog. Unfortunately, the capsule's heat-control system was damaged during the separation from its booster and the temperature in Laika's cabin rose to 40 degrees C (104 F). Only much later was it revealed that the dog had died from overheating and stress several hours after being carried into space.[2] However, the test did prove that it was possible for living animals, and presumably humans, to survive the pressures of space launch. In addition, it was now clear that the Russians were quite capable of hitting targets in the United States with nuclear missiles.

## The Advance Research Projects Agency

McElroy's predecessor as defense secretary, Charles Wilson, had been reluctant to fund basic research. 'What do I care what makes the grass green?' he had asked.[3] The results of this approach were all too evident to many Americans when in a test on 6 December 1957, two months after Sputnik I, the rocket intended as a launch vehicle for Vanguard rose four feet into the air, then fell back on to its concrete platform and exploded.[4]

Amidst the panic caused by the Sputniks in the US scientific and defense communities, defense secretary McElroy decided that the federal government would henceforth participate directly in the organization of basic research. Accordingly, on 8 January 1958, President Eisenhower sent a message to Congress requesting funds to establish the Advanced Research Projects Agency (ARPA). Rather than channel funding through the three squabbling branches of the military, the new organization would directly finance its own basic research projects. To run the agency and its $520 million budget, approved by Congress in February, McElroy recruited Roy Johnson, a vice-president of General Electric.[5]

However, Johnson's attempt to centralize all missile and space programs in the new agency aroused considerable opposition. As often happens in government, there was then a change of plans, and McElroy pulled the rug from under his appointee's feet. In the summer of 1958, the defense secretary supported a new bill that created the National Aeronautics and Space Administration (NASA), with von Braun as its director. At the same time, McElroy yielded to the armed services' demands that their research budgets be restored. ARPA was stripped of its missile and space programs, and its budget was cut back to $150 million.[6] Johnson resigned.

If basic research was to be government-financed, it would be done on a decentralized basis, with ARPA as just one of several competing funding agencies. ARPA's turn would come, but only after the Air Force had initially financed efforts to solve two apparently unrelated problems. The scene now shifts from Washington DC to California.

## The Traitorous Eight

In late June 1957, some three months before the launching of Sputnik I, a curious ritual took place in the Redwood Room of the Clift Hotel in San Francisco. Alfred 'Bud' Coyle, a partner in the New York investment bank of Hayden, Stone and Company, pulled out ten freshly minted one-dollar bills. Around the table were Cole's young associate, Arthur Rock, and eight scientists from a recently started California high-technology firm, Shockley Transistor Laboratories. The eight had had enough of their eccentric boss, Nobel laureate William Shockley, and thought they could do better on their own. At Cole's bidding, the ten men signed each of the dollar bills. These certificates were to be their contracts with one another. Two months later, after a lengthy search, Coyle and Rock found a New York venture capitalist ready to break into the production of semiconductors. Sheldon Fairchild, the largest shareholder in IBM, agreed to finance the eight as a subsidiary of his own firm, Fairchild Camera and Instrument. On 19 September 1957, two weeks before Sputnik I was launched, Fairchild Semiconductor Corporation was born.[7]

William Shockley, the boss of the firm that the eight researchers were quitting, was one of three men who had been credited with inventing the transistor a decade earlier. At that time, Shockley was working at Bell Labs in New Jersey. The transistor consisted of three layers of silicon doped with chemicals. The conductivity of each of these layers increased with its temperature. Accordingly, changes in voltage at the terminal connected to one of the transistor's layers could alter the current flowing between the terminals attached to the other two layers. The resulting device could act as an

be transmitted from a command center to a distant missile base. However, the military officers quickly rejected this proposal as insufficient. The amount of information they desired to be transmitted would easily exceed the capacity of Baran's network of radio stations.

Back at his desk, Baran wondered if this idea of a network with redundant nodes might be applied to some other technology. Meanwhile, as he worked, the Russians were busy installing weapons that could easily destroy the existing American telephone network.

## BUILDING BLOCS

Novaya Zemlya is an icy archipelago in the Arctic Ocean consisting of two large islands, each about half the size of Ireland, and many smaller companions. The mountainous island chain is an extension of the Urals, the range that divides Europe from Asia. Two days after the launching of Sputnik, on 6 October 1957, the USSR exploded a 2.9 megaton thermonuclear weapon in the atmosphere over the northernmost of the main islands.[19] This was the first test of the warhead designed for the R-7 (NATO-designated SS-6) rocket that had carried Sputnik into space. The missile could also reach sites in North American from the Soviet Union. In little more than a year, by February 1959, the world's first ICBM unit, made up of SS-6 missiles and their nuclear warheads, would be operational at Plesetsk, 500 miles (800 km) north of Moscow.

For the United States, the R-7 was not quite as threatening as might first appear. American intelligence was well aware of the missile's limitations thanks to the flights of an airplane designed exclusively for espionage. The U-2 was an adaptation of Lockheed's F-104 Starfighter to which long glider-like wings had been attached. It could consequently fly at altitudes above 70000 feet (21000 m) over long distances. From the photos taken during U-2 overflights, the Americans knew that the R-7 required over 20 hours of preparation before launching and was therefore vulnerable to attack from US bombers and missiles. Nevertheless, the activation of this deadly new weapon system added an additional element of urgency to American military research.

### The Three Worlds

The year 1957 marked the beginning of President Dwight Eisenhower's second term of office. In January, in his second inaugural address, the former commander of Allied forces in Europe had painted a glowing picture of his country's place in the world. He divided the world into three main regions. In the first of these, he said, America had never been as wealthy or powerful.

> In our nation work and wealth abound. Our population grows. Commerce crowds our rivers and rails, our skies, harbors, and highways. Our soil is fertile, our agriculture productive. The air rings with the song of our industry – rolling mills and blast furnaces, dynamos, dams, and assembly lines – the chorus of America the bountiful.[20]

To protect itself and its overseas interests in Eisenhower's First World, the United States had built up a web of alliances surrounding the Soviet Union. In the West, it had brought Canada and most countries of Western Europe into the North Atlantic Treaty Organization (NATO) to block a possible Soviet offensive. Under NATO auspices, the US would deploy Thor intermediate-range ballistic missiles with atomic warheads in Britain in 1958. In the Far East, Secretary of State John Foster Dulles had organized the Southeast Asia Treaty Organization (SEATO) to counter the influence of the Soviet Union and China. Finally, in central Asia, there was the Central Treaty Organization (CENTO), made up of Britain, Turkey, Iran, Iraq and Pakistan. Although the United States was not an official member of this group, it clearly benefited from the alliance's impact in thwarting Soviet expansion into the region.

In his address, Eisenhower proceeded to identify the principal threat to world peace and stability: 'In the heart of Europe, Germany still stands tragically divided. So is the whole continent divided. And so, too, is the world. The divisive force is International Communism and the power it controls'.[21] The principal threat to the United States and its allies was of course the Soviet Union. At the end of the Second World War, the Soviet Army had remained in the countries it had liberated from Nazi Germany. This military presence had led to the creation of a Second World of states with single-party socialist governments. To legitimize this presence, the Soviets in 1955 had organized their own alliance, the Treaty of Friendship, Cooperation and Mutual Assistance (Comecon). Not all citizens of east European states favored the imposed ties. In 1953 in East Berlin and again in 1956 in Hungary, a year before Sputnik I, the Red Army had been called in to suppress resistance to Soviet control. Finally, said Eisenhower, there were the remaining countries that some had begun calling the Third World: 'From the deserts of North Africa to the islands of the South Pacific one third of mankind has entered upon an historic struggle for a new freedom; freedom from grinding poverty'.[22]

Most of these states were former colonies of one or the other of the First World states. The Netherlands had granted Indonesia its independence in 1945. The following year, the United States had allowed the Philippines to become an independent republic. India and Pakistan had obtained their independence from Britain in 1947. More recently, Sudan, Morocco and Tunisia had reached independence in 1956 and Ghana and Malaysia would follow in 1957.

With a few exceptions like Turkey and Pakistan, the countries of the Third World were allied to neither of the great powers. China and the Soviet Union were still on favorable diplomatic terms in 1957, but relations between the two most powerful socialist states were beginning to cool because of what Beijing considered the revisionist policies of Soviet leader Nikita Khrushchev. Under the leadership of Prime Minister Nehru of India, China, Egypt, Indonesia, Yugoslavia and many other states considered themselves 'non-aligned'. The vast gap in income levels that separated these states from the developed countries of the West constituted one of the planet's principal challenges. The world's wealthiest society by far was that of the United States.

## Guns versus Butter

As 1957 began, Americans were driving their Fords, Chevrolets and Dodges on the first sections of a national network of expressways. The Federal-Aid Highway Act of 1956 stipulated that the federal government would provide 90 per cent of the funds for highways of at least four lanes with no railroad crossings at road level. The states would pick up the rest of the cost. President Eisenhower had signed the bill into law six months earlier, while in hospital recovering from a heart attack. The first section of the new Interstate network, I-70 west of Topeka, Kansas, had opened in November 1956.

Two decades earlier, in a speech in Berlin, the German propaganda minister Joseph Goebbels had argued that in an economy, there necessarily existed a tradeoff between military and civilian expenditures. Attempting to calm those who were criticizing the Nazi government for food shortages, he had insisted that when under attack, a country could defend itself without butter but not without cannon.[23] However, under Eisenhower in 1957, it seemed that America's continually rising productivity had all but eliminated this collective budget constraint. In a year of peace, the United States was able to devote ten per cent of its GNP to military spending while still financing its social security net and enormous investments in social infrastructure.[24] Not only could Americans have both guns and butter, but also they could finance research which provided hope that the rest of the world might share their prosperity.

To finance these government services, Americans paid about a quarter of their total income in taxes – a proportion that was slightly below the average for First World countries.[25] A federal tax siphoned off 48 per cent of corporate profits. But the most important government revenue source was the federal personal income tax. A progressive tax, it took about seven per cent of the median family's income, but 11 per cent of the income of a family with twice the median income.[26] In calculating the total tax burden, one must also consider the tax implied by the system of conscription. By 1957, the number of men drafted averaged about 100 000 per year, although they accounted for only a quarter of total recruitment into the armed forces.[27] Draftees were required to serve for two years. One of the most famous of all those who would be drafted between the Korean and Vietnam Wars was a young white singer from Mississippi.

**Information Systems**

On 6 January 1957, Elvis Presley made his third and final appearance on the CBS network's Ed Sullivan show. Elvis's first visit to the show four months earlier had attracted about 60 million viewers – one out of three Americans and 83 per cent of the national television audience.[28] Parents and teenagers had watched together, curious to see Elvis's controversial hip-swiveling performance. This time, anxious not to offend his family audience, Sullivan ordered the camera crews to shoot the singer 'from the waist up'. Elvis sang five songs, including 'Don't Be Cruel' and the spiritual, 'Peace in the Valley'.

During the middle decades of the twentieth century, the degree of centralization of mass media – newspapers, radio and television – in America was at its peak. Limited competition among a few channels of communication in each of these powerful media led to convergence in the content. Elvis, for example, had appeared six months earlier on the show of Sullivan's rival, Steve Allen, on the NBC network.

The centralization of decision making was evident not only in the media but also in industry and government. Just as the federal government was able to prevail over the states in determining the construction of highways, so also large firms such as AT&T, General Motors and IBM were able to dominate their sectors. Moreover, the phenomenon was true not just in the United States but also in the countries of Western Europe, where the welfare state and large corporations, many of them American subsidiaries, co-existed peacefully. In the socialist bloc of countries, of course, the centralization of power was even more pronounced.

Given the communications technologies in 1957, centralization made good sense. Reliance on written and typed documents for record keeping meant that the cost of storing information was high and therefore justified the concentration of power close to the store of data. The first generation of computers required data to be processed sequentially by expensive, delicate machines, thereby serving to accentuate this centralizing tendency. During the 1950s, computers were built with vacuum tubes. Remington Rand delivered the first commercial mainframe to the Census Bureau in 1951.[29] Punch cards were used to enter data and programs sequentially. In 1954, International Business Machines marketed the first of an eventual 1800 IBM 650 computers. The machines had a random-access memory of 2 kilobytes. Since each computer cost $500 000, only very large firms could afford to buy or rent them.

By the late 1950s, then, the countries of the world had grouped themselves into blocs along lines that corresponded quite closely to their writing systems. With the exception of Greece, the NATO countries, including Turkey, used the Roman alphabet. In the western hemisphere, a regional organization, the US-dominated Organization of American States, used the same alphabet. The Warsaw Pact group all used Russian with its Cyrillic alphabet as their lingua franca, although most of the smaller states wrote their national languages with the Roman alphabet. Meanwhile, India and China were attempting to impose a common language and writing system on their component regions – Hindi in the former and Mandarin in the latter. In the Arab world too, there was movement toward integration. The Arab League, formed in 1945, coordinated economic, cultural and political relations among Egypt, Syria and five other Arab countries where Arabic was spoken. By 1958, it included the newly independent Libya, Sudan, Tunisia and Morocco. In February 1958, Syria and Egypt agreed to form a single state, the United Arab Republic.

Within the NATO bloc, there was jostling over the relative importance of French and English. On 25 March 1957, six European countries signed the Treaty of Rome, committing themselves to forming a customs union and a common atomic energy agency. The European Economic Community (EEC) would begin to restructure Europe's economic links on coming into effect the following 1 January. The EEC group chose French as its lingua franca, at least for commercial matters, while most of the other NATO states tended to use English for communication among themselves. Britain refused to join the EEC, preferring to maintain its commercial ties with its former colonies and reluctant to sacrifice its sovereignty to a supranational body.

One other event marked the year 1957. In Jeddah, a Saudi Arabian port on the Red Sea, a son was born to a wealthy building contractor, Muhammad Awad bin Laden. The seventeenth of his father's 55 children, the boy was named Osama and was raised as a devout Sunni Muslim. The boy was expected to follow the path of commercial success set out by his father and older brothers. However, Osama's career would be knocked off course by the shock from an object too small to be seen with the naked eye.

## WHEN THE CHIPS ARE DOWN

Peering into his microscope in late 1958, Gordon Moore spied 'a fleck of crud' sitting on top of the drop of wax that formed the mesa. The tiny piece of yellow metal had broken off the transistor's canister during the sealing process and obviously, by creating a short circuit, had caused the device to fail. The discovery explained why several examples of Fairchild Semiconductor's first product had been returned to their producer. Moore, 29, who had a doctorate in chemistry and physics from Caltech, was one of the eight co-founders of the young firm. He was also the leader of the team that had developed this faulty transistor. Peering at the metal fleck, he now understood why a mere sharp tap with a pencil could cause the device to stop working. Bouncing around inside the can, such contaminants were the seemingly unavoidable result of assembling transistors by hand.[30]

When Moore's colleague, Jean Hoerni, 34, heard about the cause of this setback, he started thinking. How could one better protect the surface of a layer of semiconductor? He recalled that Bell Labs had recently demonstrated a technique for applying a coating of oxide to a semiconductor's surface. Perhaps the oxide layer could be used to protect that surface from contamination, like the enamel on a tooth. Hoerni, one of Fairchild Semiconductor's eight co-founders, was a Swiss theoretical physicist who held two doctorates.[31] In January 1959, after weeks of intense work, he developed a way of keeping the 'crud' in the transistor canister from affecting the electronic circuit. Under Hoerni's planar process, a slice of silicon was coated with a layer of oxide and then with a second layer of light-sensitive material or 'resist'. A pattern was then photographed on to the resist, and acid was allowed to eat through the light-exposed areas of resist and oxide. Finally, the exposed silicon was doped with chemicals, while the oxide protected the remaining surface of the semiconductor from dust or contaminants.[32]

Robert Noyce, now 32, the acknowledged leader of the Traitorous Eight, signed Hoerni's two-page patent disclosure as a witness. Then he in turn started thinking. Perhaps this new planar process could help to solve the problem that had been bothering him for months – the reliable linking of the components of a circuit.

### The Dawn of an Era

Even at the age of 11, Bob Noyce had been a risk taker. Together with his older brother, Gaylord, he had built a wood and cloth glider with an 18-foot (5.5 m) wingspan. It had been Bob who had jumped from the roof of a barn hanging on to their flying machine. Unhurt, he was immensely proud of having actually flown for a few seconds.[33] Noyce was born in Iowa in 1927, the third son of a Congregationalist minister and his high-school Latin teacher wife. Both of his grandfathers had also been ministers. Bob grew into a good-looking young man, five feet eight and muscular, his high school's valedictorian. Afraid of nothing, in a few hours he taught himself to do back flips into a pool from a ten-foot diving board.[34]

In his senior year at Grinnell College in 1949, Noyce and his physics professor together explored the first technical monographs prepared by Bell Labs to describe the workings of the firm's new electronic device, the transistor. The experience convinced Bob that he wanted to study the physics of semiconductors. A charismatic leader, he graduated with a double major in physics and math from Grinnell. He was also awarded the class's Brown Derby Prize for the best marks with the least work.[35] He applied to and was accepted at MIT. Four years later, he obtained his doctorate in applied physics with a thesis on the surface states of two minerals. Noyce graduated from MIT with a sound knowledge of electrons, quantum states and the properties of solids.[36] He then spent three frustrating years at Philco in Philadelphia debugging the production of transistors for the Defense Department. Early in 1956, he received a phone call. 'Shockley here', the caller began and proceeded to offer Noyce a job in California.

Now another three years had passed and the existence of Noyce's new firm was threatened by complaints about the uneven quality of the transistors it was making. Yet he took the time to reflect upon a question far from his immediate concerns as Fairchild's director of research and development. In his notebook, in January 1959, Noyce wrote the heading, 'Methods of Isolating Multiple Devices', and then proceeded to explain how the soldering problem might be solved.

Hoerni proposed to use his planar process to make identical transistors on the same wafer, their surfaces protected by oxide. Noyce added two seemingly obvious but nevertheless path-breaking refinements. First, the process could be used to make *different* components on the same piece of silicon. Second, he proposed an ingenious way of linking the devices together. The planar process inserted dopants through holes in the insulating layer of oxide. Noyce now suggested depositing liquid metal into the holes to make contact with the semiconductor. The overhang of the metal beyond the holes to connect the device with other parts would simply lie on the oxide layer, unable to affect the rest of the component. In this way, the wiring to connect the electronic components on the chip could be made as thin as desired, with no need to solder manually.

Noyce filed his patent for the integrated circuit on 30 July 1959. Meanwhile Jack Kilby of Texas Instruments had filed a patent for a similar device. Like Noyce's proposal, Kilby installed different components of an electronic circuit on the same chip. Unlike Noyce, however, he had his devices joined manually with gold wire.[37] From the production point of view, Noyce's idea was superior in that its wiring was done mechanically, with slight risk of failure.

Fairchild introduced its first integrated circuit on to the market in 1961. However, initially, sales were slow. Although the new devices were much smaller, lighter and reliable than discrete components, at $100 a piece they cost up to 50 times as much as the existing technology.[38] In the spring of 1964, with integrated-circuit sales stagnating, Noyce made a dramatic move. He slashed the price of the low-end model to below its production cost. The idea was simple. There was a cost for customers to adapt to a new technology. Unless Fairchild made the change worth their while, they would stay with the existing discrete components.

The strategy worked. In 1966, instead of the $58 million in sales that had been predicted, the industry sold $157 million worth of integrated circuits. Among the new products using the inexpensive chips were small, rugged computers from Digital Equipment and Honeywell that were soon known as minicomputers. They would play a crucial role in the development of new ways of communicating.

## The First Strands in the Net

On 1 May 1960, Captain Gary Powers sat at the controls of his U-2 spy plane flying over the Soviet missile base of Sverdlovsk, when suddenly he was shaken by a powerful explosion. A Soviet surface-to-air missile had severely damaged his fragile craft, forcing him to bail out. Powers, an employee of the US Central Intelligence Agency, would spend the next 21 months in a Soviet prison before being exchanged for an accused Russian spy. The incident led to the canceling of a planned summit meeting between President Eisenhower and Secretary Khrushchev.[39] Later that year, the USSR began testing a powerful new liquid-fuel ICBM, the R-16, that could be launched in only three hours.[40] For the first time in its history, the United States was threatened with massive destruction with virtually no warning.

It was in this context of an escalating arms race between the two superpowers that Paul Baran of the RAND Corporation was trying to devise a scheme to save the American communications system from nuclear attack. Baran, 34, was born in Poland, but his family moved to the USA when he was two. He grew up in Philadelphia and earned a degree in electrical engineering in 1949. There followed a decade of dead-end jobs and part-time studies until he finally landed his research position at RAND.[41]

As mentioned earlier in this chapter, Baran's first assignment was to solve the redundancy problem; that is, to determine the minimum amount of extra capacity required to assure that the military communications network would survive a nuclear strike. His initial proposal – to use the nation's AM radio stations to broadcast military signals – was rejected by the armed forces as providing insufficient carrying capacity. However, there existed another rapidly growing network that was dispersed widely across the country, namely, government-financed computers, many of them in universities.

In a seminal paper written in 1962, Baran distinguished three types of networks.[42] In a centralized network, all receiving stations were linked to a central broadcast node but not to one another. In a decentralized network, there were regional hubs each linked to the stations near it and to one or more other hubs. Finally, there was a distributed network, in which each node was connected to two or more other nodes for transmission and reception (see Figure 9.1). All that was needed to build such a network was to establish communications links between the nation's computers. Then even if one or more nodes were knocked out, messages could flow around them between the remaining nodes. After trial and error with simulations, Baran concluded that the optimal level of redundancy was three or four, that is, each node should be linked to three or four other nodes.[43] The upper panel in Figure 9.1 illustrates such a network.

It may be readily understood that the most efficient network structure depends on the cost of installing a transmitter relative to the cost of building communications links between stations. Suppose that initially the two costs are roughly comparable. If so, the decentralized network in the middle of Figure 9.1, with a moderate number of both transmitters and communications links, is the most efficient structure. Now imagine a rise in the fixed cost of installing the most efficient transmitter. An example from Chapter 7 is the introduction of the electric-powered rotary press. Because of the high cost of such machinery, it makes sense to reduce the number of transmitters and centralize information processing, as in the lower illustration in the figure. A subsequent fall in the cost of a transmitter would cause a reversion to the original decentralized structure.

Now imagine another type of technological shock. Suppose that a decentralized system is subjected to a sharp fall in the cost of communications links between stations. For example, think of a rise in literacy rates due to a sudden outpouring of inexpensive texts printed in the language spoken in a region. A shock of this sort occurred in many countries of Western Europe during the early-modern period (as described in Chapters 3 and 4). It is now efficient to link each station with several of its neighbors.

Baran called the resulting structure a distributed network. He argued that such a sturcture, as shown in the upper panel of the figure, was the most efficient means of assuring that the network would survive a nuclear strike. However, we can easily understand that if building such links is not cheap then the decentralized network may be the most appropriate.

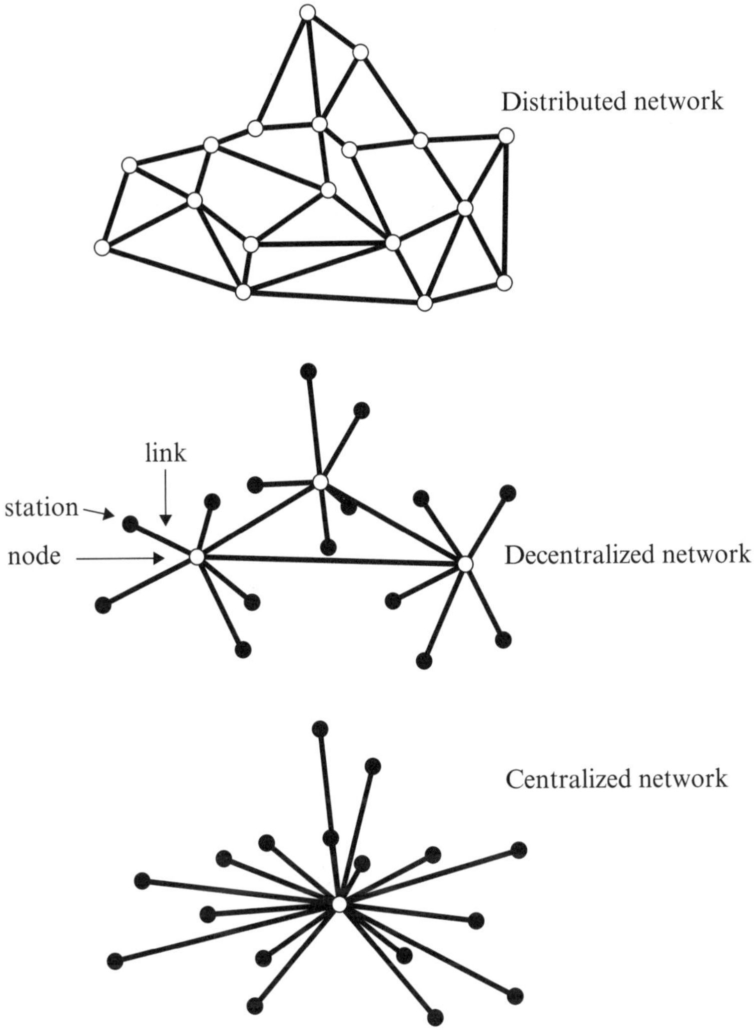


*Figure 9.1* *Three network configurations. In a 1962 paper, Paul Baran of the RAND Corporation suggested that the least expensive communication system capable of surviving a nuclear attack was a distributed network (Baran, 1964).*

In addition to the concept of a distributed network, Baran had a novel proposal for structuring transmitted information that would reduce the cost of linking stations in this fashion. Since messages were likely to come in bursts separated by periods of silence, it would be wasteful to have a dedicated line between each pair of nodes. Baran proposed that for transmission, the messages be broken up into small parts of fixed length. Not all would be sent by the same route or at the same time. At each node there would be a routing computer to assure that the message components were sent on to the proper destination. A computer at the receiving end would reassemble them. The English mathematician, Donald Davies, who proposed the same idea in 1965, would call this process *packet switching*.[44]

Finally, there was the actual coding of the messages. Analog messages, as used by the telephone system at the time, tend to deteriorate with each successive transmission from node to node. Baran concluded that the messages would therefore have to be digital.[45] Together, these ideas were brilliantly innovative. However, when Baran tried to convince civilian and military decision makers to set up the proposed system, he was unsuccessful. The most vociferous opposition came from technicians at AT&T who refused to admit that their own network was vulnerable. Finally, in 1965, he simply gave up and turned to other projects.[46]

That same year, across the continent, Bob Taylor moved into a new and larger office at the Pentagon as director of ARPA's Information Processing Techniques Office. A Texan trained as an experimental psychologist, Taylor was astonished to find near his desk three teletype machines, each linked to a different computer, one at MIT, another at Santa Monica and the third at Berkeley. Because the three ARPA-financed computers had different operating systems, they could not communicate with one another. To Taylor, an obvious project was to develop a system that would permit a user on one computer to access shared time on one of the others. After a 20-minute conversation with the agency's director in February 1966, Taylor suddenly had a million dollars in funding for such a project.[47]

At a meeting in Ann Arbor in early 1967, Taylor and his associate, Larry Roberts, proposed a system to link the agency-financed computers. However, when the university computer managers heard that their overburdened machines would have to handle new networking tasks along with the normal research work load, they were less than enthusiastic. The impasse was finally broken when Wesley Clark, director of the computer lab at Washington University, St Louis, suggested giving each site a new computer – a routing machine to handle interactions between the host mainframes and the network. In the ARPA project specification, these machines were subsequently called 'interface message processors' or IMPs.[48] It was not until a conference in Tennessee in October 1967 that the ARPA researchers learned from their British colleagues about the innovative research done on distributed networks by Paul Baran. Returning to

Washington, they found copies of his reports gathering dust on Pentagon shelves.[49]

In 1968, an initial contract for setting up a network of IMPs at four sites was granted to Bolt, Beranek and Newman (BBN), a small consulting firm in Cambridge, Massachusetts. Although a private firm was responsible for the routing computers, the design of the standards for running the network and for linking each mainframe to its IMP was largely the result of collaborative efforts by graduate students working at the designated sites. At UCLA, for example, Len Kleinrock headed a group of 40 researchers financed by ARPA.[50] The participants set up a Network Working Group that drew up the procedure by which two mainframe computers would contact each other – the Network Control Protocol.

In September 1969, BBN shipped the first of the IMPs, a reconfigured Honeywell 516 minicomputer, by air freight to Kleinrock's group at UCLA. A month later, a second rugged machine was sent out to the Stanford Research Institute. The challenge was to determine whether UCLA's Sigma-7 mainframe could communicate with SRI's 940 using the two IMPs as intermediaries. Charley Kline, an undergraduate at UCLA sent first the 'L' and then the 'O' of LOGIN, confirming each transmitted command by telephone. Then the Stanford machine tried to complete the missing 'GIN,' and the terminal program crashed. Fortunately, when the two teams tried later that day, the system worked perfectly.[51] But would electronic communication be limited to a few groups of university researchers? A third critical development was required before the new technology could be made available to society at large.

## A Computer on a Chip

In June of 1969, three months before the historic linkage of the two California mainframes, three Japanese engineers arrived at the offices of a small California semiconductor startup named Intel. The visitors were from Busicom, a Japanese calculator company, and were in Mountain View to determine the specifications for a set of integrated circuits their firm had contracted to buy for a new calculator. At the time, a typical calculator used six chips, each with fewer than 1000 transistors. However, Busicom was offering to pay Intel $100 000 to design a set of 12 chips, each with about 4000 transistors. For each set, Intel would be paid $50.

Robert Noyce, the president of the new firm, assigned a young engineer, Ted Hoff, as the liaison expert for the project. Hoff, 31, was a former postdoctoral fellow in Stanford's engineering department who had been hired by Intel the previous year.[52] A specialist in the design of computers, he quickly concluded that the project was much more complex than his boss realized. The custom-made chips that Busicom wanted could not be produced for anything near the stipulated price. Noyce wrote back to the Japanese informing them that their design would cost $300 per kit.[53] However, Hoff had an idea that by simplifying the design, he might lower the production cost.

Hoff's boss, Robert Noyce, had resigned from Fairchild in June 1968, frustrated at seeing the profits from his semiconductor division siphoned off for the parent firm's other activities. With the backing of venture capitalists, he and Gordon Moore had set up their own semiconductor firm, which they named from the first syllables of **Int**egrated **El**ectronics. Moore had earlier noted how the number of transistors that could be printed on to an integrated circuit tended to double at regular intervals – every 24 months in the current formulation of what has become known as 'Moore's Law'. In the mid-1960s, the barrier of 1000 components per chip had been crossed.[54] Thanks to this technical progress, Noyce proposed in launching the new firm that it was now possible to build computer memories on mass-produced integrated circuits rather than on hand-wired magnetic cores. By the spring of 1969, the most promising of three techniques that Intel was exploring – metal oxide silicon (MOS) – had yielded a working memory, although yields were still low.[55]

Hoff now suggested to Noyce a way of using this new memory chip to simplify the structure of the circuits for the Busicom calculator. Instead of having a separate dedicated chip for such functions as calculations, printing and display, Hoff proposed the development of a single programmable chip that would perform multiple functions. At any one time, it would download on to complementary Intel-produced memory chips the instructions it was not currently using. When Hoff explained his idea to the Japanese engineers, they showed no interest. However, with Noyce's support, Hoff prepared the designs for his circuits. His approach would cost $155 per kit – half the price of the chips in the Japanese firm's original specifications.[56] Busicom was convinced.

It took another two years, but finally, in 1971, the Busicom 141-PF calculator went on sale.[57] In November of that year, Intel announced the first microprocessor – the 4004 – a programmable computer on a single chip. Hoff's breakthrough for Busicom was being offered to the world at large. The device was so revolutionary that Noyce had to make numerous rounds of 'missionary activity', explaining its advantages to prospective clients. One skeptical listener asked what would happen if his tiny computer fell through a crack in the floor. Noyce quickly replied, 'You wouldn't care. It would just cost a few dollars to replace it'.[58]

In December 1974, a New Mexico firm called MITS began marketing a kit for building the Altair – a computer for personal use that was based on

Intel's most recent 8080 microprocessor.[59] Expecting to sell a few hundred copies, the makers were astounded to receive orders for several thousand in the first month. The following year, the Apple I, using an inexpensive chip from an Intel competitor, MOS Technology, went on sale. In 1981, IBM began selling its personal computer, at the heart of which was the Intel 8088. Since the specifications were open, the machine was quickly cloned by Compaq and other firms.

By the late 1980s, there were millions of personal computers along with thousands of minicomputers and mainframes in the United States and abroad. How could all of these machines possible be fitted into Baran's vision of a distributed network?

**The Etiquette of Conversation**

One day in 1972, Ray Tomlinson, an engineer at BBN in Cambridge, Massachusetts, had an idea. Since the 1960s, users of time sharing systems on a single mainframe had been able to leave messages for one another in the electronic equivalent of the in-box. Tomlinson himself had recently written two programs for BBN's Digital Equipment PDP-10 minicomputer that allowed people to send and retrieve messages. As yet, however, there was no easy way to send messages *between* computers. Taking advantage of having two identical PDP-10s connected to the ARPANET, Tomlinson wrote a little program that allowed a message typed on one machine to be inserted into a file on the other. Needing some means of distinguishing a person's name from the machine on which the file was to be sent, he simply separated the two parts of the address by the symbol '@'. In this way, e-mail was born.[60] By the following year, it accounted for three-quarters of all the traffic on the ARPANET.[61]

In 1973, there were several nets other than the ARPANET using the idea of packet switching. The French had the Cyclades network, while the British National Physical Laboratory had developed its own network. In the US, there was the ALHA network that used radio frequencies. Thanks to lightweight integrated circuits, there were also communications satellites that linked US military bases around the world into SATNET.[62] How could all of these networks be linked together?

One possibility was to decide on standards to be satisfied by all member networks. In 1972, ARPA arranged a meeting of representatives of the different networks who formed the International Network Working Group.[63] After contemplating the difficulties of negotiating a consensus on norms, the group's chairman, Vinton Cerf, an assistant professor of computer science at Stanford, had a clever idea. Having participated as a graduate student in the linking of ARPANET's first two nodes, Cerf realized it would be easier to let each network keep its current specifications. Special gateway computers could then serve as passages from one network to another. Together with Robert Kahn of DARPA (Defense had now been added to the agency's title), Cerf published a paper in 1974 proposing internetwork linkages via these gateway computers. In addition, the authors suggested that the transmitting host computer on one network wrap the packets of its message in an electronic envelope that would be delivered through the gateway to the receiving host computer on the other network. Thus a message of any type could be transmitted provided that it was placed in this standard container. The result was the internet.[64]

It took another three years to develop the Transmission Control Protocol to be used by the host computers. Then finally, in July 1977, the first demonstration took place. A computer in San Francisco linked to a packet radio system sent a message through the ARPANET by SATNET satellite to Norway and from there by cable to University College, London. From the British capital, the message returned to the ARPANET and was finally received on a computer at USC in Los Angeles. Not one bit of information was lost in this 94 000 mile (150 000 km) trip.[65] It would take a few years before the political and military implications of this feat began to be felt, but they would be profound.

By the late 1980s, the internet joined together not only government and university computers but also thousands of individual users who used telephone links to transmit files to one another. However, there was no standard interface to discover what was available or to gain access to it. In 1990, Tim Berners-Lee, an English researcher at CERN in Geneva, proposed a means of tying all of this information together. Those who had information to share would present it using a standard hypertext language and store it on a stripped-down computer called a server. Potential viewers could then contact the server through the internet and see these pages using a program called a 'browser' installed on their own computers. Berners-Lee wrote one version of such a program for graphic content, while a simpler text version was prepared by a colleague. This interface, that Berners-Lee called the World Wide Web, was made public in 1991. It opened up the vast resources of the internet to anyone who could type.

Meanwhile, under the seemingly inexorable progress of Moore's Law, Intel in 1982 launched its 286, the first microprocessor with over 100 000 components.[66] During the 1960s, the diffusion of the integrated circuit had been limited to the West and Japan. By the 1980s however, large numbers of consumers in Eastern Europe had access to portable radios, videocassette recorders and solid-state television sets. The various applications of the integrated circuit began to undermine the barriers that separated the world's writing systems.

## THE CLASH OF CODES

Günter Schabowski had just returned to East Berlin from vacation and was scheduled to give a televised evening press conference concerning the easing of visa regulations for travel to the Federal Republic of Germany. Just before he went on the air, he was handed a note saying that residents of the East German capital would be permitted to cross to the western sector of the city if they had the required authorization. Tired at the end of a long day, Schabowski duly read the announcement. A reporter then asked when the new regulations would take effect. The minister shuffled through his papers and replied that, as far as he knew, 'ab sofort' (immediately).

The day was Thursday, 9 November 1989. Schabowski, 60, was Politburo member and spokesperson for the East German regime. Trained as a journalist, he had been the editor of the popular party newspaper, *Neues Deutschland*, from 1978 to 1985. Unknown to him, his colleagues had intended the visa regulations to take effect only on the following day in order to allow time for preparing the border guards. However, within minutes of his press conference, huge crowds began to assemble on each side of the Berlin border crossings. Overwhelmed, the East German guards soon stopped trying to check travel documents. For the first time since the end of the Second World War, Berliners were able to move freely between the eastern and western sectors of their city. The celebrations continued through the night, all the next day and over the weekend.[67]

### The Terrestrial Satellite

Why did the East German regime suddenly ease its travel restrictions? To answer this question, it is necessary to go back some four decades. West Berlin was the fatal flaw in the agreement that Stalin signed at Potsdam in 1945. Located 110 miles (175 km) within the borders of the German Democratic Republic, the territory constituted a show window for the growing opulence of the West. Even more, by 1960, it was in effect a geostationary satellite for capitalism and democracy, continuously beaming radio and television signals that could be captured in most East German cities and towns. Although East Germans had the highest living standard in the countries of the Soviet-led Comecon bloc, the young and educated were leaving by the tens of thousands each year through West Berlin.[68] Finally, in August 1961, the East German authorities decided to erect the Wall in Berlin and an electrified fence along the rest of their border with the Federal Republic.

The Wall virtually stopped the outward flow of East Germans, but not the inward flow of information. By 1970, two out of three East German households had inexpensive black and white television sets.[69] During the 1960s, it had been forbidden to watch West German television. Informers known as *inofficielle Mitarbeiter* (IMs) employed by the *Staatssicherheit* Ministry (Stasi) kept watch on their neighbors. Then in 1971, the Socialist government took a survey to measure the effects of the electronic invasion. It found that 93 per cent of 14- to 19-year-olds watched or listened to Western radio and television. Realizing that its regulations had become unenforceable, the government in 1972 reversed its decision and allowed people to watch Western television.[70] The decentralization of desire was henceforth officially condoned.

In Estonia, Czechoslovakia and Hungary, which bordered on the West, people also had access to Western television. Elsewhere in Eastern Europe, Radio Free Europe, the Voice of America and the BBC World Service were available on inexpensive transistor radios. Thus when the whole Comecon group entered a severe economic downturn in the 1980s, most of its citizens were aware that an alternative means of organizing society existed. A crucial development was the choice of Mikhail Gorbachev, 54, trained as an agricultural economist, to be Soviet leader in 1985. Aware that major change was needed, Gorbachev introduced a series of domestic reforms known as *perestroika* (reconstruction). Factory managers were given more freedom to set production levels and sell their output, but they could no longer count on the state to finance their deficits.

In foreign policy, too, there were changes. The Soviets had been suffering heavy losses in Afghanistan since 1986, when the United States, with the help of Pakistan, began arming the Mujahideen resistance fighters with Stinger anti-aircraft missiles.[71] A lightweight heat-seeking device made possible by integrated-circuit electronics, the Stinger was used to deadly effect against Russian warplanes and helicopters. In 1988, Gorbachev decided to withdraw his country's troops from the country it had first occupied in 1979.

In 1988, a reforming group within the Communist Party of Hungary took advantage of the change in attitudes in Moscow to oust the conservatives who had ruled their country since 1956. The following spring, in Poland, the harassed government of General Jaruzelski accepted free elections for most of the seats in the two houses of the legislature. When in June 1989, the opposition Solidarity Party won all but two of the contested seats, the Communist leaders, prodded by Gorbachev, had little choice but to accept the results.[72]

Meanwhile, the Hungarian government, anxious to win approval from Western investors, had begun dismantling the electrified fence along its border with Austria. By September, there were 60 000 tourists from the German Democratic Republic camping in Hungary. A declaration by the

Hungarian foreign minister that he would not stop East Germans from crossing the border was followed by a deluge of people from the GDR voting with their feet.[73] When the Hungarians refused to stop this outflow, the East German regime, led by Erich Honecker, announced on 3 October that henceforth visas would be required for travel to Czechoslovakia, the escape route to Hungary.

Six days later, on 9 October, there were rumors of an impending police crackdown on those demonstrating after the usual Monday evening service at the Nikolaikirche in Leipzig. However, thanks to the intervention of local party leaders with the security minister, Egon Krenz, there was no repression. After the following week's service, the crowds in Leipzig increased to 100 000, while the demonstrations spread to other East German cities.[74] Then on 18 October, the Politburo members forced the ailing party leader, Erich Honecker to resign, with Krenz taking his place. It was Krenz and his new colleagues in a restructured Politburo who decided to relax the laws for visiting the West on the day before Schabowski's historic statement of 9 November.

The fall of the Berlin Wall was a signal for change across Eastern Europe. The following day, 10 November, Bulgarian party leaders pushed their aged leader, Todor Zhivkov, 78, overboard. They then announced a series of reforms, including free elections.[75] On 25 November, the leaders of the Czechoslovak Communist Party resigned. Early in December, a new non-Communist government was formed, with the dissident playwright Vaclav Hável as president.[76] Shortly thereafter, on 7 December Egon Krenz was forced to resign as East German leader. Finally, on Christmas Day, Romanian authorities executed their discredited party leader Nicolae Ceauseşcu and his wife.[77]

By 3 October 1990, when the two German states were reunited, the border between the zones dominated by the Cyrillic and Roman writing systems had been pushed east by some 600 miles (1000 km). Meanwhile, even closer to Moscow, trouble was beginning to bubble in one of the small Baltic republics that the Soviet Union had seized in 1940.

## From Union to Commonwealth

Early in January 1991, special Soviet riot-control troops were flown into the outskirts of Vilnius, the Lithuanian capital. Fearful that the Russian-dominated Soviet government would interfere in their quiet revolution, thousands of Lithuanians began to gather around the principal government buildings. The expected showdown occurred shortly after midnight on the morning of 13 January when Soviet troops, tanks and BMPs (*boevaya mshina pekhoty* – armored personnel carriers) approached the television tower and the Radio and Television building in Vilnius. Finding their path blocked by demonstrators, the Russian soldiers began firing live ammunition into the crowd, while tanks drove directly into the mass of people, crushing those in the way under metal treads. In all, 13 Lithuanians were killed and over 160 more injured.[78]

Like the citizens of the other two Baltic States, the Lithuanians had never accepted their forced integration into the USSR in 1940. Encouraged by the fall of the Berlin Wall and the dismantling of pro-Soviet regimes in Eastern Europe, the Lithuanian government declared its independence from the Soviet Union in March 1990. Then, over the following months, economic conditions in the small republic worsened as food and fuel became scarce. The Russian minority were particularly active in voicing their discontent. It was one thing for a sovereign state such as Poland to change its constitutional status, and another when one of the republics of the Soviet Union itself wanted to secede, particularly when ethnic Russians were likely to suffer as a result. On 10 January 1991, Soviet president Mikhail Gorbachev served the Lithuanians an ultimatum demanding that they restore the Soviet constitution. When this call went unheeded, the powers in Moscow issued the command to restore order in the breakaway republic.

Lithuania was one of the smallest of the 15 member states of the Soviet Union. The largest and dominant among the USSR member states was the Russian republic. Early on the morning of the Vilnius massacre, 13 January 1991, Boris Yeltsin, one of the leading politicians in the Russian Republic, flew to Tallinn, Estonia, where he met with the presidents of the three Baltic republics. As chairman of the Presidium of the Supreme Soviet of his republic, Yeltsin held a position roughly equivalent to that of majority leader of a provincial or state legislature.[79] An engineer by training, Yeltsin, 59, had a reputation as an outspoken reformer. Together the four heads of state issued a statement in which each recognized the others' sovereignty and rejected the use of armed force to solve their internal problems. Warned by his allies in the KGB that it would now be dangerous for him to return by plane, Yeltsin went back to Moscow in a small car by country roads.[80] The following day, 14 January, he held a press conference in the building of the Russian Supreme Soviet, at which he addressed the Russian soldiers in the Baltics:

> Today, when the country is in economic and political crisis, and when the healthy forces of our society seek ways out of the complicated situation using legal constitutional forms, you could be given orders to move against legally constituted state bodies, against the peaceful civilian population which is defending its democratic achievements . . . We are sure that the healthy forces in the army will not allow it to start down the anti-popular road of support for the reaction.[81]

Over the following months, events unfolded quickly. In April, the deputies at the Russian Republic's Congress voted to hold the first presidential elections in the Republic on 10 June. Later that month, Gorbachev invited the leaders of Russia's republics, including Yeltsin, to a meeting at Novo-Ogaryovo, the Union's dacha built outside Moscow during the Khrushchev reign. To the surprise of his guests, the Soviet leader offered to recognize the republics as sovereign states. A new Union Treaty, the constitution of a true federal state, would be prepared to be signed by them later that summer.[82]

In the Russian Republic's presidential election of 10 June, Boris Yeltsin defeated the orthodox Communist nominee by a wide margin. Over the following weeks, Yeltsin and Gorbachev played the major roles in drafting the final version of the Union Treaty, which was published on 14 August. The proposed constitution greatly weakened the power of the central government in favor of the republics, granting them exclusive control of the natural resources within their territory. Nevertheless, the Treaty would also give substantial powers to an elected federal president. The new federation would be named the Union of Soviet *Sovereign* Republics. Signature of the treaty was set for 20 August.[83] Gorbachev left Moscow for holidays on the Crimean coast on 4 August, intending to return on 19 August for the ceremony.[84]

It was now or never for those conservatives who wished to preserve the Communist state. On 18 August, Gorbachev was placed under house arrest. At dawn the following morning, Vice President Gennadiy Yanaev addressed the Soviet people in a radio broadcast. He declared that for reasons of health, Gorbachev was incapacitated and that a state of emergency was declared for six months. An emergency committee made up of Yanaev, the KGB chairman, the defense and interior ministers and three other prominent Communists would rule temporarily during this period.[85]

During the morning of 19 August, columns of tanks and BMPs thundered into the center of Moscow. However, counting on popular support, the authors of the coup failed to arrest Yeltsin and his followers or silence the media. No one stopped a black limousine carrying Yeltsin from entering the underground parking lot of the 'White House', the Russian parliament. Immediately, the Russian president held a press conference, declaring the putsch illegal and 'madness'. He then walked outside, climbed atop a tank and shook hands with the crew. As a number of astounded journalists looked on, Yeltsin read a declaration: 'We call on the citizens of Russia to give the organizers of the coup an appropriate response and to demand the return of the country to normal, constitutional government. It is imperative to allow the President of the country, Gorbachev, to speak to the people.'[86]

The next day, Yeltsin issued an appeal to the troops, calling on them to support the people's desire for freedom. Meanwhile, ordinary citizens pleaded with the soldiers or tried to immobilize their tanks with iron bars. Grandmothers brought them jars of home-made jam. Other citizens blocked the city streets with their cars or improvised barricades of overturned trucks and benches.[87] The stand-off lasted until the early morning of 21 August when, faced with massive popular resistance, the military leaders finally recalled their troops. On 22 August, Gorbachev was brought back to Moscow on a plane sent by Yeltsin. That same day, the members of the Emergency Committee were arrested, with the exception of one of the group who committed suicide.[88]

The Soviet Union itself struggled on lamely for another four months. But on 25 December 1991, it was finally dissolved, to be replaced with a voluntary Commonwealth of Independent States. At the same time, Gorbachev resigned.

In a little more than two years, from 9 November 1989 to 25 December 1991, the vertically organized Communist Empire of Eastern Europe had collapsed. The centrally planned economies had proven unable to produce efficiently goods that the rest of the world, or indeed their own citizens, wanted. Crippled by shortages, the economic and political system that had challenged the West since the end of the Second World War had collapsed. With information flowing ever more swiftly from west to east, the iron curtain had simply rusted away.

## The Electronic Underpinnings of Globalization

On 31 January 1990, a year before the massacre in Vilnius, the Canadian subsidiary of McDonald's Corporation had opened the largest of the firm's chain of restaurants. It was situated on busy Pushkin Square in downtown Moscow. The store had 27 cash registers and seating for 700 customers. But at 9:30 a.m., when George Cohon, the president of McDonald's of Canada, arrived to open the restaurant, there was not a customer in sight. Upon inquiry, he found to his relief that the police had obliged potential customers to form a queue around the corner. There, thousands were waiting to purchase their first 'Beeg Mahhov' with ordinary Soviet rubles. That day, the restaurant served 30 567 customers.[89]

Under a contract signed two years earlier, profits from the venture were to be split between the Soviet government and the Canadian group. Rubles earned by the foreign investors had to be spent on Soviet goods which could then be sold abroad. Despite the prices, which were high for Russians, there were long line-ups to enter the restaurant for years afterward. To circumvent the absence of reliable markets for its inputs, McDonald's set up its own local supply chain. Why was it that in Russia one organization, the Soviet Union, was destroyed while another, McDonald's, continued to thrive?

Over the first seven decades of the twentieth century, the world's most successful firms had been hierarchically organized giants like AT&T, IBM and Sears. In each case, a board of directors representing shareholders oversaw managers who in turn supervised workers, with commands flowing from the top down. Most consumer products were sold through distribution chains made up of wholesalers and retailers. Even IBM, when it began selling personal computers in 1981, distributed them primarily through retail chains and independent stores. Sears was in effect a wholesaler that owned its own retail outlets. Certain areas of consumption such as restaurants were virtually inaccessible to large corporations. Because of the distance of their decision makers from their clients, they found themselves unable to adapt their products to individual tastes. Other sectors such as bookselling were poorly served by such organizations because both the sellers and their customers had limited access to information.

In the 1980s, increasingly powerful integrated circuits began to undermine this vertical structure. Small firms with standardized software and inexpensive mini- and microcomputers linked electronically to one another could compete effectively with the specialized staff of large corporations. By permitting electronic information to be stored and processed in decentralized fashion and then shared with distant associates, suppliers and customers, the new information technology enabled nimble innovators to satisfy local demand from a globally organized supply system.

In the case of restaurants, the solution to better satisfying consumer desires was the franchise. In such a contractual arrangement, responsibility is divided between the franchisor, who supplies the business formula, and the franchisee, who applies it locally, with profits shared between the two. For a fixed initial payment and a share of revenues, the franchisee obtains a product with an established reputation. In return, the franchisor obtains a local manager who has a direct interest in assuring that the preferences of consumers in his community are satisfied. The problem for the franchisor is essentially one of monitoring – to assure that the franchisee upholds the standards that allow the chain as a whole to maintain its reputation.

In the late 1950s and early 1960s, Ray Kroc developed a system for monitoring large numbers of franchisees of a hamburger chain by imposing frequent inspections. In 1961, he bought the rights to the chain from the McDonald brothers who had founded it. At that time, there were 228 restaurants.[90] As the firm continued to grow, however, centralized monitoring proved inefficient. Kroc's successor, Fred Turner, gradually decentralized the administration of the restaurant chain. Franchise operators projected their sales weekly to a regional distribution center whose computer automatically calculated the required numbers of pickles, meat patties and ketchup packets.[91] In 1967, this regional structure allowed McDonald's to expand successfully into Canada. In 1971, the same system was applied outside North America. In that year, the firm opened restaurants in Tokyo, Amsterdam, Munich and Sydney. By 1986, there were 9300 McDonald's restaurants worldwide; 20 years later, the number exceeded 31 000.[92]

Unlike the restaurant meal, the microcomputer is a non-perishable commodity. Ironically, by assuring the product's standardization while at the same time maintaining a traditional vertical production and distribution structure, IBM helped to assure its own decline. As the product became standardized, it was no longer necessary to maintain an elaborate retail network to satisfy consumer demands. With low-cost computers to store sales information, a small manufacturer could sell directly to consumers, bypassing the wholesale and retail levels. In 1984, Michael Dell, 19, started a computer firm in his dorm room at the University of Texas at Austin. He was so successful at selling IBM compatibles built from stock parts that he gave up his plan to become a doctor and dropped out of school at the end of his freshman year. The next year, he began selling his own brand through computer magazines, either by mail or by telephone. By cutting out the middleman, Dell could bring a computer to market for $50 less than IBM or Compaq.[93] Dell took out full-page four-color ads in *PC Magazine* to inform customers about the speed of his products and their prices.[94] In 1992, Dell Computer Corporation was listed by Fortune as one of the world's 500 largest companies. By 2005, it was the largest computer manufacturer in the world.[95]

The development of the World Wide Web allowed firms to integrate consumers into their networks as active participants. In the spring of 1994, Jeff Bezos was working as a hedge fund manager for D. E. Shaw and Co. when he heard about the phenomenal growth of the internet. A Princeton graduate in computer science and electrical engineering, Bezos, 30, was alert to the impact of new technologies. When he learned that usage of the World Wide Web was expanding at 2300 per cent a year, he began to ask what product might best take advantage of this technology. Of the 20 possible products he examined, the most likely candidate was books. The number of books in print greatly exceeded the volume that could be handled by a bricks-and-mortar store. For the first time, the internet offered the possibility of maintaining easily accessible information on all of these publications. By centralizing the storage of inventory and by decentralizing access to information on them through the web, he could greatly reduce costs while expanding service. Customers could post their reviews on the web to inform other potential buyers – at virtually no cost to the seller. When the investment firm he worked for proved unwilling to back such a venture, he started his own company, Amazon.com.[96] The company turned its first profit in the final quarter of 2002. With over $10 billion in revenues and almost $400 million in before-tax income in 2006, the firm was one of the 500 members of the elite S&P500 index.[97]

Intel introduced its 486 series chips in 1989; each contained over one million transistors.[98] Thus far, the integrated circuit had had a dramatic effect on conventional warfare, on political structures and on the organization of firms in North America, Europe and Japan. By favoring the decentralization of decision making, the new technology had played a major role in the collapse of the Soviet empire. Now, as inexpensive chips carrying Western culture began to penetrate the Middle East, they threatened an information system that had successfully resisted outside attack for over a millennium.

## THE FIRST-PERSON SHOOTER

Political decision making in the Islamic world had generally been more centralized than in the West, especially under the Ottoman and Mughal empires. However, there were marginal areas in the Arabian Peninsula itself, the Sudan and Afghanistan that had rarely, if ever, been conquered by an outside power.

When Iraqi tanks rolled into Kuwait on 2 August 1990, one of the first to react was a tall, slender, soft-spoken Saudi. The young man immediately flew by private jet from his family's palatial home in the Red Sea port of Jeddah to the capital, Riyadh. There he obtained an audience with Prince Sultan, the defense minister and full brother of King Fahd. The visitor presented the prince a handwritten ten-page proposal to organize a group of 10 000 mujahideen from Saudi Arabia and elsewhere in the Middle East in order to defend the Saudi kingdom against Iraqi aggression. All the soldiers would be seasoned veterans of the Afghan War against the Soviets. Apparently convinced, the Prince told his guest to return to Jeddah to begin his preparations. He would submit the proposal to the king.[99]

### The Departure of the Native

Osama bin Laden, 33, belonged to one of the wealthiest and most influential families in the Arabian kingdom. During his studies in public administration at King Abdul Aziz University in Jeddah, one of his great pleasures had been to cruise the city streets in his canary-yellow Mercedes SL450 convertible. However, during a pilgrimage to Mecca at age 20,

Osama seems to have undergone a conversion to Islamic fundamentalism. Two years later, he left for Afghanistan, landing by helicopter on the edge of the bazaar in Peshawar in northwestern Pakistan in late 1979. There he used Saudi wealth to organize, train and equip Arab fighters who fought alongside the mujahideen. He received support from the CIA through the Pakistani Inter-Services Intelligence Agency (ISI), which channeled Stinger missiles to his fighters.[100]

With the departure of the Russians from Afghanistan after the accords of March 1988, Osama bin Laden withdrew back over the border of Pakistan to a site a short distance from Peshawar. There he was the owner of a large, well-defended stone house with outbuildings that he had named Al-Qaeda ('the base' in Arabic). Making contact with the flow of foreign combatants coming back through the mountains from Afghanistan to return to their homes, he built up a network of Islamic fundamentalist warriors, many of whom were willing to continue the struggle. In the summer of 1989, bin Laden returned to Jeddah, where he was soon recognized on the streets as a war hero.[101] Because of his open criticism of the Saudi regime, however, he was discreetly ordered not to leave the city. The Saudi authorities also seized his passport.[102] Nevertheless, in August 1990, with Saddam Hussein and his army poised to invade his own country, Osama wished to reconcile himself with the regime. After making his presentation in Riyadh, Osama bin Laden confidently flew back to Jeddah to await the official confirmation of his new command. However, the king's reply to his offer never came. Instead, on 7 August, the Saudi government announced the arrival of the first contingents of American troops to protect the kingdom's oil wells.[103] Osama bin Laden never forgot or forgave this humiliation. From that day on, he committed himself to fighting the Americans who were defiling his sacred land and the regime that had betrayed its people.[104]

The following spring, shortly after the conclusion of the Gulf War, Osama bin Laden learned that the Saudi interior minister had gone abroad on a diplomatic mission. Realizing that the time had finally come to take action, he told his elder brother, Bakr, that he needed his passport back in order to negotiate a construction contract in Pakistan. Bakr, with his spotless reputation as a businessman and philanthropist, was able to persuade the minister of the interior to return his younger brother's travel document.

In early April, 1991, Osama bin Laden flew by private plane to Karachi. He then wrote apologetically to Bakr to tell him that he was breaking his word. Knowing that he would probably never see his homeland again, Osama then flew on to Peshawar and from there over the border to an Al-Qaeda base in Afghanistan. Then, late in the year, word came that Pakistan's ISI was looking for him. It was time to move on.

## A Personal Jihad

A group of men sat talking calmly on cushions in the middle of a field, their legs folded under them, a distant city visible on the horizon. The year was 1992, and the city was Khartoum, a shabby former British garrison town, ruined by decades of inflation and civil war.[105] But this was not a prayer session. Rather, the discussion was about how best to attack the ultimate enemy of Islam, the United States. The location, a farm belonging to the tall, thin man leading the discussion, had been chosen to assure that no hidden listening devices could capture the conversation.[106]

Sudan is the largest country in Africa, with a territory greater than that of France, Germany, Italy, Spain, Sweden and the UK together. Osama bin Laden had been welcomed in Khartoum by Dr Hassan al-Turabi, speaker of the National Assembly and an ardent Islamic fundamentalist. At 60 years of age, the Sudanese political leader was a proponent of establishing the Sharia, the strict Islamic law, in all aspects of economic, political and social relations. Al-Turabi helped bin Laden to install himself in a suite of offices in one of the Sudanese capital's more modern buildings, guarded by a platoon of Sudanese soldiers. From this dusty outpost of civilization, thanks to satellite telephone communications, Osama was able to build up a network for organizing and financing Islamic militants around the world.[107]

On 26 February 1993, there was an explosion in the parking garage of the World Trade Center. A home-made bomb in a parked van killed six people and injured 1000 others, causing structural damages of $500 million to the center. Although four men were quickly arrested, it was not until two years later in Islamabad that Pakistani and American officials captured the organizer of the attack, Ramzi Yousef, a British-trained engineer born in Kuwait of a Pakistani father. Although there is some doubt as to whether Al-Qaeda was directly involved in Yousef's attack, the movement did provide him with a refuge in Pakistan after his initial hurried departure from New York.[108]

Between 1992 and 1995, Al-Qaeda operatives carried out further activities against the United States. Two bombs in Yemen in December 1992 damaged hotels where American soldiers were staying. The organization also channeled automatic weapons, rocket-propelled grenades and trained resistance fighters to General Mohamed Aidid, who opposed an American-led United Nations force in Somalia. On 3 October 1993, Aidid's forces used these weapons to down two American Black Hawk helicopters in Mogadishu. Lighting tires as a signal, the Somali commander's men then swarmed around the American rescue troops, inflicting 17 casualties on their enemy.[109] As Bruce Berkowitz observed, Aidid's irregular forces used the same tactics that had worked so well for the American-led coalition's 'Desert Storm' against Saddam Hussein in 1991: precision weapons, a network of agents able to swarm around a target of opportunity and information technology that permits a shorter decision cycle than that of the enemy.[110]

A year later, on 13 November 1994, a car bomb exploded in Riyadh next to a snack bar popular with US servicemen who were on a technical assistance mission with the Saudi National Guard. Six people, including five Americans, were killed.[111] A second bomb in the same city in the spring of 1995 was traced back to Al-Qaeda.[112] From mid-1994, Al-Qaeda also began establishing agents in several African countries. Some appeared under the cover of workers with a German-registered non-governmental aid agency, Help Africa People, while others came as import–export agents. Kenya and Tanzania were two countries chosen, in part because of their close ties to the US and Israel.[113]

Meanwhile, in the Sudan, after the bombings in Riyadh, the heat was becoming too great. In March 1996, Dr al-Turabi gently informed bin Laden that because of pressure from Saudi Arabia, Osama would have to leave the Sudan. Accordingly, on 10 May, bin Laden flew from Khartoum to Jalalabad in Afghanistan and from there by helicopter to Kandahar, center of an Islamic military movement known as the Taliban.[114] It was well that he had taken refuge in the mountains of Afghanistan when he did. On 25 June 1996, a massive bomb ripped out a wall of the Khobar Towers in Dhahran, an oil port on the Persian Gulf in Saudi Arabia. The blast killed 19 American airmen and injured 372 others, all of whom were attached to the nearby American air base that was enforcing a 'no-fly' zone in southern Iraq. Although the government of Iran was found to be the principal sponsor of the attack, Osama bin Laden may also have participated in its planning.[115]

## The Army of God

In the spring of 1994, two teenage girls from the village of Sang Hesar near Kandahar in southern Afghanistan were kidnapped by members of local mujahideen units and repeatedly raped. Word of this incident reached Mohammed Omar, a mullah (religious cleric) and former commander of pious fighters known as *taliban* recruited from the network of students of Afghan madrasas (Koranic schools). Omar gathered together 30 of his fellow warriors to attack the control post of the mujahideen. After a brief firefight, they managed to free the girls. Then as a warning to other lawless mujahideen, Omar and his men slipped a noose over the captured warrior leader's neck, attached it to the gun-barrel of a tank and slowly raised the cannon. Omar and his men then fled to the neighboring Pakistani province of Balochistan.[116]

Two years earlier, in April 1992, Najibullah, the last Afghan president named by the Russians, had been overthrown by an alliance of regional warlords. Almost immediately, the different Afghan factions began to fight among themselves for control of the capital, Kabul. By mid-1994, after more than two years of anarchy, most Afghans were willing to accept any leader, provided that law and order be restored. Mullah Omar, 35, a giant of a man who had lost an eye to shrapnel while fighting the Russians, decided that it was time to satisfy this desire for stability. He managed to recruit some 1500 pious men who were willing to fight for Islam. His group of *taliban* then offered its services to protect a convoy of trucks crossing from Pakistan to Turkmenistan. The Pakistani truck owners had bribed the local commanders along the route through Afghanistan. Nevertheless, as the convoy approached Kandahar, it was set upon and its cargo seized. In three days of fighting, Omar's force managed to rout the mujahideen and take their stronghold of Kandahar. Driving Japanese four-wheel-drive pickup trucks and armed with machine guns and rocket-propelled grenades, teams of Taliban then went from village to village. They used satellite phones to coordinate their movements, imposing the Koran by force.[117] Any warlord who refused to support them was shot.[118]

Helmand, the province around Kandahar, is one of two main poppy-growing regions in Afghanistan. With the return of peace and high opium prices, local farmers had a strong incentive to resume poppy production using new genetically enhanced seeds. Whether they wanted to or not, the Taliban had to tolerate the growing of poppies in the region they controlled. Inevitably, they began to finance their purchases of arms by taxing the production of poppies.[119] In doing so, they attracted the attention of the Pakistan ISI, whose regular funding from Washington had been cut off when the war against the Soviets came to an end and who now sought to control the drug traffic across their country's borders.[120] Toward the end of 1995, Osama bin Laden too began to channel Saudi funds to Mullah Omar.[121]

On 5 September 1995, Herat, a provincial capital in the west, fell to the Taliban. The movement now controlled nine of the country's 32 provinces. In areas under their administration, not only did the Taliban prohibit women from working but also they beat any women found in public without the full burka. In October, they began a siege of the capital, Kabul, bombarding the city daily with rockets. Finally, on 26 September 1996, after more than a year of bitter warfare, the opposing warlords pulled out of Kabul.[122] Two days later, television channels around the world broadcast images of former president Najibullah and his brother, the former pro-Soviet security chief, strung up in the center of Kabul after being dragged from their prison cells by the victorious Taliban.[123]

## Returning the Call

On the morning of 20 August 1998, Osama bin Laden used his satellite phone to call a journalist in Pakistan from a training camp he had set up in the mountains near Khost, a provincial capital south of Kabul. American intelligence agents tracking the call were able to pinpoint exactly where bin Laden had been. Three hours later, some 70 cruise missiles launched from American vessels exploded over this and three other sites used to train militants in Afghanistan. Each missile contained 166 bomblets weighing 3.3 lbs (1.5 kg) designed to kill personnel and destroy property over a wide area. Simultaneously, American missiles blew up a pharmaceutical factory near Khartoum in the Sudan that was believed to produce inputs for chemical weapons. However, bin Laden had been informed that the American government had advised its citizens to leave Afghanistan three days earlier. Neither he nor any of his key operatives were hurt.[124]

In ordering the attacks on the Sudanese factory and the Afghan terrorist training facilities, President Clinton had been acting on a promise made earlier that month. 7 August 1998 was the eighth anniversary of the arrival of American troops on Arabian soil after Iraq's invasion of Kuwait. Osama bin Laden chose that moment to activate the sleepers he had installed in Kenya and Tanzania several years earlier. Two massive truck bombs exploded within minutes of each other next to the American embassies in Nairobi and Dar es Salaam. More than 220 people were killed and over 4000 wounded. When Clinton learned of the deadly attacks, he vowed that his country would bring the perpetrators to justice 'no matter what or how long it takes'.[125]

Surprisingly, despite this concrete proof of the Americans' displeasure with Al-Qaeda and their willingness to intervene with force, Mullah Omar, the head of the Taliban government, did little to restrain the activities of bin Laden. Proof that the Al-Qaeda network was left intact would come two years later, on 12 October 2000, when two Arab suicide bombers in a small boat carrying a bomb blasted a hole in the side of the destroyer USS Cole as it refueled in Aden.[126] The stage was set for an unprecedented version of David's clash with Goliath.

In short, the link between 11/9 and 9/11 was technological. The first two decades of mutations of the integrated circuit weakened the information monopoly of the Soviet state in Eastern Europe sufficiently to bring about the fall of the Berlin Wall and the collapse of the Soviet Union itself. A third decade of advances enabled a stateless group to plan, coordinate and finance an increasingly deadly series of attacks against the United States and its allies using anonymous international financial transfers, cellular telephones and electronic timing devices.

Despite the collapse of the World Trade Center on 11 September 2001, the struggle was by no means over. By 2006, McDonald's had more than 230 restaurants in the Middle East.[127] The chain had opened its first restaurant in Saudi Arabia in 1993 – in Jeddah, Osama bin Laden's home town. Out of respect for local customs, the restaurant had set up separate eating areas for men and women. Nevertheless, as Osama bin Laden instinctively understood, the standardized characters developed at the time of Charlemagne were now engaged in a bitter struggle for hearts and minds in the Middle East. Mounted on microchips, the descendants of the Caroline Minuscule posed an unprecedented threat to the sacred script of Islam.

## NOTES

1. Hafner and Lyon (1996, pp. 15–17).
2. National Aeronautics and Space Administration (2007).
3. United States Department of Defense (n.d.).
4. University of Oregon (n.d.).
5. Hafner and Lyon (1996, p. 21).
6. Hafner and Lyon (1996, p. 22).
7. Berlin (2001, pp. 73–75).
8. Kaplan (1999, p. 48).
9. Berlin (2001, p. 70).
10. Kaplan (1999, p. 48).
11. Kaplan (1999, p. 49).
12. Kaplan (1999, p. 49).
13. Berlin (2005, p. 93).
14. Berlin (2001, p. 77).
15. Berlin (2001, p. 72).
16. Berlin (2001, p. 79).
17. Hafner and Lyon (1996, p. 54).
18. Naughton (1999, p. 96).
19. Sublette (1997).
20. United States, Government Printing Office (2001).
21. Ibid.
22. Ibid.
23. Eklof (2004).
24. Webber and Wildavsky (1986, p. 508).
25. Webber and Wildavsky (1986, p. 495).
26. Urban Institute and Brookings Institution (2007).
27. Burk (2001, p. 50).
28. Museum of Broadcast Communications (n.d.).
29. Athey and Zmud (1988, p. A-3).
30. Berlin (2005, p. 102).
31. Berlin (2005, p. 61).
32. Forester (1987, pp. 19–20).
33. Berlin (2005, pp. 8–9).
34. Berlin (2005, pp. 18–19).
35. Berlin (2005, pp. 26–27).
36. Berlin (2005, p. 42).

37. Berlin (2005, p. 109).
38. Berlin (2005, p. 136).
39. Judt (2005, p. 251).
40. Wade (2007).
41. Naughton (1999, pp. 92–94).
42. As noted in Chapter 1, the principle concepts of this paper were later included in his RAND Corporation Memorandum (Baran, 1964).
43. Hafner and Lyon (1996, p. 59).
44. Naughton (1999, p. 126).
45. Naughton (1999, p. 98).
46. Naughton (1999, pp. 106–109).
47. Naughton (1999, p. 84).
48. Naughton (1999, p. 90).
49. Naughton (1999, p. 131).
50. Hafner and Lyon (1996, pp. 140–141).
51. Hafner and Lyon (1996, pp. 151–153).
52. Berlin (2005, p. 162).
53. Berlin (2005, p. 187).
54. Suplee (2005, p. 39).
55. Berlin (2005, pp. 183, 186).
56. Berlin (2005, p. 187).
57. CPU Museum (n.d.).
58. Berlin (2005, pp. 202–204).
59. Berlin (2005, p. 226).
60. Hafner and Lyon (1996, pp. 191–192).
61. Hafner and Lyon (1996, p. 194).
62. Naughton (1999, pp. 157–158).
63. Hafner and Lyon (1996, p. 222).
64. Naughton (1999, pp. 160–162).
65. Naughton (1999, pp. 163–164).
66. Suplee (2005, p. 39).
67. Fulbrook (1991, p. 331).
68. Watson (1992, p. 190).
69. Judt (2005, p. 345).
70. Fulbrook (2005, p. 135).
71. Coll (2004, p. 11).
72. Judt (2005, p. 607).
73. Judt (2005, pp. 612–613).
74. Fulbrook (1991, p. 329).
75. Judt (2005, pp. 626–627).
76. Judt (2005, pp. 618–619).
77. Judt (2005, p. 625).
78. Aron (2000, p. 410).
79. Aron (2000, p. 384).
80. Aron (2000, p. 411).
81. Aron (2000, p. 412).
82. Brown (1996, p. 286).
83. Brown (1996, pp. 287–288).
84. Brown (1996, p. 293).
85. Aron (2000, p. 440).
86. Aron (2000, p. 445).
87. Aron (2000, pp. 448–449).
88. Aron (2000, pp. 455–456).
89. Cohon (1997, p. 215).
90. Love (1986, p. 189).
91. Love (1986, pp. 349–350).

92. Love (1986, p. 3).
93. Holzner (2006, p. 5).
94. Holzner (2006, p. 11).
95. Holzner (2006, p. 2).
96. Millennium Ventures Group (2006).
97. Yahoo! Finance (2007).
98. Suplee (2005, p. 38).
99. Robinson (2001, p. 129).
100. Griffin (2001).
101. Robinson (2001, p. 119).
102. Robinson (2001, p. 128).
103. Robinson (2001, p. 130).
104. Robinson (2001, p. 131).
105. Coll (2004, p. 267).
106. Robinson (2001, p. 159).
107. Robinson (2001, p. 138–139).
108. Robinson (2001, p. 163), Burke (2003, p. 99), Haqqani (2005, p. 230).
109. Robinson (2001, p. 151), Berkowitz (2003, pp. 115–116).
110. Berkowitz (2003, pp. 75, 116).
111. Robinson (2001, p. 174).
112. Robinson (2001, p. 176).
113. Robinson (2001, pp. 221–222).
114. Robinson (2001, p. 188).
115. Robinson (2001, pp. 187–188, 227).
116. Griffin (2001, p. 35).
117. Griffin (2001, pp. 40–41).
118. Haqqani (2005, p. 239).
119. Griffin (2001, p. 154).
120. Griffin (2001, p. 149).
121. Robinson (2001, p. 181).
122. Griffin (2001, p. 47).
123. Griffin (2001, p. 1).
124. Griffin (2001, p. 200).
125. Robinson (2001, p. 229).
126. Robinson (2001, p. 253).
127. Media Line (2006).

# Conclusion

The nine preceding chapters have presented a series of historical examples in which the introduction of a new information technology was followed by rapid social, political and economic transformation. However, we should not necessarily conclude that the technological developments in some way *caused* the social changes simply because the innovations occurred first. The timing of the two sets of events might well be accidental. Or, if such a long series of coincidences seems improbable, both sets of developments might be the consequence of some third factor.

How might we demonstrate that new information technologies which alter the importance of scale economies relative to network effects lead to revolutions in social interactions? The next section examines two experiments in which the manipulation of information available to participants provoked surprising changes in group behavior. It is then suggested that the experimenters inadvertently replicated the information revolutions observed at the outset of each epoch of the past millennium. The chapter concludes by returning to the nine questions asked in the introduction.

What follows by no means constitutes a rigorous test of the information-revolution hypothesis. For statistical tests of some of the implications of this thesis, the reader is referred to the journal articles listed in the Epilogue. Here, the question is: can the observed discontinuities in Western history be explained in a manner that is consistent with what we know of group behavior?

## ROBBERS AND PRISONERS

In order to demonstrate causality from information technology to social change, we would require evidence that changes in the way information is channeled may affect the structure of interpersonal relationships in a society. Ideally, we would like to conduct a controlled experiment where only the distribution of information is changed and then observe the impact of this development, if any, on social groups. As it happens, there are two famous experiments in which psychologists deliberately manipulated the information to which groups of subjects had access. Let us examine each in turn to learn how the individuals reacted to these changes in their information environment.

**The Robbers Cave Experiment**

One Saturday morning in June 1954, a bus picked up 11 fifth-grade boys in Oklahoma City and drove them to a campsite some 160 miles (250 km) southeast of the city. The scout camp at which they would spend the next three weeks was entirely surrounded by the densely wooded Robbers Cave state park. Although the boys were all about 11 years of age and were from middle-income families in the same city, they did not know one another, since each had been chosen from a different school. The following day, another 11 boys of the same age from similar backgrounds in the same city were picked up and driven to another site in the park, about a half mile (800 m) from the first through the forest.

Over the following week, the meal and sport times of the two groups were staggered to avoid contact between them. Only toward the end of the week did the psychologists running the experiment inform each group of the other's existence. The boys were also told that during the second week, the two groups would be competing in baseball and other activities for individual and group prizes. At about this time, the two sets of boys picked names for their groups – the 'Rattlers' and the 'Eagles'. Each team stenciled its name and a corresponding emblem on team t-shirts while at the same time developing its own leadership structure.[1]

From the start of the second week, tensions between the two groups quickly escalated. The Rattlers won the first day's baseball game and tug-of-war. Over the days that followed, the Eagles tended to come second in the sports competitions. To keep the losers sufficiently motivated, the staff juggled the points awarded in non-sports events in a manner that favored the Eagles. Nevertheless, there was resentment. On the first evening, the Eagles avenged their defeats by burning the Rattlers' team flag, which had been left on the baseball diamond. This act initiated a series of 'tit-for-tat' aggressions by the two groups. Late the following evening, the Rattlers raided the Eagles' cabin, ripping mosquito netting and overturning beds. Two days later, the Eagles retaliated by messing up the Rattlers' cabin. By the end of the week, the staff had to intervene to prevent yet another threatened raid from turning violent.

What had happed to change these two sets of boys with excellent access to food and recreational facilities from peaceful campers into rival bands of warriors determined to inflict physical harm on each other? The only thing that the organizers had modified was the youngsters' information structure. The initial position of each boy on arriving at the camp may be represented by one of the nodes in the Paul Baran's distributed network at the top of Figure 9.1 (p. 271). At the outset, we may assume that these healthy, well-adjusted boys of the same age and similar backgrounds were roughly equal. Two weeks later, as a deliberate result of intervention by the experiment's planners, each boy's information structure was much closer to that of the decentralized network in the center of the figure. Information was centered in the leaders of each of the cabins, with the low-prestige boys playing the role of followers. There was virtually no contact between individuals on different teams except through information transmitted by the staff.

The activities of the third week had the effect of breaking down this asymmetric distribution of information. Would individual contact between members of the two groups accomplish this objective? An initial joint meal in the mess hall quickly degenerated into a session of paper and food throwing. The following day another joint meal session erupted into a full-scale food fight with challenges and counter-challenges.

Only then did the planners introduce 'superordinate goals', that is, objectives desired by all that could be reached only if the two groups cooperated. First, the staff deliberately cut off the water supply, announcing to the campers that there may have been trouble with vandals. Before long, the members of both teams were working together to solve the problem, removing the sacking that had blocked a faucet. Later, the boys agreed to contribute jointly to the rental of two movies that all of them wanted to see. The following day, at a joint campsite, the boys all pushed to start a truck that supposedly had stalled, depriving them of food. By the end of the week, all the boys agreed to travel home on the same bus. In choosing their places for the ride, members of the two groups mingled. At the refreshment stop, the Rattlers, the team that had won five dollars in the contests, offered to use its prize money to buy milkshakes for all the boys in both groups.

How had the two rival groups been transformed in such a short time into a band of brothers? The simplest explanation is that the third week's structured interaction to solve common problems had the effect of breaking down the information asymmetries deliberately created during the first two weeks. Individual Rattlers and Eagles came to realize that the boys on the other team were similar to them and could be trusted to cooperate in times of common need. In the process, the decentralized network of the middle diagram of Figure 9.1 was converted into the distributed network shown in the upper diagram.

Let us now turn to a second experiment to see the effects of another quite different type of information restructuring.

## The Stanford Prison Experiment

On the morning of Sunday 15 August 1971, nine university students living in houses and residences scattered across the quiet town of Palo Alto,

California, were arrested, handcuffed and taken to the local police station. There they were fingerprinted, blindfolded and left in a temporary holding cell. A short time later, the prisoners were all transferred to the basement of the psychology department of Stanford University, where three small laboratories had been converted into steel-barred prison cells. Each young man was then stripped, sprayed with a delousing liquid and given the prison uniform he was to wear. It consisted of a smock, no underwear and a hair covering made from a nylon stocking. In addition, each had a heavy chain padlocked around his right ankle.[2] Sewn on the back and front of each prisoner's smock was his ID number, the only way by which he was to be addressed over the next two weeks.

The student prisoners had been chosen from 70 applicants who had answered an ad in a local newspaper offering $15 a day for participants in a study of prison life. In all, 24 students had been selected. Half of them were randomly given the role of prisoners and told they should be prepared to spend their days and nights in jail. The other 12 students were assigned to be prison guards who would relay one another in eight-hour shifts. At the beginning of the experiment, three prisoners and three guards were kept in reserve, in case some of the others withdrew. The guards, who had met one another before the arrests, were free within limits to set their own rules so as to maintain order in the prison. They were given khaki uniforms with mirror sunglasses, whistles and billy clubs.

On the first day everything went as the psychologists had expected, each of the students adapting to the role he had been assigned. Then, early in the morning of the second day, before the guards' change of shift, a revolt suddenly broke out among the prisoners. A video camera set up behind a wall at one end of the prison corridor captured the events as they unfolded. The prisoners took off their stocking caps, ripped off their numbers and barricaded the cell doors with their beds. Overwhelmed by what was happening, the three guards on duty called on the three students assigned as stand-by guards and waited for the next shift to arrive. Then, using cold carbon dioxide sprayed from a fire extinguisher to force the prisoners away from the doors, the guards stormed each of the three cells. They stripped the prisoners, removed their beds and threw the ringleaders into solitary confinement.

In order to prevent rebellion from reoccurring, the guards then devised a strategy to break down solidarity among the prisoners. The more docile inmates were given special privileges, being allowed to wash and brush their teeth and get their beds back. The troublemakers were deprived of food and punished with push-ups, sometimes with a guard's foot on their backs. Then, after a day of this treatment, the guards arbitrarily transferred some of the prisoners from the 'good' cell to the 'bad' cell. Were some of their new cellmates informers? No longer knowing whom he could trust, each prisoner found himself increasingly alone and isolated.

On the evening of the experiment's fifth day, Christina Maslach, a recent Stanford psychology PhD who was dating the experiment's organizer Philip Zimbardo, stepped into the psychology department basement to do some interviews. When she witnessed uniformed guards herding a group of chained prisoners to the toilet, each with a bag over his head, his hands on the shoulders of the young man in front of him, she was shocked. 'It's terrible what you are doing to these boys!' she exclaimed to Zimbardo. He and his associates were so caught up in the experiment, trying to deal with a prisoner hunger strike, uneasy parents and the possibility of a breakout aided by confederates from outside the prison that they had lost sight of the moral restraints usually placed on social behavior. Suddenly made aware of the incongruity of what he had created – a concentration camp in the middle of one of America's elite educational institutions – Zimbardo put an end to the experiment.

What was it that triggered this abrupt change in the behavior of ordinary college students? How had these well-adjusted young Americans been transformed into cringing introverts on the one hand and brutal club-wielding bullies on the other? Once again, the explanation would appear to lie in the information structure. On the first day of the experiment, the staff, the guards and the student prisoners formed three linked clusters similar to those shown in the decentralized network in the middle of Figure 9.1. By the end of the fifth day however, the network had been transformed into the centralized network at the bottom of the figure. The staff and guards were at the center of the information structure and the isolated, broken-spirited prisoners on the periphery.

Toward the end of the experiment, Professor Zimbardo had to intervene when one of the student prisoners, #819, started to sob uncontrollably. Taking him apart, Zimbardo told him, 'Listen, you are not #819 . . . This is just an experiment, and those are students . . . just like you. Let's go'. Zimbardo recalled that the student looked up at him like a child after a nightmare and immediately calmed down.

The day after the prisoners' release, Zimbardo held debriefing sessions, first with the guards, then with the prisoners and finally with all of the participants together. The prisoners were relieved that their ordeal was over, but most of the guards were disappointed to see the project cancelled ahead of schedule.

By suddenly terminating the experiment, Zimbardo had again transformed the information structure in which each participant found himself. Once more, the young men were just ordinary students and the older adults were psychology researchers, each able to communicate freely with those who shared his interests. In effect, by waving his magic wand once again, Zimbardo had reformed the clusters of the middle graph of Figure 9.1. However, all of the participants in the experiment would be marked by their experience.

In conclusion, these two experiments show how four different changes in the structure of information within small groups triggered four different types of mutations in social networks. We now explore the possibility that the experimenters were inadvertently mimicking the effects of the major innovations in information technology within Western society over the past millennium.

## REVOLUTIONARY TECHNOLOGIES

The Robbers Cave and Stanford Prison experiments demonstrate the impact of restructuring information flows on social networks. By simply manipulating the information to which boys or young men had access, the experimenters were able to trigger sudden transformations in group behavior. Might these experiments somehow have replicated the effects of the new information technologies that began to diffuse across the West at the beginning of each major period of the past millennium?

In the introductory chapter, it was suggested that the crucial characteristic of information technologies was the relative importance of scale economies and network effects. Recall that there are scale economies if the cost of processing each additional unit of information falls when the total quantity of information to be treated rises. Remember too that there are network effects if, when an additional person begins to use a technology, those who are already using the same technology benefit.

Using these definitions, let us examine once again the historical changes of the preceding chapters in chronological order. We will be on the lookout for fundamental transformations in the patterns that people use to interact with one another. Of course no society can possibly be represented by one of the pure types of network shown in Figure 9.1. There will always be some organizations that follow the authoritarian structure of the centralized network, for example, the military. Other groups such as religious organizations may tend to interact according to the flatter structure of the decentralized network. Finally, the dispersed pattern of the distributed network will tend to be more appropriate for interactions between producers and their suppliers. Nevertheless, the relative importance of these three types of network can change rapidly over a short period of time.

## The Contractual Revolution

The transformation of medieval Europe at the end of the first millennium has a close parallel in one of the experiments. At the end of the Stanford Prison experiment, the organizers allowed the prisoners and the guards to interact freely. Whereas the prisoners had previously been allowed to interact only with the guards (and their own cellmates if they were not in solitary confinement), they were now free to form links within their group. Similarly, the guards who were formerly under the orders of the organizers could now express themselves as they saw fit. The centralized network that had formed by the experiment's fifth day quickly broke down. By the debriefing sessions on the sixth day, the research staff, guards and prisoners had reformed their own parallel groups, each with its own leadership structure.

This change in information channels is similar to what may occur in a society if scale economies fall while network effects rise. In the ninth century, a new communications medium – Medieval Latin in standardized script – reduced scale economies in information storage. Each territorial lord could now afford to replicate the imperial chancellery. At the same time, by making possible a rise in literacy, the efficient new technology increased network effects, providing links between decentralized clusters of people. As the number of literate clerics and lay people increased, it became possible to share information about agricultural, manufacturing and military techniques across Western Europe.

If the Carolingian Empire in 800 may be represented by the centralized network in the lower panel of Figure 9.1, the new structure may be represented by the decentralized network in the middle of the figure. The court of each regional lord was now a node surrounded by the stations of his dependent vassals, with whom he communicated orally in the local vernacular. Linking the clusters were the educated clerics and *ministeriales* able to read and write in standardized Latin.

The result was a contractual revolution. In repeated interactions among the players, there was strong pressure to encourage each member of a group within a society to conform to a common behavioral code. As early as 842, in the Oath of Strasbourg, Louis the German and Charles the Bald swore before their assembled troops to uphold an alliance against their older brother, Lothar. By the end of the eleventh century, the practice of liegeancy had emerged. In effect, the nobles in a region recognized the division of their territory into heritable fiefs and agreed jointly to defend that territory under the leadership of one of their number. They began to conform to a code of behavior in which heritable tenure of property was recognized in exchange for regular military service.

Over the last decades of the twentieth century, there was a similar fall in scale economies relative to network effects owing to the diffusion of ever-more-powerful and less-expensive integrated circuits. In each country, the national television networks were challenged by new entrants – local channels, cable companies, satellite broadcasters, DVDs and the internet. As a result, the mass audience broke up into multiple niches. Much like the Rattlers and Eagles, each competing group was determined to defend its territory against its rivals.

**The Consensual Revolution**

The formation of nation states in the early modern period also has an analog in the psychology experiments. In the third week of the Robbers Cave experiment, the deliberate introduction of superordinate goals permitted the two groups of campers to know one another better. Over the next few days, the boys formed ties of friendship that cut across their group boundaries. Similarly, within each state in early modern Europe, the introduction of printing in a standardized vernacular caused network effects to rise while scale economies remained roughly constant. During the sixteenth and seventeenth centuries, there was a sharp rise in the percentage of lay people from different regions able to communicate with one another in a standardized written form without the intermediary of a priest or clerk trained in Latin. As a result of this consensual revolution, each major European state was transformed from a set of interlinked regions into a more or less homogeneous nation.

**The Pre-emptive Revolution**

During the nineteenth century, with the mechanization of printing, there was a great increase in scale economies of information processing and at the same time a fall in network effects. Previously, the most efficient means of communicating had been the handwritten letter or the printed pamphlet or news sheet. Any literate individual could write a letter or have a pamphlet printed in a few hundred copies to distribute among his acquaintances. As the setup costs and scale of printing rose, these low-volume letters and sheets were replaced by daily newspapers printed first in tens and then in hundreds of thousands of copies. The previous national distributed networks broke up into sub-networks whose members read the same newspapers as those who shared their interests.

The effect was analogous to the transformation that occurred at the beginning of the Robbers Cave experiment. During the first and second weeks, the boys, who were initially social equals, developed into two rival bands, each with its own leadership structure. By the end of the second week the staff members were obliged to intervene to prevent violence and to redistribute competition points from the stronger to the weaker of the two groups.

Similarly, in industrializing Europe, the distributed network of the nation state coalesced into clusters of competing networks, decentralized not by territory but by social class. With inter-class violence a growing threat, those who held power were obliged to intervene to improve conditions for the least favored groups. Factories were regulated, schools were subsidized, voting rights were extended and slavery was abolished. This mutation in which a distributed network was transformed into a decentralized network may be described as a pre-emptive revolution.

### The Prescriptive Revolution

As the nineteenth century ended, further improvements to printing technology and the push toward universal literacy continued these trends. Scale economies in newspaper publishing rose further, while tensions between property owners and workers became more acute. In the first days of the Stanford Prison experiment, the blocking of information flows between the student prisoners and the outside world led to a restructuring of the participants into a highly centralized network. Similarly, within Western societies, urban workers cut off from their families and traditional support groups were forced to rely on the mass media for information and on the state or large corporations for their material needs. This prescriptive revolution transformed a decentralized society into a centralized structure.

It may be seen, then, that the four types of startling changes in group behavior observed in two famous psychology experiments had counterparts in the history of the West. In each case, the arbitrary decisions of the experimenters seem to have replicated the effects of new technologies that changed the relative importance of scale economies and network effects in information processing. Equipped with this conceptual structure, let us now try to draw some conclusions from the nine detailed case studies.

## THE QUESTIONS ANSWERED

Using the network illustrations of Figure 9.1, we may summarize the contents of this book. Each of the first four pairs of historical chapters began with a society in which one of three basic network structures – centralized, decentralized or distributed – was dominant. A search for a means of lowering the cost of processing information then altered the relative importance of scale economies and network effects. The result was a mutation in the dominant pattern of social interaction. There were four types of revolution – contractual, consensual, pre-emptive and prescriptive – each corresponding to the transition from one of three basic network structures to another. Initially, in each revolution, there was a phase of creative destruction. Subsequently, however, as the new technology diffused, a period of wrenching rebirth began. Consider now the questions asked in the introduction.

## The Contractual Revolution

### 1. Why did the Carolingian Empire collapse?

In the late eighth century, Charlemagne faced the high cost of preserving information accurately over time in a primarily oral society. He therefore hired the Anglo-Saxon clergyman Alcuin to instruct the young Franks at his court how to read and write in Latin. However, not only did Alcuin teach but also he brought together the best existing practices to develop a standardized procedure for preserving information. In reducing information storage costs, this innovation had unforeseen consequences for both Charlemagne's dynasty and Western civilization. The decline in scale economies and rise in network effects led to a contractual revolution in which the centralized Carolingian information network broke up and regional leaders formed their own decentralized scriptoria, armies and fiscal agents.

### 2. Why were the Normans able to conquer and hold on to the Kingdom of England?

The spread of literacy during the tenth and eleventh centuries permitted the compilation of legal codes based on Roman law and more recent precedent. Eventually, after repeated conflict with one another, the squabbling nobles in each region realized that they all had something to gain by cooperating with one another. Gradually conventions arose that restricted opportunistic behavior within each of the three social orders – those who prayed, those who fought and those who worked. The presence of literate clergy and *ministeriales* helped to assure the respect of these behavioral codes. Cooperation proved favorable to the search for better ways of doing things. As Joel Mokyr has compellingly shown, the first centuries of the new millennium saw a burst of innovation in Western Europe.[3]

One of the first leaders to take advantage of the new communications technology was Duke William II of Normandy. In a series of local victories in the 1040s and 1050s, he succeeded in dominating the other nobles of his duchy. Realizing that force alone would not be sufficient to maintain their allegiance, he worked out an arrangement with his principal barons. They would be allowed to transfer the rights to their property to their heirs;

in return, they were expected to provide their duke with regular military service. Under this new feudal system, the Norman landholders had an incentive to master the costly technology of cavalry warfare and stone castles. At Hastings in 1066, thanks to their technological superiority, the Normans and their French allies were able to wear down and envelop the shield wall of Saxon infantrymen. The castles the Norman nobles then erected in the conquered land enabled them to suppress revolts and discourage other invaders. With King John's acceptance of the Magna Carta in 1215, the contractual revolution was complete. Although John himself refused to recognize the conditions of the charter with his barons, his heirs respected it. It would become the basic constitutional document of the United Kingdom.

### The Consensual Revolution

Consider next the situation of the ruler of a small German state such as Electoral Saxony in the mid-fifteenth century. Although he might have objected to the gold and silver that the Catholic Church collected on his territory, any attempt to break away from the Church would have led to excommunication for the ruler and his subjects. Temporal sanctions from the German emperor might also be applied. In the early fifteenth century, therefore, each territorial prince had an incentive to remain within the medieval social structure.

**3. Why did Luther's movement to reform the practice of Christianity succeed where the earlier attempts of John Wycliffe and Jan Hus had failed?**

In 1415, the Council of Constance had suppressed the writings of would-be church reformers John Wycliffe and Jan Hus. Wycliffe's bones were dug up and burned, while Hus himself was burned at the stake. At the time then, the Church was still powerful enough to stifle heresy. However, in 1450, Pope Nicholas V authorized the sale of letters of indulgence to help defend Cyprus against the Turks – and, incidentally, to finance the Vatican library. The German Church requested Johannes Gutenberg to produce hundreds of copies of these letters by a new process of printing with movable type. On the promise of further orders to print missals and Bibles, Gutenberg was able to obtain loans to finance his costly venture of printing the Bible. Little did Pope Nicholas V and Cardinal Nicholas of Cusa realize that this new technology would eventually destroy the religious monopoly of the Catholic Church.

As a result of Gutenberg's invention, the cost of reproducing an extra page of text fell by more than two orders of magnitude. However, since few were able to read the vehicular language, Medieval Latin, the immediate effect of the new technology was slight. Then in the late fifteenth century, the printers and writers in each cultural area performed a priceless service by beginning to standardize the written forms of the vernacular languages. For example, the Saxon court dialect used by Luther in his translations of the Bible in the 1520s became the basis for High German. As more and more people learned to write in these standardized forms, there was a considerable increase in network effects. In this way, the high initial expense of making written information available to large numbers of people triggered a pair of innovations that sharply reduced coding and decoding costs. At the same time, the scale of operations remained modest, since the investment in human capital required to train a group of scribes for copying manuscripts was roughly equal to the investment in physical and human capital required to set up a printing shop. The availability of printing in national languages enabled first Luther and then Calvin to establish churches independent of Rome. Rulers of North European states were only too happy to cooperate by seizing the assets and fiscal privileges of the Catholic Church in their jurisdictions. The reaction of the Church to their coordinated challenge was too little and came too late to avoid creative destruction.

## 4. Why did Charles I of England lose his kingdom – and his head?

We pass now to the diffusion phase of the consensual revolution. At the time of Shakespeare, the vocabulary, grammar and pronunciation of English were still evolving. Only a quarter of the male population in England could read and write in 1600. Shortly after his coronation in 1603, King James I decided that the best way to unite his three kingdoms was to promote a standardized Bible that Scots, Irish and English could all accept. The English version of the Bible that he authorized in 1611, soon printed in Roman type, became the basic work used to promote literacy in Britain. By 1700, almost half of English men could read and write. The turn of the century also marked the appearance of present-day English in a form that has changed little in the past three centuries.

A society bound by rigid codes of social behavior was transformed into a more individualistic structure where people felt free to interact with those who shared their interests. The newly literate English squires, merchants and artisans, whose power depended on their wealth rather than on their birth, insisted that their voices be heard in political decisions. When Charles I refused to heed the wishes of Parliament, he was overthrown and executed. However, neither the parliamentary leader, Oliver Cromwell, nor his eventual successor, James II, realized that the game itself had changed. Both were unwilling to compromise sufficiently with elected legislatures.

Only in 1688, when William III and his wife Mary II agreed to accept parliamentary sovereignty by signing the Bill of Rights, did the long struggle come to an end. As soon as the literate English realized that they and not their sovereign held the ultimate power, the English nation state came of age. Its citizens were no longer bound by convention or precedent. The consensual revolution was complete. Medieval English society had mutated into the distributed network of the nation state.

**The Pre-emptive Revolution**

By 1797, even though half the English population could read and write, it was expensive to reach large numbers of them with an identical message because of the slow Gutenberg wooden press. In that year, Prime Minister William Pitt raised a tax on each printed sheet from 2 to 3½d. Pitt's intention in setting the tax, apart from raising revenue, was to put papers hostile to the government out of business. Friendly papers would be discreetly subsidized to keep them afloat. However, the effect was not quite what he anticipated. The tax provided a convincing inducement to search for ways to increase the size and lower the cost of production of each sheet.

A first improvement came shortly after 1800, when British newspapers began using the all-metal Stanhope press. This device both lowered the cost per page by reducing the effort required to operate the press and in addition allowed a 40 per cent increase in the size of the sheet, so that more advertising could be printed on each copy. A decade later, in 1814, *The Times* was the first to publish using a second and even more profound improvement – Friedrich Koenig's steam-powered press, which could print five times as many sheets per hour as the manual press. In England after the Napoleonic Wars, newly literate and informed strata of the population threatened to revolt if they were not granted the right to vote. A society based on trust among members of the same linguistic group was now increasingly split into sub-groups with distinct interests.

**5. Why did the British Parliament pass the Great Reform Bill of 1832?**

Since the new high-speed metal printing machines were more expensive to acquire than the old wooden Gutenberg-type presses, there was an increase in the scale economies of newspaper publishing. As circulations rose, the government found that it could no longer afford to bribe the press. Information could now circulate freely. When the new technology was applied to the publishing of books, it made reading material more accessible to those of modest incomes. Illiteracy, which had remained quite stable in England from 1750 to 1810, began to fall sharply. However, the new readers of William Cobbett's *Political Register*, excluded from voting, had tastes and interests different from those of the bourgeois readers of *The Times*. As the literate public divided itself into distinct markets by income, network effects fell sharply.

In 1832, a majority of those Britons who already had the right to vote approved a reduction in the property qualifications for voting in order to avert revolution. Nevertheless, the creative destruction of the institutions of early-modern England would continue for another half-century. Meanwhile, across the Atlantic, the new printing technology would amplify the existing social divisions between the slave-owning south and the free north.

### 6. Why did the Northern states not let the Deep South secede in April 1861?

For slavery to function effectively within a society, free people who did not own slaves had to be prepared to respect the rights of slave owners over their human property. Until 1840, largely through ignorance, there was toleration of slavery in the northern states. For example, President Martin Van Buren, who came from New York, had owned a slave as a young man.

Technological developments in the second quarter of the nineteenth century altered this initial equilibrium. For one thing, the production rates of steam-powered printing presses continued to improve rapidly. For another, during the 1840s and 1850s, the invention of the telegraph brought information from distant places instantly into the smallest towns of the United States.

Ironically, both the device's inventor, Samuel Morse, and his backer, Fog Smith, were opposed to emancipation, as was John Tyler, the slave-owning president who signed the bill that financed their first telegraph line. However, thanks to cheaper newspapers and books and the more rapid circulation of information, the horrid details of the slavery system and the arbitrary measures taken to uphold it quickly became widely known. As more and more northerners felt uncomfortable supporting the institution of slavery, network effects within the Union fell. In 1848, Van Buren ran for the presidency at the head of a third political party opposed to the extension of slavery – and lost.

After the 1860 election, slave owners in the Deep South realized that with the growing strength of the abolition movement, it was only a matter of time before the northern states refused to uphold their human property rights. Accordingly, their states insisted on secession. The departure of these seven states alone did not seriously threaten the northern states. However, if the breakaway seven had been joined by all of the Border States, the resulting slavery-based federation would have been a serious rival for the remaining Free States.

Lincoln's provocative supply mission to Fort Sumter combined with his assurances that slavery would be respected where it was currently practiced may be seen as a pre-emptive move designed to persuade as many as possible in the Border States to remain within the Union. In so doing, he in effect obliged the Confederacy to fire the first shot. With the North acting as the injured party, he could call for volunteers to defend the Union. As a result, Missouri, Kentucky, Maryland, Delaware and the breakaway western part of Virginia refused to secede.

Deprived of a critical mass of population and resources and forced into a war it could not win, the southern confederacy was doomed. Once the North was confident of victory, Lincoln could emancipate the slaves of the breakaway states. The Thirteenth Amendment to the United States Constitution, ratified in December 1865, altered the contractual basis of the Union by abolishing the institution of slavery altogether. The market for human beings was henceforth constrained by codified law, although for generations to come, North and South would remain distinct societies. The pre-emptive revolution was complete, the United States having shifted from a distributed to a decentralized network.

## The Prescriptive Revolution

Several key developments in the second half of the nineteenth century – paper from wood pulp, stereotype plates, the linotype machine and the electric motor – further increased the scale economies of newspaper publishing. Joseph Pulitzer and William Randolph Hearst in the United States along with Alfred Harmsworth in Britain developed a New Journalism designed to make their publications appealing to those who previously had not been regular newspaper readers. As daily circulations approached the million mark and newspaper chains began to spread, individual publishers obtained enormous power to shape public opinion. They did so in ways that raised their own profits by attracting more readers. Information processing became increasingly centralized, leading to a decline in the value to individual citizens of their contacts with one another. As a result, network effects fell. Citizens demanded that the State take the lead in steps to increase their collective welfare. In return, they were willing to sacrifice an increasing share of their income through taxation. Once more, the dominant type of interaction between individuals was vertical, one player commanding and the other submitting.

### 7. Why did the United States declare war on Spain in 1898?

William McKinley was the first American politician to make effective use of mass-circulation newspapers. In his victorious 1896 presidential campaign, the Republican candidate remained in his home town of Canton Ohio and let the press diffuse his messages to the American people. However, he failed to foresee that rather than retain an instrumental role in his career, the press would finish by calling the shots.

A pacifist, McKinley hoped to bring a peaceful end to the bitter civil war in Cuba. Nevertheless, at a crucial moment in the spring of 1898, he ceded the initiative in foreign policy to Congress, where anti-Spanish sentiment had been stirred up by the jingoist press. The result was a war with Spain, although the Spanish government had been prepared to make important concessions.

Even more remarkable was the change in American attitudes toward imperialism. After the inevitable Spanish defeat, McKinley decided to keep Puerto Rico and the Philippines as American protectorates (along with the island of Guam and the naval base of Guantánamo Bay in Cuba). Over the following three-quarters of a century, the political life of most Americans would be dominated by the effects of this sudden leap of their country on to the world stage. Meanwhile, domestically, they insisted that their government do more to protect them from the vicissitudes of the market economy. McKinley's larger-than-life image through the media undoubtedly attracted the attention of the anarchist who shot and killed him in 1901.

**8. Why did the United Kingdom enter the First World War?**

Mass-circulation newspapers made their appearance in Britain with only a slight delay compared to the United States. In 1896, Alfred Harmsworth, later Lord Northcliffe, modeled his *Daily Mail* after the New York papers he had seen on a visit to the United States two years earlier. The main difference with the American situation was that in Britain, one man was able to gain control of almost 40 per cent of the national daily press. Not only was Harmsworth anti-Semitic and anti-German but also he was a populist who supported measures that would improve the lives of ordinary Britons. During the decade from 1904 to 1914, when his influence was most felt, the British Parliament instituted an Aliens Act that sharply cut the entry of Jewish immigrants from Eastern Europe. Britain also formed an alliance with its former enemies, France and Russia, to defend against their potential enemy, Germany. In addition, Parliament approved heavy tax increases to finance the first programs of the welfare state. When war broke out, thanks in part to Northcliffe's persuasive powers, Britons volunteered in massive numbers to fight a country that posed no direct threat to their own nation.

By the middle of the twentieth century, the United Kingdom, with its welfare programs and nationalized industries, had reached a situation analogous to that of the Frankish Empire under Charlemagne. With decision making centralized, citizens' lives and property were protected by an all-powerful state, as portrayed in Baran's centralized network. The prescriptive revolution was complete.

## Another Contractual Revolution

The launching of the Soviet Union's Sputniks in 1957 triggered a massive government-financed research and development program in the United States. The control of ballistic missiles required a greatly improved capacity to store information in decentralized sites. Two spin-offs of this research were the integrated circuit and the internet. As use of these innovations spread into civilian life, the optimal size of organizations fell and multiple interest groups formed at a level below that of the state. Another contractual revolution was under way.

### 9. Was there a connection between 11/9 and 9/11?

If there was a link between the fall of the Berlin Wall (11/9) and the destruction of the World Trade Center (9/11), it was surely technological. This time round, the gravitational pull of innovations to the Roman writing system began dragging many other cultures along with it, whether they were willingly or not.

By the 1980s, the West held a commanding lead over the Soviet Union and its allies in the civilian and military applications of the integrated circuit. The collapse of the Comecon bloc on 11 November 1989 was not the result simply of a bungled plan for visa reform in East Germany. Rather, it was the consequence of an increasing gap in information technology between producers in East and West and a relentless barrage from Western media that informed East-European citizens of their predicament. The resulting destruction of the Soviet state's information monopoly drove the zone of penetration of the Cyrillic alphabet some 600 miles (1000 km) back east.

Similarly, the installation of the Roman alphabet on Saudi soil was a reflection of American mastery of the applications of the new electronic technologies. Both the McDonald's restaurant in Jeddah and the American Air Force units stationed at the oil port of Dhahran were a challenge to the pride of Arab nationalists. Ironically, the methods Osama bin Laden used to exact revenge for this intrusion – from the satellite phone to what Francis Fukuyama has called the 'aestheticization of violence' – were borrowed from the West.[4] The integrated circuit allowed bin Laden to recruit, coordinate and finance his far-flung agents in the attacks leading up to 9/11 without the backing of a major state.

Both the comedy of 11/9 and the tragedy of 9/11, then, signaled the remarkable success of the writing system whose elements were brought together by Alcuin some 1200 years ago. By the early twenty-first century, the characters he chose had penetrated into the far corners of the planet, from the teaching of Chinese to non-Mandarin speakers in the People's Republic to the writing of Turkic languages in former Soviet republics of central Asia. Despite the violent resistance that these incursions have generated in recent years, particularly in those cultures strongly attached to Arabic script, the further spread of the Roman alphabet and the Western culture it carries would appear virtually inevitable.

It is surely no accident that the Times Roman typeface in which this book is printed is a direct descendant of the Caroline Minuscule. The use here of titles, periods, capitalized initial letters, paragraphs, word separation and chapter breaks replicates the structure standardized by the ninth-century monks who prepared the Tours Bibles.

## NOTES

1. Sherif *et al.* (1988).
2. Zimbardo (n.d.). Zimbardo (2007) retells the story of the famous experiment, explaining its relevance to other social situations such as the Abu Ghraib prison in Iraq.
3. Mokyr (1990, pp. 31–56).
4. Fukuyama (2006, p. 73).

# Epilogue

This book is based on a number of academic papers, some containing formal modeling of the information-revolution theory and others statistical tests of hypotheses generated by this approach. As noted below, several of these texts were written with co-authors. All may be consulted on the author's web site, www.fas.umontreal.ca/sceco/u/dudley/cv-dept/.

## INFORMATION TECHNOLOGIES AS AGENTS OF REVOLUTION

'Space, Time, Number: Harold Innis as Evolutionary Theorist', *Canadian Journal of Economics*, **28** (1995), 754–769.

This article offers solid grounds in evolutionary theory for Innis's argument that economic progress is generated by an oscillation between technologies that conserve information over time and those which transmit it over distance.

'Communications and Economic Growth', *European Economic Review*, **43** (1999), 595–619.

Economic growth in Europe over the past millennium is shown to have taken place in a series of waves generated by new technologies that reconfigured communication networks.

## THE CONTRACTUAL REVOLUTION

'Standardized Latin and Medieval Economic Growth', *European Review of Economic History*, **7** (2003), 213–238, with Ulrich Blum.

Between 1000 and 1300, the diffusion of Medieval Latin was accompanied by a decentralization of urban growth and an increase in the production of human capital.

## THE CONSENSUAL REVOLUTION

'Religion and Economic Growth: Was Weber Right?', *Journal of Evolutionary Economics*, **11** (2001), 207–230, with Ulrich Blum.

The great economic leap forward of northern Europe during the early-modern period is explained by the formation of networks of cooperating individuals in the Protestant regions.

'Religion, Politics and Luck: Explaining the Rise of Sustained Innovation', *Homo Oeconomicus* (2008), forthcoming.

Tests on a sample of 116 successful inventions between 1700 and 1850 suggest the existence of two types of innovations: non-cooperative innovations are largely the result of chance, but cooperative innovations require culturally-specific signals of willingness to cooperate.

## THE PRE-EMPTIVE REVOLUTION

'The Rationality of Revolution', *Economics of Governance*, **1** (2000), 77–103.

Periods of rapid social, political and economic change over the past millennium are explained by new information technologies that changed the optimal strategies of interacting agents.

## THE PRESCRIPTIVE REVOLUTION

'Arms and the Man: World War I and the Rise of the Welfare State', *Kyklos*, **57** (2004), 475–504, with Ulrich Witt.

The doubling of the peacetime share of the state in total spending in a number of Western countries during the interwar period is explained by an increase in people's willingness to share with their fellow citizens that resulted from World War I.

## ANOTHER CONTRACTUAL REVOLUTION

'The Two Germanies: Information Technology and Economic Divergence', *Journal of Institutional and Theoretical Economics*, **155** (1999), 710–737, with Ulrich Blum.

The discrepancy between reported and actual economic growth in East Germany during the two decades prior to 1989 is explained by a technological shock to which the country was unable to adapt.

'Fast Convergence: Institutions and Economic Growth in the New East Germany', *Jahrbuch für Wirtschaftswissenschaften/Review of Economics*, **49** (1998), 124–143, with Ulrich Blum.

During the first five years after reunification, convergence of productivity, hours worked and the percentage of population in industry between East and West Germany was an order of magnitude faster than that observed previously within Western economies.

'The Great Realignment: How Factor-Biased Innovation Reshaped Comparative Advantage in the US and Japan, 1970–1992', *Japan and the World Economy*, **19** (2007), 112–132, with Johannes Moenius.

The integrated circuit enabled the United States and Japan to reshape their trade by tailor-made innovations that augmented each country's most abundant factor.

# References

Adamson, J.S.A. (1990), 'Oliver Cromwell and the Long Parliament', in John Morrill (ed.), *Oliver Cromwell and the English Constitution*, London: Longman, pp. 49–92.

Almedingen, E.M. (1968), *Charlemagne: A Study*, London: Bodley Head.

AngliaCampus (2007), 'The Great Fire of London – 1666', www.angliacampus.com/education/fire/london/history/greatfir.htm, 27 August 2007.

Architect of the Capitol (n.d.), 'A Brief Construction History of the Capitol', www.aoc.gov/cc/capitol/capitol_construction.cfm, 28 August 2007.

Aron, Leon (2000), *Yeltsin: A Revolutionary Life*, New York: St Martin's Press.

Ash, Timothy Garton (1994), *In Europe's Name*, New York: Vintage.

Ashley, Maurice (1987), *Charles I and Oliver Cromwell*, London: Methuen.

Aspinall, A. (1949), *Politics and the Press, c. 1780–1850*, reprinted (1973), Brighton, UK: Harvester Press.

Asquith, Ivon (1978), 'The Structure, Ownership and Control of the Press, 1780–1855', in George Boyce, James Currand and Pauline Wingate (eds), *Newspaper History: From the 17th Century to the Present Day*, Beverley Hills, US: Sage, pp. 98–116.

Athey, Thomas H. and Robert W. Zmud (1988), *Introduction to Computers and Information Systems*, second edition, Glenview, US: Scott, Foresman and Co.

Bacon, Francis (1620), *Bacon's Novum Organum*, edited by Thomas Fowler (1878), Oxford: Clarendon Press.

Bairoch, Paul, Jean Batou and Pierre Chèvre (1988), *The Population of European Cities, 800–1850*, Geneva: Librairie Droz.

Baran, Paul (1964), 'On Distributed Communications: I. Introduction to Distributed Communications Networks', Rand Corporation Memorandum RM-3420-PR, Santa Monica, CA: Rand.

Barber, Charles (1993), *The English Language: A Historical Introduction*, Cambridge, UK: Cambridge University Press.

Barlow, Frank (1972), *The Feudal Kingdom of England, 1042–1216*, third edition, London: Longman.

Barraclough, Geoffrey (1984a), *The Origins of Modern Germany*, New York: W.W. Norton.

Barraclough, Geoffrey (1984b), *The Times Atlas of World History*, Maplewood, US: Hammond.

Barrett, James Wyman (1941), *Joseph Pulitzer and His World*, New York: Vanguard Press.

Bates, David (1982), *Normandy before 1066*, London: Longman.

Bates, David (2004), *William the Conqueror*, Stroud, UK: Tempus.

Baylé, Maylis (1997a), 'L'Architecture Romane en Normandie', in Maylis Baylé (ed.), *L'Architecture Normande au Moyen Âge, vol. 1*, Caen: Presses universitaires de Caen, pp. 13–36.

Baylé, Maylis (1997b), 'Structure Murales et Voûtements dans l'Architecture Romane de Normandie', in Maylis Baylé (ed.), *L'architecture Normande au Moyen Âge, vol. 1*, Caen: Presses universitaires de Caen, pp. 49–61.

Bechtel, Guy (1992), *Gutenberg et l'Invention de l'Imprimerie*, Paris: Fayard.

Berkowitz, Bruce (2003), *The New Face of War: How War Will Be Fought in the 21st Century*, New York: Free Press.

Berlin, Leslie (2001), 'Robert Noyce and the Rise and Fall of Fairchild Semiconductor, 1957–1968', *Business History Review*, **75**, 63–101.

Berlin, Leslie (2005), *The Man behind the Microchip: Robert Noyce and the Invention of Silicon Valley*, Oxford: Oxford University Press.

Bertrand, Claude-Jean (1969), *The British Press: An Historical Survey*, Paris: O.C.D.L.

Bingham, Caleb (1797), *The Columbian Orator*, updated and revised in a new edition by Val J. Halamandaris (ed.) (1997), Vero Beach, FL, US: Caring Publishing.

Bischoff, Bernhard (1990), *Latin Paleography: Antiquity and the Middle Ages*, Cambridge, UK: Cambridge University Press.

Black, M.H. (1963), 'The Printed Bible', in S.L. Greenslade (ed.), *The Cambridge History of the Bible*, Cambridge, UK: Cambridge University Press, pp. 408–475.

Bloch, Marc (1939), *La Société Féodale*, reprinted (1994), Paris: Albin Michel.

Blumenthal, Uta-Renate (1988), *The Investiture Controversy: Church and Monarchy from the Ninth to the Twelfth Century*, Philadelphia: University of Pennsylvania Press.

Bookrags.com, Biography (n.d.), 'Arthur Brisbane Literary Biography', www.bookrags.com/biography/arthur-brisbane-dlb/, 29 August 2007.

Bourne, Richard (1990), *Lords of Fleet Street: The Harmsworth Dynasty*, London: Unwin Hyman.

Boyle, Leonard (1993), *The Vatican Library and its History*, www.ibiblio.org/expo/vatican.exhibit/exhibit/History.html, 24 August 2007.

Bresnahan, Timothy F. and Manuel Trajtenberg (1995), 'General Purpose Technologies: Engines of Growth?' *Journal of Econometrics*, **65**, 83–108.

Briggs, Asa (1959), *The Making of Modern England 1783–1867*, reprinted (1965), New York: Harper and Row.

Briggs, Asa (1967), *William Cobbett*, Oxford: Oxford University Press.

Brown, Archie (1996), *The Gorbachev Factor*, Oxford: Oxford University Press.

Brown, Charles H. (1967), *The Correspondents' War: Journalists in the Spanish-American War*, New York: Charles Scribner.

Brown, Giles (1994), 'Introduction: The Carolingian Renaissance', in Rosamond McKitterick (ed.), *Carolingian Culture: Emulation and Innovation*, Cambridge, UK: Cambridge University Press, pp. 1–51.

Brown, R. Allen (1984), *The Normans*, Woodbridge, Suffolk: Boydell Press.

Brown, Richard (2000), *Revolution, Radicalism and Reform: England, 1780–1846*, Cambridge, UK: Cambridge University Press.

Bullough, D.A. (1991), *Carolingian Renewal: Sources and Heritage*, Manchester: Manchester University Press.

Burk, James (2001), 'The Military Obligations of Citizens since Vietnam', *Parameters*, **31**, 48–60.

Burke, Jason (2003), *Al-Qaeda: Casting a Shadow of Terror*, London: I.B. Tauris.

Butt, John J. (2002), *Daily Life in the Age of Charlemagne*, Westport, US: Greenwood Press.

Calvert, James B. (2004), *History of the Electromagnetic Telegraph*, www.mysite.du.edu/~jcalvert/tel/morse/morse.htm, 25 November 2007.

Cannadine, David (1993), 'Churchill and the Pitfalls of Family Piety', in Robert Blake and W. Roger Louis (eds), *Churchill*, Norton: New York, pp. 9–20.

Carlton, Charles (1983), *Charles I: the Personal Monarch*, London: Routledge and Kegan Paul.

Cavanaugh, Cam, Barbara Hoskins and Frances D. Pingeon (1981), *Invention of the Telegraph*, www.parks.morris.nj.us/speedwell/tel/tel.html, 27 August 2007.

Chamberlin, Russell (1986), *Charlemagne: Emperor of the Western World*, London: Grafton Books.

Christie, Ian R. (1982), *Wars and Revolutions: Britain, 1760–1815*, Cambridge, US: Harvard University Press.

Churchill, Randolph S. (1966), *Winston S. Churchill, vol. I, Youth, 1874–1900*, London: Heinemann.

Cipolla, Carlo M. (1969), *Literacy and Development in the West*, Harmondsworth, UK: Penguin.

Clanchy, Michael T. (1979), *From Memory to Written Record*, London: Edward Arnold.

Cohen, Michael J. (2004), *Churchill and the Jews*, second, revised edition, London: Frank Cass.

Cohon, George (1997), *To Russia with Fries*, Toronto: McClelland and Stewart.

Coll, Steve (2004), *Ghost Wars: The Secret History of the CIA, Afghanistan, and bin Laden, from the Soviet Invasion to September 10, 2001*, New York: Penguin.

Collins, Roger (1998), *Charlemagne*, Toronto: University of Toronto Press.

Conant, Kenneth John (1966), *Carolingian and Romanesque Archicture*, Harmondsworth, UK: Penguin.

Cornell University Library, Division of Rare and Manuscript Collections (2002a), *Plate 22, Signal Tower. Elk Mountain, Overlooking Battle-Field of Antietam, Maryland*, http://rmc.library.cornell.edu/7milVol/plate22.html, 29 August 2007.

Cornell University Library, Division of Rare and Manuscript Collections (2002b), *Plate 73, Field Telegraph Battery Wagon*, http://rmc.library.cornell.edu/7milVol/plate73.html, 29 August 2007.

Coupland, Simon (1995), 'The Vikings in Francia and Anglo-Saxon England to 911', in Rosamond McKitterick (ed.), *The New Cambridge Medieval History, Volume II, c.700–c.900*, Cambridge, UK: Cambridge University Press, pp. 190–201.

Coward, Barry (1991), *Cromwell*, London: Longman.

CPU Museum (n.d.), *Busicom 141-PF*, www.cpu-museum.com/4004_e.htm#Busicom%20141-PF, 30 August 2007.

Craig, Gordon A. (1989), *Europe 1815–1914*, third edition, New York: Harcourt Brace Jovanovich.

Craig, Gordon A. (1993), 'Churchill and Germany', in Robert Blake and W. Roger Louis (eds), *Churchill*, NewYork: Norton, pp. 21–40.

Cranfield, Geoffrey Alan (1978), *The Press and Society: From Caxton to Northcliffe*, New York: Longman.

Cressy, David (1980), *Literacy and the Social Order: Reading and Writing in Tudor and Stuart England*, Cambridge, UK: Cambridge University Press.

Curran, James (1978), 'The Press as an Agency of Social Control: An Historical Perspective', in George Boyce, James Curran and Pauline Wingate (eds), *Newspaper History from the Seventeenth Century to the Present Day*, London: Constable, pp. 51–78.

Cutler, William G. (n.d.), *The Pottawatomie Massacre*, www.assumption.edu/ahc/Kansas/CulFranklinCounty.html, 28 August 2007.

Davies, Norman (1996), *Europe: A History*, Oxford: Oxford University Press.

Davis, J.C. (1990), 'Cromwell's Religion', in John Morrill (ed.), *Oliver Cromwell and the English Constitution*, London: Longman, pp. 181–208.
de Boüard, Michel (1984), *Guillume le Conquérant*, Paris: Fayard.
Delogu, Paolo (1995), 'Lombard and Carolingian Italy', in Rosamond McKitterick (ed.), *The New Cambridge Medieval History, Volume II, c.700–c.900*, Cambridge, UK: Cambridge University Press, pp. 290–319.
De Long, J. Bradford and Andrei Shleifer (1993), 'Princes and Merchants: European City Growth before the Industrial Revolution', *Journal of Law and Economics*, **36**, 671–701.
Depreux, Philippe (2002), *Charlemagne et les Carolingiens*, Paris: Tallandier.
Desmond, Robert W. (1978), *The Information Process: World News Reporting to the Twentieth Century*, Iowa City: University of Iowa Press.
Did You Know (n.d.), 'Gutenberg was not the first to invent the printing press', www.didyouknow.cd/words/gutenberg.htm, 24 August 2007.
Dillard, Dudley (1967), *Economic Development of the North Atlantic Community*, Englewood Cliffs, US: Prentice-Hall.
Dodge, Martin (2004), 'An Atlas of Cyberspaces', www.cybergeography.org/atlas/historical.html, 3 August 2007.
Donald, David Herbert (1995), *Lincoln*, New York: Simon and Schuster.
Douglas, David C. (1966), 'William the Conqueror: Duke and King', in Dorothy Whitelock (ed.), *The Norman Conquest: Its Setting and Impact*, London: Eyre and Spottiswoode, pp. 45–76.
Douglass, Frederick (1855), *My Bondage and My Freedom*, reprinted (1987), Urbana, US: University of Illinois Press.
Duby, Georges (1974), *The Early Growth of the European Economy: Warriors and Peasants from the Seventh to the Twelfth Century*, London: Weidenfeld and Nicolson.
Duby, Georges (1978), *Les Trois Ordres ou l'Imaginaire du Féodalisme*, Paris: Gallimard.
Duckett, Eleanor Shipley (1951), *Alcuin, Friend of Charlemagne*, New York: Macmillan.
Dudley, Leonard (2008), 'Religion, Politics and Luck: Explaining the Rise of Sustained Innovation', *Home Oeconomicus*, forthcoming.
Dudley, Leonard and Ulrich Witt (2004), 'Arms and the Man: World War I and the Rise of the Welfare State', *Kyklos*, **57:4**, 475–504.
Edited Appletons Encyclopedia (2001), *Jedidiah Morse*, www.famousamericans.net/ jedidiahmorse/, 27 August 2007.
Eggenberger, David (1985), *An Encyclopedia of Battles*, New York: Dover Publications.
Eginhard (1966), 'Life of Charlemagne', in A.J. Grant (ed.), *Early Lives of Charlemagne*, New York: Cooper Square, pp. 8–56.

Eicher, David J. ( 2001), *The Longest Night: A Military History of the Civil War*, New York: Simon and Schuster.
Einhard the Frank (1970), *The Life of Charlemagne*, London: The Folio Society.
Eisenstein, Elizabeth L. (1979), *The Printing Press as an Agent of Change*, Cambridge, UK: Cambridge University Press.
Eklof, Todd F. (2004), *Dancing with Your Opponent*, www.cliftonunitarian.com/toddstalks/dancingwithyouropponent.htm, 29 August 2007.
Encyclopedia Britannica (2004), 'Pogrom', *Encyclopedia Britannica CD-ROM*.
Evans, Eric J. (1985), *Political Parties in Britain 1783–1867*, London: Methuen.
Fassett, Will (2003), *University of Rochester Frederick Douglass Project*, *The North Star, 1847–1849*, www.lib.rochester.edu/index.cfm?PAGE=2524, 25 November 2007.
Fennell, Barbara A. (2001), *A History of English: A Sociolinguistic Approach*, Oxford: Blackwell.
Ferguson, Niall (1999), *The Pity of War: Explaining World War I*, New York: Basic Books.
Ferguson, Niall (2004), *Empire:How Britain Made the Modern World*, New York: Basic Books.
Ferris, Paul (1971), *The House of Northcliffe: The Harmsworths of Fleet Street*, London: Weidenfeld and Nicolson.
Folsom, Ed (n.d.), *Whitman, Dickinson, & the Fugitive Slave Law*, www.classroomelectric.org/volume2/folsom/fugitive/index-critintro. html, 29 August 2007.
Foran, John (2005), *Taking Power: On the Origins of Third World Revolutions*, Cambridge, UK: Cambridge University Press.
Forester, Tom (1987), *High-Tech Society: The Story of the Information Technology Revolution*, Cambridge, US: MIT Press.
Freeborn, Dennis (1992), *From Old English to Standard English*, London: Macmillan.
Friedman, Thomas L. (2005), *The World is Flat: A Brief History of the Twenty-First Century*, New York: Farrar, Straus and Giroux.
Fukuyama, Francis (2006), *America at the Crossroads: Democracy, Power and the Neoconservative Legacy*, New Haven, US: Yale University Press.
Fulbrook, Mary (1991), *The Divided Nation: A History of Germany 1918–1990*, Oxford: Oxford University Press.
Fulbrook, Mary (2005), *The People's State: East German Society from Hitler to Honecker*, New Haven, US: Yale University Press.
Fyfe, Hamilton (1930), *Northcliffe: An Intimate Biography*, London: George Allen and Unwin.

Gaffney, Thomas L. (1979), *Maine's Mr. Smith: A Study of the Career of Francis O.J. Smith Politician and Entrepreneur*, PhD Thesis, University of Maine at Orono.

Ganshof, François Louis (1952), *Feudalism*, London: Longman's Green and Co.

Ganshof, François Louis (1971), *The Carolingians and the Frankish Monarchy: Studies in Carolingian History*, Ithaca: Cornell University Press.

Ganshof, François Louis (1982), *Qu'est-ce que la Féodalité?* Paris: Tallandier.

Ganz, David (1987), 'The Preconditions for Caroline Minuscule', *Viator*, **18**, 23–44.

Gaur, Albertine (1984), *A History of Writing*, London: The British Library.

Gentles, Ian (1998), 'The Civil Wars in England', in John Kenyon, Jane Ohlmeyer and John Morrill (eds), *The Civil Wars: A Military History of England, Scotland, and Ireland 1638–1660*, Oxford: Oxford University Press, pp. 103–155.

Gibson, Margaret (1978), *Lanfranc of Bec*, Oxford: Clarendon Press.

Gies, Frances and Joseph Gies (1987), *Marriage and the Family in the Middle Ages*, New York: Harper and Row.

Giessel, Jess (n.d.), *Black, White and Yellow: Journalism and Correspondents of the Spanish-American War*, www.spanamwar.com/press.htm, 28 August 2007.

Glanz, Johannes and Lothar Häusler (1993), 'Das Frankenreich Karls des Grossen', in Heinrich Pleticha (ed.), *Deutsche Geschichte, Band 1*, Gütersloh: Bertelsmann, pp. 21–64.

Gobry, Ivan (1991), *Martin Luther*, Paris: La table ronde.

Gobry, Ivan (1999), *Charlemagne Fondateur de l'Europe*, Paris: Éditions du Rocher.

Godman, Peter (1982), *Alcuin: The Bishops, Kings and Saints of York*, Oxford: Clarendon.

Goldstone, Jack A. (1991), *Revolution and Rebellion in the Early Modern World*, Berkeley, US: University of California Press.

Goldstone, Jack A. (2001), 'Toward a Fourth Generation of Revolutionary Theory', *Annual Review of Political Science*, **4**, 139–187.

Goodwin, Jeff (2001), *No Other Way Out: States and Revolutionary Movements, 1945–1991*, Cambridge, UK: Cambridge University Press.

Graff, Harvey J. (1987), *The Labyrinths of Literacy: Reflections on Literacy Past and Present*, London: Falmer.

Graff, Harvey J. (1991), *The Legacies of Literacy: Continuities and Contradictions in Western Culture and Society*, Bloomington, Ind.: Indiana University Press.

Greenslade, S.L. (1963), 'English Versions of the Bible', in S.L. Greenslade (ed.), *The Cambridge History of the Bible*, Cambridge, UK: Cambridge University Press, pp. 141–176.

Gregg, Pauline (1981), *King Charles I*, Berkeley, US: University of California Press.

Greif, Avner (2000), 'The Fundamental Problem of Exchange: A Research Agenda in Historical Institutional Analysis', *European Review of Economic History*, **4:3**, 251–284.

Greif, Avner (2003), *Institutions and Impersonal Exchange: The European Experience*, Department of Economics, Stanford University.

Greif, Avner, Paul Milgrom and Barry R. Weingast (1994), 'Coordination, Commitment, and Enforcement: The Case of the Merchant Guild', *Journal of Political Economy*, **102**, 745–777.

Griffin, Michael (2001), *Reaping the Whirlwind: The Taliban Movement in Afghanistan*, London: Pluto Press.

Guelzo, Allen G. (2004), *Lincoln's Emancipation Proclamation: The End of Slavery in America*, New York: Simon and Schuster.

Hafner, Katie and Matthew Lyon (1996), *Where Wizards Stay Up Late: The Origins of the Internet*, New York: Simon and Schuster.

Hail, H.G. (1977), 'Luther as Renaissance Writer', in Gerhart Hoffmeister (ed.), *The Renaissance and Reformation in Germany*, New York: Frederick Ungar, pp. 141–156.

Haqqani, Husain (2005), *Pakistan: Between Mosque and Military*, Washington, DC: Carnegie Endowment for International Peace.

Harding, Robert S. and Alison Oswald (2001), *Western Union Telegraph Company Records 1820–1995*, http://invention.smithsonion.org/resources/fa_wu_index.aspx, 27 August 2007.

Harris, Michael (1978), 'The Structure and Control of the Press, 1620–1780', in George Boyce, James Curran and Pauline Wingate (eds), *Newspaper History from the Seventeenth Century to the Present Day*, London: Constable, pp. 82–97.

Häusler, Lothar (1993), 'Der Hof Karls des Grossen', in Heinrich Pleticha (ed.), *Deutsche Geschichte, Band 1*, Gütersloh: Bertelsmann, pp. 65–75.

Haythornthwaite, Philip (1983), *The English Civil War 1642–1651: An Illustrated Military History*, reprinted (1994), London: Arms and Armour Press.

Heer, Friedrich (1975), *Charlemagne and His World*, New York: Macmillan.

Helpman, Elhanan (1998), *General Purpose Technologies and Economic Growth*, Cambridge US: MIT Press.

Hernandez, José M. (2002), *Cuba in 1898*, Hispanic Division, Library of Congress, www.loc.gov/rr/hispanic/1898/hernandez.html, 28 August 2007.

Holborn, Hajo (1982), *A History of Modern Germany: The Reformation*, Princeton: Princeton University Press.

Hollis, David W., III (1996), 'The Reform Bill of 1832', in Frank W. Thackeray and John E. Findling (eds), *Events that Changed the World in the Nineteenth Century*, Westport, US: Greenwood Press, pp. 62–74.

Hollister, C. Warren (1968), *Medieval Europe: A Short History*, Second Edition, New York: Wiley.

Holzner, Steven (2006), *How Dell Does It: Using Speed and Innovation to Achieve Extraordinary Results*, New York: McGraw-Hill.

Houston, S.J. (1973), *James I*, London: Longman.

Howarth, David (1977), *1066: The Year of the Conquest*, London: Collins.

Howell, Roger, Jr. (1977), *Cromwell*, Boston, US: Little, Brown.

Huntington, Samuel (1986), 'Revolution and Political Order', in Jack A. Goldstone (ed.), *Revolutions: Theoretical, Comparative and Historical Studies*, New York: Harcourt, Brace Jovanovich, pp. 39–47.

Hutt, Allen (1973), *The Changing Newspaper: Typographic Trends in Britain and America, 1622–1972*, London: Gordon Fraser.

Innis, Harold A. (1950), *Empire and Communications*, Oxford: Clarendon.

Innis, Harold A. (1951), *The Bias of Communication*, Toronto: University of Toronto Press.

Japan, National Diet Library (2004), *What Are Incunabula?*, www.ndl.go.jp/incunabula/e/chapter 1/, 24 August 2007.

Jenkins, Roy (2001), *Churchill: A Biography*, New York: Farrar, Straus and Giroux.

Joda, Robert (1977), 'Nicholas of Cusa: Precursor of Humanism', in Gerhart Hoffmeister (ed.), *The Renaissance and Reformation in Germany*, New York: Frederick Ungar, pp. 33–50.

John, Eric (1996), *Reassessing Anglo-Saxon England*, Manchester: Manchester University Press.

Johnson, Paul (1997), *A History of the American People*, New York: HarperCollins.

Judt, Tony (2005), *Postwar: A History of Europe since 1945*, New York: Penguin.

Kaplan, David A. (1999), *The Silicon Boys and Their Valley of Dreams*, New York: William Morrow and Company.

Kapr, Albert (1987), *Johannes Gutenberg: Persöhnlichkeit und Leistung*, Munich: C.H. Beck.

Kapr, Albert (1996), *Johann Gutenberg: The Man and His Invention*, Aldershot, UK: Scholar Press.

Keller, Randolf E. (1978), *The German Language*, London: Faber and Faber.

Kennedy, Paul (1987), *The Rise and Fall of the Great Powers*, New York: Random House.

Kershen, Anne (2005), 'The 1905 Aliens Act', *History Today*, **55:3**, 13–19.
Kloss, William (1988), *Samuel F.B. Morse*, New York: Harry N. Abrams.
Knight, Stan (1996), 'The Roman Alphabet', in Peter T. Daniels and William Bright (eds), *The World's Writing Systems*, Oxford: Oxford University Press, pp. 312–332.
Kontzi, Reinhold (1978), *Zur Entstehung der romanischen Sprachen*, Darmstadt: Wissenschaftliche Buchgesellschaft.
Koss, Stephen (1984), *The Rise and Fall of the Political Press in Britain, Vol. 2, The Twentieth Century*, Chapel Hill, NC: University of North Carolina Press.
Kurzman, Charles (2004), *The Unthinkable Revolution in Iran*, Cambridge, US: Harvard University Press.
Lee, Alan J. (1976), *The Origins of the Popular Press in England, 1855–1914*, London: Croom Helm.
Lemmon, Charles H. (1966), 'The Campaign of 1066', in Dorothy Whitelock (ed.), *The Norman Conquest*, London: Eyre and Spottiswoode, pp. 77–122.
Lenhart, John (1935), *Pre-Reformation Printed Books: A Study in Statistical and Applied Bibliography*, New York: Joseph F. Wagner.
Library of Congress (1995), *The Temple of Justice and Faith: The Capitol's East and West Porticoes and Dome*, www.loc.gov/exhibits/us.capitol/s3.html, 27 August 2007.
Linn, Brian McAllister (2000), *The Philippine War, 1899–1902*, Lawrence, US: University Press of Kansas.
Lipsey, Richard G., Kenneth I. Carlaw and Clifford T. Bekar (2006), *Economic Transformations: General Purpose Technologies and Long Term Economic Growth*, Oxford: Oxford University Press.
Lockyer, Roger (1989), *The Early Stuarts: A Political History of England: 1603–1642*, London: Longman.
Loewenich, Walter von (1986), *Martin Luther: The Man and His Work*, Minneapolis: Augsburg Publishing House.
Lohse, Bernard (1997), *Martin Luther: Eine Einführung in sein Leben und sein Werk*, third edition, Munich: C.H. Beck.
Love, John F. (1986), *McDonald's: Behind the Arches*, New York: Bantam.
Loyn, H.R. (1962), *Anglo-Saxon England and the Norman Conquest*, London: Longmans.
Mabee, Carleton (1943), *The American Leonardo: The Life of Samuel F.B. Morse*, New York: Alfred A. Knopf.
MacCulloch, Diarmaid (2003), *The Reformation: A History*, New York: Viking.
Macdonald, A.J. (1944), *Lanfranc: A Study of His Life, Work and Writing*, London: Society for Promoting Christian Knowledge.

MacGregor, Geddes (1959), *The Bible in the Making*, Philadelphia: Lippincott.

Maddison, Angus (2001), *The World Economy: A Millennial Perspective*, Paris: OECD.

Man, John (2002), *The Gutenberg Revolution: The Story of a Genius and an Invention that Changed the World*, London: Headline Book Publishing.

Manchester, William (1983), *The Last Lion: William Spencer Churchill, Visions of Glory, 1874–1932*, Boston, US: Little, Brown and Co.

Marty, Martin (2004), *Martin Luther*, New York: Penguin.

Massie, Robert K. (1991), *Dreadnought: Britain, Germany and the Coming of the Great War*, New York: Ballantine.

Mathew, David (1967), *James I*, London: Eyre and Spottiswoode.

McCord, Norman (1991), *British History 1815–1906*, Oxford: Oxford University Press.

McCrum, Robert, William Cran and Robert MacNeil (1986), *The Story of English*, New York: Viking.

McEvedy, Colin and Richard Jones (1979), *Atlas of World Population History*, Harmondsworth, UK: Penguin.

McEwen, Neal (1997), *Morse Code or Vail Code? Did Samuel F.B. Morse Invent the Code as We Know it Today?*, www.telegraph-office.com/pages/vail.html, 27 August 2007.

McFeely, William S. (1991), *Frederick Douglass*, New York: Norton.

McKitterick, Rosamond (1989), *The Carolingians and the Written Word*, Cambridge, UK: Cambridge University Press.

McKitterick, Rosamond (1994), 'Script and Book Production', in Rosamond McKitterick (ed.), *Carolingian Culture: Emulation and Innovation*, Cambridge, UK: Cambridge University Press, pp. 221–247.

McLuhan, Marshall (1962), *The Gutenberg Galaxy: The Making of Typographic Man*, Toronto: University of Toronto Press.

McNeill, William H. (1963), *The Rise of the West*, Chicago: University of Chicago Press.

McPherson, James M. (1988), *Battle Cry of Freedom: The Civil War Era*, Oxford: Oxford University Press.

Media Line (2006), *America's Middle East Economy*, www.themedialine.org/news/news_detail.asp?NewsID=13340, 19 May 2007.

Millennium Ventures Group (2006), *The World's Cyber Mall*, www.innovationthinktank.org/nmay06v1/, 30 August 2007.

Mills, Brian (1983), *Some Abraham Darby Companies 1717–1784*, www.booneshares.com/SomeAbrahamDarbycompanies.htm, 27 August 2007.

Millward, C.M. (1988), *A Biography of the English Language*, Orlando, US: Harcourt Brace Jovanovich.

Modelski, Andrew M. (1984), *History of Railroads and Maps*, http://memory.loc.gov/ammem/gmdhtml/rrhtml/rrintro.html, 27 August 2007.
Mokyr, Joel (1990), *The Lever of Riches: Technological Creativity and Economic Progress*, New York: Oxford University Press.
Mokyr, Joel (2002), *The Gifts of Athena: Historical Origins of the Knowledge Economy*, Princeton, US: Princeton University Press.
Monk of St Gall (1966), 'Life of Charlemagne', in A.J. Grant (ed.), *Early Lives of Charlemagne*, New York: Cooper Square, pp. 8–56.
Moran, James (1973), *Printing Presses: History and Development from the Fifteenth Century to Modern Times*, Berkeley, US: University of California Press.
Morrill, John (1990), 'The Making of Oliver Cromwell', in John Morrill (ed.), *Oliver Cromwell and the English Constitution*, London: Longman, pp. 19–48.
Mott, Frank Luther (1962), *American Journalism, A History: 1690–1960*, third edition, New York: Macmillan.
Museum of Broadcast Communications (n.d.), *The Ed Sullivan Show*, www.museum.tv/archives/etv/E/htmlE/edsullivans/edsullivans.htm, 29 August 2007.
Musicant, Ivan (1998), *Empire by Default: The Spanish-American War and the Dawn of the American Century*, New York: Henry Holt and Company.
Nasaw, David (2000), *The Chief: The Life of William Randolph Hearst*, Boston, US: Houghton Mifflin.
Nash, Gary B., Julie Roy Jeffrey, John R. Howe, Peter J. Frederick, Allen F. Davis and Allan M. Winkler (eds) (1986), *The American People: Creating a Nation and a Society*, New York: Harper and Row.
National Aeronautics and Space Administration, National Space Science Data Center (2007), *Sputnik 2*, http://nssdc.gsfc.nasa.gov/database/MasterCatalog?sc=1957–002A, 29 August 2007.
Naughton, John (1999), *A Brief History of the Future: The Origins of the Internet*, London: Weidenfeld and Nicolson.
Nelson, Janet L. (1995), 'The Frankish Kingdoms, 814–898: The West', in Rosamond McKitterick (ed.), *The New Cambridge Medieval History, Volume II, c.700–c.900*, Cambridge, UK: Cambridge University Press, pp. 110–141.
Nicolson, Adam (2003), *God's Secretaries: The Making of the King James Bible*, New York: HarperCollins.
North, Douglass C. (1981), *Structure and Change in Economic History*, New York: Norton.
North, Douglass C. (1990), *Institutions, Institutional Change and Economic Performance*, Cambridge, UK: Cambridge University Press.

North, Douglass C. and Robert Paul Thomas (1973), *The Rise of the Western World: A New Economic History*, Cambridge, UK: Cambridge University Press.

North, Douglass C. and Barry R. Weingast (1989), 'Constitutions and Commitment: The Evolution of Institutions Governing Public Choice in Eighteenth-Century England', *Journal of Economic History*, **49**, 803–832.

Norton, Rictor (2004), *Queen James and His Courtiers*, www.infopt.demon.co.uk/jamesi.htm, 24 August 2007.

O'Brien, Patrick (1988), 'The Costs and Benefits of British Imperialism 1846–1914', *Past and Present*, **120**, 163–200.

O'Gorman, Frank (1982), *The Emergence of the British Two-Party System 1760–1832*, London: Edward Arnold.

Olsen, Kirstin (1999), *Daily Life in 18th-Century England*, Westport, US: Greenwood Press.

O'Toole, G.J.A. (1984), *The Spanish War: An American Epic – 1898*, New York, W.W. Norton.

Patterson, W.B. (1997), *King James VI and I and the Reunion of Christendom*, Cambridge, UK: Cambridge University Press.

Pirenne, Henri (1927), *Les villes du Moyen Âge*, reprinted in 1971, Paris: Presses Universitaires de France.

Plant, David (2006), *The Storming of Leicester and the Battle of Naseby*, www.british-civil-wars.co.uk/military/1645-leicester-naseby.htm, 24 August 2007.

Poly, Jean-Pierre and Éric Bournazel (1991), *La Mutation Féodale Xe–XIIe Siècle*, Paris: Presses universitaires de France.

Pope, Franklin Leonard (1888), 'The American Inventors of the Telegraph, with Special References to the Services of Alfred Vail', *Century Illustrated Magazine*, **35**, (April) 924–45, http://cdl.library.cornell.edu/cgi-bin/moa/moa-cgi?notisid=ABP2287-0035-212, 27 August 2007.

Pound, Reginald and Geoffrey Harmsworth (1959), *Northcliffe*, London: Cassell.

Presser, Helmut (1967), *Johannes Gutenberg in Zeugnissen und Bilddokumenten*, Reinbek bei Hamburg: Rowohlt.

Preston, Dickson J. (1985), *Young Frederick Douglass: The Maryland Years*, Baltimore, US: The Johns Hopkins University Press.

Public Broadcasting Service (n.d.), *Bleeding Kansas*, www.pbs.org/wgbh/aia/part4/4p2952.html, 28 August 2007.

Quintrell, Brian (1993), *Charles I, 1625–1640*, London: Longman.

Reid, James D. (1879/1974), *The Telegraph in America: Its Founders, Promoters and Noted Men*, New York: Arno Press.

Reuter, Timothy (1985), 'Plunder and Tribute in the Carolingian Empire', *Transactions of the Royal Historical Society. Fifth Series*, **35**, 75–94.

Reuter, Timothy (1990), 'The End of Carolingian Military Expansion', in Peter Godman and Roger Collins (eds), *Charlemagne's Heir: New Perspectives on the Reign of Louis the Pious (814–840)*, Oxford: Clarendon Press, pp. 391–405.
Reuter, Timothy (1991), *Germany in the Early Middle Ages c. 800–1056*, London: Longman.
Robinson, Adam (2001), *Bin Laden: Behind the Mask of the Terrorist*, New York: Arcade Publishing.
Roberts, J.M. (1983), *The Pelican History of the World*, Harmondsworth, UK: Penguin.
Rolt, L.T.C. and J.S. Allen (1977), *The Steam Engine of Thomas Newcomen*, Hartington, UK: Moorland Publishing Company.
Rosewater, Victor (1930), *History of Cooperative News-Gathering in the United States*, New York: D. Appleton and Co.
Rowland, Peter (1976), *David Lloyd George*, New York: Macmillan.
Rubinstein, William D. (2004), 'Review of Harry Defries, "Conservative Party Attitudes toward Jews"', *The Jewish Quarterly Review*, **94:1**, 225.
Saenger, Paul (1990), 'La Naissance de la Coupure et de la Séparation des Mots', in Henri-Jean Martin and Jean Vezin (eds), *Mise en Page et Mise en Texte du Livre Manuscrit*, Paris: Éditions du Cercle de la Librairie-Promodis, pp. 447–449.
Sambrook, James (1973), *William Cobbett*, London: Routledge and Kegan Paul.
Scannell, T.B. (1911), 'Pope Nicholas V', *The Catholic Encyclopedia*, www.newadvent.org/cathen/11058a.htm, 24 August 2007.
Schama, Simon (2000), *A History of Britain: At the Edge of the World? 3000BC–AD1603*, New York: Hyperion.
Schama, Simon (2001), *A History of Britain: The Wars of the British, 1603–1776*, New York: Hyperion.
Schama, Simon (2002), *A History of Britain: The Fate of Empire 1776–2000*, New York: Hyperion.
Schumpeter, Joseph A. (1950), *Capitalism, Socialism and Democracy*, third edition, New York: Harper.
Seel, G.E. (1999), *The English Wars and Republic, 1637–1660*, London: Routledge.
Seitz, Don C. (1924), *Joseph Pulitzer: His Life and Letters*, New York: Simon and Schuster.
Shakespeare, William (1602/1906), *The Tragedy of Hamlet, Prince of Denmark*, New York: American Book Co.
Sherif, Muzafer, O.J. Harvey, B. Jack White, William R. Hood and Carolyn W. Sherif (1988), *The Robbers Cave Experiment: Intergroup Conflict and Cooperation*, Middletown, CT: Wesleyan University Press.

Skocpol, Theda (1979), *States and Social Revolutions*, Cambridge, UK: Cambridge University Press.
Skocpol, Theda (1986), 'France, Russia, China: A Structural Analysis of Revolutions', in Jack A. Goldstone (ed.), *Revolutions: Theoretical, Comparative and Historical Studies*, New York: Harcourt, Brace Jovanovich, pp. 68–88.
Slocombe, George (1961), *William the Conqueror*, New York: G.P. Putnam.
Smiles, Samuel (1884), *Men of Invention and Industry*, London: John Murray.
Smith, Jean Edward (2001), *Grant*, New York: Simon and Schuster.
Somerville, Johann (1990), 'Oliver Cromwell and English Political Thought', in John Morrill (ed.), *Oliver Cromwell and the English Constitution*, London: Longman, pp. 234–258.
Spartacus (n.d.), *Fugitive Slave Law*, www.spartacus.schoolnet.co.uk/USASfugitive.htm, 29 August 2007.
Speck, W.A. (1988), *Reluctant Revolutionaries: Englishmen and the Revolution of 1688*, Oxford: Oxford University Press.
Stenzel, M.J. (2006), *A Brief Overview of NY in the Spanish American War*, www.dmna.state.ny.us/historic/articles/spanamer.htm, 28 August 2007.
Stephens, Mitchell (n.d.), *History of Newspapers*, www.nyu.edu/classes/stephens/Collier's%20page.htm, 27 August 2007.
Stevenson, David (2004), *Cataclysm: The First World War as Political Tragedy*, New York: Basic Books.
Stock, Brian (1983), *The Implications of Literacy: Written Language and Models of Interpretation in the Eleventh and Twelfth Centuries*, Princeton, US: Princeton University Press.
Sublette, Carey (1997), *Soviet Atmospheric Tests*, http://nuclearweaponarchive.org/Russia/Sovatmtest.html, 29 August 2007.
Sulloway, Frank J. (1997), *Born to Rebel: Birth Order, Family Dynamics, and Creative Lives*, New York: Vintage Books.
Suplee, Curt (2005), 'The New Spin on Circuitry', *Discover*, **26:10**, (October), 38–39.
Swanberg, W.A. (1967), *Pulitzer*, New York: Scribner.
Taylor, S.J. (1996), *The Great Outsiders: Northcliffe, Rothermere and the Daily Mail*, London: Weidenfeld and Nicolson.
Theosophy Trust, Theosophy Library Online (2006), *Nicholas of Cusa*, http://theosophy.org/tlodocs/articlesTeacher.php?d=NicholasOfCusa.htm&p=90, 26 November 2007.
Tilly, Charles (1986), 'Does Modernization Breed Revolution?' in Jack A. Goldstone (ed.), *Revolutions: Theoretical, Comparative and Historical Studies*, New York: Harcourt, Brace Jovanovich, pp. 47–57.

Tilly, Charles (1990), *European Revolutions, 1492–1992*, Cambridge: Blackwell.

United Kingdom, Royal Household (n.d.), *History of Jubilees: Queen Victoria*, www.royal.gov.uk/output/page929.asp, 29 August 2007.

United States, Bureau of the Census (1977), *Historical Statistics of the United States*, Cambridge, UK: Cambridge University Press.

United States, Bureau of the Census (1998), *Population of the 100 Largest Urban Places: 1890*, www.census.gov/population/documentation/twps 0027/tab12.txt, 28 August 2007.

United States, Department of Defense (n.d.), *Neil McElroy*, www.defenselink.mil/specials/secdef_histories/bios/mcelroy.htm, 29 August 2007.

United States, Government Printing Office (2001), 'Dwight D. Eisenhower: Second Inaugural Address, Monday January 21, 1957', in *Inaugural Addresses of the Presidents of the United States: from George Washington to George W. Bush*, www.bartleby.com/124/pres 55.html, 29 August 2007.

University of Oregon, Electronic Universe (n.d.), 'Vanguard', in *Sputnik/Vanguard*, http://zebu.uoregon.edu/~js/space/lectures/lec09.html, August 29 2007.

Urban Institute and Brooking Institution, Tax Policy Center (2007), *Historical Federal Income Tax Rates for Family of Four*, www.taxpolicy-center.org/taxfacts/displayafact.cfm?DocID=226&Topic2id=20&Topic3 id=22, 29 August 2007.

van Werveke, H. (1971), 'The Rise of the Towns', in M.M. Postan, E.E. Rich and Edward Miller (eds), *The Cambridge Economic History of Europe, Volume III, Economic Organization and Policies in the Middle Ages*, Cambridge, UK: Cambridge University Press, pp. 3–41.

Verger, Jacques (1999), 'The Universities and Scholasticism', in David Abulafia (ed.), *The New Cambridge Medieval History, Volume V c. 1198–c. 1300*, Cambridge, UK: Cambridge University Press, pp. 256–278.

Vocke, Roland (1993), 'Vom Frankenreich zum deutschen Reich', in Heinrich Pleticha (ed.), *Deutsche Geschichte, Band 1*, Gütersloh: Bertelsmann, pp. 123–151.

Wade, Mark (2007), *R-16*, www.astronautix.com/lvs/r16.htm, 29 August 2007.

Watson, Alan (1992), *The Germans: Who Are They Now?* London: Thames Methuen.

Webber, Carolyn and Aaron Wildavsky (1986), *A History of Taxation and Expenditure in the Western World*, New York: Simon and Schuster.

Wells, C.J. (1985), *German: A Linguistic History to 1945*, Oxford: Oxford University Press.